P9-DVT-672

THE LIFE OF MY TEACHER

A Biography of Kyabjé Ling Rinpoché

The Sixth Ling Rinpoché,
Thupten Lungtok Namgyal Trinlé (1903–83)

THE LIFE
OF MY TEACHER

A Biography of Kyabjé Ling Rinpoché

His Holiness the Dalai Lama

Translated by Gavin Kilty
Introduced by Thupten Jinpa

Wisdom Publications
199 Elm Street
Somerville, MA 02144 USA
wisdompubs.org

© 2017 Yongzin Lingtsang Labrang
All rights reserved.

No part of this book may be reproduced in any form or by any means,
electronic or mechanical, including photography, recording, or by any
information storage and retrieval system or technologies now known
or later developed, without permission in writing from the publisher.

Library of Congress Cataloging-in-Publication Data is available
Names: Bstan-'dzin-rgya-mtsho, Dalai Lama XIV, 1935– author. | Kilty, Gavin, translator.
Title: The life of my teacher: a biography of Ling Rinpoché / His Holiness the Dalai Lama;
    translated by Gavin Kilty; introduced by Thupten Jinpa.
Description: Somerville, MA, USA: Wisdom Publications, [2017] | Includes bibliographical
    references and index. |
Identifiers: LCCN 2016044496 (print) | LCCN 2017016073 (ebook) | ISBN 9781614293439
    (ebook) | ISBN 1614293430 (ebook) | ISBN 9781614293323 (alk. paper) | ISBN 1614293325
    (hardcover: alk. paper)
Subjects: LCSH: Thub-bstan-lung-rtogs-bstan-'dzin-'phrin-las, 1903–1983. | Dge-lugs-pa
    lamas—China—Tibet Autonomous Region—Biography. | Tibet Autonomous Region
    (China)—Biography.
Classification: LCC BQ990.H63 (ebook) | LCC BQ990.H63 B7813 2017 (print) | DDC
    294.3/923092 [B] —dc23
LC record available at https://lccn.loc.gov/2016044496

ISBN 978-1-61429-332-3   ebook ISBN 978-1-61429-343-9

21 20 19 18 17
5 4 3 2 1

Front cover photograph by Nicholas Vreeland. Cover and interior design by Gopa & Ted2, Inc.
Set in Garamond Premier Pro 11/14.16.

Wisdom Publications' books are printed on acid-free paper and meet the
guidelines for permanence and durability of the Production Guidelines
for Book Longevity of the Council on Library Resources.

🌸 This book was produced with environmental mindfulness.
For more information, please visit wisdompubs.org/wisdom-environment.
Printed in the United States of America.

Contents

Publisher's Acknowledgment

The publisher gratefully acknowledges the generous help of the Hershey Family Foundation in sponsoring the production of this book.

Preface

It is a profound joy to me that the biography of my late tutor Kyabjé Ling Rinpoché is being published in an English translation. There is a longstanding Tibetan custom for students to compose biographies of their teachers, and it has been my privilege to write this one, with assistance from another of Ling Rinpoché's closest disciples, Ratö Khyongla Rinpoché. I am pleased that readers not familiar with the Tibetan language will also now be able to learn about him.

Kyabjé Ling Rinpoché Thupten Lungtok Namgyal Trinlé was one of the most accomplished Tibetan lamas of the twentieth century, a true embodiment of the ideals of the Nālandā tradition—a conscientious monk, a rigorous scholar, and a dedicated practitioner. Born in 1903 in Kyishö, a day's journey northwest of Tibet's capital, Lhasa, Ling Rinpoché was recognized as the reincarnation of his predecessor when he was barely four years old. He studied at the renowned Loseling College of Drepung Monastic University and obtained his lharam geshé degree at the age of twenty-one. He then joined Gyütö Tantric College, where he rose through the ranks of the monastic system, eventually emerging as the Ganden Throneholder, the head of the Geluk school, and a custodian of Tibet's great spiritual heritage.

It was my good fortune that Kyabjé Ling Rinpoché was my principal tutor from my early childhood. A landmark in my training took place in 1954 when, during the Great Prayer Festival, I received full ordination as a Buddhist monk before the statue of Buddha Śākyamuni in the Jokhang. On what was for me very moving occasion, Ling Rinpoché officiated.

In guiding me through my education Ling Rinpoché was like a loving father to me, and it was under his watchful eye that I passed my final geshé examinations at the Great Prayer Festival in Lhasa in February 1959. In the early years of our lives as refugees in India, too, Ling Rinpoché's supportive presence was something I could always rely on.

Since he had been the greatest influence on my life, when Ling Rinpoché passed away in December 1983, I felt as if the solid rock I had leaned on for so long had suddenly vanished. I missed him deeply. But rather than fall into despair, I determined that the greatest tribute I could pay to his memory was to try my best to fulfill the hopes and aspirations he had for me.

Kyabjé Ling Rinpoché lived an exemplary, meaningful life that it has been my honor to record. I am immensely grateful to Ratö Khyongla Rinpoché for his assistance in this work. It gives me great satisfaction to know that the events of my teacher's life and the qualities he abided by will now be accessible to interested readers across the world. I would also like to thank Gavin Kilty, who has translated this book, Thupten Jinpa for his editorial role, and members of Ling Labrang, especially the young Ling Rinpoché, for facilitating the translation and its publication in English.

Dalai Lama Tenzin Gyatso
December 21, 2016

Introduction

KYABJÉ LING RINPOCHÉ was a towering figure among the great Tibetan spiritual masters of the twentieth century. Born in 1903—the very year of Colonel Younghusband's short-lived British incursion into Tibet—and passing away in India in 1983, Ling Rinpoché's life of eight decades witnessed the unfolding of the Tibetan nation's tragic twentieth-century history.

The augustness of Ling Rinpoché's position, especially in the Geluk school of Tibetan Buddhism, goes back to the early eighteenth century. The First Ling Rinpoché, Hor Döndrup Gyatso (1655–1727), became the Forty-Eighth Ganden Tripa, or Ganden Throneholder, the holder of Tsongkhapa's seat at Ganden Monastery, and also served as the main spiritual teacher to the Sixth Dalai Lama, Tsangyang Gyatso. The Second Ling Rinpoché (1728–90) was a close disciple of the Seventh Dalai Lama and a renowned scholar. The Third Ling Rinpoché passed away young, at the age of nineteen, according to one source. The fourth, Ngawang Lungtok Yönten Gyatso (1811–55), was a formidable master who became the Ganden Throneholder at age forty-one and served as a tutor to the Eleventh Dalai Lama. The Fifth Ling Rinpoché, Losang Lungtok Tenzin Trinlé (1856–1902), was a famed yogi of Vajrabhairava, an important cycle of esoteric teachings in Tibetan Buddhism. He also served as a tutor to the Thirteenth Dalai Lama.

The Sixth Ling Rinpoché, the subject of our biography, was also a truly great master. A consummate scholar of Buddhist thought, he was a kind and inspiring teacher, a dedicated practitioner, and a highly accomplished yogi. In his youth Ling Rinpoché studied at the great Loseling College of Drepung, reputedly the largest monastery in the world in 1959 when many Tibetans fled into exile in India along with His Holiness the Dalai Lama. He received teachings from the Thirteenth Dalai Lama and was mentored by the famed Geluk master Phabongkha Dechen Nyingpo (1878–1941)[1] to be a custodian of numerous transmissions of Tibet's sacred teachings. In

1940, Rinpoché was formally appointed a tutor to the young Fourteenth Dalai Lama. Together with his colleague Kyabjé Trijang Rinpoché, Ling Rinpoché accompanied the Dalai Lama during his official visit to China in 1954–55 and during his subsequent, clearly more joyful, visit to India to celebrate the twenty-five-hundredth anniversary of the Buddha's nirvana. Part of this India trip included pilgrimage to the Buddhist holy sites of central India. In March 1959, Ling Rinpoché again accompanied the Dalai Lama to India, this time into exile, never to return to his homeland Tibet. In 1965, Rinpoché ascended to the throne of Jé Tsongkhapa (1357–1419), becoming the Ninety-Seventh Ganden Tripa, and thus the head of the dominant Geluk school. By then, hardly a single member of the Geluk school had not received teaching from this great Tibetan master.

When Ling Rinpoché passed away on December 25, 1983, he remained seated cross-legged in *thukdam* for thirteen days—a state in which all vital signs have ceased yet the body remains without decomposition. According to Tibetan Vajrayana tradition, Rinpoché was at that time in the state of the clear light of death, when all gross levels of mind have ceased with only the subtle pure luminosity remaining. Tica Broch, who was one of the few Western disciples of Ling Rinpoché, describes her firsthand experience of being in the presence of Rinpoché remaining in thukdam. She writes, "When he went into meditation on December 25, the atmosphere of the house changed completely. It was hard to describe; I remember trying to convey the sensation by saying it felt like being in an igloo—such a feeling of light and peace, clarity, and stillness; everything seemed clear-cut and pure."[2]

THE TEACHER, THE YOGI, AND THE HIGH LAMA

What I aim to do in these few pages of introduction is, first and foremost, to offer the contemporary reader a larger context to help appreciate the life and legacy of this remarkable Tibetan teacher. For those interested in the teachings and practices of Tibetan Buddhism, in particular, I hope that this introduction will also help them to relate to the life of traditional Tibetan teachers, such as the subject of this biography, in a way that illustrates what it means for someone to dedicate their entire being to the service of the Dharma.

My first personal interaction with Kyabjé Ling Rinpoché took place in February 1970, when I was eleven. The monastery I was a member of then,

The Sixth Ling Rinpoché, posing for a formal portrait

Dzongkar Chödé, was located in Dharamsala, and as was customary for all monks, I went to receive blessings from Rinpoché on the first day of Tibetan New Year. Known as Chopra House, Rinpoché's residence was located on the edge of a flat base on the crest of the wooded hill overlooking the then-small town of McLeod Ganj. I recall the view from the garden as breathtaking.

We all rushed into Rinpoché's audience room, prostrated ourselves, and took turns offering Rinpoché the ceremonial white scarf. He placed the scarf back on our bent necks and gave each a blessed red string. To an eleven-year-old boy, Rinpoché looked impressive. He had a heavy-set body, a shiny clean-shaven head with long ears, a large forehead and high cheek-bones, and his eyes with fleshy upper lids looked almost squinting. In brief, he looked formidable, and I felt a mix of both awe and terror. A few weeks later, I was back in his presence, this time to receive my formal novitiate vows, which involved nervously having to repeat phrases after him. This was when I received my monastic name Thupten Jinpa, Thupten being the first part of Rinpoché's personal name, Thupten Lungtok Namgyal Trinlé.

The Sixth Ling Rinpoché in the garden of his residence, Chopra House, Dharamsala

The seventies and early eighties were the heyday of Tibetan cultural and spiritual revitalization in India. Having just completed a decade of hectic work resettling a large number of Tibetan refugees, opening new schools, and establishing a functioning central administrative structure in Dharam-sala, the Tibetan exile community was ready for major cultural revitalization. This began with the consecration of the main prayer hall in Dharamsala and the Dalai Lama's first Kālacakra ceremony in Dharamsala in 1970, when

Ling Rinpoché, left, and the Fourteenth Dalai Lama, right, consecrating a new
Akṣobhyavajra statue at the Thekchen Chöling main prayer hall, Dharamsala

around thirty thousand devotees gathered at the small foothill town. The
two tutors of the Dalai Lama, Kyabjé Ling Rinpoché and Kyabjé Trijang
Rinpoché, also began conducting formal public teachings in Dharamsala
and began traveling to the major Tibetan settlements in different parts of
India. I remember attending many of these formal teachings in Dharamsala,
with Ling Rinpoché conducting empowerment ceremonies belonging to
the so-called father tantras, such as Guhyasamāja and Vajrabhairava, while
Trijang Rinpoché focused on mother-tantra teachings like the Cakrasaṃvara cycle.[3]

For those in the Geluk tradition of Tibetan Buddhism in particular, to be
able to receive an empowerment and the associated guide to Vajrabhairava
practice from Ling Rinpoché is considered most auspicious. The Ling reincarnation lineage has a special connection with this particular Vajrayana
practice, and there is a unique set of teachings associated with the Ling
lamas on how to engage in the three-year retreat focused on Vajrabhairava.
These instructions, known as the "eighteen steps" (*them skas bco brgyad*),
are part of the sealed instructions open only to the initiate.

By the time I had the good fortune to receive teachings from Kyabjé Ling
Rinpoché, he was already a highly revered lama and the senior tutor, or
yongzin, to the Dalai Lama himself. Ling Rinpoché was particularly famed
for his empowerment ceremonies, guiding initiates through a series of

visualizations, often with long pauses of silent meditation. For a twelve-year-old young monk, to be part of such collective silence amid hundreds of people felt quite powerful.

At times though, when some of these afternoon sessions went on for hours, way beyond sunset, I remember becoming quite restless as the thought of having to walk back in the dark through the wooded area to our monastery loomed large in my mind. Once I grew older, I was able to appreciate the preciousness of these ceremonies, and the feeling they produced of being guided through powerful, deeply absorbed states of mind. Some classical texts speak of "savoring the taste of meditative states" (*ting nge 'dzin gyi ro nyong ba*), and this is something Ling Rinpoché was a master at invoking for his disciples during these empowerment rites.

Many came to view Ling Rinpoché as a great yogi whose identity had become fused with that of the meditation deity Vajrabhairava. I grew up hearing the Tibetan lamas referring to Ling Rinpoché as "Vajrabhairava in the flesh" (*rdo rje 'jigs byed sku sha rlon pa*). The late Chogyé Trichen Rinpoché reported to His Holiness the Dalai Lama that when he was attending Ling Rinpoche's commentary on the single-deity Vajrabhairava in 1976, he had a vision of Ling Rinpoché in the aspect of Vajrabhairava with blue

Ling Rinpoché conducting a Vajrabhairava initiation in exile.

ornamented horns. Alexander Berzin, who had served on occasions as the translator at those rare teachings Ling Rinpoché gave to Western students, describes this widespread perception of Rinpoché as Vajrabhairava in the following: "As a widely recognized human embodiment of Vajrabhairava, the forceful form of Mañjuśrī, the buddha figure incorporating the clarity, intelligence, and wisdom of all the buddhas, Yongzin Ling Rinpoché exuded this forceful energy of clarity around him while being a solid rock of support."[4]

On the personal level, Ling Rinpoché remained humble and kind-hearted throughout his life. Dagyab Loden Sherab, a high-ranking Tibetan reincarnate lama, shares a moving story. Ling Rinpoché and Trijang Rinpoché were waiting for the Dalai Lama to begin a formal ceremony in Tezpur in eastern India, the first major town reached following his arrival on Indian soil in 1959. A room had been prepared for the two tutors, and on a table sat a plate filled with fruit. Ling Rinpoché called the young Dagyab Rinpoché in and gave him a banana, saying, "This fruit is called banana, and it's delicious as well as good for health. Come, take it." Dagyab Rinpoché had never tasted banana before and was surprised at the unique taste of this tropical fruit. He also relates how, on their long trek from Lhasa to the Indian border, every now and then Ling Rinpoché and his colleague Trijang Rinpoché would insist on traveling by foot so that their horses were not too taxed.

The presence of Ling Rinpoché and Trijang Rinpoché—referred to as *kyabjé namnyi* (literally "the two chief refuges")—close to the young Dalai Lama was a source of profound comfort and confidence for many Tibetans during their early years of exile in India. Growing up as a child in northern India, I always saw the photographs of the trio—His Holiness flanked by his two tutors—in almost every home or monk's cell I visited. I later found out that both tutors would receive on a daily basis any Tibetan devotee—monastic or lay—that would turn up to seek blessing or spiritual counsel. According to Jhampa Shaneman, who occasionally interpreted for Ling Rinpoché between 1971 and 1983, Rinpoché set aside Wednesdays for Western visitors and students to visit. He was always kind and patient, even when the questions and requests involved things that were culturally quite alien to him.

Ling Rinpoché served the Dalai Lama, counseled the major monasteries, gave comfort to ordinary Tibetans, and maintained his own personal development on the path to enlightenment. He also conducted regular formal teachings in Dharamsala and the major monasteries in southern India as well as taught annually in Bodhgaya, the holy site sanctified by the Buddha's attainment of enlightenment under the Bodhi Tree. The famous *Guru Puja* by the First Panchen Lama, memorized by all young monks in the Tibetan Geluk tradition, contains the following lines, which capture the devotion many felt toward Ling Rinpoché:

> When due to time's dictates Buddha Shakyamuni's sun has set,
> you urgently perform the enlightened deeds of the buddhas
> for so many beings bereft of protector and refuge.
> I entreat you, O most compassionate refuge and protector.

In 1968, five years before the Dalai Lama was able to travel to the West, Ling Rinpoché joined Trijang Rinpoché on their first European tour. Beginning in Switzerland, where the two tutors consecrated the newly built Tibetan monastery at Rikon, they visited Germany, France, and England, giving teachings to the Tibetan Buddhist communities in these countries. Twelve years later, Ling Rinpoché traveled to the West for a second time, this time visiting North America as well.

I had the fortune to attend Ling Rinpoché's last major public teaching. This was his exposition of Tsongkhapa's *Great Stages of the Path to Enlightenment* (*Lam rim chen mo*) at Sera Monastery in South India in January 1983. When Ling Rinpoché would explain important points of the Buddhist philosophy of emptiness from Tsongkhapa's classic, he would often close his eyes, pause, and speak with total absorption, as if describing the intricacies of his own personal experience. I was then a student at Ganden Monastic University and already exposed to classical Buddhist philosophical thinking, hence in a position to appreciate the depth of Ling Rinpoché's profound teachings. This particular teaching, taught by a Ganden Throneholder and thus a successor of Tsongkhapa himself, was profoundly meaningful. Many in attendance felt how special this teaching was, a true transmission from a great master's heart to his disciples. When Rinpoché passed away in December 1983, his loss was felt powerfully by the entire Tibetan community, not least by the Dalai Lama himself, who writes in his preface here, "When he passed away in December 1983, I felt as if the solid rock I had leaned on for so long had suddenly vanished."

Ling Rinpoché teaching under the Bodhi Tree, Bodhgaya

UNIQUE SIGNIFICANCE OF THIS BIOGRAPHICAL WORK

This book, although composed in the traditional style of a Tibetan religious biography or hagiography, has the singular distinction of being the only biographical work ever written by the present Dalai Lama. For the Tibetan Buddhist world, the work has rare status, not just due to the importance of the subject but due to the fact that its author is none other than His Holiness himself. In composing this biography (assisted by Ratö Khyongla Rinpoché, another senior student of Kyabjé Ling Rinpoché), the Dalai Lama was honoring the age-old Tibetan tradition of disciples writing about the lives of their spiritual teachers.

Ling Rinpoché was the senior tutor to the Dalai Lama, responsible primarily for the young Dalai Lama's philosophical training, and he was also the master from whom the Dalai Lama received his full monastic ordination. In 2004, on the fiftieth anniversary of this ordination, His Holiness himself would bestow the same lineage upon the present Ling Rinpoché in India. In addition to philosophical teachings on Tsongkhapa's *Great Stages of the Path* and so forth, His Holiness also received from Ling Rinpoché major tantric teachings and initiations. For example, over three days in 1952 in the Potala Palace, His Holiness received the Kālacakra initiation from

Ling Rinpoché—the same initiation that His Holiness has since bestowed more than thirty times around the world.

The book opens with verses of salutation paying homage to important objects of reverence such as the Buddha and invoking inspiration for the writing. Since Rinpoché's life story is here being composed by a devout student, the Dalai Lama, and also given the memory of the subject's sanctified status as a great guru, even the opening paragraph stating the author's intention to write the work carries recognizably devotional tone. Even from the opening section, Ling Rinpoché is referred to in honorific terms, rarely using his personal name. Rinpoché's life is treated as an illustration of the journey to spiritual awakening, with major life events acquiring significance beyond that of an individual. In fact, the Tibetan word for lamas' biographies, *namthar*, literally means "thoroughly liberating," conveying that the primary purpose of such works is to inspire the devout and lead them to true liberation. In a sense, traditional Tibetan lama biographies such as this one can be viewed in line with religious art, whose purpose exceeds its status as a mere work of art. The following sentences from the Dalai Lama's colophon capture the kind of larger religious aspiration behind this book:

> I was formally requested by the Ling Labrang[5] manager Losang Lungrik to compile for the benefit of future disciples a biography of the life and deeds of this incomparably kind tutor, the Vajradhara throneholder and Ling incarnation whose very name is difficult to speak but out of necessity I mention is the most venerable and glorious Thupten Lungtok Namgyal Trinlé. These deeds in the eyes of his ordinary disciples consisted of entering the gateway of the precious teaching of the Buddha, followed by study, contemplation, and meditation on the vast ocean of scripture, composition, teaching, and debate, and working for the Buddha's teaching and sentient beings through his wisdom, pure ethics, and compassion. . . . May all who see, hear, recall, or come into contact with this work be joyfully cared for by a Mahayana spiritual mentor such as this great master.[6]

For devout Tibetan Buddhists, especially the direct students of late Kyabjé Ling Rinpoché, one of the most important aspects of this biography is the detailed records it presents of the formal teachings Rinpoché himself received as well as the dates and places where he transmitted these teachings. This information, gleaned from the extensive diaries kept by Rinpoché himself or a close personal attendant, offer students crucial information about the transmission of important spiritual instructions, which require unbroken lineage traceable all the way back to their origins. Any disciple who may later be in a position to transmit the teachings to his or her own students needs to consult a biography such as the present one, to see whether he or she has received the transmission of that particular instruction from Ling Rinpoché. Once students can discern that, they can then check it against Rinpoché's own record of teachings received to see from whom Rinpoché himself received the transmission. So, for a serious student of Tibetan Buddhism, the biography of the lama and his "record of teachings received" (*gsan yig*) are important resources to authenticate the lineage of the important instructions.

For a student of Tibetan cultural history such as myself, a unique merit of this biography lies in its meticulous accounts of the rites of passage at Gyütö Monastery. Gyütö is one of two tantric colleges of the Geluk school, the other being Gyümé. These two colleges sustain the formal study and practice of the rituals associated with the Vajrayana aspect of Mahayana Buddhism. Gyütö was founded in 1475 by Kunga Döndrup, a major religious figure of fifteenth-century Tibet. Until 1959 Gyütö was the custodian of the Ramoché temple in Lhasa. Ramoché once housed the sacred statue of the Buddha believed to have been brought to Tibet by Wencheng, the Chinese princess who married the seventh-century Tibetan emperor Songtsen Gampo.

Ling Rinpoché rose through the ranks of Gyütö Monastery, assuming the roles of its proctor and deputy abbot, and eventually becoming the tutelary head. Never have I read such intricate details of the life of a monk at Gyütö and how a calendar year at this monastery was structured in Tibet around specific studies, practices, and rituals. I have no doubt that this biography will remain an important historical resource as well as a guidebook to the members of Gyütö Monastery. For scholars and students of Tibetan Buddhism, too, this specific part of the biography will offer a valuable chance to appreciate how, in practical terms, the members of the Geluk monastic tradition combined the sutra teachings of general Mahayana and the esoteric Vajrayana Buddhism.

FOR THE MODERN READER

Beyond the details of one man's life, this work can be read as a detailed account of how an important religious teacher in Tibet was formally groomed and trained. From identification of a child as a reincarnate successor of an important predecessor to the training as a young monk, and from the study of key classical Buddhist texts to how such traditional education is structured, and finally to how, after obtaining the famed *lharam geshé* degree (equivalent to a doctorate in divinity), a lama enters into formal Vajrayana training—all of these can be understood in the context of the training of Kyabjé Ling Rinpoché. The book, therefore, offers the discerning contemporary reader a chance to appreciate how the intellectual and philosophical thinking of an elite Tibetan scholar monk comes to be formed.

Earlier, I spoke of how one key purpose of the biography is to record the formal teachings Ling Rinpoché received and gave. An important dimension of such teachings is the platform they provide for forging and strengthening relationships between a lama and his close disciples and benefactors. It's commonly a benefactor or benefactors who formally request teachings and sponsor them, thus providing opportunities for many students to receive these teachings. Some of these students may emerge as future upholders of the lineage of these important teachings. A well-known prayer by the Seventh Dalai Lama alludes to this symbiosis:

> May the lamas, the glory of the Dharma, live long.
> May the holders of Dharma pervade the face of the earth.
> May the benefactors of Dharma enjoy status and prosperity.
> Through such auspiciousness, may the Dharma long endure.

Perhaps the most significant contemporary relevance of this biography is its role in helping us understand the influences on the present Dalai Lama, especially in his formative years as a student. Rinpoché was known for his mastery of the great Indian classics, his expertise in philosophical debate, and his laser-like focus in meticulously following intricate chains of thought. We can observe all these same attributes unmistakably in the Dalai Lama today. In speaking of Ling Rinpoché's role as a tutor, the Dalai Lama writes:

In terms of my own temperament and natural talents, I think I am closer to Ling Rinpoché than to any of my other tutors. It's perhaps fair to say that Ling Rinpoché has been the greatest influence on my life.[7]

In his special relationship with the Dalai Lama, first as a teacher and later as a close colleague and a confidant, we can imagine how Ling Rinpoché must have served as a powerful anchor for the Dalai Lama as he gradually emerged as a spiritual and global leader. One area where the Dalai Lama's close collegial relationship with Ling Rinpoché proved to be a powerful source of strength was the Dalai Lama's initial dealings with the controversy surrounding the so-called Shugden practice.[8] His Holiness has told me that the fact that Ling Rinpoché never had any association with the Shugden practice was a source of comfort and confidence for him. In His Holiness the Dalai Lama's grateful devotion to Ling Rinpoché and his strong identification of him as his key teacher, we see a side of the Dalai Lama—the deeply devotional and traditional Tibetan Buddhist—rarely observable in the contemporary literature on the Dalai Lama.[9]

For cultural historians of twentieth-century Tibet, in particular, an appreciation of the role of Ling Rinpoché is a must. Just like his colleague Trijang Rinpoché, Ling Rinpoché lived at the critical crossroads of old and new Tibet, overlapping the tenures of two Dalai Lamas. In between, Rinpoché also had substantial dealings with Tibet's two controversial regents, Radreng and Takdrak, whose personal conflicts split the Tibetan establishment and led to an unfortunate period of infighting. This inward turn left little space to appreciate the dangerous historical and political forces gathering momentum to the east. By the time the Tibetan establishment awoke to the threat of Communist China, it was too late.[10]

Second to Ling Rinpoché's relationship with the Dalai Lama was that with his close colleague and fellow tutor of the Dalai Lama, Trijang Rinpoché. The two tutors not only shared a dedication to the education of the Dalai Lama, they also received formal teachings from each other. The biography shows us how close and special this particular relationship was, and how the death of Trijang Rinpoché in 1981 weighed heavily on Ling Rinpoché's mind. Reading Ling Rinpoché's biography side by side with Trijang Rinpoché's autobiography gives a powerful sense of the special relationship between these two remarkable Tibetan teachers, who together shaped the

The Thirteenth Dalai Lama on his teaching throne
at the Norbulingka summer palace

life, character, and thought of an entire generation of Tibetan teachers and scholars that continue to dedicate their lives to preserving and disseminating Tibet's cherished spiritual and cultural heritage.

In brief, whether serving the Dalai Lama as his senior tutor, traveling and conducting public teachings at the request of his students, deepening his own meditative realizations, or strengthening the bonds between teachers, disciples, and benefactors, Kyabjé Ling Rinpoché's life was dedicated to one thing: serving the Dharma to help others find genuine peace and happiness. In a brief autobiographical note composed about a decade before his death, Ling Rinpoché wrote, "Until now I have dedicated my stay in India to restoring the waning Buddhadharma and to preserving the teachings of the second Buddha Jé Tsongkhapa, which are like a refined gold and present a stainless union of sutra and tantra."[11]

It has been both an honor and a profound joy to be part of the team bringing the biography of Ling Rinpoché to the English-speaking world. I offer my deepest thanks to the present Seventh Ling Rinpoché, Tenzin Lungtog Trinley Choephag, for inviting me to be part of the team as the general editor. I thank the translator Gavin Kilty for excellently rendering the original Tibetan work into English, no small task given all the specific cultural and technical references to intricacies of Tibetan monastic life.

Ling Rinpoché and Trijang Rinpoché in Switzerland, 1968

My gratitude goes also to Dakpo Rinpoché, a senior teacher in the Geluk tradition and a former student of Kyabjé Ling Rinpoché, for funding the translation of this important biography. I would also like to thank the Ing Foundation for its patronage of the Institute of Tibetan Classics, which has enabled me to have the time to edit this precious book as well as write this introduction. Finally, I must express my deep appreciation to our dedicated team at Wisdom Publications, including especially our incisive editor David Kittelstrom and our publisher Tim McNeill.

May the publication of this biography of Kyabjé Ling Rinpoché be a source of inspiration to many travelers on the path of awakening.

Thupten Jinpa
A humble student of the late Kyabjé Ling Rinpoché

Translator's Note

WHEN I WAS asked to translate the biography of Kyabjé Ling Rinpoché, my mind went back to Dharamsala in the 1970s and 80s to a small wooded area above the little village of McLeod Ganj. There, in a large bungalow called Chopra House that had been built during the days of the Raj, lived Ling Rinpoché, who by then was in his seventies. Around him were his attendant, Losang Lungrik, or Kungo-la as he was called, and other attendants and servants. In those days there were no fences or wire sealing off properties, and one could roam freely over the area. More than once I made the mistake of stumbling into his presence as he sat on his balcony around four in the afternoon. He usually waved me away with a smile.

My wife, Jacquie, and I, along with our two small children, lived very close by in a small stone-wall house. It was at that time a peaceful area, whose tranquility would only be shattered occasionally by a pack of brown monkeys that breezed through noisily, or by dogs barking at nothing in particular. This hill was dominated by Chopra House and bounded by Rishi Bhavan, where Geshé Rapten lived for a while, Tushita Meditation Centre, where Lama Yeshe and Lama Zopa gave regular teachings to Westerners, and Elysium House, where we lived in a detached room.

Everybody knew that Kyabjé Ling Rinpoché lived in Chopra House. He was the great lama on the hill, but he was rarely seen. He would often say that he was retired, and that his work of teaching His Holiness the Dalai Lama was finished. Consequently, he did not give regular teachings in Dharamsala, although, as this biography makes clear, he would teach and grant ordination every winter in the monasteries in South India and in Bodhgaya in Bihar, the site of the Buddha's enlightenment.

However, he never refused to give teachings when requested, and occasionally he was invited to Tushita close by to teach Westerners there. I personally remember attending his teachings there and in the Thekchen Chöling temple in McLeod Ganj. Often he would grant private audiences to his Tibetan disciples, many of who were revered lamas in their own right. Once a week he saw Westerners who queued up outside his room in Chopra House. Like the Canadian monk Jhampa Shaneman, I was fortunate enough to interpret for him on occasion. He was a lama of few words, but they were always prescient and to the point.

One vivid recollection involved me and my family personally. For weeks our little room in Elysium House had been plagued by bedbugs. Anyone who knows anything about bedbugs knows that they can withstand anything thrown at them. Our two little children would wake crying in the night as these creatures emerged from crevices in the beds and attacked their soft skin. In the morning we were all covered in red welts. We tried various ways to get rid of them. We scrubbed the beds and stood them outside with the legs in tins of water. We searched the cracks and crevices to pry the bugs out, but they were devious and had hid themselves well. We were at our wits' end. So I thought to ask Ling Rinpoché for advice. I don't quite know what I thought he would say, but we were desperate.

One day I walked the few minutes over to Chopra House. There I saw Kungo-la with a big smile on his face. I asked if I could see Rinpoché. "He is busy now," came the reply.

My dejected look must have caused him to ask, "What is it you want?"

I told him of our bedbug predicament. "Wait here," he said. "I will ask Rinpoché."

A minute later Kungo-la emerged and said, "Rinpoché says he knows nothing about bedbugs."

I returned home in despair. We had tried every method known, short of burning the beds, to free ourselves from these little devils, and now our last hope had gone.

That night we went to bed in resignation. The following morning not a red welt was to be seen on any of us. No one had awoken in the night crying and scratching. We were astonished, but not too hopeful. And yet, from that day on, we never had another bedbug in our home again!

To me, this story encapsulates a particular quality of Ling Rinpoché. He was reserved and not given to small talk. And yet underneath must have burned bright the fire of high attainments and profound insight. Although we lived a few hundred meters from Chopra House, I cannot say that I knew him. Those fleeting glances when interpreting for him, accidently meeting him as I stumbled around Chopra House, seeing him at public events, and receiving teachings from him afforded glimpses of the great yogi, but the door was only slightly ajar.

Imagine then my delight as I made my way through the life of this great lama by way of translating his biography. Here was revealed a lama whose learning, discipline, kindness, total dedication, patience, and humility were laid before me. Although, as His Holiness points out, only a fraction of his attainments can be perceived from the outside, it was enough to fill in many missing pieces that had remained hidden from me while living in his vicinity.

Here was a lama who did more than make a few bedbugs disappear. Here was one who guided and nurtured a young Tenzin Gyatso, Holder of the White Lotus, helping him to become the confident Dalai Lama that he is today. His Holiness loved him so much that he feared that when his root lama passed away he would be left like a baby bird alone in the world. However, the world these days is blessed with the presence and kindness of a fearless Dalai Lama. We revere him and give thanks that he is in the world. But he himself talks of the kindness of his teacher Ling Rinpoché, calling it a kindness that until enlightenment he will never be able to repay.

Even now as on occasion I walk by Chopra House, I think about the reserved but straight-talking lama that used to live there. But now I fill in the picture with the fulsome colors taken from the paint box of his remarkable life. I pray that this translation goes some way in displaying that picture in all its glory.

Acknowledgments

I felt honored to be asked to translate this biography by Geshé Thupten Jinpa and was equally grateful that he took the time to review this translation. Many terms peculiar to the Tibetan monastic environment I was unfamiliar with, and he kindly corrected any errors.

As His Holiness notes, he requested Ratö Khyongla Rinpoché to compile the book by writing down the day-to-day events of Rinpoché's life and to interview his attendant Losang Lungrik. Fortunately, Khyongla Rinpoché was in Dharamsala during some of the times I was there, and I was able to take advantage of his presence to clear up one or two points. Although of an advanced age, and though I often felt I was pestering him like an annoying mosquito, he was unfailingly gracious and kind with his time.

Being in Dharamsala often means that I am able to avail myself of the great learning that dwells within the many Tibetan inhabitants here. Often I would seek out a more knowledgeable soul than myself to resolve a query about an expression or term. Those I am indebted to for this range from Losang Yeshé, present abbot of Drepung Loseling, to monk and lay friends that I would meet in the streets and cafés of this little town. To them all I offer appreciative thanks.

Much of the information in the glossary was taken from the recently published *Gomdé Tibetan-to-Tibetan Dictionary* (*sgom sde tshig mdzod*), painstakingly compiled over sixteen years by Gomdé Lharampa Geshé Thupten Samdrup, formerly of Sera Monastery. It is truly a treasure mine of Buddhism-related information.

Sharpa Tulku Tenzin Trinley made a draft translation of this biography, and I have relied upon it throughout. It would be remiss not to acknowledge the effort made by this devoted student of the Sixth Ling Rinpoché.

The photographs that adorn this work are here thanks to the work of long-time friend Jane Moore. By trade Jane is a professional photo researcher and editor and happily gave of her time to meticulously work on gathering and selecting the best photos for this book. As a devoted student of the Dalai Lama, she put her heart and soul into this task, and the book is so much the better for it.

Without an editor the reader would tire of the grammatical errors, convoluted expressions of simple points, inapt word choices, and so on that would plague my efforts. It is indeed fortunate then that Wisdom Publications has the services of editor David Kittelstrom. Over the many years that I have worked with David, he has nudged my attempts at translation to a clarity that far better reveals the meaning of the text.

Finally, I want to express my gratitude to Thupten Tsering, known affectionately to all as TT-la, a member of staff of Ling Labrang of the former and present Ling Rinpoché. He told me more than once that he wanted to see this book translated before he passed to his "heavenly realm." Although still weakened by the effects of the serious car crash he suffered with the present Ling Rinpoché, he always managed to encourage me to persevere with the translation, even when successful publication seemed distant.

TECHNICAL NOTE

The title of the Tibetan text translated here is *'Jam mgon rgyal ba' rgyal tshab skyabs rje yongs 'dzin gling sprul rdo rje 'chang rje btsun thub bstan lung rtogs rnam rgyal 'phrin las dpal bzang po'i thun mong ba'i mdzad rnam mdo tsam brjod pa nor bu'i do shal,* which can be translated as *Jewel Pendant: A Brief Account of the Commonly Perceived Deeds of Mañjunātha, the Regent of the Buddha, the Protector and Great Tutor, the Vajradhara Ling Incarnation, Venerable Thupten Lungtok Namgyal Trinlé Palsangpo.*

The text used for translation was the latest book-format edition, published by Yongzin Ling Labrang in Dharamsala in 2009 to mark the fiftieth anniversary of the nonviolent uprising in Lhasa and the mass exodus into exile that followed.

Some of the text that is not chronologically bound, as well as that section which portrays Rinpoché's character, daily routine, teachers, and so on, has been moved to the front of the book. Chapters and sections have been reformed to make reference easier. Except in some cases of titles frequently mentioned, works mentioned in the translation have wherever possible had the author's name added by the translator. All footnotes are those of the translator.

The phonetic transcriptions of Tibetan words are those developed by the Institute of Tibetan Classics and Wisdom Publications. These reflect approximately the pronunciation of words by a modern Central Tibetan. Transliterations of the phoneticized Tibetan terms and names used in the text can be found in the index. Exceptions to the above system of phonetic transcription are those modern proper names whose owners have spelled them according to their own preference. Drakyap Rinpoché, therefore, is rendered Dagyab Rinpoché. Sanskrit diacritics are used throughout except for Sanskrit terms that have been naturalized into English, such as samsara, nirvana, sutra, stupa, Mahayana, and mandala.

Pronunciation of Tibetan phonetics
ph and *th* are aspirated *p* and *t*, as in *pet* and *tip*.
ö is similar to the *eu* in the French *seul*.
ü is similar to the *ü* in the German *füllen*.
ai is similar to the *e* in *bet*.
é is similar to the *e* in *prey*.

Pronunciation of Sanskrit

Palatal *ś* and retroflex *ṣ* are similar to the English unvoiced *sh*.

c is an unaspirated *ch* similar to the *ch* in *chill*.

The vowel *ṛ* is similar to the American *r* in *pretty*.

ñ is somewhat similar to the nasalized *ny* in *canyon*.

ṅ is similar to the *ng* in *sing* or *anger*.

Jewel Pendant

The Biography of the Sixth Ling Rinpoché

༄༅། །འཇམ་མགོན་རྒྱལ་བའི་རྒྱལ་ཚབ་སྐྱབས་རྗེ་ཡོངས་འཛིན་

གླིང་སྤྲུལ་རྡོ་རྗེ་འཆང་རྗེ་བཙུན་ཐུབ་བསྟན་ལྱུང་རྟོགས་རྣམ་རྒྱལ་འཕྲིན་ལས་

དཔལ་བཟང་པོའི་ཐུན་མོང་བའི་མཛད་རྣམ་མདོ་ཙམ་

བརྗོད་པ་ནོར་བུའི་དོ་ཤལ།

HIS HOLINESS
THE FOURTEENTH DALAI LAMA,
Tenzin Gyatso

1 | Homage and Introduction

Oṃ sati.
Precious vessel composed of the elements of enlightenment
filled with the golden particles of the wisdom of every buddha,
most exceptional deity renowned as Mañjuśrī,
grant me the gift of the confidence of limitless speech.

Rising as the slayer of Yama's demigod-like armies
in their outer, inner, and secret forms,
sole protector of the god-like fortunate beings,
Bhagavan, lord of the gods, bestow your auspicious abundance.

In these degenerate times, the master of the enemy of time,[12]
through the magic of the dance of the ordinary,
puts on the wondrous spectacle of a great festival
of high rebirth and renunciation for countless beings.

Amid the golden mountains of those spiritual masters,
wise in preserving the Mighty Sage's doctrine,
you are hailed as a great citadel of scripture and insight,
made delightful by the twin ornaments of the sun and moon
of your enlightened deeds, victorious in every direction.[13]

With its foliage of bodhisattva deeds spread far and wide,
hung low with its fulsome fruit that benefits living beings,
the wish-granting tree of your succession of lives
has beautified the earth of the teachings of all traditions.

In particular, with the firm hands of teaching and practice,
you have skillfully placed the wish-fulfilling jewel of the Geluk tradition
upon the topknot of the head of samsara and nirvana
and many have made your teachings their own.

Every representation of your extraordinary three mysteries,
whose reach equals that of the brilliant sun,
are phenomena to be understood only by the omniscient;
how can the mind of a child encompass these?

Nevertheless, a few fragments of his deeds,
instances depicted to guide ordinary beings,
will be created here with the brushes of the three unshakable types
    of faith
as a portrait to delight the intelligent.

With these verses offered in homage to a sacred object, the medium of speech has been rendered virtuous.

This great guide of ours completed the three practices of perfection, maturation, and cultivation countless eons ago. He actualized by way of the three equalities the ultimate stage of development of the buddhas of the ten directions, and through spontaneous and uninterrupted enlightened deeds, he has displayed manifestations appropriate to those who are to be tamed and as numerous as the living beings pervading the realms of space. All these and other mysteries are beyond conception, an internal experience shared by those great beings who have merged with the pervasive dharmakāya. It is difficult for ordinary beings to discern such phenomena.

Also, his fully accomplished past lives were like a string of pearls in that he appeared as a succession of beings who were great scholars and practitioners, beginning from Arhat Udayin, the great disciple of the Buddha who was supreme in taming the minds of the lay population, up to the glorious Losang Lungtok Tenzin Trinlé, the previous incarnation. There are limitless accounts, all worthy of mention, of their activities performed for the sake of the teachings without differentiating between the old and new tantra traditions, and so on. However, I will not take on the hardship of writing of them here but instead speak of the topic at hand, of how this particular incarnation, through his remarkable activities of study, contemplation, and meditation within the doctrine of the Buddha, and his teaching, composition, and debate, illuminated the true and excellent path for his discerning followers and those endowed with the treasure of intelligence.

2 | Some Reflections on Ling Rinpoché's Personality

M Y PRECIOUS TUTOR[14] usually maintained a humble and modest demeanor. In times of crisis for the country and the Buddha's teaching, however, he was not modest and revealed a powerful and decisive side. Here is one example. In 1951, when we were staying in Dromo, there were conflicting opinions in the Tibetan government on whether we should proceed to India or return to Lhasa. A divination was performed to see which course of action was better. The divination came out for returning to Lhasa. Nevertheless, some still voiced their opinion strongly that returning to Lhasa would be too dangerous. The precious tutor gave me the following advice, "The unfailing guru is the Three Jewels, and in a divination request made to the Three Jewels, the answer has come out for returning to Lhasa, and so that is what we should do. If His Holiness finds this difficult to do, then it is perfectly fine to ignore what I say." This decisive advice was given without a trace of hesitation. Later, when I reflected on this, I marveled at how decisive and resolute the precious tutor was.

Normally, whenever I visited Rinpoché in the labrang or invited him to my rooms, it was to receive teachings on sutra and tantra and so on. Occasionally, however, I would ask for advice on other matters, and so over time we had much discussion. On all those occasions, I never heard the precious tutor find fault with others, make sarcastic remarks, or grumble about his personal situation. He was always content and reserved, a happy person.

Having the responsibility of the Tibetan people resting on my shoulders, I would sometimes share my troubles with Rinpoché. Whatever the problem, he would always discuss it with me. Sometimes he would make me laugh. He would make the problem seem smaller and was skillful in comforting and reassuring me. This greatly benefited my mind. Sometimes he told me in an easygoing manner and with great joy that in this day and age, I was like "specially ordered brocade," in that I was perfectly suited for

Sakya Trizin, Ling Rinpoché, the Dalai Lama, and Trijang Rinpoché sit
and Drukpa Thuksé Rinpoché, Düdjom Rinpoché, and Kalu Rinpoché stand
in front of the Mahabodhi stupa in Bodhgaya, early 1960s.

both the religious and secular world, and that there was no need to worry,
whatever the situation. These words would reassure me greatly.

Not only when I had a problem, but whenever I visited the precious
tutor, I would always feel happier afterward and retain a definite and special
joy. This was his inconceivable kindness. Alongside that was the knowledge
that one day the precious tutor might no longer be with us. How would I
be able to face that situation? How would I be able to bear it? Such fears
and torment began to arise in my mind a few years ago. Therefore, as this
biography makes clear, I put a lot of effort into making repeated requests for
him to live long, performing longevity rituals, and so on.

The precious tutor kept his qualities decidedly hidden, and as a result, his
inconceivable qualities of body, speech, and mind are far beyond our comprehension and powers of description. Nevertheless, I have seen firsthand
that he possessed a clairvoyance capable of clearly foreseeing future events.
I will recount a couple of those occasions.

While the precious teacher was receiving the textual transmission of the combined *Kālacakra Root Tantra*, *Kālacakra Condensed Tantra*, and Butön Rinpoché's *Annotations on the Kālacakra Stainless Light Great Commentary* from Kumbum Minyak Rinpoché, this lama did not remember exactly which other texts were needed to be brought together to complete this transmission. Therefore, in Tibet I had only received the transmission of Butön Rinpoché's *Annotations* and had not been given the combined transmission that included the root tantra and the commentary. When we arrived in India, I remarked to the precious tutor that the transmission lineage of the Kālacakra root tantra and commentary has probably come to an end, and what a loss that would be. The precious tutor replied, "The lineage has definitely arrived in India. We must search for it." He spoke with complete certainty that it was in India, but none of us knew who had this lineage. Later, after much investigation, it was found that the complete teaching lineage was with Kīrti Tsenshap Rinpoché. This news was reported to the precious tutor. Kīrti Tsenshap Rinpoché passed the lineage to Serkong Rinpoché,[15] and I subsequently received it from Serkong Rinpoché. Therefore I was able to receive this transmission that had been close to dying out. Rinpoché had stated with total certainty that this lineage was in India before it had been discovered, and this is one extraordinary example of his clairvoyance.

Also, when I asked for advice on my practice and other matters, Rinpoché would usually approve of my line of thought, whether in the religious or secular domain, saying it was based on good reasoning. Sometimes, however, he would give me advice that ran counter to my ideas and wishes in that moment. Later, after some time had passed, I saw that the advice the precious tutor had given me turned out to be perfect for that situation and that my own ideas clearly would not have worked.

Owing to experiences like these, I came to suspect that the precious tutor had clairvoyance. Consequently, at a meeting with him, I once said, "It seems the precious tutor is clairvoyant. Is that true?"

He replied, "Sometimes I wonder if that is not the case." If we look at these words of such a guru, one who would never commit the monastic downfall of "the lie of elevating oneself above the ordinary,"[16] it was as if he were actually asserting that he had clairvoyance. I have something like pride in noting that it is of no inferior merit to be cared for by such a guru.

It was the precious tutor's nature to be reserved, and he was not prone to sudden displays of either elation or sadness. However, whenever he was aware of a living being in distress, such as on hearing the cries of a dog being beaten, his eyes would well up and he would say, "Ah, poor thing!" This was a sign that he possessed the quality of great compassion.

As recounted in this biography, the precious tutor told Ratö Khyongla, "I only requested teachings that I thought I could practice." That was certainly true. In Tibet a monk called Ngawang Nyendrak, who spent his time in retreat at Taklung Drak Hermitage, would inform Rinpoché whenever Takdrak Vajradhara was giving important teachings. Once Takdrak Rinpoché was giving the initiations of the Hundred Practices of Mitrayogi, and Ngawang Nyendrak informed the precious tutor and wondered aloud whether he would attend them. Rinpoché reflected that he would be unable to do the practices and so did not receive the initiations. This consideration of whether he would be able to do the practice, not just collecting teachings, is an example to us all and a wonderful teaching on the need for practice.

3 | Daily
Routine

G URU VAJRADHARA'S daily routine was as follows: He woke up at five
o'clock and practiced the yoga of rising. He went to the bathroom and
washed his hands and face while practicing the ceremonial cleansing yoga.
He then drank a cup of warm milk and went outside for a short walk. He
sat on the veranda and recited the seven-limb prayer that begins with the
line "To the venerable and noble Tārā . . ." and then chanted the Tārā prayer
thirty-five times. Returning inside he made three preliminary prostrations
to the compassionate Buddha before reciting the lines of reviewing the
vows, concluding with three more prostrations. Sitting on his seat he would
perform a self-generation using the *Longevity Ritual for Self and Others by
Way of Cittamaṇi White Tārā* composed by Phabongkha Dechen Nyingpo.
Afterward he recited the *Torma Offering Rites.*

At half past seven Rinpoché had breakfast with Losang Lungrik, the
labrang manager. Rinpoché ate *tsampa* and drank three cups of tea. Before
eating he would offer the food. To the Three Jewels he made offerings with
the lines "For myself and those around me, in all our lives . . ." and so on. To
the lamas from whom he had received teachings he offered with the lines
"The actual embodiment of all the buddhas and deities . . ." and so on. To
the venerable Tārā, the deity of enlightened activity, he made offerings with
the lines "Savior from samsara, *tāre ma* . . ." and so on. To the meditation
deity Vajrabhairava he offered with the lines "Supreme form, supremely
wrathful . . ." and so on, and to the Dharma protectors, he offered with the
lines "Those who had vowed in the presence of the Buddha . . ."

Then he returned to his meditation room. Usually until half past eleven
he would undertake his practices and perform many times the offering of
the mandala that he himself constructed. At noon he would perform the
practice of offering the first portions of lunch while reciting the *Remembering the Three Jewels Sutra* and then perform the inner-offering blessing

before having lunch with Losang Lungrik by way of the yoga of eating. At the end of the lunch he cast some food to the hungry ghosts and gave to the spirit Hāritī, dedicating with the lines beginning "By the merit of offering this food..."

From two o'clock onward, Rinpoché received visitors of all kinds. He received them all with a smile and asked them briefly about their health. Any questions on the Dharma he would answer in great detail. On Wednesdays he gave audience to Westerners, and through an interpreter would answer any questions. At three o'clock tea was served, and Rinpoché would drink three cups of tea. The attendants would place the cup and tea on the table, and he would serve himself from the teapot.

When there were no visitors Rinpoché would read texts. At four o'clock he would retire to his meditation room, and there he would recite a few pages from the *Perfection of Wisdom in Eight Thousand Lines*, repeat Tsongkhapa's *miktsema* verse, the hundred-syllable Vajrasattva mantra, and the *maṇi* mantra. At six o'clock he had dinner by way of the yoga of eating. Afterward, he would sit on the veranda and talk for a while with the labrang manager and attendants. On occasions he would speak about going to the assemblies and teachings at Drepung and the tantric college, about the lamas he had received teachings from, their great qualities, even down to imitating their voices. He would speak of past events that served as methods to tame the minds of disciples and so on. He only spoke of Dharma-related topics. No one ever heard or saw him speak with anger, attachment, and so on.

Around eight o'clock he went to his room, where he performed the Vajrabhairava protector offering ritual, the torma offering to Nechung, and so on. After this he recited prayers and dedicated his virtuous deeds for enlightenment. Then, with the following verse, he prayed a long time for all those he had connections with:

> By the power of these virtuous deeds,
> may my parents, who nurtured me with kindness,
> my lamas and masters, from whom I received the bodhicitta,
> my vajra brothers, with whom I share the pledges,
> those persons with whom I have made connection in material ways,
> those animals used for my transportation, killed for my use,
> whose milk I have drunk and flesh I have eaten,
> may they all soon attain the state of enlightenment.

After this verse Rinpoché made three prostrations and then went to his bedroom to sleep with the practice of sleep yoga. This was his daily routine as printed in his autobiography.[17]

As indicated by the divination performed by Vajradhara Phabongkha, Rinpoché took single-deity Vajrabhairava, who is elevated by five special qualities, for his special meditation deity. Concentrating on the practice involving the combination of the peaceful and wrathful forms, the yoga of Vajrabhairava was his main practice. He also performed the extensive form of the blessings of the four initiations by way of the Guru Puja ritual in conjunction with this meditation deity. He also performed the daily sādhana self-generations of Heruka body mandala, Vajrayoginī, and Guhyasamāja. Practicing these three equally was in keeping with the practice tradition of Tsongkhapa, the Dharma sovereign within the three realms.

Rinpoché also recited the name mantras of twenty-nine lamas that he had received direct teachings from. They were:

1. His reading master, Ngawang Lhundrup of Gyütö
2. The attendant of the previous Ling Rinpoché, Jampa Losang
3. Tutor Geshé Tenpa Chözin of Nyakré
4. The Great Thirteenth Dalai Lama, Ngawang Losang Thupten Gyatso
5. Phabongkha Jampa Tenzin Trinlé Gyatso
6. Buldü Vajradhara Losang Yeshé Tenpai Gyaltsen
7. Tutor and former abbot of Ratö Monastery Losang Samten
8. Takdrak Vajradhara, Ngawang Sungrap Thutop Tenpai Gyaltsen
9. Khangsar Vajradhara Ngawang Thupten Chökyi Wangchuk
10. Choné Geshé Rinpoché Losang Gyatso
11. The Mongolian geshé Palden Sangpo
12. Trijang Vajradhara Losang Yeshé Tenzin Gyatso
13. Kangyur Lama Losang Dönden
14. Former throneholder Minyak Yeshé Wangden
15. Simok Rinpoché Jampa Ngawang Kunga Tenzin
16. Lhatsun Vajradhara Losang Thupten Gelek Rapgyé
17. Kumbum Minyak Ngawang Lekshé Gyatso
18. Sikgyap Rinpoché Losang Palden Chökyi Wangchuk of Tashi Lhunpo
19. Yeshé Rapgyé of Gyütö
20. Gyütö assistant to the ritual monks Tsultrim

21. Deyang Monastery assistant tutor Tenzin Trinlé Öser Rinpoché
22. Throneholder Khyenrap Yönten of Changyap
23. Tengyé from Gyütö
24. Shaphel Tulku Ngawang Damchö Losang
25. Ngakrampa Losang Nyima of Gyütö
26. Khunu Lama Rinpoché Tenzin Gyaltsen
27. Throneholder Thupten Nyinjé
28. Ratö Drakyap Dongkong Tulku Thupten Gelek Gyatso
29. Trinlé Wangdrak of Yerpa

Various texts were kept separately in a box that Rinpoché used for his regular recitations and readings. From this it can be concluded that he would practice them when he was not busy. They included:

Speaking the Names of Mañjuśrī
Tamboura of Devotion and Respect: Requests Invoking the Essence of Ārya Cittamaṇi Tārā
Mantras of oath-bound protectors to be recited daily, taken from the Rinjung Cycle and Surka Cycle of sādhanas
Losang Gyaltsen Sengé's *Vajra Diamond: Sādhana of Wisdom Ḍākinī Siṃhamukha*
Mahākāla Who Enters the Heart: Requests Made to the Guru and Mahākāla as One—A Hook that Draws in the Attainments
Secret Teachings on Four-Faced Great Vajra Mahākāla, Protector and Robber of Strength
Prayer of Samantabhadra
Dedication chapter of Śāntideva's *Guide to the Bodhisattva's Way of Life*
The outlines to the *Stages of the Path to Enlightenment*
Könchok Tenpai Drönmé's *Way to Study the Texts of Sutra and Tantra*
Könchok Tenpai Drönmé's *Ramblings of an Old Man*
Dakpo Losang Jinpa's *Review Meditations on the Stages of the Path, Encompassing All Essential Points*
Gungthang's *Summary of Advice on the Three Vows*
Notes on quiescence (*śamatha*) meditation
Teachings on the Vajrabhairava completion stage

Core instructions on mind training

Thuken Chökyi Nyima's *Way to Follow the Instructions for Repairing Weakened Pledges by Relying Upon the Five Yamāntaka Families Performed in Conjunction with the Guruyoga of Glorious Vajrabhairava*

Yangchen Drupa Dorjé's *Pillar of the Indestructible Life Force: The Way to Perform a Longevity Ritual by Way of Yellow Bhairava*

Removing All Opposing Hindrances: An Unelaborated Curse-Weakening Ritual

Drawings of the ritual implements that no tantric practitioner must be without

Drawings of the energy channels

Jamyang Shepa's *Precious Garland of the Oral Transmission: Annotations on the Vajrabhairava Seven-Chapter Root Tantra*

PART I

Childhood and Early Monastic Life, 1903–24

4 | Place of Birth

THIS LAND surrounded by a wall of cooling snow mountains is divided up into Tibet and Greater Tibet. In earlier times, during the reigns of the three great ancestral Dharma kings,[18] Tibet was also divided into the four regions of Ütsang.[19] Of these four, he was born in the central region of Uru. His actual birthplace was Kyishö, a place replete with all the qualities of the ten virtues, otherwise known as Yaphu, famed as the abode of Cakrasaṃvara and consort and a day's journey northwest of the capital, Lhasa. There the land is shaped like a triangular *dharmodaya*.[20] The mountains in the distance resemble a heap of jewels. On the sides of the surrounding hills are shapes of vowels and consonants. Sitting amid the foreground hills, which resemble draped silk, is the hermitage of Ratsa. Of its many sacred objects, the main one is a statue of Vajrayoginī, the meditation deity of the great Paṇchen Nāropa, which many times has given spoken replies to questions asked of it, thereby endowing it with the powerful blessing of "liberation through seeing." There is a small and delightful shortcut known as the Ḍākinī hill path between his birth village of Karbok and Ratsa hermitage.

On the mountains in the distance can be seen a stack of rocks known as the Palace of Cakrasaṃvara (plate 5), and because of this feature the name of this region is Yap.[21] This means that a constant stream of devout pilgrims—ordained and lay, men and women—come from Lhasa and elsewhere to make offerings. Moreover, there are very many accounts of the arising of realization and experiences in several great beings that have practiced in this place.

It is difficult for an ordinary being like me to gauge precisely the intention of this great being. However, were I to speculate why he took birth in that place, I would say that in the eyes of his ordinary disciples, this root guru of ours had achieved advanced spiritual stages by relying on the vajra paths of Śrī Cakrasaṃvara with consort and Vajrabhairava. The master was now instructing his followers that should they also wish to quickly gain the stage of union endowed with its seven features,[22] it is proper to rely upon such meditation deities. Also, he would be able to care for the people of this area through their seeing, hearing, remembering, and coming into contact with him.

I have not found a reliable source from whom I can enquire about the family background of our master's mother and father. However, he was born into a very poor household in Karbok, subjects of the private Yuthok Drachen estate that was the household of the Tenth Dalai Lama. His father was Kunga Tsering and his mother Sönam Dekyi. Great beings take birth in royal families such as the Shing Sala family, as well as in rich, poor, and moderately well-off households, for special reasons. I think the reasons that this holy being deliberately took birth in a poor family was firstly to care for two beings who had fostered roots of virtue over many lifetimes and who had prayed to be the parents of this great and holy being. Secondly, he was teaching that preserving and spreading the teachings of the Buddha do not depend upon family lineage but upon the qualities of study, contemplation, and meditation. As the Buddha himself said, "In my doctrine, lineage and family are not the main considerations. Dharma practice is."

Our master was born in the year 1903,[23] or in the water-rabbit year of the fifteenth sixty-year cycle, in the very early morning of the sixth day of the eleventh month. It is said that he emerged still inside the amniotic sac and his mother hesitated, not knowing what to do. At that moment he cried out "A-ye!" and with the movement of his arms, became free of the amniotic membrane.

His predecessor, Venerable Losang Lungtok Tenzin Trinlé, exhibited passing away on the eighth day of the eighth month of the water-tiger year, when he was forty-seven years old (1902). From one point of view it appears as if he did not complete a full life. However, the reality is that he returned as the display of a supreme incarnation to be the guide for the doctrine and for living beings such as myself. At a time when the sun of the doctrine of the Buddha was shining brightly in the Dharma land of Tibet, he listened and received all the initiations, transmissions, core instructions, and so on in the presence of many learned and adept masters. He became the master of the doctrine of scripture and insight, thereby sustaining the teachings of the Buddha Śākyamuni in general, and specifically those of the second Buddha, Tsongkhapa Losang Drakpa. His incarnation was therefore timely. In particular, from the time I learned how to read and write, he bestowed upon me, who is the fourteenth in the lineage of the Holder of the White Lotus,[24] the complete teachings of sutra and tantra in the manner of a pot being filled to the brim. In particular, after the doctrine had been reduced almost to a point where its name had vanished in the Dharma land of Tibet, in keeping with the prophecy of the Buddha that the doctrine would go from north to north and then would spread again in the central region, the master clearly took on the form of regent of the second Buddha Tsongkhapa in the noble land of India, and he ensured that the doctrine shone like the sun. Without a doubt it is for these reasons that he took birth at such time.

This glorious lama was the eldest son of the parents mentioned above. They also had a son Öser and a daughter Bakdro. While this great being was still in his mother's womb, his father traveled to the Lhasa district to sell dung, and there his load-carrying mules died. I think that this and other troubles that occurred were the work of Makaradhvaja[25] and his cohorts, who set out to obstruct the extensive activities that this great being would go on to perform for the doctrine of the second Buddha and others. As the saying goes, "When the Dharma is profound, the hindrances will be profound." I am not clear about the time and circumstances of his father's passing, but Rinpoché told those around him that he had never met his father.

There can be no doubt that, even at such a tender age, the nature of this great being far surpassed that of ordinary beings. However, as to the details of the master's early childhood, I have found no reliable source, so I cannot write more about it here.

The Thirteenth Dalai Lama on his throne
at the Potala Palace

5 | Searching for the Reincarnation

AFTER RINPOCHE'S PREDECESSOR had passed away, Jampa Losang, who was the predecessor's nephew and attendant, approached the Great Thirteenth for a divination and the two oracles of Nechung and Gadong for a prophecy concerning his reincarnation. The replies came back: "Not far, directly northwest of the temple of the Kalsang Palace in the Norbulingka . . ."[26] Also:

> In the south, as considered from
> the time of the predecessor,
> will be found the unmistaken reincarnation,
> the enlightened body, speech, and mind as one.

The great Dharma protector of Gadong also declared that the place would be Yap. Thus it was clear that this would be the birthplace, and any doubt about the area in which to conduct the search for the incarnation was resolved. Yaphu was northwest of the Norbulingka Kalsang Palace and south of Phenpo Rakma, the birthplace of his predecessor. It was between the two.

When making a detailed search for children with special signs born in the small settlement of Yaphu, three were identified. They were Losang Gyatso, son of Jangkha Lhopa, who was an official in the general revenue office of Drepung Monastery; Sönam Wangden, a child from Karbok; and Yeshé Namdak, the son of a tenant of Phukpoché estate. A request for divination was made to the Gadong protector asking for identification of the correct incarnation from these three. Without saying clearly which child this was, the response from the protector was that to resolve this issue, they should go to the lands of China and Mongolia, where the great master Meaningful to Behold[27] was visiting. Accordingly, the attendant Jampa Losang and a party set out from Lhasa.

Prior to leaving, Jampa Losang invoked the great Gadong protector through the oracle and requested that, when making this long journey to China and Mongolia for the purposes of identifying the correct incarnation, there be no obstacles and their task be successful. The reply came, "There may be a few hindrances, but as in the past, I the spirit will help you." In keeping with this prophecy, a few of the servants did not want to make such a long journey. They conspired together, and one night on the northern plains they cut the ropes of the tents, threw stones, and so on. However, not much damage was done, and those servants suspected of being involved were sent back at once. The attendant Jampa Lobsang was someone who believed resolutely in the protector Nechung and consequently had brought with him the little statue of Nechung, which he usually kept in his room. It is said that at this time the small bells that adorned the brocade on the statue began to ring.

Whatever the case, because of the unfailing assistance produced by the four types of activities[28] that are performed by the vast ocean of oath-bound protectors, they arrived safely in the Tashi Lhunpo Ling Monastery of Khadro Chingwan Dākhural in Mongolia, where the previous Dalai Lama was staying. They at once made their prostrations and presented to him a detailed account of their search for the precious incarnation. They requested a divination through the vision of his exalted wisdom on who was worthy of being the unmistaken reincarnation from among the three children. In response he placed his seal of approval upon the name of Sönam Wangden, the boy from Karbok, as being the unmistaken incarnation and gave him the name Thupten Lungtok Namgyal Trinlé. The Great Thirteenth also composed a long-life prayer entitled *Nectar for the Supreme Granting of All Wishes*. In the colophon of this long-life prayer, found in the collected works of the Great Thirteenth, it says, "Although I have not received any entreaty for assistance from the manager of the Ling Labrang in the search for the incarnation, I remember the kindness of my holy tutor and have trust in the divination request made to the Mahārāja."[29] The manager of Ling Labrang at that time was a monk from Dargyé Ling of Lhokha district. There was a child from Lhokha who could have been the incarnation, and he had high hopes that this was indeed the case. It seems that the manager did not pay as much attention to the other candidate children.

As mentioned previously, the birthplace of the previous incarnation was Phenpo Rakma, while the birthplace of this present incarnation is Ratsa.

Thus the names of both birthplaces contain the syllable *ra*. It is said that this illustrates that Rinpoché is a manifestation of Ra Lotsāwa.[30]

The Great Thirteenth gave careful instructions to the attendant Jampa Losang on the relevant ceremonial duties to be performed around the enthronement. Accordingly, when Rinpoché arrived in Lhasa, he was offered a set of robes and led to Garpa Hermitage (plate 6), where he was enthroned on the high Dharma throne that had been blessed by his previous incarnations. When he was being escorted from his birthplace in Karbok in the early morning, he reached the circumambulation path around the Ramoché temple at the same time that the morning assembly gong was being struck at Gyütö Monastery. According to the senior monks this was clearly an auspicious sign that this great being would later enroll in the glorious Gyütö Monastery, complete his study, contemplation, and meditation within the vast ocean of tantras to rise as a great teacher of tantra endowed with the two sets of ten principles,[31] and preserve and spread the teaching of mantra as if vajra-holder Kunga Döndrup[32] himself had come again.

Gyütö Monastery's main temple in Lhasa, also known as Ramoché.

6 | Childhood

ALTHOUGH I AM not sure of the exact dates and times, it was probably around the age of four when his reading tutor Ngakrampa Ngawang Lhundrup, from Phukhang House of Gyütö Monastery, started tutoring him in reading the vowels and the consonants, which is the gateway to all learning, the basis of all expression in words and sentences, and the fundamentals of the great treatises. After about eight months, this scholar had to leave for China and Mongolia under the orders of the former Dalai Lama as one of a party of eight ritual monks from Gyütö. Therefore the attendant Jampa Losang had to serve as teacher for his study and contemplation. Rinpoché memorized texts, such as *Speaking the Names of Mañjuśrī*, Maitreya's *Ornament of Realization*, and Candrakīrti's *Entering the Middle Way*.

Ngakrampa Ngawang Lhundrup was born in Tsakhalho. He was entered into Karda Monastery, where he memorized the various liturgical texts. He later came to central Tibet and joined Gyütö Monastery and became very skilled at chanting and recitations, such as the long-and-low tone chanting. When the previous Dalai Lama entered into the great retreat on the meditation deity Vajrabhairava, Ngawang Lhundrup was one of the eight monks from the two tantric colleges that sat in on the retreat in the Norbulingka Palace. He had sat at the feet of many lamas studying and contemplating the sutras and tantras and had developed a successful meditative practice. Therefore, when he died at the age of seventy-eight, he did so in a joyful state. When Rinpoché was eight, he gave Ngawang Lhundrup one of his baby teeth. This tooth today resides as an inner component of a statue of Kunga Döndrup, one of the principal sacred objects of the present Gyütö reestablished at Tenzin Gang in Mön.[33]

In 1909, the earth-bird year, the previous Dalai Lama returned to the great capital of Lhasa from his visits to China and Mongolia. When he had reached the place called Nakchu Tratsangla, Rinpoché went specially to greet him, even though he was only seven years old. The Dalai Lama afforded him great respect and honor, such as coming out of his residence and standing in the door as Rinpoché was being led in through the cordon of the military bodyguards. The previous Ling incarnation had been a tutor to this Dalai Lama, and this was an indication that later this young incarnation would become an object of great veneration for me. Once inside the residence, Rinpoché made three preliminary prostrations and offered to the Dalai Lama the mandala and the three representations of the enlightened body, speech, and mind. During the audience the Dalai Lama put him at ease with smiles and a joyful nectar-flow of speech.

His teacher Ngawang Lhundrup had returned with the Dalai Lama. Rinpoché recognized him at once and called out to him, "Gen-la!" which means "venerable teacher."

On the way back Rinpoché visited Radreng (a.k.a. Reting) Monastery, the source of the stream of Kadam teachings, and paid homage to the sacred objects there, such as the central statue of Jowo Jampel Dorjé. There he had a relaxed audience with the fourth Radreng incarnation.

Until he was about eight or nine he alternated his residence between Garpa Hermitage and the Ling Labrang in Lhasa. One time the all-knowing Paṇchen, the eminent Thupten Chökyi Nyima Gelek Namgyal, came especially to Garpa Hermitage for a pilgrimage visit. After Rinpoché had offered the mandala and the three representations, the two spent their time in pleasant conversation.

In the year 1911, the iron-pig year, when Rinpoché was in his ninth year, Geshé Tenpa Chözin of Drepung Nyakré House, or Phuntsok as he was known, a true master of scholarship and meditative practice, was invited to be Rinpoché's tutor. He began training in the dialectical path of Collected Topics,[34] learning how to propose and respond to syllogisms as well as memorizing the opening sections of *Ratö Collected Topics* composed by Jamyang Lama Choklha Öser.

Geshé Tenpa Chözin was born to a family from Metö Darutsang, which was under the domain of the Drakyap branch monastery. His father was Sherap Gyaltsen and his mother Kunga Tsomo. He was ordained as a monk at an early age and studied in Drepung Monastery, where he earned the title of geshé lharampa. He received extensive initiations, transmissions, and teachings from many great beings and put them into practice perfectly.

Through this he became a teacher giving classes on classical texts to the students at the monastery. At this time, Ling Labrang offered his name as well as that of Kunga from Nyakré House of Loseling College, who had a great reputation as a scholar, to the great protector Gadong as worthy candidates for being the tutor of the young incarnation. The former was deemed the better choice and so became the tutor and took up residence at Ling Labrang. After a while Geshé Tenpa Chözin returned to the land of his birth and was conferred the title of throneholder of both the main and branch monasteries of Drakyap, where he turned the wheels of Dharma. With this and other duties he served as a great being performing extensive deeds for the propagation of the Buddha's teaching.

7 | Initial Studies

I CANNOT BE SURE of the exact date, but sometime in 1912, in the water-rat year, when Rinpoché had reached the age of ten, he first set foot in the glorious and great monastery of Drepung, that great Dharma lake of study and practice where millions of white swan-like scholars and practitioners beat their wings of scripture and logic to fulfil their desires. (plates 7 and 8) In Lhasa, this year came to be known as "the water-rat year of Chinese war" because of the troubles that had erupted at that time between Tibet and China. Because of this the attendants from Ling Labrang had to smuggle Rinpoché from the hermitage to the monastery very early in the morning. Later Rinpoché recounted to others how he had heard gunfire in Lhasa when the group reached the corner of Pari Hill.

When Rinpoché's feet first adorned the residence at Ling House in Drepung, where the previous incarnations had pursued their studies and contemplations, he was served tea, ceremonial sweet rice, and so forth. After this the governing assembly of the monastery, the abbots and officials of Drepung Loseling, Ling House, and others presented Rinpoché with offering scarves and the three representations, which were joyfully accepted. Keeping with tradition, Ling Labrang presented gifts to the Drepung governing body, the college officials, and others.

On the morning of an auspicious day, when Rinpoché was to enter into the great assembly hall, the attendant Döndrup, nephew of Jampa Losang, the attendant to Rinpoché's predecessor, placed the monastic robe on his shoulder and carried it as far as the entrance of the assembly hall. Rinpoché then took the robe himself and entered the hall, where he sat on a monastic mat laid out at the head of the back row on the right. Because he had memorized them previously, Rinpoché was able to recite the prayers together with the monastic assembly. After tea in the great assembly he went to

Drepung Loseling assembly hall and sat at the head of the front row on the right. There too he recited prayers with the monks. The monastery entrance offerings and so forth, made to the assembly and Loseling College, were far greater than usual.

When the formal debate session began, Rinpoché attended and sat in front of that master of scripture and reasoning, abbot Minyak Jamyang Yönten, and listened to him recite from the beginning of the *Ratö Collected Topics*. Rinpoché then repeated from memory what the abbot had recited from that text. After that he went to the classroom, where he sat in front of the class with a companion and recited the *Ratö Collected Topics*. Then a monk from the class put forward some points of debate, to which Rinpoché replied.

After the day's debate session was over, Rinpoché went and sat on the prepared throne in the assembly hall. At that time, the Dalai Lama was still in India, and Ganden Throneholder Tsemönling Rinpoché Ngawang Losang Tenpa Gyaltsen was serving as regent. Accordingly, a Potala representative of the Dalai Lama offered Rinpoché a ceremonial scarf and a protection cord, followed by a representative of the regent also presenting a ceremonial scarf. Rinpoché stood up on the throne and graciously received these two scarves around his neck. He then sat down on the throne, and the abbot of Drepung made three prostrations and offered the mandala and the three representations. After this Rinpoché received with great joy offerings of scarves from the dignitaries of the Drepung governing body, the abbot and officials of Drepung Loseling, the teachers of the monastic houses of Ling, Nyakré, Trehor, and so on, and other invited guests. At the conclusion of these ceremonies, Ling Labrang offered an elaborate banquet to all the assembled guests and made extensive offerings of gifts, donations, tea, thukpa soup, and rice porridge to the residents of Ling House and neighboring monastic houses.

A few days later Rinpoché went for an audience with the current administrator of Tibet, Tsemönling Rinpoché, and visited Losang Gyaltsen, the former Ganden Throneholder. Both advised Rinpoché to follow the example set by the previous Ling Rinpoché by continuing to cultivate without decline all activities of study, contemplation, and meditation, as well as exposition, debate, and composition. Rinpoché then continued his training on the dialectical path of the Collected Topics.

The Drepung Loseling assembly hall, in the 1930s

In his *Treasury of Abhidharma* the master Vasubandhu states:

> Living properly, endowed with study and contemplation,
> apply yourself well to meditation.

Therefore, in accordance with a request made earlier in 1913, on the eighth day of the first month of the water-ox year, when he had reached the age of eleven, Rinpoché received the preliminary ordination of the complete lay vows followed by those of the intermediate ordination and finally the vows of a novice monk. This took place at the Potala Palace in the chamber called Victorious in the Three Realms, with the crown jewel of all Vinaya holders in this land of snows, the Great Thirteenth Dalai Lama, acting as ordination abbot. Although Rinpoché was very young at that time, because of the awakened imprints from familiarity over many lives, he did not take the vows from resolve alone but followed to the best of his ability the practices of observance and abandonment pertaining to the thirty-six precepts of a novice monk.

The prime duty of the ordained who go forth from home to homelessness is to study and contemplate the three precious scriptural collections (the Dharma of scripture) and to immerse themselves in the practice of the path of the three trainings (the Dharma of insight). From these two, as is universally extolled in the tantras, sutras, and treatises, study is initially the most important. Accordingly, Rinpoché determined that he would devote himself properly to the study of the treatises that present the tenets of Buddhists and non-Buddhist schools in general, and in particular, the great classics of the six ornaments and two supreme beings,[35] who beautify the world and are unerring in the core instructions and scriptures that bring about the development of the three trainings in the mind. Therefore, after he had completed his training in Collected Topics, Rinpoché began his study of the treatise *Ornament of Realization* composed by Maitreya, successor to the Buddha. This work determines the presentation of Mahayana practice and explicitly sets forth the practices of the eight themes and seventy points that constitute the hidden meanings of the Perfection of Wisdom sutras. Rinpoché had memorized this root text earlier, and so he sat in front of his great tutor and listened to a clear and direct explanation from the vast commentary to that treatise called *Lamp Illuminating the Meaning of the Mother Wisdom: An Overview of the Perfection of Wisdom* composed by Panchen Sönam Drakpa,[36] a master vastly learned in sutra and tantra. On the debating grounds with other critically trained students, he strove in his study through careful examination of the points found within the great texts.

When he was studying the topic of the definitive and the provisional meanings of the scriptures, Rinpoché memorized Jé Tsongkhapa's *Essence of Excellent Explanation: Differentiating the Definitive and the Provisional*. While engaging in the interclass debates, Rinpoché also sat with other classes of a similar level and listened to Minyak Amé, or Yeshé Wangden, a master of dialectics who later became the Ninety-Third Ganden Throneholder. I heard that Rinpoché told others that this master would develop debates based upon the difference between the way superimpositions are refuted in the two works *Differentiating the Middle Way and the Extremes* by Maitreya and *Stages of the Bodhisattva* by Asaṅga.

During the debates between the higher and lower classes, Rinpoché would take on the responsibility of putting forward and answering debate points. In between classes and debate sessions, he would go to the roof of the labrang at night and engage in memorization until late. Every day in front of his tutor, Rinpoché had to recite as a test all that he had newly memorized. Tutor Phuntsok lived at Ling Labrang but sometimes was called away for a few days to perform ceremonies. At such times Rinpoché performed his recitation tests in front of Geshé Buyak of Nyakré House, who was well known to the tutor and was a frequent visitor to the labrang.

When asked how he played as a child, Rinpoché replied, "I would often look out from the roof of my residence. Other than that, I spent my time reading texts, biographies, and so on. If I were very naughty, the venerable attendant Jampa Losang would scold me." He also delighted in making clay models of the monastic disciplinarian and so on. Sometimes tents were erected for a few days on the Denbak picnic ground at Drepung, and during the breaks Rinpoché was invited, where he would play games like king and vassals.[37] He was also very skilled in playing games with stones. On those days Tenpa-la, the labrang manager, and others would be immersed in their gambling games of dice and dominoes. Rinpoché would remark how he was amazed that when they were gambling, it all seemed so important, and so completely were they caught up in their playing that even when they went to the toilet they would return straight away, with no time at all spent looking around!

Labrang possessions and some scroll paintings and items used in offering rituals were kept at the monastery and at Garpa Hermitage, but all valuable items and documents belonging to the labrang were kept in Rinpoché's chambers at the labrang house in Lhasa. During the water-rat year of Chinese war, the buildings of the Lhasa labrang burned down. As a result, the labrang became rather impoverished. This meant that the regular meals made for Rinpoché, while not devoid of quality, were certainly not prepared from the best food. Also, of all the reincarnate lamas at Loseling College, Rinpoché wore the poorest quality monastic robes. However, as he had acquired familiarity over many lives with the four characteristics of a lifestyle of a noble one,[38] it did not concern him at all.

Rinpoché always attended the prayer and debate sessions. Except for the evening sessions attended by the abbot when there was no debate, he would never miss the evening ceremonies.

One time at Tibetan New Year, when Rinpoché was about twelve years old, the Nechung oracle, Gowo Chösur, came to visit. During the audience Nechung suddenly entered the oracle and seemed to speak about the possibility of there being obstacles to Rinpoché's health that year and of the need to have specific rituals performed to counter them. Because of the commotion of the unexpected event, everyone present was distracted and could not concentrate on what the protector was actually saying. After the protector had left the oracle, those present asked each other what the predictions had been, but no one was able to say. After some discussion, it was agreed that the protector should be invited again. This was done and the protector was requested, "When you gave your predictions just now, we were so distracted we cannot recall it. Please repeat it clearly for us." The protector with great concern repeated the predictions in a relaxed but detailed manner. Although the recommended rituals given by the protector were performed assiduously, Rinpoché was plagued by a bile-related fever for quite some time that year, but gradually his health fully recovered. This story was told to me by my precious tutor himself in the course of a conversation. This was probably around the time when it was known that Gowo Chösur had been punished by the government and was forbidden from inviting and making requests of Nechung. However, it seems that a few within his inner circle had been inviting the protector in secret. If we consider the significance of Nechung suddenly appearing like that, it may be that the precious tutor had a special relationship with Nechung from an early age.

One time a senior monk asked Rinpoché, "Have you heard the news these days?"

To which Rinpoché replied, "I've heard nothing."

The monk then added, "I've been hearing people say, 'The managers of the Tsawa, Phu, and Do[39] houses should beware.'"

Rinpoché replied, "This may refer to the surfacing of certain documents that indicate these three had a strong connection with the Chinese military, and to the government's expelling them from the monastery and imprisoning them."[40] Upset about the arrest of these managers and other incidents, a few thoughtless monks who could not be subdued by monastic officials stirred up trouble. Several Loseling monks took to a platform at the Norbulingka Palace, where they prostrated, shouted out their appeals, and so on. This went against the laws of the country, and Takdrak Rinpoché,[41] who was a high-ranking incarnate monk and at the time held no government post, came specially to the managers' office in the monastery out of concern for the Buddha's teaching, and he strongly advised that it was wholly improper for lamas, tulkus, and anyone else to rise up against the government. While giving this advice, Takdrak Rinpoché's upper garment slipped down to

Takdrak Rinpoché

reveal something like a large wheel that he was wearing on his waist. Rinpoché remarked that it was probably a ceremonial wheel of control.[42]

Because of the turmoil in the monastery brought about by the provocative actions of those rash Loseling monks, there was much disquiet. Therefore Rinpoché's manager decided to move the most valuable assets of the labrang to Lhasa. A light brown Mongolian horse, purchased from the government, was saddled with an ornate saddle with Chinese woven underlay and saddle seat, when it suddenly reared up for no reason and the saddle was damaged. Rinpoché remarked that this looked as if the protectors were angry at the decision to move these items to another place, and that it indicated that there was no need to move them.

Much later, after that horse had died, its skull was placed over the stables at the labrang's estate in Gangtö Changra Jang. Rinpoché would often ask manager Losang Lungrik if the horse's head were still there. The manager said that he believed it to have been no ordinary horse.

The previous Dalai Lama had commanded the great *tenma* female protectors in their chapel to send birds such as nightingales to the Norbulingka. As a sign that the spirits obeyed his command, Rinpoché told manager Losang Lungrik that he had seen birds fly to Norbulingka in the morning and leave in the evening.

In 1914 Rinpoché received a transmission and teachings on Tsongkhapa's *Great Stages of the Path to Enlightenment* given by the Dalai Lama in response to a request from Bārin Lama Rinpoché. This lasted for ten days beginning from the fourth day of the sixth month of the wood-tiger year. The teachings took place under a canopy erected in a grove to the east of the Norbulingka's Kalsang Palace. At that time, Rinpoché said that in his studies and debate he had reached the topic of bodhicitta.

After that the Dalai Lama went on a pilgrimage to the sacred place of Yerpa. On his return he visited Garpa Hermitage. There he made offerings and so forth in front of the precious reliquary of the previous Ling Rinpoché, the great tutor and holder of the Ganden Shartsé throne, the venerable and glorious Losang Lungtok Tenzin Trinlé. One day when the Dalai Lama was sitting happily in a meadow at the back of the hermitage, Rinpoché was also invited. Some small pet dogs belonging to the previous Ling Rinpoché were barking, and Rinpoché said, "Be quiet!" The Dalai Lama told him that he should be more respectful and say, "Please be quiet." Rinpoché often told this story.

Sometime later Kyabjé Phabongkha Rinpoché was invited to the hermitage, where Rinpoché received from him the great initiation of the single-deity Vajrabhairava, the glorious Yamāntaka, and the four-initiation blessing of Vajrayoginī of the Nāropa lineage. From that day on, in keeping with the tradition, Rinpoché practiced on a daily basis the *sādhanas*, or self-generation rites, of these two supreme deities as well as the six-session guruyoga.

I am not sure of the exact date, but Vajradhara Phabongkha was asked to perform a divination to determine which meditative practice Ling Rinpoché had a strong karmic connection with and which wisdom deity he should rely on. The following verses came as the reply:

Sole father, the wisdom dance of all the buddhas,
having abandoned his striking youthful form,
assumed a saffron-clad manifestation,
peaceful and well tamed, to become the glory of this land.
May he, the conqueror Losang,[43] care for you.

Your qualities are those of a sacred being,
nurtured to completion through a succession of lives,
and even in youth you are worthy of praise.
Supreme glory, supreme incarnation,
I have received the white lotus of your words of praise
like a beautiful gift of nectar overflowing;
you revere as a golden crown jewel
one who is but a clod of earth.

Your hidden wishes and intentions
cannot be discerned by one as ignorant as me,
but please think on these signs that have appeared
from single-pointed requests to the guru-deity.

The glorious master of the enemy of time,
deity of the two stages, single-pointedly meditated upon
from Ra Lotsāwa up to the previous incarnation,
alone supreme: hold him as your meditation deity.

The two stages of Guhyasamāja, Cakrasaṃvara, and Vajrabhairava:
hold each in your heart without abandoning the others.
This is the essence of the mind of Mañjunātha.

The sole father with a body like moonlight,
who brings forth the treasure of sharp and swift wisdom,
is nowhere better found than in the tradition of Mati.[44]
Develop wisdom, therefore, from this practice.

It is important also to strive in
the uncommon points of the practice
of the peaceful and wrathful aspects combined
found in the oral transmission built on experience,
through which even a glance meditation
will create wisdom that blazes like fire.

Constantly practice the rituals that will produce
the phenomena of the vajras of the three secrets
by gathering at the center of your heart
the glorious immortality ambrosia of samsara and nirvana.

Take the meanings from a vast study,
bring them into the stages of the sutra and tantra paths,
and with meditation carrying the load of experience,
penetrate to the vital points.

Teach living beings compassionately
the path on which you have traveled,
and by doing so let your sun illuminate
the degenerated tradition of Losang Drakpa.

The drumbeats of my prayers resound
"May your aspirations be perfectly fulfilled,"
and together with this pure white silken scarf,
I offer this with a pure and joyful mind.

In 1917, the fire-snake year, in Drepung Hardong's tantric hall, Rinpoché received from the great Vajradhara Kyabjé Buldü Rinpoché the initiation of the five-deity Cakrasaṃvara of the Ghaṇṭapāda tradition, the great initiation of the Hayagrīva secret accomplishment, initiations from the Rinjung Cycle and the Surka Cycle, teachings on the six-session guruyoga, Aśvaghoṣa's *Fifty Verses on the Guru*, and others.

While he was studying the Perfection of Wisdom, not only did he study Maitreya's *Ornament of Realization* and its related monastic textbooks but also the commentary to the *Ornament* composed by Ācārya Haribhadra entitled *Clarification of the Meaning*, as well as commentaries to Maitreya's four other works, such as the *Uttaratantra*. Rinpoché combined the study of these texts with associated commentarial works, such as *Golden Garland of Excellent Explanation* by the all-knowing Jé Tsongkhapa, *Essence Ornament* by Gyaltsap Darma Rinchen, and so on. Furthermore, Rinpoché showed extra effort by comparing and contrasting monastic textbooks from the other colleges as well. In this way he was able to comprehend perfectly the meaning of the Perfection of Wisdom texts. Rinpoché mentions in his own short autobiography,[45] and told the same with great humility to the former abbot of Shakor House of Drepung Loseling, Nyima Gyaltsen, "When I was studying the Perfection of Wisdom, I felt that I could compose a commentary to Panchen Sönam Drakpa's *Overview of the Perfection of Wisdom*. Why would I think that!"

It was the custom at Drepung Monastery that during the study of the topic of Buddha lineage, the brightest minds of Loseling and Gomang colleges could choose to stand up amid the great assembly hall and, subject to the approval of the master of studies, engage in a formal stand-up debate on a topic of their own choosing. Our master chose to debate on topics related to the fourth chapter of *Ornament of Realization*. Prior to this formal debate, from the great spring session of the second Tibetan month until the actual debate day, as it is the tradition, Rinpoché, accompanied by Nyakré Tashi Namgyal, a jewel among logicians, took part in the debates held in the various Drepung Loseling houses and classes and, in the summer sessions, in the assembly courtyards. During the latter, Mongolian Tenpa, a renowned scholar of Gomang College, and others would come and would engage in debates beginning from the section [from the fourth chapter of *Ornament*] on how all the aspects of the "three knowledges" are summarized and meditated upon. Nevertheless, I heard from scholars who were witnesses to the debates that Rinpoché gave without hesitation answers that would please the learned ones.

On the eighth day of the seventh month, during the great nāga ritual festival, Rinpoché and Kumbum Gakshing Shapdrung, or Mangra Shapdrung, of Gomang College engaged in the actual assembly stand-up debate in front of most of the monks of four colleges during the great tea offering. Gakshing began the debate with two lines that relate to the qualifications relevant to those who are suitable to listen to the Perfection of Wisdom sutras:

> Having performed exceptional devotions for the buddhas,
> and therefore having accumulated roots of virtue . . .[46]

Rinpoché opened his debate with the lines that begin with "They destroy the power of Māra."[47]

8 | Higher Studies

AFTER HE HAD completed studying the Perfection of Wisdom, Rinpoché's studies included the following: He studied six works on Madhyamaka, or Middle Way philosophy, by the great pioneer Nāgārjuna. These works establish the levels of emptiness, which is the explicit subject matter taught in the Perfection of Wisdom sutras. In addition, Rinpoché studied *Entering the Middle Way* with its autocommentary, composed by the great Indian master Candrakīrti, which engages with Nāgārjuna's *Verses on the Fundamental Wisdom of the Middle Way* from the above six works, in terms of its profound meaning as well as the vast bodhisattva practices; *Ocean of Reasoning: The Great Commentary* and *Clarifying the Intention*, both by Tsongkhapa; and Panchen Sönam Drakpa's *Middle Way Overview* and *Middle Way Analysis*. Apart from studying these works on Madhyamaka in general, he also studied in great detail the various difficult points of Madhyamaka within these texts, including rebuttal of the consequence,[48] the two truths, critique of foundationalist epistemology, and negation of self.

The study and contemplation of the texts of Pramāṇa, or Logic and Epistemology, are indispensable for determining the profound view of the Middle Way. As it is said, "The intertwined necks of the lions of Madhyamaka and Pramāṇa." For the pursuit of this study, there was a monastery primarily dedicated to the teaching and study of Pramāṇa texts called Taktsang Rawatö (Ratö) in Nyethang, and each year at the beginning of the eleventh month, for a month and a half, the monks of this monastery would hold a great monastic winter gathering at Jang to the west of Lhasa. When this great winter debate session at Jang is held, students from the great monasteries would attend this gathering in order to pursue their study of the Pramāṇa texts. Accordingly, our master and his precious tutor would also attend. The monks from the Drepung houses of Nyakré and Ling would stay with the monks from Ratö Nyakré on the upper floor of the Nyakré communal rooms and enjoy the mix of Dharma practice and festivities.

In the beginning Rinpoché attended the classes on the science of reasoning, where he studied typology of cognition and the ways of reasoning. After that he attended classes on advanced Pramāṇa and studied and contemplated the meaning of the relevant texts, which include the *Treatise of Valid Cognition (Pramāṇavārtika)* composed by the master of logic and epistemology, the glorious Dharmakīrti. This is the most important text of Dharmakīrti's seven works on Pramāṇa and is in fact an explanation of the *Compendium of Valid Cognition* by Ācārya Dignāga, who was a student of Vasubandhu, the second omniscient one. Dignāga is famed as having become more learned than Vasubandhu in the field of Pramāṇa. He also studied the commentary to Dharmakīrti's classic *Treatise of Valid Cognition* by Gyaltsap Darma Rinchen entitled *Illuminating the Path to Freedom* as well as Panchen Sönam Drakpa's *Elucidation of the Difficult Points*.

When debaters discuss with each other the themes from the five great topics [Pramāṇa, Perfection of Wisdom, Madhyamaka, Abhidharma, and Vinaya] they employ physical gestures and movements and clap their hands together. This is a practice initiated by the masters of reasoning of the past. During the gathering at Jang it was winter, and the cold in that place was intense. Consequently, when Rinpoché was in dialectical discussion with the other debaters, the combination of the constant clapping of his hands and the intense cold meant that his fingers would crack and bleed. However, as he was immersed in the debates, he was unaware of it, and only when he returned to his quarters and warmed his hands did he notice the pain. Rinpoché remarked that this would happen quite often.

In the monastic house, during the night debates, he would sit as position defender and because of his swift and profound responses, many of the debaters were rendered speechless.

Toward the end of the winter debate gathering, Rinpoché, together with Drakyap Dongkong Tulku, who later was the first scribe of Phabongkha Rinpoché's *Liberation in the Palm of Your Hand*, performed a formal stand-up debate in front of the college. Dongkong Tulku started the debate beginning with the following citation from one of the Ratnakuṭa sutras:

> Kāśyapa, just as prostrations are to be made to the new moon
> and not to the full moon, likewise those who have faith in me

prostrate to the bodhisattvas and not to the tathāgatas. Why is that? From bodhisattvas come the tathāgatas. Similarly, from the tathāgatas come the śrāvakas and the pratyekabuddhas.[49]

Rinpoché then replied to the debate, and the discussion ensued.

When the winter gathering had come to a close, Rinpoché visited Nyethang Ratö, where he spent one day in an upper room in Nyakré House. Paying homage in the temples, he offered prayers for the long-term continuation of the Pramāṇa teachings and so on. He then returned to Drepung.

I am not sure about the specifics of other activities he undertook, such as how often he attended the winter gatherings at Jang, but back in Drepung he took on the extracurricular activity of studying the texts on Pramāṇa. In this way he came to understand the views of the non-Buddhist Indian schools: namely, how some held that suffering had no cause whereas some held that suffering had a cause but that it arose from such incongruous causes as a primal source, or Īśvara, and so on; the extreme and meaningless ascetic practices; the empowerments from Īśvara; and other tenets that posited non-paths as paths, non-liberation as liberation, and so on. In short, he understood how their erroneous tenets pertaining to the basis, paths, and results were formed, and how the Buddhists with their stainless reasoning had refuted them.

About halfway through his Madhyamaka studies, his main tutor Geshé Tenpa Chözin returned to his district, and Geshé Losang Samten, or Loyak Rinpoché as he was known, of Drepung Nyakré House took on the role of tutor. He was born in a household from Metö Reda Gyangtré, which was under the domain of the Drakyap branch monastery. I am not certain about his father's name, but he was a great yogi from the Nyingma school. His mother was Tsultrim Drölma. He entered the teachings of the Buddha at an early age and studied at the great monastery of Drepung. He was renowned for his great ascertainment of the meanings of the texts and for his compassionate nature.

Some said that textual explanations from this geshé were far easier to understand than those of other teachers. Students learned in the scriptures not only from Loseling but also from the great monasteries of Sera and Ganden sat at his feet. After Rinpoché had attained the title of geshé, the Great Thirteenth granted Geshé Losang Samten the abbacy of Ratö College, where he remained for ten years engaged solely in the teaching of classical texts. After that he served as the shapdrung of Sangphu Lingtö Monastery for three years. Then he returned to his home, where he lived at Sakar Hermitage, giving explanations of classical texts and so on. In this way his legacy was clearly one of great benefit to the Buddha's teachings.

After Rinpoché had finished his Madhyamaka studies, he pursued the study of monastic discipline, or Vinaya. These works teach primarily the disciplined behavior that is the inner treasure of the Buddha's teachings. They include the *Individual Liberation Sutra* for monks and nuns, and the four scriptural collections on Vinaya. The intent of these root and explanatory sutras is to teach how to receive vows not yet taken, how to guard vows that have been taken, how to repair vows that have become degenerated, and so on. These can be summed up as (1) that which is prohibited, (2) that which is to be implemented, and (3) that which is allowed. All the points involved in training in these three are explained in the *Vinaya Sutra* by Ācārya Guṇaprabha, its commentary entitled *Sunlight Explanation* by the all-knowing Tsonawa, *Precious Garland: A Commentary on Vinaya* by the First Dalai Lama Gendun Drup, and Panchen Sönam Drakpa's *Analysis of Vinaya*. With these works as fundamental texts, Rinpoché studied the monastic discipline texts in general and specifically the seventeen key elements of Vinaya, which include the five sets of rites, the common downfalls to be avoided, the five categories of infraction, general presentation of the precepts, and the three basic rites pertaining to rectifying broken precepts.

After that he studied the fundamental texts on the Abhidharma. These include Vasubandhu's *Treasury of Abhidharma*, which explains the thinking of the seven great works on Abhidharma that establish the presentation of the practices of the Lesser Vehicle; commentaries such as Chim Jampaiyang's *Ornament of Abhidharma*, and the noble Gendun Drup's *Illumination of the Path to Freedom*. In doing so Rinpoché came to be trained thoroughly in the extensive topics of the lower Abhidharma: namely, the specific and general characteristics of the five fundamental categories of existence,[50] the ways of engaging in the forward and reverse sequences of the four truths, the paths, the persons [in stages of development], as well as the knowledge of the resultant states, a study of the śrāvaka and pratyekabuddha paths, the shared and exclusive qualities, and so on.

During the breaks between the terms, Rinpoché's teacher Loyak Rinpoché would give him explicit teachings, sometimes lasting all day, on every word of Chim Jampaiyang's *Ornament of Abhidharma* and Tsonawa's commentary on Vinaya. Because of this Rinpoché remarked that in debates on Vinaya and Abhidharma, there were hardly any passages he was not familiar with.

In his autobiography Rinpoché writes:

> At that time, I was very young. I liked to distract and amuse myself and was very lazy. However, both my great attendant and my wonderful spiritual teacher with their great kindness would use both peaceful and forceful skillful means to make sure my body, speech, and mind were meaningfully engaged. Moreover, they were very kind in the way they thoroughly encouraged me to pursue my study and contemplation. Also, my intelligent debating classmates used straight-talking reasoning and scripture to give me much help in many different ways in developing an understanding of the difficult points in the classical texts and so forth. Because of this, through my meager efforts in study and contemplation for twelve years, I have been able to ascertain within my mind the rough meanings of the vast ocean of the great treatises. Even now I remember from my heart the kindness of those sacred spiritual friends.

9 | Full Ordination

I N 1922, at the age of twenty, inside the Potala Palace (plate 9) room named Victorious in the Three Realms, during the period of the Great Prayer Festival in Lhasa, with the Great Thirteenth Dalai Lama as both the ordination master and the preceptor, in the assembly of the required number of monks as objects of veneration, and with rites conducted in perfect accordance with the required tradition, Rinpoché received the vows of a fully ordained monk, which constitute the complete foundation of spiritual practice.

One day that year the Loseling abbot Gowo Lodrö Gyaltsen invited Rinpoché to his residence in order to offer him candidacy for the title of geshé. Rinpoché went to the abbot's quarters on the upper floors in the college. There, with three prostrations, Rinpoché presented the abbot with a ceremonial scarf and representations of the enlightened body, speech, and mind. The abbot praised Rinpoché's studies so far and went on to say that in the forthcoming wood-rat year, during the Great Prayer Festival in Lhasa, Rinpoché would be formally sitting for the title of *lhaden rapjampa* (lharampa).[51] "Therefore even now you must continue to strive in your studies as before." With this the abbot presented Rinpoché with a ceremonial scarf.

In the following year, from the beginning of the great spring session, Rinpoché would attend classes on whatever texts he was studying and sit in debates holding the position of the defender. As was the practice, he would attend classes in some of the other monastic houses, where he sat in the higher classes about three times and in other classes at least twice. Once when he sat as the defender at Trehor House of Loseling College, Yama Tsepak, a renowned scholar, began the debate on the "ninefold division of obtainment" according to the Abhidharma system, and Rinpoché found it difficult to answer. Also, during the great debate sessions on Abhidharma and Vinaya held jointly by Gomang and Loseling colleges, Mongolian

Tenpa took the place of the defenders while Rinpoché and others debated on the connections between all occurrences of the word "other" in the *Treasury of Abhidharma* root text. Tenpa responded, "I did not come here to recite the Abhidharma root text. So if you have anything to debate, then do it!" Without any companion to help him with the answers, he soon became tired. These anecdotes were related later by Rinpoché himself.

In the fifth month of that year, Rinpoché with other lharampa candidates who were due to partake in the intermonastic gathering of Lhasa's Great Prayer Festival in the forthcoming wood-rat year attended the debate examinations held in the Sunlight Room of the Norbulingka Palace. These debates were monitored by the Ganden Throneholder, the Sharpa Chöjé and Jangtsé Chöjé (deputy Ganden throneholders), the Sera Jé abbot Ngawang Phuntsok of Jadral House, Gomang abbot Mongolian Öser Dorjé, and the Deyang Monastery assistant tutor and Nyal incarnation Tenzin Trinlé Öser. The candidates were not allowed to choose their own debating topics but had to debate on the sections from the texts and the difficult topics chosen by the tsenshap. When Rinpoché sat as thesis defender, he took the position, as formulated in the Loseling textbooks, that according to the Prāsaṅgika Madhyamaka school, the truth of cessation is an ultimate truth but it is not emptiness. To this Sera Jé Jadral Ngawang Phuntsok, Lawa Yeshé, and others responded with some extraordinary debate, but Rinpoché succeeded in defending his position.

In the past, the practice was that the title of geshé was awarded by the abbots of the individual monastic seats; the government took no part in any examinations. However, a few years previously, in an effort to improve teaching standards at the monastic centers, the Great Thirteenth had initiated these debate examinations in the Sunlight Room. Those who did not reach the standard required by the examination were eliminated from the candidacy. With this in mind, tutor Loyak Rinpoché offered Rinpoché the following advice: "When some of the candidates who are a little weaker debate with you, and you hold very firmly to your position, and when you initiate a debate against them and you present compelling proofs and refutations, this could mean that some of those candidates may not be able to join the ranks of lharampa geshés. That would not be good. It is better if you can avoid that."

This can be seen as a true sign that both teacher and student held the bodhicitta practice of cherishing others more than oneself as the very heart of their spiritual practice and is worthy of great praise.

During the great winter session Rinpoché made high-quality offerings of communal tea and donations to the monks of the Drepung great assembly, and tea, thukpa soup, rice porridge, money, and general offerings to Drepung Loseling and its various houses.

When Rinpoché formally sat as thesis defender in a two-day debate in the Drepung Loseling courtyard, Rinpoché invited his classmates and geshés to the labrang at the time of the communal tea serving in the great assembly. There they were served tea, tsampa, and softened cheese. About nine o'clock in the morning, sweet potato with melted butter was provided followed by a good lunch and dinner.

Except when he attended the debate, Rinpoché remained with his guests discussing the various points from the classical texts. Not only did he work on answers for defending positions in his own debate, but he also coached those geshés who needed help coming up with answers for when they sat as defenders.

10 | Receiving the Geshé Degree

I N THE WOOD-RAT year of 1924, on the tenth day of the first month, during the Great Prayer Festival at Lhasa, the intermonastic debate gathering was finally convened amid a congregation of thousands of monks that included the abbots, lamas, tulkus, karampa geshés,[52] monks skilled in logic, and many other scholars of the three monastic centers and the two tantric colleges. In the morning in the discourse courtyard, the best of the beginner students debated with Rinpoché on the Collected Topics, types of cognition, the science of reasoning, and themes from Dharmakīrti's *Treatise of Valid Cognition*. In the afternoon in the Kalsang Khyamra courtyard,[53] the best students from the intermediate classes debated with him on Madhyamaka philosophy and the Perfection of Wisdom. During the evening debates karampa geshés primarily debated with Rinpoché on Abhidharma and Vinaya. In these debates, no matter how difficult the topic was, Rinpoché responded at once with answers that would delight the wise, all the while a smile sitting naturally on his face and a demeanor that was both gentle and conscientious. In this way, his reputation of being learned and of having moral integrity and a compassionate disposition grew extensively.

The next day, the Drepung governing body, the college abbots, the monastic houses, the monastic disciplinarian, the sponsors, and other associated parties presented ceremonial scarves of congratulations. A few days later Rinpoché followed the convention for all geshés in performing the short discourse debate, the debate involving the presentation of the syllogisms and the relevant text, and the offering of communal tea in the morning, afternoon, and evening long prayer sessions, and he attended the interassembly debate, the teachings, and the afternoon prayers.

On the day of the twenty-fourth, after the Great Prayer Festival torma-casting rite had been performed, the awards and grades were given to the top candidates in the Sunlight Room, above the Kalsang Khyamra courtyard,

Procession of the torma during the Great Prayer Festival
torma-casting rite on the twenty-fourth day of the new year

in the presence of the Great Thirteenth Dalai Lama, as was customary. First
place was awarded to Lodrö Rapyang of Jadral House at Sera Jé Monastery.
Second place was given to our master, the precious tutor. Third place went
to Lawa Yeshé of Sera Jé, who would later become Sharpa Chöjé, a deputy
throneholder. A monastic official from the lord chamberlain's office read
out the full list at the entrance to the Sunlight Room, and the geshés proceeded in order into the chambers to receive from the Dalai Lama gifts and
awards in keeping with their placement.

PART 2

Later Monastic Life and Appointments,
1924–53

11 | Entering the Upper Tantric College

RINPOCHÉ DECIDED that having completed his studies and contemplations of the great philosophical literature of the sutras, he should embark on the study and contemplation of the Vajrayāna in general, and specifically of the tantras of the highest yoga class, which present to the fortunate in this degenerate era the flawless and complete methods for swift attainment of the Vajradhara stage of union in a single short lifetime. Then by engaging properly in their practices, he would quickly liberate all kind mother sentient beings, extensive as space, from the dangers of samsara and nirvana. Therefore, following in the footsteps of most of his previous incarnations, Rinpoché entered Gyütö Monastery, the upper tantric college. In the fifteenth century, the great tantric practitioner Kunga Döndrup, who was the heart disciple of both Jetsun Sherap Sengé and Jinpa Palwa, taught the glorious Guhyasamāja, king of tantras, to a group of disciples, whose number [thirty-two] matched that of the Guhyasamāja mandala, in a place called Jampa Ling in Upper Central Tibet. This gradually expanded to become Gyütö, as it is known these days.

Three weeks before his enrollment in that great source of tantric learning, in the second month of the wood-rat year in 1924, the ngakrampa geshé Ngawang Lhundrup of Phu House, who was the teacher who first taught Rinpoché the alphabet, sent a formal request to tantric college officials stating that Rinpoché was ready to enter the tantric monastic community. On the morning of the last day of those three weeks, in keeping with tantric monastic tradition, Rinpoché dressed in robes made from ordinary Tibetan wool and not from expensive material or imported silks and cottons, and proceeded to Ramoché.[54] His teacher from Phu House acted as his guide and led him to the rooms of the abbot and the *lama umzé*, or deputy abbot. There he made three prostrations and presented offering scarves. After that he went to the outside assembly area. There he sat on the Longdöl stone platform. This was the place where the seventeenth-century great ascetic and master practitioner Longdöl Lama Ngawang Losang sat when he came to the assembly area. After the morning assembly had finished, Rinpoché went with the monks to the mid-morning assembly in the prayer hall. There he sat on the left at the back of the geshé row facing the chant master. That day was the same day that Kyabjé Trijang Rinpoché was leaving the tantric college, and the two of them sat together for the duration of one assembly.

The Phu House ritual assistant Yeshé Rapgyé acted as Rinpoché's guide. As well as accompanying him to the assembly for the first three days, he instructed Rinpoché on what new entrants can and cannot do. These include not clapping during recitations until the admission tea for the monastic officials had been offered, taking the corners of the left-hand side of the upper robe and folding them over the left arm when coming and going, and not entering or leaving the assembly area by the main entrance in between prayer sessions. He also instructed him on Gyütö's internal discipline and codes of conduct.

After three days, following the mid-morning assembly, the admission tea was offered to the monastic officials. This is tea of good quality. While this was happening, Rinpoché and the reporting instructor[55] stood barefoot inside the assembly hall to the left of the entrance. After the serving of the tea was over, the officials gave their permission for Rinpoché to sit at the head of the row as was customary for great-assembly tulkus. He was also allowed, like former disciplinarians, to request permission to miss the monastic assemblies. However, for a whole year Rinpoché always attended the assemblies as the ordinary monks did and held it as important to not request a leave of absence. On that day during lunch, the labrang offered to the whole assembly two helpings of tea together with rice porridge, donations to the monastery, and donations to each individual monk.

In the third month Rinpoché went to the tantric college spring session in Chumda in Ütö (Upper Central Tibet). It was the custom that the monks had to walk to various places in and around Lhasa and also to these out-of-college sessions. However, those who were chronically ill or who were great-assembly tulkus, if they submitted a request to the officials, could receive permission to travel by horse. Rinpoché did this and journeyed to Chumda on horseback. However, on the day of the monks placing their mats, not far from the monastic quarters, Rinpoché joined the other monks in the procession to the assembly hall escorted by the disciplinarian holding sticks of incense. He walked in a calm and peaceful manner like that of Ārya Aśvajit[56] to the entrance, carrying a text holder on his back, a begging bowl, a cloak, a tantric eating bowl the width of a hand, and a small bag of tsampa.

There the disciplinarian gave an unhurried introduction to the Chumda monastic sessions, after which the monks went barefoot inside to place their mats. They returned to the courtyard, put on their robes, cloaks, and so forth, and returned inside. Rinpoché sat in the front row on the right near the altar and performed the recitations in the prayer assembly with the other monks. Afterward, the monks returned to the dwellings of their respective monastic houses. Rinpoché went to the Kharngön residence on the nearby Losempa estate, as arranged by the labrang.

In the larger monastic sessions it was the custom for the new geshés to sit in debate as thesis defenders over three days. Accordingly, in the evenings Rinpoché went to the debate ground and sat in debate while the elder monks debated with him. At about ten o'clock Rinpoché went to sleep in the lion position with the rest of the monks. Following the lead of the great beings of the past who never allowed any breach in precepts to remain for longer than a day, it was customary to confess and purify at night just before sleeping those wrongs collected in the daytime, and to confess and purify in the morning those wrongs collected at night. Therefore, every dawn after he had risen and washed, Rinpoché would make prostrations outside the assembly hall and recite the confession ritual three times. After that he recited the review of the monk's vows and went inside the assembly hall, where he recited with the others the self-generation of the Guhyasamāja meditation deity and so on.

From the third day onward, after the morning session, Rinpoché sat in an assembly that included the Sera Jé geshé Lawa Yeshé and Rinpoché's own root tutor, the Drepung Loseling Nyakré geshé Loyak Rinpoché, and listened to the precious abbot Minyak Yeshé Wangden teach from the textbook of Gyütö—the commentary on the *Guhyasamāja Tantra* by the revered Kunga Döndrup. In the afternoon, after the assembly, they listened to instructions based on interwoven readings of the four commentaries on the glorious *Guhyasamāja Root Tantra*, the king of tantras, whose seventeen chapters focus particularly on the methods for developing the illusory body, which is the uncommon and substantial cause of the form body at the stage of buddhahood, the ultimate goal of those who strive for freedom. The commentaries are: (1) *Bright Lamp* composed by the glorious Candrakīrti, who reveals with clarity the enlightened intention underlying the "six facets and four modes" of interpretation that seal this tantra; (2) interlinear annotations that clarify the difficult points of Candrakīrti's commentary; (3) an analysis of specific points entitled *Precious Sprout*; and (4) a summary outline of the *Guhyasamāja Root Tantra*. The latter three are all by the most revered Mañjunātha Tsongkhapa. These are the four commentaries. The days were spent in this manner.

In the evenings Rinpoché attended debate sessions where the monks recited the *Guhyasamāja Root Tantra* and took part in the detailed analysis of the meanings of the tantra.

Around that time, it is said, a newly enrolled monk was being persistently troubled by a spirit that had possessed him. When no treatment proved effective, someone suggested asking Ling Rinpoché for some purifying substances that could be burnt in front of the monk. Once this was done, the spirit was never able to possess the monk again.

Ganden Monastery. Tsongkhapa's mausoleum is the red-painted building in the center, and to the right of this is the main assembly hall.

After the spring session had ended, Rinpoché traveled with the tantric college monks to Ganden Monastery, whose full name is Drok Riwoché Genden Namgyal Ling, the special seat of the all-knowing master Tsongkhapa.

There Rinpoché joined the assembly and continued his studies and contemplations. In between the assemblies and the sessions, he stayed, as was the custom, at an affiliated house, which in this case was above Ganden Shartsé's Lhopa House, arranged by the monastic house itself.

On the second day Rinpoché journeyed to Yangpachen Monastery with several monks from Phu House of Gyütö. In front of the reliquary of the all-knowing Tsongkhapa (plate 12), Rinpoché made prostrations, presented a ceremonial scarf, and made limitless offerings, real and visualized. On the following days also he visited the precious reliquary many times, performing prostrations and circumambulations and making intensive prayers for the successful completion of his studies and contemplations pertaining to the vast ocean of tantra. Moreover, he made offerings together with ceremonial scarves to the sacred objects in Yangpachen, such as the icon of Buddha Śākyamuni known as Tsultrima (embodiment of pure ethics), and to the main shrine objects in the assembly halls of Shartsé and Jangtsé colleges of Ganden Monastery. To the great assembly of Ganden, to its two colleges, to Lhopa House, and elsewhere, Rinpoché made extensive offerings of tea, food, and money. He went on the circumambulation route of Ganden Monastery and examined with great curiosity the self-arisen objects found there.

He climbed to the peak of Wangkur (Enthronement Hill), so called because it marks the site where Lokeśvara in the glorious human form of King Songtsen Gampo, the thirty-third emperor of Tibet honored by many, was enthroned in the seventh century. There Rinpoché hung prayer flags and satisfied the superior and inferior nonhuman guests with an offering cloud of purifying incense. After this he returned to Lhasa, where he rested in his residence for a few days.

He returned to Ramoché to attend the monastic sessions, and at the end of the seventh month, he attended monastic sessions at Sera Monastery. There he sat as defender in the evening debates while the best students of Sera Jé and Sera Mé colleges debated with him. As he did in Ganden, Rinpoché attended the assemblies, visited sacred sites, and made communal tea offerings and gave donations to the assembly, colleges, and affiliated monastic houses.

Drak Yerpa was a very special place that had been visited by, and therefore blessed by, many great and holy beings past and present. These included scholars and practitioners, such as the Dharma king Songtsen Gampo, the master siddha Tsokyé Dorjé (Padmasambhava), and the incomparable Atiśa

Sera Monastery, 1936

and his disciples. In this place, on the fifteenth day of the seventh month, Rinpoché and the other tantric monks took the precepts for the late rainy-season retreat. From the precious abbot he listened to transmissions and teachings on three texts combined. These are (1) the glorious *Cakrasaṃvara Condensed Tantra* in fifty-one chapters, which focuses on the development clear light as the exclusive substantial cause for the dharmakāya of resultant buddhahood, (2) the commentary to the root text by the great Mañjunātha Tsongkhapa entitled *Elucidation of All Hidden Points*, and (3) the summary outline of this commentary.

In the presence of the ngakrampa geshé Losang Nyima from Amdo House, a ritual assistant who had become a master in creating grids, colored sand mandalas, torma making, and so on, he learned how to draw the mandalas of Guhyasamāja, Cakrasaṃvara, and Vajrabhairava and how to make the grid drawings necessary for the fire-offering rituals of the four feats. Rinpoché said that he had heard that Geshé Losang Nyima liked tea and consequently would offer him top-quality strong tea during the grid-drawing lessons. Rinpoché also perfected the art of creating three-dimensional mandalas under the guidance of ritual assistant Tsultrim from Amdo House.

During the great grid-drawing examination, which was a three-day exam-

Drak Yerpa monastic complex with outlying caves

ination held by the abbot and the deputy abbot on the grids, colored sand drawings, and the creation of three-dimensional mandalas, together with the symbolism of these creations, Rinpoché gave excellent answers to every question he was asked.

Sometimes Rinpoché visited and made offerings to the temple housing the great statue of Maitreya erected by Matön Chökyi Jungné, to the Avalokiteśvara statue built by Rikzin Kumara, and in the moon cave of the Uḍḍiyāna second Buddha (Padmasambhava), and so on. He also made communal tea offerings, donations, and so on to Yerpa College.

On the thirtieth day of the eighth month, the ceremony for the end of the rainy-season retreat was performed, and on the way back to Lhasa, Rinpoché stayed for a few days at Garpa Hermitage. Back in Lhasa he attended

Spectators and cavalry in ancient uniform at the main entrance
to the Jokhang temple during the Great Prayer Festival

two autumn monastic sessions, a Potala session, the Ganden winter sessions,
and the Drepung session.

During the year that they traveled together to the various monastic
sessions, Rinpoché developed great affection for his Dharma friend geshés.
During tantric monastic sessions held at the great monastic centers, it was
the custom for tantric college monks formerly of that monastery to offer
food and drink to one's Dharma friends. Accordingly, one day at Drepung
Monastery Rinpoché invited his geshé colleagues and put on an extensive
feast, and they passed the time in relaxed conversation.

After New Year during the Great Prayer Festival [of 1925], except for
attending the afternoon assemblies and so on, Rinpoché stayed at the
labrang and often attended the evening debate sessions in the Kalsang
Khyamra courtyard to debate on Abhidharma or Vinaya with the lharampa
geshés learned in those texts.

On the twenty-fourth of the first month, which was the day of the Great
Prayer Festival torma-casting ritual, Rinpoché watched the torma-offering

rituals and the military parades of ancient uniforms. During this time he focused on the complete pacification of the perverse actions and intentions of all those who harbor harmful wishes bent on destroying the happiness of living beings and the Buddha's teaching.

On the morning of the twenty-fifth, a statue of Maitreya, the fifth Buddha of this eon, is carried on a palanquin around the middle circumambulation routes. This is done to establish an auspicious connection so that when the sun of the doctrine of the fifth great savior shines in the future, we will be born as the first among his disciples, and having had the lotus of our mind opened, we will be satisfied like a swarm of bees with a great nectar feast of Maitreya's vast and profound teachings. Rinpoché specially attended this procession and made prayers. He also enjoyed watching the ancient traditional sports of wrestling, weightlifting, horse racing, and other athletic events.

During the fifteenth-day offerings [of Tibetan New Year] Rinpoché went to the shop known as Nepalese Pearls and viewed the great offerings from there.[57] On another day a young attendant monk escorted him along the circumambulation route, from where he viewed all the offerings. He also went to witness the erecting of the Ganden prayer flagpole[58] and the Eastern Dawn prayer flagpole. I have heard that, in his youth, Rinpoché enjoyed these spectacles.

As was the tradition, at the end of the second month of the wood-ox year [spring 1925], Rinpoché attended the tantric monastic session at the college in Kyormolung Monastery. This monastery is one of a group renowned as the six great monastic centers of central Tibet that were built during the early spread of the Kadampa tradition. These were Kyormolung, Gadong, Sulpu, Dewachen Ratö, Sangphu, and Tsal Gungthang. In the presence of the abbot, like the other geshés at the sessions, Rinpoché listened to the recitation of texts in the mornings, teachings on tantric commentaries in the afternoons, and attended the reading of root tantras in the evenings. While at Kyormolung Rinpoché made offerings to the sacred site of the remains of the "meditative concentration pillar," so called because it was at the foot of this pillar in the fourteenth century that Jé Tsongkhapa sat absorbed in meditation on the four facets of emptiness while the monks were chanting the *Heart Sutra* in the assembly hall. Because of his meditation, Tsongkhapa was unaware that the chanting had ended and remained there long after the entire assembly departed. Later this pillar was placed inside the golden reliquary of the Great Fifth Dalai Lama.

Rinpoché also made offerings to the monks of Kyormolung. He visited the place known as the Pool of Celestial Water and fed the fish there. This was a pool miraculously created in the eighth century by Guru Rinpoché [Padmasambhava] to provide a source of water.

In all the outside tantric gatherings that he attended for a year, as well as in other events, Rinpoché became an object on whom the monks of the tantric college cast the flowers of praise. Primarily he analyzed thoroughly the meanings of the tantras with stainless reasoning. At the same time he trained to perfection in the rituals of the college, such as the self-generation, front-generation, and vase rituals for Guhyasamāja, Cakrasaṃvara, and Vajrabhairava, propitiation of the Dharma protectors, torma rituals, consecration rituals, and so on.

Lharampa geshés who had sat tantric examinations at Gyütö had to attend examinations at the Norbulingka, and in 1925, a wood-ox year, Rinpoché was notified accordingly by the abbot. In the Norbulingka, in front of debate monitors that included the precious Ganden Throneholder, the Sharpa Chöjé, and the Jangtsé Chöjé, Rinpoché first sat as defender. Two geshés took it in turn to debate with him on the six great topics, namely, Pramāṇa, Perfection of Wisdom, Madhyamaka, Vinaya, Abhidharma, and Tantra. Then other geshés sat as defenders and Rinpoché posed them question on the relevant topics.

The result of the debate examinations was that this great being was awarded first place. Therefore that year he would have to sit again in debate examinations on tantra. Consequently, he memorized about half of Panchen Sönam Drakpa's work on the Guhyasamāja completion stage, as well as Gyütö's textbook. He trained himself well in works on the four classes of tantra, including *Great Exposition of Secret Mantra* and *Lamp to Illuminate the Five Stages*, both by the great Tsongkhapa, as well as many other treatises and their explanations composed by great Indian and Tibetan scholar practitioners.

During the Yerpa summer retreat, on the twenty-fifth day of the eighth month, Rinpoché attended the noon assembly and sat at the head of the left front row facing the deputy abbot. The chant master led the assembly into a recitation of supplications to Kunga Döndrup. After this the whole assembly listened with joy, faith, and delight to Rinpoché's beautiful and gentle uplifting tones like deer transfixed by a sound, as he recited from memory and without the slightest error a combined reading from Candrakīrti's commentary *Bright Lamp* and its exposition by Kunga Döndrup. Rinpoché ceased the recitation when signaled by the abbot. This was at a point in *Bright Lamp* on the section dealing with the benefits and faults of knowing and not knowing the suchness of the two syllables *e-vaṃ*. The particular passage read:

> Those who know the reality of the two-syllable *e-vaṃ* mudrā that seals the meanings of the 84,000 heaps of scripture, and who practice according to that knowledge, will very soon become buddhas who will turn the wheel of Dharma for all sentient beings.

Immediately after Rinpoché ceased his recitation, the deputy abbot stood up on his seat and initiated a short debate on the completion stage. That day the labrang made more than the usual offerings of tea, thukpa soup, sweet rice, and individual and collective donations. After lunch and in the evening, Rinpoché sat as defender in the debates. Also, in a five-day period, Rinpoché sat in debate while those who had traveled to Yerpa, beginning from the senior ranks, debated with him. This was repeated over five days back at the Lhasa Ramoché debating courtyard, where all the geshés, including the rapjampas, debated with Rinpoché. Whatever questions were asked of him, Rinpoché gave replies without hesitation, and the many unbiased scholars there cast flowers of praise his way.

12 | Appointment as Disciplinarian

I N 1926 the time came for our great tutor Rinpoché to join the ranks of disciplinarian. At an audience with the previous Dalai Lama, Rinpoché asked for advice on whether it would be proper to ask to be excused from this duty. The Dalai Lama replied:

> You should definitely become a disciplinarian. You should develop a good familiarity and confidence concerning the rules and regulation of the tantric college. After that you should go on to become deputy abbot and then abbot.

At another audience I heard that the previous Dalai Lama said:

> Recently I have introduced the custom of reciting the extensive *Individual Liberation Sutra* during the rainy-season retreat. During our regular bimonthly waxing- and waning-moon confession sessions, only the introductory part is recited, and for the rest—the sections relating to downfalls and so on—the following statement is included: "These appear in the recitation of the *Individual Liberation Sutra* every half month, so they were either heard previously or will be heard in future." If the extensive sutra is never recited, however, then it seems one should say, "These were not heard previously and will not be heard in future either!"[59]

Generally this Dalai Lama took a very serious view about the business of governing as well as the sacred bond between lama and disciple. He did not give that many public Dharma discourses, but he took an intense interest in overseeing the studies of the monastic centers. Also every year he performed the ceremony for bestowing novice and full-ordination vows on thousands of willing candidates from all over the country. His legacy in terms of propagating the precious teaching of the Buddha, both in its forms of scripture and realization, has been immense.

Although not even a year had passed since Rinpoché sat for the tantric debate exam, because he had gained first place, on the morning of the eighth day of the tenth month of the fire-tiger year, in 1926, the abbot sent the assistant to the disciplinarian to notify Rinpoché that he was to become the disciplinarian for the winter session. Immediately Rinpoché went to the abbot and the deputy abbot, and the matter of strictly maintaining monastic rules, disciplining, and so forth was discussed. Then on the morning of the tenth day, the assistant to the disciplinarian again went to Rinpoché's quarters. Taking Rinpoché's cloak, robe, scripture holder, begging bowl, and so on, he escorted Rinpoché to the temple of the Lion-Face Ḍākinī protector, where he waited for a while. After the morning assembly had finished, Rinpoché was accompanied by the outgoing disciplinarian for an audience where he knelt on one knee before the abbot and the deputy abbot. From there he went to the assembly hall. From the center of the front row, he made three prostrations and cast handfuls of grain into the air, visualizing them as vast clouds of offerings made in the presence of the buddhas and bodhisattvas. He placed a ceremonial scarf over the precious scroll painting of the protector Mahākāla and invoked his assistance to be able to perform excellent service to the monastic community. He then made three prostrations to the representation of Mikyö Dorjé,[60] offered a superior quality scarf, touched his head to both knees of the statue, and remained in prayer for some time. (plate 11)

He went to the top of the Ramoché main temple. There the outgoing disciplinarian handed over the gong, and Rinpoché beat it three times. They descended to the assembly hall, and after the outgoing disciplinarian had sat on his throne, Rinpoché requested from him permission to lay his own mat upon the disciplinarian's throne, to place the ceremonial hat upon his shoulder, to carry the disciplinarian's whip, to make the rounds of the monks' rows, and the general permission to exercise discipline by laying down what the monks could and could not do. After Rinpoché had sat upon the disciplinarian's throne, the outgoing disciplinarian respectfully requested permission to move his mat to the rows, to join the ranks of former officials, to which Rinpoché agreed. Then teachers from the individual houses presented Rinpoché with requests for leaves of absence due to sickness, leave for a number of days, for a year, and so on. The college steward listed the requests for leaves of varying lengths from the monastic staff old and new. Rinpoché then proceeded to the debate area, escorted by the assistant to the disciplinarian, where he made three circumambulations of the abbot's throne. He then went to the entrance to the assembly hall. The midmorning gong was sounded from the roof, and the entire assembly filed into the courtyard, where they waited. Rinpoché signaled with his right hand for the assembly to enter the assembly hall, beginning with the chant leader followed by the senior monks. After everyone had entered, Rinpoché went among the rows to see if the assembly were sitting in order of seniority in the seven-point meditative posture of Buddha Vairocana.

When the time came for tea, Rinpoché made three prostrations in between the two front rows and requested permission for those present to partake of the tea offering with the words: "Pray grant with great compassion your permission to those who are worthy of partaking in the tea offering." To this, the assembly responded aloud in unison, "So be it." He then read out the names of the faithful who had made offerings, with their requests for prayers.

After mid-morning tea Rinpoché returned to his quarters, where those close to him presented ceremonial scarves for auspiciousness. In the evening about nine o'clock, he returned to Ramoché temple. The temple manager gave the signal to indicate the time to sleep, and the monks assembled at the entrance to the assembly hall. There they made prostrations while reciting confession prayers, thereby performing the daily ritual of declaring and purifying their infractions. Then, with a lamp in his left hand and a signal from his right hand, Rinpoché respectfully ushered the monks inside. After the monks had laid down without making any unnecessary noise, Rinpoché went among the rows to check that the monks were in order of seniority and were following the proper ways of going to sleep, such as lying in the lion position described in the sutras and tantras. Then in front of the precious scroll painting and with sticks of incense in his hand, Rinpoché invoked the assistance of the protector Mahākāla for the propagation of the teachings and practice through harmony and pure monastic discipline among the monks. From the back of the rows, he made three prostrations to the monks and laid down to sleep upon the disciplinarian's seat.

Around dawn the next day, Rinpoché rose through the call of the chief food server. He made three prostrations to the sleeping monks from the back of the rows and recited the review of the vows and so on. To represent being awoken from the clear light of sleep by the songs of the four goddesses, he struck the stone gong, increasing the volume gradually to rouse the monks from their clear light of sleep. In the morning assembly, during the first tea break, he walked repeatedly through the rows seeing that the monks were performing the recitations and so on, and rousing sleeping monks from their slumber. After the mid-morning session, he went to the debate courtyard to see that those who had been enrolled at the college for fewer than nine years were at their stone slabs engaged in study and contemplation.

In this way, apart from breaks, Rinpoché was with the monks day and night for four months, from the tenth day of the eleventh Tibetan month to the tenth day of the third month of the following year. Showing no signs of fatigue in making the rounds of the rows and so on, he took on the responsibility of enforcing the rules and regulations of the monastery. He did not shrink from reprimanding, handing out corporal punishment, and so forth to those who, through a lack of conscientiousness, transgressed monastic rules. Once a monk from Minyak House called Sherap Dorjé who was afflicted by a nāga disease received severe corporal punishment from Rinpoché and as a result was freed of his illness. Later he came for an audience with Rinpoché and thanked him. This is testified to unanimously by those in the monastery at that time.

A man known as the woodsman from Shang, whose nickname was the Turtle, had died and was reborn as a spirit that was bringing much trouble to many people. They came to Rinpoché for help, and soon after this spirit was liberated from its birth and things were peaceful again. Also at this time, Rinpoché initiated a monk-increasing rite at Drepung Monastery, and as a result the number of monks clearly increased. These are things I have heard from older monks.

On the morning of his last day as disciplinarian, during the first tea break, Rinpoché stood in the middle of the assembly and, as was the tradition, asked for forgiveness if during his tenure he had caused any offense to the monks through his own mishandling or lack of awareness. Initiated by the chant leader, the monks recited the confession prayers while Rinpoché made many prostrations at the ends of the rows. Before the mid-morning session had ended, the deputy abbot met with the house teachers at the meeting place on the monastery roof and asked them about Rinpoché's tenure as disciplinarian. All replied that it was unparalleled in its excellence. The deputy abbot then presented Rinpoché with a superior quality ceremonial scarf and lavishly offered his praises for a task well done.

Phabongkha Rinpoché

13 | Receiving Teachings from Phabongkha Rinpoché

T HE GREAT Thirteenth Dalai Lama had hoped to be able to pass on all the initiations, transmissions, and textual explanations that he had received to the incarnations of his two tutors, Phurchok Rinpoché and Ling Rinpoché. Likewise, Rinpoché had hoped to be able to receive teachings from the great Dalai Lama like a vase being filled to its brim. However, the political duties of the previous Dalai Lama were great, and such opportunities for giving teachings were rare. Therefore the Dalai Lama instructed that henceforth Rinpoché should request teachings from Phabongkha Rinpoché.

Consequently, when Rinpoché had completed his duties as disciplinarian [in 1927], he sent an attendant to Phabongkha Rinpoché close to the time when Phabongkha was scheduled to give an initiation of and teachings on the Cakrasaṃvara body mandala of the Ghaṇṭapāda tradition with a request seeking permission to attend the teachings. Phabongkha Rinpoché replied that he had already performed the preparatory empowerment that day, but if Ling Rinpoché were to come the next day, he would conduct the preparatory rite separately for him. Immediately Rinpoché set out for Tashi Chöling, and that morning Phabongkha Rinpoché specially conferred the preparatory rites on Ling Rinpoché. In the afternoon, together with the large assembly gathered there, he received the body-mandala initiation. The initiation ceremony did not finish until about ten at night. Nevertheless, there followed an elaborate chanting of the verses of auspiciousness and so on, conducted with long melodious tunes, to the accompaniment of cymbals and other instruments.

At those teachings was the great scholar Choné Rinpoché[61] from Tashi Khyil Monastery in Amdo, from whom Phabongkha Rinpoché himself had received teachings on many of the classical texts. Choné Rinpoché was very learned, and without doubt he had received the Cakrasaṃvara body-mandala initiation before this time. Ling Rinpoché said that Choné Rinpoché was probably receiving it again because the Guru Vajradhara (Phabongkha) had a special connection with Cakrasaṃvara.

The master Phabongkha specially gave the preparatory rite to this great being, our master, even though he had already conducted it for the assembly undoubtedly because it was so rare to find a student greater than this jewel-like disciple in whom all necessary qualities are complete. As the glorious Candrakīrti's *Bright Lamp* states:

> Of pure ethics, learned and capable,
> of intelligence, and single-minded,
> one who, having learned, teaches it well:
> such a person is known as a "jewel."

After this initiation Rinpoché sat and received many related experiential teachings from Phabongkha Rinpoché. These include three works on the Cakrasaṃvara generation stage, which were taught simultaneously: *Lamp Illuminating Great Bliss* by Changkya Yeshé Tenpai Drönmé,[62] who in the eighteenth century achieved great levels of realization by relying on the two stages of the Cakrasaṃvara body mandala; *Secret Path of the Vehicle of Means* composed more recently by Kalsang Khedrup, also known as Chökyi Dorjé, a great scholar and practitioner of Dakpo Shedrüp Ling; and *Increasing Great Bliss: Actualization of the Bhagavan Cakrasaṃvara Body Mandala in the Tradition of the Mighty Siddha Ghaṇṭapāda*, by Phabongkha Rinpoché himself. With respect to the completion stage, Rinpoché simultaneously received experiential teachings on the prose teachings on the Ghaṇṭapāda five stages that were included in the sealed teachings of Panchen Losang Chökyi Gyaltsen, the crown jewel of scholars and practitioners in the seventeenth century; explicit teachings on the body mandala completion stage by Kalsang Khedrup; and teachings possessing the pure core instructions, which almost expose the heart blood of the ḍākinīs of the twenty-four places and which are aimed primarily at the practice of beginner yogis. Other teachings Rinpoché received were an experiential explanation of the profound path known as the Six Yogas of Nāropa, which constitute the very essence of Panchen Nāropa's instructions, given by way of *Guide Endowed with the Three Convictions* by Jé Tsongkhapa, and the instruction text written by Losang Tenpa Dargyé of Trehor Naktsang. Rinpoché also received direct instructions on the yogic exercises that train the body. As was the custom of the lineage lamas of the past, every morning and evening Rinpoché would integrate the main points of these teachings.

After these teachings Rinpoché received the initiation into the Chö (cutting-off) practice stemming from the Ensa oral tradition lineage. This was followed by explanations of the Chö text entitled *Navigator for Those Who Seek Liberation* on the basis of *Instructions on the "Navigator for Those Who Seek Liberation"*, a work composed by the great eighteenth-century practitioner Drupchok Losang Namgyal, and Kalsang Khedrup's guide entitled *Chö Text: Beautiful Adornment to the Teaching of the Ganden Practice Lineage.*

One day Phabongkha Rinpoché was giving instructions in his room to a few tulkus and geshés on the melodies of Chö chanting. Rinpoché said that he was sitting at the front and was very nervous and did not master the chanting. However, afterward he practiced again with Phabongkha Rinpoché's attendant, Jamyang, and improved somewhat. Rinpoché remarked that years later, even when he was old, the beautiful but powerful melodies of Chö that he would occasionally chant in his spare time could naturally bring on feelings of deep faith.

There was once a Sera Jé monk called Tsawa Phuntsok who originally was something of a *dopdop*[63] monk at the monastery. Having received extensive core instructions on the path, he meditated for a long time at Yerpa, and later he became known as Mahāsiddha Phuntsok. Close to his death this meditator decreed that the few possessions he had be put to good use by requesting a grand teaching by Vajradhara Phabongkha Rinpoché at Yerpa Monastery. Accordingly, in response to continued requests by the monastery, from the twenty-eighth day of the eighth month of the fire-rabbit year of 1927, to an audience of over five hundred monastics and laypeople, including geshés, tulkus, and so on, who came specially from the three monastic centers and elsewhere, Phabongkha Rinpoché gave experiential teachings on the stages of the path to enlightenment for over a month. This he did by combining the two works *Oral Transmission of Mañjuśrī: Instructions on the Stages of the Path to Enlightenment*, by the Fifth Dalai Lama Ngawang Losang Gyatso, and *Swift Path Direct Instructions*, by the all-knowing Panchen Losang Yeshé, who was born in 1667.[64] At the end of the teachings a small statue of Maitreya was brought from the Maitreya temple, and Phabongkha Rinpoché conducted the ceremony for taking the

Drak Yerpa assembly hall

aspiration and engaged bodhicitta vows. Rinpoché attended these teachings and made notes.

The place where our precious tutor was staying had many religious paintings displayed on all four walls, and in the teaching Guru Vajradhara said that when sleeping, you should not lie with your feet pointing toward representations of the buddhas and bodhisattvas. Rinpoché said that he felt that these words were being directed at him and became anxious. After this, when he retired for the night, not only at the labrang but in the houses of others too, he made sure that all paintings that might be in the direction of his pointing feet were placed elsewhere.

After the teachings on the stages of the path, and with teachings on Aśvaghoṣa's *Fifty Verses on the Guru* as a preliminary, Rinpoché received initiations into the thirty-two-deity Akṣobhyavajra mandala of the Ārya tradition of Guhyasamāja, the five-deity outer mandala of the Cakrasaṃvara Ghaṇṭapāda tradition, the thirteen-deity Vajrabhairava mandala, the thirty-seven-deity Vairocana mandala, the nine-deity Akṣobhya mandala, the great initiation of Eleven-Faced Avalokiteśvara of the Bhikṣuṇī Lakṣmī tradition, the permission initiation of the Guhyasamāja, Vajrabhairava, and Cakrasaṃvara mantra formulation, and the initiation of the sixteen drops of the Kadampa. During the preparatory rituals for the Guhyasamāja initiation when Rinpoché cast the divination stick, it remained upright. Everyone present regarded this with astonishment.

After the initiations Rinpoché listened to teachings on the six-session guruyoga, the fourteen root tantric vows and the eight faults, as well as Candragomin's *Twenty Verses on the Bodhisattva Vow*, all of which were specially requested by Rinpoché himself. Though he had received these teachings before from Buldü Vajradhara, those who pledge to train on the Mahayana path do so with the buddhas and bodhisattva as their witnesses, and so this must be done correctly by knowing thoroughly how to uphold the commitments they have taken. If this is not done, such people would be Mahayana practitioners in name only. Moreover, it is taught that those who wish to train in Vajrayāna in general, and especially in the path of highest yoga tantra, should hold guru devotion as a fundamental practice of even more importance than how it is explained in the general Mahayana path, and that they should protect the pledges and vows of tantra as they would their own eyes. Therefore there can be no doubt that Rinpoché particularly sought out these teachings again because of the importance of guarding the vows and pledges.

Rinpoché asked Phabongkha Rinpoché whether it would be appropriate for him to listen to teachings from Choné Geshé Losang Gyatso from Tashi Khyil Monastery. Phabongkha Rinpoché replied that Choné Rinpoché was someone who had sat at the feet of the most revered Sherap Gyatso,[65] who was a treasure house of core instructions from the oral tradition, and so was definitely worthy of receiving teachings from. Therefore, from the twenty-first of the tenth month of that year, together with Phabongkha Rinpoché and others, Rinpoché received from Choné Rinpoché teachings and transmission on the *Abridged Perfection of Wisdom* combined with Maitreya's *Ornament of Realization*, as well as teachings and transmissions on Candrakīrti's *Entering the Middle Way*. From the twenty-second of the eleventh month, he received teachings and transmissions including *Essence of Excellent Explanation: Differentiating the Definitive and the Provisional*, by Jé Tsongkhapa, and Jamyang Shepa Ngawang Tsöndrü's root text on classical Indian philosophies.

While Phabongkha Rinpoché was receiving teachings on these classical texts from Choné Geshé, in the morning and during evening breaks, in response to requests by the great Sakya Trizin, by Simok Rinpoché, and others, he gave extensive oral explanatory instruction in his room on Anubhūti's *Sarasvatī Grammar Treatise* to several geshés and tulkus, including Rinpoché.

In 1928, from the twelfth of the fourth month of the earth-dragon year, in the Chusang assembly hall, and with Phabongkha Rinpoché as sponsor, Rinpoché listened to teachings from Choné Geshé Rinpoché, which included explanation and transmissions of Jé Tsongkhapa's *Great Exposition of Secret Mantra*, *Annotations on the Emptying the Lower Realms Tantra*, and *An Elucidation of the Meaning of the Mandala Rite for the Complete Emptying of the Lower Realms by Way of Vairocana*; *Letter to a Friend* by Nāgārjuna; a combined explanation and transmission on *Cakrasaṃvara Tantra*, its commentary called *Elucidation of All Hidden Points*, and the outline to this work [both by Tsongkhapa]; a work on the Kālacakra generation stage by Detri Jamyang Thupten Nyima of Tashi Khyil Monastery; and the explanation and transmission of a work by Choné Rinpoché himself: *Interwoven Praise Based upon Tsongkhapa's Praise of Dependent Origination: Opening Wide the Door to the Limitless Skies of Treasure That Is Its Explanation, a Great Cloud of Melody from a Golden Age*.

Rinpoché said many times that Choné Rinpoché's poetic compositions were excellent and consequently were very beneficial to his mind. Examples from *Interwoven Praise* that Rinpoché would regularly cite even in conversation are:

> The Ever-Cool Lake[66] of the perfection of wisdom,
> very essence of the mind of the buddhas,
> ruled over by the nāga emperor Nāgārjuna,
> its valley suffused by the moon of Candrakīrti,
> drunk in by the Ganges of the mind of Losang Drakpa.[67]

Also:

> "Dependent" does not discard the ultimate nature;
> "arising" is in keeping with the world.

Also:

> When beings of today reach the end of their journey
> on the road carved by the wheels of the chariot
> of the *Wish-Fulfilling Tree*, the king of poetics,
> what companion will they travel on with?

While receiving the above teachings from Choné Rinpoché alongside other geshés and tulkus, Rinpoché also received teachings from Phabongkha Rinpoché. They included: Gungthang Tenpai Drönmé's *Powerful Weapon Wheel: Protection Circle and Repelling Torma Ritual of the Ten Wrathful Protectors* and his *Profound Instructions on Drawing and Executing Ensnaring Yantras*; teachings and transmission on the commentary on the learned Daṇḍin's *Mirror of Poetics* called *Melody to Delight Sarasvatī* by the Great Fifth Dalai Lama; and instructions on *Guru Yoga: Blessings That Are a Treasury of All Desires* by Phabongkha Rinpoché himself.

During the lessons on poetics, Rinpoché composed a few examples himself and showed them to Phabongkha Rinpoché for correction. Phabongkha Rinpoché told Rinpoché, "If you want to perfect your study of poetry, it is important to study Kṣemendra's *Wish-Fulfilling Tree of the Bodhisattva's Lives*."[68] Accordingly, at a later date Rinpoché borrowed two volumes on this work from the Phabongkha Labrang and studied them thoroughly. They were the annotations by Pang Lotsāwa Lodrö Tenpa on *Wish-Fulfilling Tree of the Bodhisattva's Lives* as well as the black-ink annotations by Sotön Jikmé Drakpa, and the red-ink annotations by Lha Jikten Wangchuk. He had planned to make copies of these texts, but that was put aside for the time being. Generally, Rinpoché did not make small talk, but he would tell stories of the Buddha's previous lives and so on, of which he had a very firm grasp.

Rinpoché also listened to Choné Rinpoché's teaching on Drati Rinchen Döndrup's explanation of Thönmi Saṃbhota's grammar treatise, *Thirty Verses*. Rinpoché mentioned that the reference for the particle *na* being used for the locative case was a line from Vasubandhu's *Treasury of Abhidharma*, "In the first meditative absorption, all . . ."[69]

After this, Phabongkha Dechen Nyingpo gave the transmissions and teachings on the generation-stage work *Ocean of Attainments* by the all-knowing Khedrup Jé and the completion-stage work *Lamp to Illuminate the Five Stages* by the omniscient Tsongkhapa. These teachings were given to an audience of about three hundred in the assembly rooms of Tashi Chöling Hermitage and were requested by the Mongolian geshé Nyendrak from Sera Jé Hardong monastic house. Rinpoché attended and received these teachings in their entirety.

One time, in response to a request from Ling Rinpoché, Phabongkha Rinpoché gave teachings on *Wonderful Wish-Granting Vase Sādhana* by

Minling Terchen Dharma Śrī, and the life entrustment of the great five king emanations (Nechung) using a work by Thuken Chökyi Nyima. At this time, Phabongkha Dechen Nyingpo told Rinpoché, "Last night I had a dream in which a red man came to me and exhibited great joy. The five king emanations is very committed to you."

In 1930 Rinpoché attended teachings on the profound path of the *Guru Puja* given by Phabongkha Rinpoché in Chusang Monastery debate ground. When he arrived at the section on the single-pointed prayer, a delegation from Thösam Dargyé Ling Monastery in Yartö arrived to escort Rinpoché to the monastery. (plate 18) As this had been a long-standing request, Rinpoché had to postpone listening to the discourse. There are existing annotations of the discourse up to this point. Later, Rinpoché received teachings on the *Guru Puja* again from Kyabjé Lhatsun Rinpoché, and also from Trijang Rinpoché, as will be described later.

As requested, Rinpoché spent six months in southern Tibet. At Thösam Dargyé Ling Monastery he gave experiential instructions on stages of the path using Panchen Losang Yeshé's *Swift Path Direct Instructions* and ending with the bodhicitta ceremony. This was the first time in this particular life that he had given teachings on the stages of the path. Similarly, he gave teachings at Yasang Monastery and made extensive offerings to both monasteries. He made visits to holy places in Yarlung to make offerings and prayers, including Tradruk Temple, Takchen Bumpa Hermitage, Yumbu Lagang Palace, the cave of Rechungpa, Namgyal Temple, Ngachö Monastery at Tsethang, as well as the Migyur Lhundrup temple of Samyé. Also, in response to their wishes, he gave teachings to many monastics and laypeople in that region, thereby bringing great benefit to the people and the doctrine.

While Rinpoché was staying in Dargyé Ling Monastery, his attendant Jampa Losang, nephew of Rinpoché's predecessor, contracted a severe stomach ailment akin to "bull-like worms,"[70] from which he would not recover. While his attendant placed himself in a virtuous frame of mind, Rinpoché made offerings for his passing. This attendant had been with Rinpoché from an early age, teaching him how to read and write, pushing him to memorize the prayers, and so on. He had become like his inner teacher, and Rinpoché counted him among his gurus. Moreover, whenever Rinpoché mentioned him, he would always respectfully refer to him as Kushap Sölpön-la, "the late venerable attendant."

Yumbu Lagang in the Yarlung Valley

While Rinpoché was staying at Tsethang Ngachö Monastery, the future manager of the labrang, Losang Lungrik, who at that time was only ten years old, was brought before Rinpoché by his aunt. Later, when he was eighteen, he would enter the labrang as a servant. At that first meeting he offered Rinpoché five freshly minted coins as a token. Rinpoché wrote the date on the paper they were wrapped in and put them away for safe keeping in a small box that he used for his personal effects. This act was as if he were seeing with his clairvoyance that Losang Lungrik, in accordance with Rinpoché's wishes, would serve him all his life.

In Takdrak Samten Monastery Rinpoché also received from Kyabjé Takdrak Vajradhara Ngawang Sungrap Thutop Tenpai Gyaltsen the great empowerments of forty-five mandalas. These comprised the forty-two deities from the great Ācārya Abhayākaragupta's *Vajra Garland Mandala Procedures*, supplemented by the "three mandalas for auspiciousness" from *Compendium of Activities* composed by Pandit Darpaṇa Ācārya.[71]

Rinpoché mentioned that one day, during these initiations, as Ekajong Tulku was performing the purification ritual on the students, Rinpoché bent forward and the incense holder struck him on the face, causing a small nosebleed.

Rinpoché requested Phabongkha Rinpoché for a teaching on Śāntideva's *Guide to the Bodhisattva's Way of Life*. Phabongkha replied that someone had already requested this teaching, and he had accepted to teach it. Therefore it would be excellent if Rinpoché would attend. Unfortunately, however, circumstances conducive for this event to take place never arose.

The Mongolian geshé Palden Sangpo from Tashi Khyil Monastery had received many teachings and consequently was invited to Lhasa by Lhatsun Rinpoché. Along with Kyabjé Takdrak Rinpoché, Khangsar Rinpoché from Gomang College, and others, Rinpoché received from him the initiation into the thirty-three white, peaceful deities of the Amitāyus inner practice from the Niguma tradition, the twenty-three red and wrathful deities of the secret practice, the nine red deities of the very secret Rechung Gongkhuk lineage, the nine white deities that grant immortality, the seventeen deities of Sitātapatrā, and many others, all based upon the manual of the famous nineteenth-century Mongolian geshé Losang Tayang from Dhakhural.[72]

Rinpoché remarked that one time he was receiving experiential instruction on the single-deity Vajrabhairava generation and completion stages from Palden Sangpo, and because of the strong Mongolian accent, he found it a little difficult to understand. However, he felt sure he would be able to receive the transmission later from Khangsar Rinpoché, who listened to the entire teaching. Therefore he went instead to the Shedra family house to receive the transmission on the *Miktsema Compendium*[73] from Kangyur Lama Losang Dönden.

Rinpoché listened to transmissions of the collected works of Panchen Chökyi Gyaltsen, the writings of the eighteenth-century[74] master Phakgo Lama Yeshé Tsöndrü, the collected works of Thuken Losang Chökyi Nyima,[75] and the collected works of the more recent master Akhu Sherap Gyatso, crown jewel of all scholars and practitioners from Tashi Khyil Monastery. Rinpoché often praised Kangyur Lama Losang Dönden as possessing the twin qualities of scholar and practitioner. He too regarded Rinpoché as a great pillar that would hold up the teachings of the Buddha and made him his heart disciple. From Shaphel Rinpoché, also known as the younger Kangyur Lama, Rinpoché received a few transmissions that had been missing.

Khangsar Rinpoché

Rinpoché also received other teachings, the dates of which I cannot be sure of. He took all of Jé Phabongkha's teachings. These include: experiential teachings on the generation and completion stages of Vajrabhairava using Tsongkhapa's *Jewel Box Sādhana of the Thirteen-Deity Vajrabhairava*, a deity that in these degenerate times is superior to other deities in five ways; profound teachings on the eleven yogas of the generation stage of Vajrayoginī of Nāropa using the instruction text on Vajrayoginī called *Stairway of Refined Vaidūrya* composed by Takphu Losang Tenpai Gyaltsen; the *Quick Path to the Ḍākinī Realm* by the former throneholder of Shalu Riphuk Monastery, Losang Khyenrap, and the annotations of Ngulchu Dharmabhadra; profound instructions on the completion stage from the shorter *Teachings on the Central Channel* of Amé Shap, together with exclusive and inconceivable core instructions, and teachings on the union of cutting of the knots of superimposition and the practice of holding the mind from the tantric pupil-instruction practices of the Sakya masters. He also attended most teachings given by Kyabjé Takdrak Vajradhara, Khangsar Rinpoché of Gomang College, Kangyur Lama Losang Dönden, the Mongolian Palden Sangpo from Tashi Khyil Monastery, and Choné Geshé Rinpoché Losang Gyatso, known also as the Dharma Wish-Fulfilling Cloud.

To sum up, from the time of completing his duty as disciplinarian at Gyütö until the performance of his duties for the previous Dalai Lama's golden reliquary, Rinpoché remained insatiable in his quest for teachings on the stages of the path, mind training, tantric initiations, and instructions. Through this he became a great treasure house of core instructions from the oral traditions. However, because the record of the teachings he received was left behind in Tibet, I cannot write of them in too much detail.

At the end of the summer of 1933 in Chusang Hermitage, in response to a request by Trijang Rinpoché, Phabongkha Rinpoché gave the permission empowerment of Four-Faced Robber of Strength, Vajra Mahākāla of Seventeen Aspects. Rinpoché attended these teachings. Mahākāla teachings that he did not receive at this time he received later, after Phabongkha had passed away, from Simok Rinpoché at Ling Labrang. These included the permission empowerments of two aspects of Four-Faced Mahākāla. They were the secret-practice Mahākāla, which is the preliminary for the very-secret and strict-secret instruction practice, and the empowerment known as the black-brahman entrustment, in which Mahākāla is used as a servant. He also received the secret Mahākāla instructions.

Also Rinpoché often received long-life initiations, obstacle-removing rituals, and so on. Rinpoché held Simok Vajradhara to be someone who had reached a high level of attainment and mentioned this to others.

14 | Funeral Arrangements for the Thirteenth Dalai Lama

IN 1933, on the thirtieth of the tenth Tibetan month, the Great Thirteenth Dalai Lama displayed the act of passing away. The instruction came from the lord chamberlain's office at the Norbulingka residence that Rinpoché was to assume the responsibilities of helping with the work of preparing the exalted body, washing it, changing the embalming salts, and so on. At that time one high government official joked, "The oath-bound are tied to their oath."[76] Rinpoché says that on that day a personal attendant to the Dalai Lama, Thupten Kunphel, was about to be arrested and there was a general commotion around the Norbulingka, with soldiers and others milling around.[77]

Rinpoché went to Phabongkha Rinpoché to seek advice about these funeral duties, and it is clear from the notes he made at that time that, with the assistance of Trijang Rinpoché and others, he flawlessly carried out the funeral ceremonies, laid down the foundation grid for the building of a new golden reliquary, and made the necessary preparations for the mantras to be placed inside the reliquary.

There was quite some time between the completion of the funeral rituals in the morning and the second session in the afternoon, and as there was no separate place to rest in the Potala, Rinpoché was somewhat tired. However, together with Trijang Rinpoché, he spent the days looking at the murals on the Potala walls. Later they became friends with Namgyal Monastery's chant leader, who was from the Trimön family, and they would take rest in his room.

Rinpoché spent a year and a half performing the funeral duties. After the reliquary had been constructed, Rinpoché together with Kyabjé Takdrak Rinpoché assumed the responsibility of creating the murals in the mausoleum. Gyaltsen, the chief artist, would speak highly of Kyabjé Rinpoché's great knowledge of working with colors, the grids of various deities, and

A section of the Thirteenth Dalai Lama's mausoleum,
completed in 1936, at the Potala Palace

so on. Not only could he produce good drawings of flowers, birds, deity implements, and so on, but he loved to do woodwork and metalwork. Consequently, he kept toolboxes in the Lhasa labrang and the hermitage containing tools such as various size planes and saws for making practical items such as tables and small boxes. Sometimes Rinpoché would sharpen the blades of the plane.

The Mongolian monk Puré Sangpo of Drepung Gomang gave Rinpoché a camera and showed him how to take photographs and develop them. In this way Rinpoché was able to produce good photographs. Sometimes he would develop photographs taken by his attendants. However, he did not involve himself in these kinds of activities regularly. Rinpoché liked cameras, watches, telescopes, and so on. He did not like to wear a watch and kept about ten good-quality watches in a white box and would wind them once a month. Apart from these, he did not take much interest in having special possessions. He liked arranging such things as artificial flowers for offerings on the altars. (plate 10)

Before he became the deputy abbot at the tantric college, Rinpoché lived in Lhasa, and each day he would walk the outer circumambulation route and often visited the various temples. One year he visited the Jebum temple, the Riksum, and all other temples in Lhasa, where he made offerings and prayers. In the *vaiśākha* month[78] he would order *tsampa* to be brought in from the labrang's estate in Gangtö and distribute it to the beggars while walking the outer circumambulation route. He also liked to listen to the *lama maniwa*, or religious storytellers, on the street. From an early age he would clean his room himself and offer the water bowls, as was the custom of the lamas of the past and which was part of the six preliminary practices. He said that once after he had gone to bed when staying at the hermitage, he heard a scratching sound coming from the wooden framework. He thought it probably was a mouse. However, in the morning, as he was putting away his bedding and cleaning the room, he saw a scorpion, which gave him a scare. Once he did a hundred thousand full-length prostrations in the courtyard of the main temple, and although he became quite tired, he exceeded the required number.

Rinpoché's innate intelligence was acute, and his imprints from past training were highly pronounced. This meant that without the need of many years of training in the textual traditions, as was the case for others, he traveled to the far shore of the great ocean of sutra and tantra, of Buddhist and non-Buddhist tenets. Through the proper application of the teachings in these texts, he attained great levels of insight. Moreover, his predecessor's predecessor, Trichen Ngawang Lungtok Yönten Gyatso, was the tutor of the Eleventh Dalai Lama. After that, his immediate predecessor, Jetsun Losang Lungtok Tenzin Trinlé, became the Sharpa Chöjé, a deputy throneholder, and was also tutor to the Great Thirteenth Dalai Lama for seven years and became probably the foremost lama among the renowned holders of the Riwo Genden[79] tradition at that time. Because of this the monks at the tantric college had high hopes that this great being too would become a deputy abbot. Moreover, it was the tradition to offer deputy-abbot candidacy to high-ranking lharampa geshés who had sat in the tantric debate examinations, and Rinpoché from his side had been to the debate examinations a few times. However, the Thirteenth Dalai Lama while he was alive did not appoint Rinpoché to the post of deputy abbot. There were many reasons for this. He was still young and such a duty might interfere with him being able to continue with receiving initiations, transmissions, instructions, and so on. But the prime reason was the Dalai Lama foresaw that in the future, after the ruthless Chinese occupation and repression in 1959 had almost reduced the teaching of the Buddha to just a name, Rinpoché would rise up as the regent of Tsongkhapa, Mañjunātha the second Buddha, and resurrect the doctrine from its ashes. Therefore, as it is said, "If asked why? Because the protector sees the time."[80]

However, it was necessary for him to become the deputy abbot at some time. This can be understood from the Dalai Lama's response to Rinpoché asking to be excused from taking on the role of disciplinarian, as mentioned previously. His response was that it was necessary to become disciplinarian because familiarity with the rules and regulations would be important when he became the deputy abbot later on.

15 | Becoming the Deputy Abbot

I N 1936 Drepung Loseling Nyakré Geshé Tashi Namgyal completed his tenure as the deputy abbot, and as the time approached for him to become the abbot, the regent Radreng Rinpoché summoned the candidates for the post of deputy abbot. In the ensuing examinations, this great being took first place. Also, seeing that the timing was appropriate, the regent placed his seal of approval on his name and appointed him to the post of deputy abbot.

On the morning of an auspicious day, a ceremony was held in the labrang. Requested by the five teachers of the monastic houses, Rinpoché ascended a throne in the reception room. The house teachers offered the regent's letter of appointment to Rinpoché, and as was the tradition, he stood up and received it respectfully with both hands. Representatives of the labrang, Gyütö, Drepung Loseling, the monastic houses, and many others presented ceremonial scarves and representations of the body, speech, and mind. The labrang gave all guests tea and rice.

A few days later, early in the morning on the day of the actual inauguration ceremony, the Gyütö disciplinarian, the chant leader, the teachers from the five houses, as well as many of the faithful who were close to him welcomed him and escorted him with incense as he arrived at Ramoché. Rinpoché wore his ceremonial yellow robe and carried a begging bowl and on his back a scripture holder containing the *Guhyasamāja Root Tantra* and other texts. After the morning assembly had finished and before the mid-morning session began, Rinpoché went to the assembly hall. From about the midway point of the front row, he cast flowers and made prostrations. He went to the Ramoché Buddha statue, where he made prostrations, offered a scarf, and made prayers. Then he offered a scarf to the great painting of the protector Mahākāla, after which he proceeded to sit on the throne where

Radreng (Reting) Rinpoché

all previous deputy abbots have sat. The scripture holder was placed against the pillar behind the throne.

The chant leader began the chanting, and together with the disciplinarian and the five house teachers, he performed the instantaneous generation of Guhyasamāja followed by the blessing of the bell, vajra, and inner offering. Then the college served tea and rice to all present. The chant leader began the verses of tea offering, which begin "Unequaled guide . . . ," and the sweet rice offering, which begins "Beautiful and varied offerings . . . ," and on their completion Rinpoché drank the tea and ate one portion of the sweet rice. Those who escorted him with incense went outside. Monks came into the assembly hall, and the chant leader led them into a recitation of Khedrup Jé's praise to Tsongkhapa, which begins "Glorious being, sole eyes for the beings of the three worlds. . . ." The college and the labrang then presented Rinpoché with representations of the enlightened body, speech, and mind. While the monks took tea, Rinpoché read out the offering dedications. Then the incense bearers escorted Rinpoché to the Medicine Buddha temple on the roof of the assembly hall, where an elaborate ceremony was performed. After that Rinpoché went to the Potala for tea and an inauguration meeting with the regent and officials. He returned to the deputy abbot's quarters under the pagoda roof of Ramoché. There representatives of the tantric college, the houses, and many disciples of his present and previous incarnations, both lay and ordained, came to present scarves of auspiciousness, which he joyfully received and returned with knotted protection cords.

During the preparations for the ceremonies, a throne table was borrowed from the labrang of former Ganden Throneholder Ngawang Norbu of Sungchu House of Drepung Gomang. When it was being returned, a pair of yellow boots that had been regularly worn by the famous throneholder Ngawang Norbu was discovered inside. This was regarded by all the helpers involved as an auspicious sign that Rinpoché would one day become the Ganden Throneholder.

Those who were to become deputy abbot without first serving as disciplinarian had to buy themselves out of the role of disciplinarian by offering three helpings of tea and thukpa and a donation of five *kar*.[81] Those who had previously held the position of disciplinarian did not need to make such an offering. However, Ling Labrang made the best-quality offerings of tea, thukpa, and money all day long to the assembly.

It was the tradition that the new deputy abbot should spend three evenings at the head of the tantric-text recitation assembly and should sleep alongside the monks in the temple. Therefore, at the time of the tantric-text assembly, the monks gathered in the debate courtyard, and Rinpoché arrived and entered the temple with the chant leader. The chant leader and Rinpoché sat down on the floor facing each other without any cushions or seats. The monks passed a vajra and bell from one to another and finally offered it to Rinpoché. The recitations began with the three-part torma ritual, followed by the tantric-text recitation, and then the prayer for the "flourishing of the doctrine" (*bstan 'bar ma*). Then the retiring gong was sounded. Rinpoché joined the assembly and lay down to sleep in the lion position. The next morning Rinpoché rose before the monks at about three o'clock, recited the review of daily duties, went to the morning assembly, and so on. This he did for the next three days.

For a whole year a new deputy abbot has to attend all Gyütö's outside sessions. First, Rinpoché went to Kyormolung in the second Tibetan month. After he had laid out his mat in his quarters on the top floor of the monastery's house, he attended the assembly, and that evening he slept alongside the monks in the assembly hall. The next day he rose before the monks, washed, and went to the morning assembly. While the monks were taking tea Rinpoché delivered a lecture to the assembly, in which he spoke in general terms of how the community of tantric practitioners who hold all three vows should guard the precepts of the three vows as they would their eyes, and with that as a basis, how they should strive in learning by way of the wheel of listening and contemplation, and in eradication of mental afflictions by way of the wheel of concentration. Specifically, he listed for the assembly the rituals and ceremonies to be performed there in the sessions at Kyormolung.

On the second day the new abbot performed the text recitation and Rinpoché, acting as the repetition master, repeated the text once. After that, the geshés and other students of that class formed a group in one part of the courtyard, where Rinpoché repeated the text recitation three times. In the afternoon he joined the monks for the classes given by the abbot and for the tantric-text recitation assembly in the evening.

On the way back to Lhasa after the week-long session had finished, Rinpoché went to take teachings from the great Takdrak Vajradhara, the all-pervading master of a hundred buddha families, at his residence in Takdrak Hermitage. There he made the Takdrak Dzomo enclosure his quarters. At that time Losang Lungrik was his attendant. Phenpo Drakyap Rinpoché from Sera Mé also attended these teachings, and Rinpoché met with him many times. Together they practiced long tone chanting and drew grids.

Based on this description, maybe they were receiving teachings on the iron-fortress torma ritual, but I cannot be sure. After these teachings Rinpoché returned to Lhasa.

Every year at Ramoché it was the tradition to hold a week-long ritual of self-empowerment into the Lūipa tradition of Cakrasaṃvara using a colored-sand mandala. On the day of the ground-preparation ritual, Rinpoché attended the assembly and gave a talk on this self-empowerment ritual and so on. After the mandalas had been constructed by the ritual assistants, Rinpoché walked around to examine if the measurements and colors matched those described in the tantras.

In the third month Rinpoché went to Chumda. He stayed on the Kharngön estate, where he had stayed on previous out-of-college sessions. On the day after the laying of the mats, Rinpoché gave a talk on the various activities the monks would be participating in during their stay in Chumda, thereby maintaining without decline the traditional procedures.

At the end of the fourth month Rinpoché was invited to Drigung Mangra Monastery, the seat of Geshé Jayulwa Shönu Ö, chief disciple of the master practitioner Chenga Tsultrim Bar, and first lineage holder of the Kadam oral instructions.[82] (plate 17) He stayed in quarters on the top floor of the temple, and although the rooms were not that comfortable, Rinpoché was very cheerful and relaxed. He gave extensive teachings in keeping with the requests of the ordained community and the laity and made generous offerings to the monks. One day Rinpoché was treated to a monastic ritual dance called the Mangra Setor, which included a dance involving sixteen monks holding staffs and wearing yellow large-brim hats and a dance involving Vaiśravaṇa and his eight attendant horsemen. After that he enjoyed folk operas put on by residents of Nyibak and Lower Dzongkha.

In this area there was a local deity called Pomchen. Rinpoché traveled to its abode, and as was customary, the deity was invoked through a medium. Rinpoché offered this deity an upper garment, an apron, and a hat all made from good-quality brocade and bade the protector to do whatever it could to make the rains come on time, and to give good counsel to the people of the area on the best course of action in various matters. Pomchen replied, "Even though the stupa is turned upside down, its terraced part remains in the middle."[83]

There is a story concerning a mule belonging to the labrang. It was playing with a horse, and they were chasing each other around when the mule fell onto a pile of wood. A piece of wood pierced its body, causing the animal much suffering. At the suggestion of the local people, this local deity was invoked through an oracle. The deity through the medium took a long sword, which he heated over a fire, and then licked its blade. He placed the blade over the wound, uttered a mantra, and this was very helpful in the animal's recovery.

The main sacred object in the monastery is an extraordinary statue of Jayulwa made of medicinal clay. The elders of the area say that whenever an incarnation of Ling Rinpoché is in good health and his activities are extensive, the face of this statue turns upward to the sky. When an incarnation shows signs of ill health, the head of the statue is bent down. It was said that at this particular time the statue was especially radiant and facing the sky. It is as if Rinpoché had taken birth in the eleventh century as Jayulwa Shönu Ö in order to promote the Kadam doctrine of Atisa.

From about that time onward a deity would often spontaneously enter the body of attendant Thupten Rikzin, who was in the employ of the labrang and was son of the caretaker of Gyütö's monastic house at Yerpa. Rinpoché remarked this was probably the Yarlha Shampo deity,[84] as there was no medium for this protector at present. Hearing this, people from Lhokha who relied upon this deity requested Rinpoché to allow this attendant to become the medium for Yarlha Shampo. Rinpoché said it was best to be sure and sent the attendant to Demo Rinpoché for an "opening the doors of the channels" ceremony. After this Thupten Rikzin was confirmed as the oracle for Yarlha Shampo and sent to Lhokha. Not only with this incident, but whenever cases of seeming spirit possession were brought before him, Rinpoché always referred them to Demo Rinpoché, and never did he perform exorcisms or oath-swearing rituals and the like.

When the ceremonies at Mangra had finished, Rinpoché proceeded to Ganden Monastery. On the way he set up camp for three days near the Lhodrak Bumpa reliquary. This was a shrine to the great Lhodrak practitioner Namkha Gyaltsen.[85] In reality he was the venerable Vajrapāṇi, the keeper of the secret tantras in human form. Even to the eyes of his ordinary disciples he was being cared for by this meditation deity and could receive instructions and teachings from him whenever he wished as if they were meeting face to face. Moreover, from him Jé Tsongkhapa received the stages of the path teachings according to the explanation tradition of the Kadam oral instructions as well as that of the Kadam stages of the path lineages. In this place Rinpoché made the required 150 rounds of the circumambulation route in silence and in bare feet while making prayers that the people be unharmed by malevolent forces above, below, and on the ground, and that the shared and exclusive insights of the path be quickly born in the minds of the limitless living beings just as they were born in the mind of this great practitioner. Blisters broke out on his feet, and for a few days after he was tired. In the beginning all the attendants set out with Rinpoché on the circumambulation, but only Losang Lungrik completed the course with him.

Rinpoché then proceeded on to Ganden Monastery, where he stayed in rooms on the top floor of Lhopa House. He maintained the duties of a deputy abbot by attending the assemblies in the tantric house. He made pilgrimage to the great reliquary of Jé Rinpoché and performed the thousand-offering ritual as well as other offerings. This was something he did every time he went to Ganden. After the Ganden summer sessions had finished, Rinpoché left for Lhasa. On the way they passed a place called Den, where the great eleventh-century tantric practitioner Ra Lotsāwa Dorjé Drak lived for a long time, as is clear from the account of the past lives of Rinpoché.[86] Rinpoché stopped for a time and looked toward Den, while recounting to his attendants and disciples the practices of this master, some of the teachings Ralo gave during his life, and so on.

On the fifteenth of the fifth Tibetan month, which was World Purification Day, Rinpoché arrived back at his rooms on the top floor of Ramoché temple. In the temple the entire Gyütö assembly was performing the yearly consecration ritual known as the Causing the Rain of Goodness to Fall,[87] which alternated between the rituals of Guhyasamāja, Cakrasaṃvara, and Vajrabhairava. Rinpoché, as per tradition, united the wisdom beings with the *samaya* beings through the performance of a flawless rite.[88]

At the end of the sixth month, the tantric college went to Sera Monastery, where Rinpoché maintained the traditions of deputy abbot. On the fourteenth day of the seventh month, Rinpoché traveled to Yerpa. Along with the Gyütö and Yerpa monks, he took the pledges of the late rainy-season retreat and distributed the counting sticks[89] to the monks, as was the tradition. He listed the rules, assigned sleeping quarters, handed out bedding, and so on, as described in the summer-retreat Vinaya manuals. After seven days of mandala-drawing training came the three days of the drawing examination, during which Rinpoché went round the drawing areas of each monastic house. He thoroughly tested the geshés on the three-dimensional mandalas and their symbolism, the ritual assistants on the colored grids of the mandala, and the novices on their knowledge of the grid manuals. During the three days of chant training, Rinpoché went to the courtyard to examine the students, with each of the front-row chanters beginning a long tone chant and Rinpoché joining in.

During his first year in office, Rinpoché, as was customary for the deputy abbot, handed out debate topics on pieces of paper to the geshés who were to engage in the tantric debates; they could not choose their own topics. On the twenty-fifth of the eighth month, Geshé Wangdü Gyaltsen of Loseling's Nyakré House was sitting as thesis defender in tantric debate in the assembly hall. Rinpoché posed questions to him on the body mandala that the geshé later said he found difficult to answer. Thereafter, for five days in Yerpa and for five days in the first autumn session of the ninth month, Rinpoché always attended the tantric debates from beginning to end as monitor. There he decided the length of time each challenger would have, and sometimes he participated in the debates himself.

Rinpoché then returned to Lhasa. The twenty-second of the ninth month was the day commemorating the Buddha's return from the celestial realms. On that day the college received the customary invitation from the government. Consequently, a procession consisting of the deputy abbot and the monks in the correct order of seniority, escorted by a monk government official holding incense, proceeded in a peaceful and pleasing manner, reminiscent of the Ārya Aśvajit, to the great reception hall called Glories of Samsara and Nirvana in the Potala Palace. After the laying down of the mats, they performed the evening assembly and returned to Lhasa. From the next day onward, Rinpoché attended all the assemblies for the torma ritual of Mahākāla. On the final day, Rinpoché was the vajra master as the torma-casting ritual was performed in front of the Potala outside Shöl main gate. After the torma ceremony had finished, Rinpoché returned to the Potala to complete the concluding activities, such as the benediction.

In the second autumn sessions during the tenth month, Rinpoché attended the tantric debates continually for a week. The twenty-fifth of that month commemorates the day that Dharma king Mañjunātha Tsongkhapa actualized the complete-enjoyment illusory body in the intermediate state. On that day in the Potala, the robes of the Great Thirteenth were brought out, and the regular official tea gathering was attended by the regent Hothokthu[90] Radreng and by the council of ministers. As was the custom,

Rinpoché attended this winter audience with the entire Gyütö assembly. After the tea gathering had finished, Rinpoché visited at his leisure the statues of Ārya Lokeśvara, the reliquary of the Great Fifth Dalai Lama that was known as the "sole ornament of the world," and other sacred objects, where he offered scarves and made prayers.

During the Ganden winter sessions when entrants were admitted to the tantric college, new generation-stage[91] monks had to gather at the entrance to the assembly hall. The deputy abbot had previously entered the hall and was sitting with the chant leader. As the door was opened, everybody started to chant in a clear and distinct voice the *Guhyasamāja Root Tantra* from its opening words, "In the language of India . . . ," as they noisily sat on the floor around the front rows. They recited slowly the *Guhyasamāja Root Tantra* up to the end of the twelfth chapter, the first verse of the *Cakrasaṃvara Tantra*, the self-generation of Guhyasamāja, and the verses of benediction. After this test, Rinpoché gave a short speech in which he talked about the purpose of entering this great seat of tantric learning, the fundamental need to maintain all their vows and pledges, and monastic discipline, and to devote themselves to the integrated study, contemplation, and meditation of sutra and tantra in general, and specifically of the paths of Guhyasamāja, Cakrasaṃvara, and Vajrabhairava, and so on.

Seniority in the tantric colleges was usually determined by the time of enrollment. However, in Gyütö those entrants who took the recitation test all enter at the same time. Therefore it was the custom for the disciplinarian's assistant to gather the rosaries from each new student and hide them under his robe. He would then pull them out one by one for identification, and this would determine the order of seniority for sitting in the assembly and so on.

After the recitation the deputy abbot would return to his rooms and grant permission for the new entrants to join the tantric monastic community, as listed by the teachers of the individual.

At the end of the eleventh month, Rinpoché left for the Ganden winter session. On the evening of the first day, he went to the assembly hall and, after laying down his mat, slept alongside the other monks. In the morning during the first tea, he outlined the ceremonies to be performed while at Ganden. During the great protector propitiation ritual at Yangpachen hall, Rinpoché occupied the main seat of the assembly, as was the custom.

In the twelfth month Rinpoché left Ganden Monastery for Lhasa.

During the great iron-fortress torma ritual at Ramoché, Rinpoché looked carefully to ensure that the grid for the nine-point iron fortress, the offering tormas, and so on had been constructed by the ritual assistant according to the tantras. On the last day of the ritual he attended the assembly sessions from the morning onward. In the assembly hall the self-generation of the Thirteen-Deity Vajrabhairava and the torma invocation of the oath-bound protector Kālarūpa were performed. Outside on the stone floor by the entrance, the nine-weapon "liberation" rituals and so on were executed, after which the pouring ceremony of the iron-fortress ritual was performed. At first the fire would not light and there was only thick black smoke. Suddenly, a huge ball of fire burst forth and burned the effigy. Again a great fireball erupted in the sky with a loud explosion. The ritual attendants, the monks, and the onlookers all gasped with astonishment. After that Rinpoché cast the tormas into the fire and so on, exactly as it was done by the great masters of the past.

On the first day of the first month of the fire-ox year (1937), during the New Year celebrations held in the great reception hall of the Potala Palace, Kyabjé Rinpoché and Song Tulku of Phu House, who was the abbot of Ganden Shartsé, stood up in the assembly to perform a debate. Song Rinpoché began his debate by citing a verse from Vasubandhu's *Treasury of Abhidharma*:

> This is the way to Brahma.
> It is the wheel of Brahma,
> turned by Brahma.[92]

One day, in his first year as deputy abbot, Rinpoché was on the roof of Ramoché and saw a butcher about to slaughter a sheep just outside the circumambulation route. He immediately sent an attendant to pay the butcher what he wanted for the sheep and saved its life. He gave it the name Tsering (long life). Because of the monastic rules the sheep could not be kept at Ramoché, so it was kept at the labrang.

At that time Kyabjé Takdrak Rinpoché had compiled the writings of the previous Dalai Lama and composed the catalogue on the construction and the contents of his reliquary named Golden Reliquary Granting All That Is Good. He asked Rinpoché for help with editing and correcting. Consequently, in the times when he was not busy attending assemblies and so on, Rinpoché would seek out some peace and quiet by taking a seat and a canopy to Chapzing Park, find a place where there were few people, and set up the canopy. Tsering the sheep would sit nearby. There he would work on the editing of the texts. Rinpoché was told by close friends that because he was coming to the park often, some monks from the monastery were remarking disparagingly, "Our deputy abbot does not spend much time in his own rooms but is always going to the park." Rinpoché replied, "They do not know the reason why I go to the park. That's a shame." And he paid no more attention to it.

Around this time, Khunu Lama Rinpoché Tenzin Gyaltsen, a master of all teachings regardless of their affiliations, had heard of Kyabjé Rinpoché's glowing reputation for being learned, of pure ethical discipline, and of compassionate conduct and came to visit him at Ramoché. In their discussions on the Dharma, they were both impressed with the other's knowledge and qualities. They also gave each other teachings. Kyabjé Rinpoché had previously received teachings from Vajradhara Phabongkha on Sanskrit grammar using Anubhūti's *Sarasvatī Grammar Treatise*. However, Khunu Rinpoché was known for having reached the pinnacle of scholarship in the study of Sanskrit grammar. Therefore, for one day in a room on the top floor of the labrang, Rinpoché listened to lessons on Sarvavarmā's *Kalāpa Sutra* grammar, using the fourteenth-century commentary composed by the scholar Sasang Maṭi Paṇchen, who was Jé Tsongkhapa's Sanskrit grammar teacher. Rinpoché also received teachings from Khunu Lama Rinpoché on composition and poetry using the root text on poetics. Their minds had become as one, and later when Rinpoché was in India, teachings between the two continued. Rinpoché repeatedly praised Khunu Lama Rinpoché as not only a great master who had totally renounced the world and made bodhicitta the very heart of his practice but as someone who could answer any question on the common and exclusive sciences and so on.

In his second year of taking on the responsibilities of the deputy abbot, Rinpoché completely studied the creation of astronomy charts during the Yerpa summer retreat with the Yerpa astronomer Trinlé Wangdrak, who had graduated from the Astro-Medical Institute. Rinpoché praised this man as a gentle person and very learned in astronomy.

After receiving teachings on astronomy, Rinpoché gave the initiation of single-deity Vajrabhairava, complete with a preparation day, to about forty people in the rooms of a hermit known as the Jomo meditator. This hermit was a good Dharma practitioner who before living in Yerpa had previously lived for many years in Jomo Lhari. The initiation had been requested by a Gyantsé monk official in charge of restoring the Yerpa temple. Rinpoché liked this hermit very much, and whenever he visited, Rinpoché would always serve him food. Because the hermit liked Chinese egg noodles, whenever this dish was being made at the Yerpa labrang, Rinpoché instructed his attendant to hang a red monk's shawl on a pole on top of the labrang. This was a signal that egg noodles were being cooked that day. The story goes that one day the hermit asked a disciple to cook momos, and after he had eaten the momo the hermit died.

Except for geshé and rapjampa entrants, all new entrants into the tantric college had to take the test of reciting many texts from memory, including the *Guhyasamāja Root Tantra* up to the end of the twelfth chapter, the first chapter of the *Cakrasaṃvara Tantra*, and the Guhyasamāja sādhana. However, some monks had fallen victim to the thieves of forgetfulness, and as a result the chanting had become muddled. In Śāntideva's *Guide to the Bodhisattva's Way of Life* it says:

> Study, contemplation, and meditation
> in the mind of one who lacks awareness,
> like water in a leaky pot,
> will not remain in the memory.

Those who participate in the recitation have to be able to chant the texts on their own. Rinpoché gave warnings in the assembly that unless everyone corrected their forgetfulness, there would be a test, and those who could not recite the texts correctly would be punished. Three times he gave this warning, after which he put the monks to the test. For several days on the Ramoché assembly hall veranda, Rinpoché, the chant leader, and the disciplinarian tested monks in groups of seven. If it was felt that anyone was unable to recite the text individually, he was singled out and asked to chant it by himself. He asked one monk to recite from the section on the creation of the Guhyasamāja celestial palace in the sādhana. As he began to recite, he muddled up the Guhyasamāja, Cakrasaṃvara, and Vajrabhairava celestial palace creations, and so Rinpoché asked him to begin from the Guhyasamāja praise. "What is the praise?" he asked. "It begins from 'Akṣobhyavajra of great exalted wisdom," Rinpoché replied. The monk was so anxious he could only recite "I prostate to the realm of secrets" and could not remember the two intervening lines.[93] Rinpoché laughed but then showed him a stern face.

Those who did not pass the test had to carry sand from the riverbanks to their own quarters, and as the time for the communal assembly approached, they were made to stand in the courtyard with the bags of sand on their backs while the deputy abbot observed them. He told the disciplinarian to hit one particular monk with his strap. At this time some of the monks took to slandering Rinpoché, saying that with such punishment they were being treated like mules. However, the quality of the chanting improved greatly by tackling the matter in this way, and the elder monks praised Rinpoché for this. Moreover, at that time there was a smallpox[94] epidemic in the country, and it is said that those monks who had to ferry the bags of sand, apart from one or two, all recovered from the disease.

Once, during the Cakrasaṃvara self-initiation ritual, the abbot could not attend the midday communal session, and so Rinpoché acted as the ritual master. For father tantra deities the offerings are arranged from right to left, and for mother deity tantras from left to right. Rinpoché noticed that the ritual assistant had arranged the offerings according to the Vajrabhairava self-initiation. As well as giving him a severe reprimand, Rinpoché ordered the disciplinarian to give him a few lashes of the strap. During the preparations for the great self-initiation ritual using the sand mandala, the ritual assistant made a mistake when setting down the mandala colors. Rinpoché made him circumambulate the rows of monks holding aloft the colored-sand container. Also, once the chant leader of the protector temple fell asleep during the morning session. First Rinpoché told the disciplinarian's assistant to put a butter lamp in front of the chant leader. However, he continued to fall asleep again and again. A vajra was placed in hand and he was made to stand up until the session had ended. In this way, Rinpoché was very firm with monastic discipline. The Manchu Chinese invasion of Tibet around 1910 brought about troubled times, and this had resulted in some laxity in Gyütö monastic discipline. Kyabjé Rinpoché's extraordinarily kind deeds to restore this discipline were highly praised by the monastery.

16 | Becoming Abbot

IN EACH OF his first two years of service as deputy abbot, Rinpoché held examinations in Yerpa on the drawing and colors of the mandalas of Guhyasamāja, Cakrasaṃvara, and Vajrabhairava. In his third year he had intended to hold examinations on the construction of new three-dimensional mandalas, which would have been a test of the teachings the students had been receiving on the practice of constructing these mandalas. However, in 1938 the incumbent abbot Tashi Namgyal passed away suddenly. Consequently, the regent Radreng Rinpoché told Rinpoché that he had to take the position of abbot there and then.

I am not sure of the exact date, but on the morning of an auspicious day, in between the morning and mid-morning assemblies, Rinpoché was escorted from the deputy abbot's residence above the college by an incense-led procession, at the head of which was a painted representation of the *sipaho* elemental divination diagrams,[95] and which included the teachers of the five houses, the chant leader, and the disciplinarian. He entered the Changrak great reception hall through the back door by way of the offering temple. There he ascended the throne of the venerable Kunga Döndrup, and immediately the college offered representations of enlightened body, speech, and mind followed by tea and sweet rice offerings. The investiture ceremonies began here. As the monks gathered for the mid-morning assembly Rinpoché left the Changrak great hall through the main door. In a corner of the courtyard, the inscription on the back of the *sipaho* was read, and then the incense-led procession entered the assembly hall, where it formed a line from the right of the altar to the head of the rows. Standing under a parasol banner and from the head of the front row, Rinpoché made three prostrations on a hand-knit red woolen mat. He cast into the air flower petals and barley grains dyed in Kashmiri saffron. In front of the precious Mahākāla painting, he offered a ceremonial scarf. The assistant to the disciplinarian handed him the Langdöl butter lamp—so called because it was offered by the master renunciate Langdöl Lama Ngawang Losang—filled with melted butter. Rinpoché lit the lamp and offered it with prayers.

Rinpoché took his cloak, and when the entire assembly reached the point in the front-generation ritual that reads "From the realm of Akaniṣṭa, the buddhas are invited, and they come to reside in the space in front," he ascended the throne previously occupied by those masters of Dharma, the lineage of Gyütö abbots, who had no fear when it came to explaining precisely the meaning of the tantras. The representatives of Gyütö, Ling Labrang, Drepung Loseling, and so on made offerings of the three representations. Those close to him and other devotees came up and offered ceremonial scarves, which Rinpoché joyfully accepted. That day the labrang made extensive offerings to the main sacred objects in the monastery and served food to the entire assembly of monks for the whole day, together with donations and offering scarves. The monks chanted the twenty-five-heap mandala offering, and at the point "Body, speech, and mind of myself and others," the tantric chant leader offered the heaped mandala to Rinpoché. Rinpoché led the recitation of the refuge and bodhicitta verse three times, and beginning with the words "Gods, demigods, humans, rulers of the nonhumans . . ." urged those gods, nāgas, and so on who delight in the virtuous to listen to the Dharma. After this he read for a while from the beginning of the *Guhyasamāja Root Tantra*. Finally, Rinpoché led the assembly in the verses of dedication of virtue, in which the virtue arising from listening and teaching the Dharma is dedicated for the spread of the teachings and for the welfare of living beings.

The usual quarters of the abbot were very small. Therefore arrangements had been made to house Rinpoché for the tenure of his abbotship in larger rooms nearby called Ramoché Desal owned by the college. Accordingly, after the ceremonies a monastery official escorted him there in an incense-led procession. After this he went to the Potala for his inaugural audience. He visited the sacred objects housed in the Potala chapel called the Celestial Palace of the Self-Arisen Avalokiteśvara, where he made offerings and prayed that his deeds of improving the teaching of mantra to its highest limit would ripen to nurture the doctrine and living beings that pervade the reaches of space.

In the third month Rinpoché went to Chumda, where he stayed in rooms above the main gate of the monastery house. On the morning of the twenty-sixth he went to the monastic courtyard. The geshés and senior-generation stage students who were participating in the Chumda sessions made three prostrations to Rinpoché. The chant leader stood up and initiated the mandala offering. After this, Rinpoché put on the ceremonial hat, and starting at the beginning of the Guhyasamāja commentary, he read about half a folio very slowly, with clear pauses between sentences to ensure that the meaning would be generally understood. This he did twice. Then he removed his hat and, without omitting a single word, gave a word-by-word commentary, using the elaboration of scripture and reasoning. After that Rinpoché listened with pleasure as the new deputy abbot, Trau Chözé from Loseling Minyak House, repeated the text. Then Rinpoché recited texts in the other classes. In the second class he used the Guhyasamāja commentary mentioned above. In the third he used Panchen Sönam Drakpa's Guhyasamāja completion-stage commentary, and in the fourth class the Guhyasamāja generation-stage commentary by the same author.

After lunch Rinpoché again ascended the throne. The chant leader led the assembly in the teaching torma offerings. Then Rinpoché led the assembly into the *Heart Sutra* followed by the verse for expelling hindrances beginning "May the eighty types of hindrances be pacified..." The assembly recited the supplication prayer to the lineage masters. When the supplications reached the name of the former Ganden Throneholder Minyak Yeshé Wangden, from whom he had received the teachings on the four commentaries of Guhyasamāja combined, Rinpoché opened the scripture holder and proceeded to give a preliminary teaching on the complete practices of the shared and exclusive stages of the path. Then he began giving transmission and teachings of the four commentaries combined. He continued teaching in this way for several days. It was customary to have a short break at a certain point in the text, which had been initiated by an event during the time of Kunga Döndrup. In the fifteenth century Lhasa was threatened by a flood, and the government invited the great tantric practitioner Kunga Döndrup to come to Lhasa. He was giving a tantric teaching at the time. When he came to the line "Walk on the water,"[96] it is said he placed his monk's mat on the river and journeyed to Lhasa. Therefore, as was customary, at this point in the teaching Rinpoché broke the session. After the teachings had finished I heard that Rinpoché undertook a meditation retreat, but I do not know which deity he focused upon.

On the fifteenth day of the seventh month at Yerpa, Rinpoché gave a reading of the extensive *Individual Liberation Sutra* to a congregation consisting of all the monks of the tantric college and of Yerpa Monastery. After that he appointed the summer retreat leaders, took the counting sticks, and so on. A few days later he continued the unfinished portion of the four Guhyasamāja commentaries combined, as well as a transmission and explanation of the *Cakrasaṃvara Root Tantra* combined with Tsongkhapa's commentary entitled *Elucidation of All Hidden Points*. Also, for one day he was invited to the teaching hall where he taught Jé Tsongkhapa's *Great Yoga of the Completion Stage* and other works to those who were doing meditation retreats on Guhyasamāja, Hayagrīva, and so on.

At this time in the mornings and evenings Rinpoché was engaged in a retreat on Guhyasamāja Akṣobhyavajra. When he had finished this retreat, he officiated at the Guhyasamāja fire offering performed by the entire assembly. He used this fire offering as the supplementary fire offering for his own retreat.

In Lhasa during the first and second autumn session Rinpoché gave transmissions and teachings on Khedrup Jé's generation-stage work *Ocean of Attainments* and Tsongkhapa's completion-stage work *Lamp to Illuminate the Five Stages*. In the winter session during the great iron-fortress ritual, he gave the transmission and teaching on the *Seven-Chapter Vajrabhairava Root Tantra*. In recent times the custom of teaching this work to the monks had declined, but this great being restored this tradition, and it continues to the present day. The work of a deputy abbot is the enforcing of monastic discipline, and the prime function of an abbot to give teachings. Consequently, Rinpoché took on the great responsibility of the monastic education. Once while he was giving teachings on the Guhyasamāja generation and completion stages, some geshés who were attending the out-of-college sessions that year reported that they had planned to go to their own monasteries for special meals and had asked permission to be excused from attending the teachings. Later Rinpoché would often speak about how sad that had made him.

I cannot be sure of the year, but on the fifteenth of its third month, in the great hall of the Glories of Samsara and Nirvana in the Potala, Rinpoché received the complete initiation of Kālacakra from the glorious Khangsar Vajradhara Ngawang Thupten Chökyi Wangchuk of Drepung Gomang Monastery, alongside Kyabjé Takdrak Rinpoché and others. Rinpoché spoke about this event by mentioning how Khangsar Rinpoché opened with the verse that reads "How fortunate to engage in this . . ." and went

The mandala tent camp at Dögu Thang where the Fourteenth Dalai Lama
was received prior to entering Lhasa in 1939

on to offer the introductory discourse. Rinpoché also had taken notes from
this teaching.

At a later date, in the residence of Chakdrung Tawang together with
approximately three hundred others, including Mokchok Rinpoché Yeshé
Jampa Tenpai Gyaltsen, Rinpoché received from Khangsar Rinpoché experiential teachings on the generation and completion stages of single-deity
Vajrabhairava. Rinpoché visualized and developed the points of the discourse as it was given, as was the practice of the great beings of the past. His
tutor Loyak Rinpoché, the former abbot of Ratö, also attended these teachings, and Rinpoché accompanied him to and from the teachings conversing
on topics vast and profound.

Another time the disciplinarian's assistant handed Rinpoché a silver butter
lamp for the regular evening offering in the presence of the precious painting
of Mahākāla, and as he requested Rinpoché to make the prayers, suddenly for
no reason a white milk-like liquid fell onto Rinpoché's lap. Rinpoché only
remarked how strange that was, but it was evidently a good omen.

On the sixth of October 1939,[97] which was the twenty-third of the eighth
Tibetan month, when I first reached Lhasa from Domé Amdo, Rinpoché
had already entered the late summer retreat with the monks at Yerpa. However, along with the entire government, current and former abbots, throneholders, and so on, he arrived at Dögu Thang. There, in the Great Peacock

A portrait of infant Lhamo Döndrup shortly after his recognition
as the Fourteenth Dalai Lama

Tent where I was staying (plates 14 and 14), I first had the great pleasure of looking upon the face of this great being, meaningful to behold, and with whom I had established a connection for many lifetimes through the power of karma and prayer.

The fifth incarnation of Amdo Jamyang Shepa had founded a branch of Gyütö in Tashi Khyil Monastery and had requested for teachers to be sent there to ensure that the mandala-grid drawing, the colors, the rituals, and so on were the same as those of the main college. Accordingly, Rinpoché sent the Drakyap ritual assistant Tenpa Chöden from Drakpa House, and the front-row monk Yeshé Döndrup from Amdo House. These two monks were the first to establish the practices from the main Gyütö Monastery in Tashi Khyil.

I had arrived safely in the capital, and having been examined and recognized as the incarnation of the previous Dalai Lama, the government said to Rinpoché that he should go at once to Chökhor Gyal to offer thanks to Palden Lhamo as well as the other oath-bound protectors. Therefore,

Palanquin of the young Dalai Lama approaching
the Jokhang temple, Lhasa, 1939

at the beginning of the tenth month, with a government monk official as
a guide, staff from the labrang, and mules and their keepers, he arrived at
Gyal Methok Thang.

Chökhor Gyal Monastery was founded in 1509 by the all-knowing
Gendun Gyatso, the Second Dalai Lama, and its full name is the Temple
of Spontaneous Auspiciousness, a Grove Proclaiming All Excellent Explanation. The party stayed there for about thirteen days. With the monks of
the monastery they made thousands of offerings for many days to Machik
Rematī, the personification of the enlightened activities of all the buddhas.
They entrusted her with the enlightened activity of ensuring that I would be
able to serve the Buddha's teaching and living beings in a way that matched
the combined activities of all the previous Dalai Lamas. One day Rinpoché

Ölkha Chölung Hermitage, in the 1930s

climbed a hill overlooking Muliding Lake.[98] Rinpoché said that he did not see any visions at all. Whether that was because the oracle lake was half frozen over or because Rinpoché was keeping it to himself I cannot say. A monk was sent to the lakeside to offer a vase to the waters, but the path was frozen and he could not complete the journey. The vase was offered in the Palden Lhamo temple instead. The labrang made extensive offerings of donations, tea, and so forth to the monks of the monastery, and the temple was filled with offerings for the main sacred objects there.

The party then proceeded by yak to Gyal Lhathok Hermitage. There in the assembly hall known as the Innermost Heart of the Ḍākinī, he made offerings to the hermits. In front of the statue of Tharpa Gyaltsen, the great practitioner who actualized in one lifetime the state of union that is Vajradhara, Rinpoché offered a ceremonial scarf and spent a long time in prayer.

On the twenty-fifth of the tenth month, Rinpoché arrived at the sacred place of Ölkha Chölung, where Jé Tsongkhapa spent a long time in the practices of purification, accumulation of merit, and so on. The hermits were in the assembly hall, and just as the chant leader intoned "From the sphere of great bliss I arise as the guru-deity . . . ," which are the opening lines of *Guru Puja*, Rinpoché arrived in the assembly hall. This was seen as a sign that Rinpoché was not only in reality Vajrabhairava endowed with the threefold wrathfulness performing the great dance of the vajra holder, but in the eyes of ordinary beings also it was as if the all-knowing Tsongkhapa had returned and through his great enlightened deeds would work for the great purpose of the teaching and living beings. Rinpoché made prostrations and offered a mandala using hand gestures. As the assembly hall was small, the hermitage practitioners offered Rinpoché a separate small room where he rested, very happy and relaxed.

Then the party left for Densa Thil and Sangri Khangmar. There he offered a ceremonial scarf and made offerings to, among others, the statue of Machik Lapdrön, who was instrumental in the propagation of the Shijé tradition. From there they went to Tsethang Monastery, where he stayed on the top floor of Ngachö College. That day coincided with a particular dance ceremony, and so Rinpoché watched the event.

On the way home Rinpoché made a pilgrimage to Tradruk. He made offerings to the sacred objects there, as exemplified by the speaking Tārā statue, by repainting them with gold paint. He then visited the college of Thösam Dargyé Ling, which belonged to the labrang and to which he had been invited. He stayed here for a few days, making offerings to the monks and giving teachings and advice to the people of the area. While Rinpoché was staying at Dargyé Ling, the regent Radreng Rinpoché issued a decree that he should return to Lhasa at once to become my assistant tutor. Consequently, Rinpoché left for Lhasa. On the way, he paid a pilgrimage visit to Samyé, where he made offerings in the temple.

17 | Appointment as Assistant Tutor and Junior Tutor

O N THE twenty-second of February 1940, or the fourteenth of the first month of the iron-dragon year, in the great reception hall of the Potala called Glories of Samsara and Nirvana, the ceremony of my ascending the throne that had been blessed by the previous Dalai Lamas took place. It was during this ceremony that Rinpoché received his inaugural audience as an assistant tutor and sat at the head of the row of senior monastic officials.

Because he was still abbot of Gyütö, occasionally he would seek permission to be excused, but otherwise he always attended the daily governmental tea gathering. Sometimes with Kyabjé Keutsang Rinpoché and sometimes alone, he would teach me reading and writing and help me with memorizing prayers and so on. He never neglected the duties of an assistant tutor in conducting exams for the lharampa and tsokrampa geshés, overseeing the lharampa debates at the Great Prayer Festival, and so on. Similarly, he maintained all his duties as abbot by teaching the monks at the tantric college and so on.

As an assistant tutor he was offered an official residence in the Norbulingka palace. However, because he was still the abbot, he continued to stay at Ramoché Desal except for times he was actually engaged in the work of an assistant tutor. Around this time the labrang manager Trinlé Chöphel passed away, and Losang Lungrik was appointed to the post.

In the eighth month of that year, after the usual discourses at Drak Yerpa, Rinpoché gave teachings on the stages of the path to enlightenment using Tsongkhapa's *Song of Experience* in the assembly hall of Yerpa College. After this he bestowed the initiation of single-deity Vajrabhairava and gave teachings on the generation and completion stages. This was probably the first time Rinpoché gave teachings on single-deity Vajrabhairava generation and completion stages.

On the twenty-fifth of the tenth Tibetan month, during Gyütö's annual winter audience in the Potala, a long-life ritual was performed for me. Rinpoché gave the mandala-offering exposition,[99] and I accepted the representations of the enlightened body, speech, and mind that he offered me. After the ceremonies had ended, Rinpoché submitted a letter announcing the completion of his duties as abbot by way of the government offices. A few days later, after the reply accepting his resignation had been received, the labrang made offerings to the whole college of tea and good-quality sweet rice, a general offering of embroidered-brocade pillar hangings of dragons and clouds, and to each monk they gave three silver *sang* coins. They also printed and distributed copies of the prayer composed by Phabongkha Rinpoché that interweaves Rinpoché's name. It reads:

> Like a second Buddha with regard to the **doctrine** of the
>   **Mighty Sage**,
> unparalleled in preserving the sacred Dharma of **scripture**
>   and **realization**,
> whose **victorious enlightened deeds** rule the three worlds,
> I pray to the venerable lama.[100]

The actual assembly recitation at that time was the Guhyasamāja initiation ritual. However, the lineage prayer was recited also, and the above verse of praise was newly inserted at its correct place. Then the *Guhyasamāja Root Tantra* was recited from the beginning up to the line "Blessed as being the four-sided, non-sand mandala of the great *samaya* holder. . . ." Then the following lines from the tantra were recited three times:

> The nature of that clarity
> is filled with various forms,
> pervaded by clouds of buddhas,
> wrathful rays of light shooting forth,
> with mandalas of light and so forth,
> the abode of all the buddhas.[101]

After lunch the college officials, the disciplinarian, the chant leader, and others, all in their best attire, formed an incense procession and escorted Rinpoché into the teaching courtyard. There he gave a very brief combined discourse on the four Guhyasamāja texts, after which he returned briefly to the top floor of the college. After the monks had finished their afternoon assembly, Rinpoché was led out by the officials of each house in an incense-led procession and, as was the custom, was escorted on horseback to the labrang. On arrival, just as he stepped off the mounting stool, a teacher from Phu House suddenly collapsed and died, as if his vital winds were suddenly blocked. Rinpoché made prayers.

His overseeing of monastic discipline during his tenure as deputy abbot and his teaching activities during his three years as abbot made him an object of devotion to the intelligent and unbiased, and many monks came to his rooms to offer ceremonial scarves of gratitude.

One time Rinpoché requested Phabongkha Rinpoché for teachings on some of his own compositions, such as *Heart Scalpel: Evoking the Awareness of Impermanence*. Phabongkha Rinpoché replied that his eyes were not so good at that moment. Ling Rinpoché asked if he could make the request later, to which Phabongkha Rinpoché answered that since these texts were his own compositions, there would not be any difficulty and proceeded to teach. However, Rinpoché only gave explanation on two lines of text and nothing else. These were, "A 'precious corpse' may be covered with fine embroidery, but it will still be placed on the cremation ground." On this Phabongkha Rinpoché said, "This is actually being said for us lamas." Ling Rinpoché later said, "Maybe when I made the request for teachings, I said it in such a low voice that Rinpoché did not hear it correctly."

At Tashi Chöling Hermitage, together with Kyabjé Trijang Rinpoché and others, Rinpoché received from Phabongkha Rinpoché profound teachings on the root texts on Cittamaṇi Tārā according to the pure vision of Takphu Rinpoché, combined with Phabongkha Rinpoché's own composition on the generation and completion stages entitled the *Jewel Pendant of Cittamaṇi*. He also received, together with Kyabjé Trijang Rinpoché and others, instructions and transmissions that included the core instructions on a longevity practice through the wind yoga of vajra recitation, in conjunction with the yoga of Cakrasaṃvara in the form of a white longevity deity. After these teachings a long-life ritual to turn away the escorting ḍākinīs, using the Cakrasaṃvara white longevity deity practice, was offered to Phabongkha Rinpoché, together with the Guru Puja *tsok* ritual.

Around the twentieth of the twelfth month, in response to a request from the Ninety-Fourth Ganden Throneholder, Lhundrup Tsöndrü of Sera Jé Monastery, Phabongkha Rinpoché went to the Lhalu estate[102] to give the initiation of the Cakrasaṃvara body mandala. Although Rinpoché had received the complete initiation, transmission, and instructions on this practice, and was therefore already practicing it, nevertheless, he went to Lhalu and requested to attend in order to receive the initiation again. Phabongkha Rinpoché replied that the sponsor, the Ganden Throneholder, had specified a very small number of attendees, and it would be better if he did not attend now but that it would acceptable to receive it at another time.

Up to this time my main tutor had been the Takdrak Vajradhara. However, Radreng Rinpoché had asked to be relieved from his political duties, and so in 1941 on the first day of the first month of the iron-snake year, Kyabjé Takdrak Rinpoché took on the responsibility of political leadership of the country. Therefore a joint proposal from the council of ministers and the secretariat was submitted to and approved by the precious regent that Ling Rinpoché, assistant tutor and former abbot of Gyütö, should take on the responsibilities of junior tutor to me. Accordingly, a monk official from the chamberlain's office came to Rinpoché's rooms in the Lhasa labrang and presented him with the letter of appointment. At that time Takdrak Rinpoché was staying in Lhasa Kunsang Palace, and on that same day Rinpoché went to see him. He expressed his concern that it would be difficult for him to take on the duties of a tutor and asked for advice. Takdrak Rinpoché replied that the previous Ling Rinpoché, Losang Lungtok Tenzin Trinlé, had the opportunity to serve as tutor to the Thirteenth Dalai Lama for only seven years, so now Rinpoché should definitely complete the work of his previous incarnation.

After the Great Offering Ceremony[103] of that year was completed, Rinpoché traveled to Lhalu to visit Phabongkha Rinpoché close to the time that Phabongkha was leaving for Dakpo Shedrup Ling, Lhokha, and elsewhere. He gave Rinpoché a gift of an oil lantern newly made in America. They held discussions on profound and vast topics. Then Phabongkha Rinpoché stood up and presented Rinpoché with a ceremonial scarf and expressed great joy and delight that soon he would assume the responsibilities of being a tutor to the Dalai Lama.

The first day of the sixth month of that year in Dakpo district was the last time that Kyabjé Phabongkha performed his enlightened activities. When Rinpoché heard the news of his passing, he was profoundly saddened. He made extensive offerings in the various temples and elsewhere, while simultaneously making prayers that the profound and untainted aspirations of this great guide and protector be fulfilled, and that his unmistaken incarnation would be quickly discovered. Except for the classical monastic works on philosophy, Phabongkha Rinpoché had been his main source of teachings, and because of him Rinpoché had developed a surge of common and exclusive spiritual realizations. Therefore, just as Atiśa revered Serlingpa as without comparison from among his 150 gurus, Ling Rinpoché held Phabongkha Rinpoché as his principal lord and master. When teaching others Rinpoché would mainly refer to Phabongkha Rinpoché's teachings and practice. Generally, whenever Rinpoché spoke about those masters belonging to the Sakya, Geluk, Kagyü, and Nyingma traditions of Tibetan Buddhism from whom he had received teachings, he would never use their actual personal names. In particular, whenever he spoke of Phabongkha Rinpoché he always referred to him as Guru Vajradhara (Tib: Lama Dorjé Chang). To those who visited him he always said Guru Vajradhara would do such and such, and he would talk about what he used to say. There were strong indications that he was never separate from the guru. There was a small photo of a young Phabongkha Rinpoché impressed with his thumbprint that Rinpoché had placed inside a golden amulet. Until the day he died, Rinpoché took it with him everywhere. Rinpoché commissioned a silver frame embossed with gold and bordered by the sixteen offering goddesses for a photograph of Phabongkha Rinpoché and placed it on the altar in his room in Garpa Hermitage. The original notes of the stages of the path text entitled *Liberation in the Palm of Your Hand* were written down by Ratö Drakyap Dongkong Tulku, who had attended these stages of the path discourses by Phabongkha Rinpoché, and wherever he lived Rinpoché kept a copy of these notes until it was properly published.

Kyabjé Khangsar Vajradhara had been ill for some time, and the swelling in his feet began to worsen not long after Phabongkha Rinpoché had shown the act of passing away. As soon as Rinpoché heard of this he went to this Vajradhara's rooms in Drepung. There with prostrations he offered a ceremonial scarf and a representation of the body, speech, and mind and earnestly requested that Rinpoché remain for a long time as a guide and protector for living beings and the teachings. Kyabjé Khangsar Vajradhara replied by saying, "As I have often said, you should definitely work to propagate the Kālacakra initiation," and offered other advice on performing great deeds for the teachings and living beings. He also requested that Ling Rinpoché perform prayers for him. After that Khangsar Rinpoché went to stay at Tharpa Chöling, where on the eighth day of the ninth month he enacted the deed of passing away, and on the receipt of an earnest request, Rinpoché immediately made extensive offerings and prayers.

Sometime that year Rinpoché's tutor Loyak Rinpoché returned to his birthplace in Drakyap. Before his tutor's departure, Rinpoché presented him with extensive parting gifts and asked to be remembered in his prayers. As described earlier, Loyak Rinpoché became tutor to Rinpoché in the second year of his Madhyamaka studies. Rinpoché received from him teachings on the remainder of Madhyamaka and detailed word-by-word explanations of Tsonawa's commentary on Vinaya, and Chim Jampaiyang's exposition of Vasubandhu's *Treasury of Abhidharma*. Consequently, Rinpoché regarded this lama as the main source of teachings and training in philosophy. Whenever he spoke his name, he would repeat, "To him I go for refuge." Rinpoché would speak highly of him as being very good-natured with a definitive understanding of the texts and would even mimic his voice when saying how he would give such and such advice. When Loyak Rinpoché was teaching Ling Rinpoché at Drepung Monastery, he said that Rinpoché should memorize the third chapter of Dharmakīrti's *Treatise of Valid Cognition* while he was away at the monastic winter sessions at Jang. When Loyak Rinpoché returned from Jang, Rinpoché would immediately offer to be tested on his memorization. Because of this and other acts, Loyak

The Norbulingka summer palace of the Dalai Lamas

Rinpoché would often tell others that Rinpoché was a very special being, without equal in the guru-devotion practice of doing exactly what the guru says. Moreover, it is certainly the case that later on Loyak Rinpoché received teachings from our precious tutor and held him in great reverence. Whenever Loyak Rinpoché came to the labrang, he and Rinpoché would sit on seats of equal height.

Rinpoché had planned to construct a likeness of Nyakré Phuntsok Dampa, who was the philosophy tutor from whom Rinpoché's first learned Perfection of Wisdom topics, Dharmakīrti's *Treatise of Valid Cognition*, and Madhyamaka, but no photograph could be found.

On the morning of the twenty-ninth of the sixth Tibetan month at the Norbulingka, Rinpoché was presented with official notification of his appointment as junior tutor. That day coincided with the first day of the Shotön or "yogurt" folk opera festival, and this was considered to be an auspicious omen. I cannot be sure of the actual date, but in the first part of the morning on the actual day of the investiture as junior tutor, Ratö Chubar Tulku, accompanied by the Gyütö ritual monks, performed a long-life ritual involving the mandala-offering recitation in the Lhasa labrang. Rinpoché was offered the eight auspicious emblems and the eight auspicious substances, and the auspicious words of truth for the appointment were recited. After these private ceremonies were completed, a horseback

Ling Rinpoché at his Lhasa labrang

The Dalai Lama's throne in the Kalsang Palace at the Norbulingka

procession consisting of the labrang staff, monastic and lay government officials, and guards proceeded to visit the two main Lhasa temples. There, in front of the two main statues of the Buddha and other sacred objects, Rinpoché made the thousand five-senses offerings together with prayers. Then he proceeded to the Kalsang Palace at the Norbulingka, and there in my room he prostrated and offered me the mandala and the representations. I immediately offered a mandala and the three representations in return and requested teachings. Then, as was the custom for the inaugural audience, Rinpoché offered the three representations and so on to me, the senior tutor, and the administrator of the country, Takdrak Vajradhara, in the Sunlight Room. When he had taken his place on the tutor's seat, the government presented him with a congratulatory scarf together with an arrangement of special Tibetan pastries. At the same time a procession of dignitaries, including the four ministers, the highest monk official, and other monk and lay government officials, as well as representatives of various departments, all offered ceremonial scarves. After the official tea

The Norbulingka stables with frescoes.
Near them were Ling Rinpoche's living quarters.

gathering, Rinpoché visited the Potala and made offerings to the Self-Arisen Avalokiteśvara and other sacred objects there. He then returned to the Lhasa labrang, where government staff, the abbots of the monastic centers, monastic officials, tulkus, geshés, and so on lined up to offer their congratulations. A special envoy sent from Tashi Lhunpo offered a set of woven scrolls from China depicting the successive lives of the all-knowing Panchen Rinpoché.

The winter residence of the precious tutor, the Losang Dunsa rooms, was situated below the Potala chambers. These rooms had been blessed and lived in for a long time by many great beings, such as the Eighth Dalai Lama's tutor Yeshé Gyaltsen. Except when receiving visitors and giving teachings, Rinpoché spent his time in one small cold bedroom, which had one small window facing north toward the Lukhang, Lhalu, Sera Monastery, and so on. There, on a low cushion topped by a red cloth, Rinpoché performed his meditations and daily practices. In the summer he would stay in rooms above the Norbulingka stables.

When he was residing at the Potala and he came to teach me, I would sit on a wooden-frame seat in front of a table, on which the text was placed. In front of that the precious tutor would sit on a raised seat with no supporting cushions or backboard. As soon as Rinpoché arrived, the chief attendant would always serve tea in a large drinking bowl. As I was still very young, my elder brother Losang Samten would be my companion in these classes.

Whether it was an old custom or was something contrived by my personal attendants I cannot say, but there were two cane-handle horse whips, one with a silk cord strap, the other with a leather strap, and both bound with leather. In the Potala they were usually hanging on a pillar in the room known as Perfect Convergence of Wishes, and in the Norbulingka they were on a hook by the north window of the washroom. I think one whip was for me and the other for Losang Samten. When the lesson began one whip was placed beside the precious tutor's seat. The usual time for the morning lesson was from the end of the official tea gathering until lunch, and the afternoon lesson was from three o'clock until a little after five. In these lessons I would be tested by having to recite the texts I had memorized. Rinpoché would also give a little explanation. He would also give me new texts to memorize. Sometimes, when Losang Samten did not meet the text-recitation standard, Rinpoché would scold him and scare him. Sometimes he would even lightly touch Losang with the whip. One day the precious tutor took Losang outside and made out that he was going to whip him. The chief attendant pleaded with Rinpoché to relent. I clearly remember sitting in my room terrified. Whenever I was unable to recite the texts properly, he would reprimand me somewhat but he never scowled at me. I was just an unthinking little child, and whenever he scolded me I felt a little sad.

When he stayed in the Norbulingka he would sometimes stroll around. Once I was sitting under the Mahākāla temple eating walnuts and the precious tutor suddenly appeared around a wall, giving me a huge fright!

As mentioned, Rinpoché would come twice a day to teach, and during those times he would not waste even a minute but would teach in a strict way from beginning to end concentrating solely on the lesson and not engaging in conversation at all. At the Norbulingka a large monkey was kept in the stables and a smaller one outside the saddling rooms. Whenever Rinpoché came to teach me, he would regularly feed these monkeys fruit. Sometimes the monkeys would put their hands inside Rinpoché's bag to look for food. In midsummer he would sometimes go to a quiet place beside the river at the Nakha meadows,[104] where he would bathe and sit for a long time under a large parasol. He would take his meals there and relax.

In 1942, on the tenth day of the first month of the Tibetan water-horse year, when I received the preliminary vows of a novice monk from my tutor Takdrak Rinpoché, the ruler of the country, in the main Lhasa temple, this great being performed the role of the time-ritual assistant. On the fifteenth of that month, I was required to confer geshé status on Hothokthu Taktsak Rinpoché of Kundeling Monastery. I also had to move to the head of the Lhasa Great Prayer Festival assembly. In the morning I gave a preliminary Dharma discourse and teachings on Āryaśūra's *Garland of the Buddha's Birth Stories* in the discourse courtyard to thousands of monks, and in the afternoon I took part in the communal recitation of the *Prayer for the Teachings to Flourish*,[105] Tsongkhapa's *Prayer for Rebirth in Sukhāvatī*, and so on. In all these events the precious tutor had given me pertinent advice and instruction in the preceding year. I had practiced by following his instructions precisely and was able to carry out these required activities well. After the events were over, the precious tutor told his reading and writing master Phukhang Ngawang Lhundrup of Gyütö that so far I had carried out my responsibilities well. As this was my first discourse, it seems that he had been very concerned.

Drakri Rinpoché explained to the precious tutor that the lineage of the *Vairocana Enlightenment Tantra* passed on from Phabongkha Rinpoché in central Tibet today rested solely with Lhatsun Rinpoché of Shungpa House in Sera Mé Monastery. Therefore it was very important that he receive the initiation from him. Accordingly, when Lhatsun Rinpoché gave the *Vairocana Enlightenment Tantra* initiation sometime that year under the sponsorship of Kundeling Taktsak Rinpoché, the precious tutor went specially to receive it.

Later, Rinpoché invited Lhatsun Rinpoché to his residence at the Norbulingka. There, over the next month, he received many sutra and tantra teachings from Lhatsun Rinpoché, who had in turn received them from the Tashi Khyil Mongolian dorampa geshé Palden Sangpo and the Dākhural geshé Losang Tayang. These teachings included the generation and completion stages of Guhyasamāja, Cakrasaṃvara, and Vajrabhairava by Akhu Sherap Gyatso, Jamyang Shepa Jikmé Wangpo's commentary to Changkya Rölpai Dorjé's *Recognizing My Old Mother: A Song on the View*, *Prayer for the Flourishing of Tsongkhapa's Teachings* by Gungthang Tenpai Drönmé, and so on. At that time the precious tutor gave an explanation of Phabongkha Rinpoché's composition on the Cittamaṇi Tārā generation and completion stages to a geshé from Dākhural. At the request of the Drepung

Loseling abbot Yeshé Jinpa from Tsang House, Rinpoché composed a supplication to Panchen Sönam Drakpa. In response to a request from Gyütö monks engaged in the extensive generation-stage retreat on single-deity Vajrabhairava, Rinpoché gave the single-deity Vajrabhairava initiation, together with the preparatory empowerment, in the Lhasa labrang's great reception room to about three hundred monks, including Kachen Ngawang Nyima of Tashi Lhunpo, who would later become the tutor to the Panchen Rinpoché.

18 | Assisting the Dalai Lama in His Studies

I N 1947 I would begin my religious education in Drepung and Sera monasteries and would have to debate with past and present abbots. Therefore, in the second month of the preceding year, tutor and ruler Takdrak Rinpoché and tutor Ling Rinpoché came to the Ganden Yangtsé room in the Potala to help me in my studies. For an auspicious start they chanted together with the assistant tutors and myself Rendawa's *Extensive as Space*[106] prayer, *Speaking the Names of Mañjuśrī*, and so on. After this ceremony had finished, tutor Takdrak Rinpoché, using the text on Collected Topics composed by Phurchok Jampa Gyatso, began giving me instructions on the subjects within the Collected Topics, such as the dialectically structured posing of questions and responses on topics such as the colors, categories of existence, and isolates, and many other subjects.

When the incarnation of Kyabjé Phabongkha Rinpoché, Ngawang Losang Tenzin Trinlé, was being escorted from his birthplace in Drigung in Upper Central Tibet, Rinpoché set up a special tent at Lungpa Darling Labrang near Garpa Hermitage to welcome him. There he presented the whole party with food, drink, and ceremonial scarves. When this supreme incarnation was enthroned at Tashi Chöling Hermitage, Rinpoché specially sent his labrang manager, Losang Lungrik, to present him with gifts, a ceremonial scarf, and so on. A few days later Phabongkha Tulku came to the Potala, and Rinpoché went to meet him. Because the previous incarnation had been the precious tutor's main master, Rinpoché constantly showed him great reverence by insisting that he sit in the head seat and so on. Later the manager of Phabongkha Rinpoché's household, Trinlé Dargyé, appealed to Rinpoché, saying, "Although Master Dechen Nyingpo was Rinpoché's root guru, this present incarnation has already taken teachings from Rinpoché and now is his disciple. Therefore please do not show so

The Fourteenth Dalai Lama at age twelve

much reverence." Nevertheless, whenever he came to Rinpoché's rooms at the labrang to have meals, they sat together on the same seat.

In the sixth month of that year, Kyabjé Trijang Rinpoché developed a serious illness that appeared to be an intestinal inflammation. Rinpoché went to visit him to wish him well and to plead that he live for a long time.

After I had trained in Collected Topics and so on, Rinpoché gave me teachings on the Perfection of Wisdom. This was done by memorizing the two root texts Maitreya's *Ornament of Realization* and Candrakīrti's *Entering the Middle Way*, as well as passages from Haribhadra's commentary *Clarification of the Meaning of the Ornament of Realization*, and the Great Fifth Dalai Lama's *Exegesis of Ornament of Realization and Its Commentaries: Ornament to the Thought of Losang Drakpa*. I memorized about half a folio each day, which I then had to recite as a test. After that the precious tutor would point out passages from the Fifth Dalai Lama's *Boat to Enter the Great Ocean of the Mahayana*, Tsongkhapa's *Essence of Excellent Explanation: Differentiating the Definitive and the Provisional*, Dharmakīrti's *Treatise of Valid Cognition*, Guṇaprabha's *Vinaya Sutra*, and the summary verses from the *Vinaya Sutra*. Whatever Rinpoché had marked I would memorize. Close to the time I sat for the geshé debate examination, I enthusiastically memorized Vasubandhu's *Treasury of Abhidharma* on my own. Although the memorization did not reach to the standard required for an examination, I memorized it anyway. It was not, however, one of the texts earmarked by the precious tutor.

When I was studying debate, immediately after the precious tutor had finished the lesson, the junior or senior assistant tutor would come in, and I would have to practice debating with them. Around that time Trijang Rinpoché would occasionally visit and he suggested that it would be good to ask the precious tutor for instructions on particular points of the generation and completion stages. From time to time the precious tutor would give me brief teachings and transmissions on these topics.

At that time, as I was very young and quite incapable of making any efforts by myself, I was like a boat cut adrift. The precious tutor from his side gave me advice and did the best he could to instill good qualities in me. His kindness, therefore, was immense.

In 1947, in the sixth Tibetan month, in response to a request from the Shokdruk Kyapgön of Lithang, Rinpoché gave teachings and transmissions at his residence at the Norbulingka to an audience of about thirty lamas, tulkus, geshés, and so on over a number of days on Khedrup Jé's *Ocean of Attainments*, which deals with the Guhyasamāja generation stage, Tsongkhapa's *Lamp to Illuminate the Five Stages*, which presents the completion stage, Tsongkhapa's *Great Exposition of Secret Mantra*, and a combined teaching of the *Cakrasaṃvara Root Tantra* and Tsongkhapa's commentary *Elucidation of All Hidden Points*.

In the eighth month of that year, I began my religious education at the various colleges at Sera and Drepung and had to engage in debate and give teachings. My precious tutor kindly gave me reassuring words of congratulations for how I performed in consideration of my age.

In the tenth month in response to a request from Ratö Khyongla Tulku, Rinpoché gave teachings and a transmission to a number of recipients on Khedrup Jé's *Ocean of Attainments* on the Guhyasamāja generation stage.

Geshé Losang Samdrup Rinpoché had sponsored the creation of two-story statues of Tsongkhapa and his two chief disciples inside the assembly hall of Gyütö. After the statues were installed, monks of Gyümé, the lower tantric college, performed an extensive consecration ritual using the thirteen-deity Vajrabhairava. Rinpoché was requested by the sponsor and the college to preside over the consecration ceremony. In between the sessions Geshé Samdrup came to Rinpoché, and the two conversed for a long time. The precious tutor then said, "Geshé-la, isn't it time now to do the recitations?" He replied that he had forgotten the recitations. Rinpoché wondered if that remark meant that he had reached a level of realization where recitation is no longer needed. Otherwise, how was it possible to forget the recitations? Rinpoché told others that it seemed that Phabongkha Rinpoché believed that Samdrup Rinpoché has reached a high level of realization.

In 1949, in the third Tibetan month, at the request of the Gyütö abbot Losang Chöjor of Sera Jé Monastery, Rinpoché gave teachings and transmission of the four Guhyasamāja texts combined and the *Cakrasaṃvara Root Tantra* and Tsongkhapa's *Elucidation of All Hidden Points*, as well as a long-life initiation of White Tārā in the Ramoché courtyard to an audience of a few thousand, including the entire Gyütö assembly, most of the monks from Gyümé Monastery, headed by the abbot and the deputy abbot, lamas, tulkus, and geshés from other monastic centers, as well as lay men and women,

To Ratö Khyongla Tulku he gave an explanation and transmission of the great Fifth Dalai Lama's commentary to Daṇḍin's *Mirror of Poetics* entitled *Melody to Delight Sarasvatī*. Rinpoché also consulted *Compendium of Poetic Examples* compiled by Lama Orgyenpa from Sikkim when teaching the second chapter of Daṇḍin's root text. He also tested Khyongla Tulku on the poetic examples. In his conversation with Khyongla Tulku, Rinpoché mentioned incidentally a verse from *White Mahākāla Treasure Vase Accomplishment* by the Radreng throneholder Tenpa Rapgyé, which reads in its current edition:

> Although the lion of the naturally pure mind
> has his abode in the snow mountains of the three pure vows,
> I openly confess the breach of my precepts caused
> by being pierced by the five arrows of mental affliction.

Rinpoché corrected the first line to "Although Śiva of the naturally pure mind." This he did by citing the background story.[107]

At the request of Deyang College, Rinpoché added a supplement to the supplication prayer to the successive lineage of abbots. In response to a request by Gephel Hermitage, he edited a propitiation of the *tenma* protector goddesses. To Tulku Jungar Rinpoché of Tashi Khyil Monastery and Ratö Khyongla Tulku he gave teachings on Sanskrit grammar up to the five classes of *sandhi*[108] using Anubhūti's *Sarasvatī Grammar Treatise* and its commentary Gyurmé Tsewang Chokdrup's *Hundred Rays of Light*. In response to a request from Geshé Wangdü Gyaltsen of Drepung Loseling's Nyakré House, Rinpoché gave teachings and transmissions of Khedrup Jé's *Ocean of Attainments* on Guhyasamāja generation stage, and Tsongkhapa's *Lamp to Illuminate the Five Stages* on the completion stage, to a few disciples in his residence at the Norbulingka. At that time, Kyabjé Trijang Rinpoché also received teachings on Guhyasamāja generation stage from Guru Vajradhara. These two lamas discussed and resolved many of the most difficult points. Rinpoché also debated often with Geshé Wangdü Gyaltsen. As Rinpoché had already received his geshé degree, he did not have much opportunity to debate others. Therefore he said it was important to engage in debate at times like these.

At the request of Jampa Chösang, my chief household attendant, Rinpoché composed the closing dedication prayers for a new edition of the Loseling textbook *Utpala Garland* of Panchen Sönam Drakpa, dealing with the difficult points of differentiation between the provisional and definitive meanings of scriptures. When the most eminent regent and tutor Takdrak Vajradhara gave me the complete collection, including the initiations, transmissions, instructions, and so on, of *Pure Visions: The Sealed Secrets* by the all-knowing Great Fifth Dalai Lama in the Norbulingka, the precious tutor also attended the initiation and transmission. At that time the tutor Takdrak Rinpoché was somewhat advanced in his years, and during a long initiation and teaching, he would become tired. One time he said to me that Ling Rinpoché was an exceptional lama and recommended that I should receive the great initiations, such as Guhyasamāja, from him.

Every winter, when I lived in the Potala, I would regularly do a generation-stage retreat on a particular meditation deity. In the beginning Takdrak Rinpoché would stay with me to assist me in the retreat, but later the precious tutor would assist me every year.

In response to the combined request of the Tsarong steward and Drepung Loseling Monastery, in the seventh month of the Tibetan calendar, Rinpoché gave an experiential fourfold-explanation[109] instruction on the stages of the path using Panchen Losang Yeshé's *Swift Path Direct Instructions* for about fifteen days in Drepung Loseling assembly hall to an audience of about five thousand, including past and present abbots of the monastic centers, the Dedruk Hothokthu, Takphu Rinpoché and other lamas and tulkus, as well as geshés, students, and so on. Afterward, he performed the bodhicitta ceremony and then conferred the single-deity, single-vase longevity initiation of Amitāyus according to the Niguma tradition. After this several benefactors sponsored a long-life ritual in conjunction with a Guru Puja *tsok* ritual for Rinpoché, which he accepted.

During his tenure as abbot of the tantric college, Rinpoché had sent Nyakré geshé Tenpa Chöden and Rongpa Yeshé Döndrup[110] to Amdo Tashi Khyil Monastery to teach the ritual practices, the grid drawing, colors, and so on to the newly established branch of Gyütö there. They had now completed their task and had returned to Lhasa. When they came to visit Rinpoché in his residence, he was very pleased to see them and asked enthusiastically about the lamas and top geshés in Amdo and about any new lineages the pair might have received during their stay. Rinpoché was very pleased to receive from Tenpa Chöden gifts of the collection of works by Palmang Könchok Gyaltsen, Shang Tenpa Gyatso, and others, which were rare in Central Tibet at that time. Rinpoché never showed much interest in the gifts he received from disciples, no matter the quality, but was always pleased when someone arrived with rare texts.

In response to a request from Tsawa Sersang Tulku of Ganden Jangtsé, Rinpoché gave a transmission of the collected works of Thuken Losang Chökyi Nyima to several lamas, tulkus, and geshés in the Norbulingka. At another time he gave a transmission of what he had received of the collected works of Akhu Sherap Gyatso and an explanation and transmission of the Kālacakra generation-stage sādhana by Detri Rinpoché. In response to a request from me, Rinpoché gave an experiential instruction on stages of the path using *Swift Path Direct Instructions* and the Fifth Dalai Lama's *Oral Transmission of Mañjuśrī* combined, in the Jangchup Gakhyil central temple at the Norbulingka.

In 1949, in response to a request from Namgyal Monastery, the monastery associated with the Dalai Lama, Rinpoché gave the Guhyasamāja initiation followed by a very extensive teaching and transmission of Khedrup Jé's *Ocean of Attainments* on Guhyasamāja generation stage and Tsongkhapa's *Lamp to Illuminate the Five Stages* on the completion stage to an audience of over a thousand, including the monks of Gyütö and Gyümé.

Around that time Ratö Khyongla asked Rinpoché if he could attend teachings being given at the Potala. Rinpoché replied that he should definitely attend the teaching on Śāntideva's *Guide to the Bodhisattva's Way of Life* to be given at Tengyé Ling Monastery by the Ganden Throneholder Lhundrup Tsöndrü. This was without doubt a teaching stressing the importance of training in the common path. Also, Khyongla often asked Rinpoché if it were important to request such and such teaching because its lineage was so rare. Rinpoché replied with a reprimand saying, "Whenever I requested a teaching in the past, I did so because I thought I might be able to practice it a little. I did not do it with the thought of selling it to others." This is also mentioned in his autobiography.

Once Rinpoché listed the names of the lamas he had received teachings from and asked Khyongla to count them. He said that while he was attending the Jang winter sessions, others had told him that Dongkong Tulku was learned in Dharmakīrti's *Treatise of Valid Cognition* and that it would be beneficial to have conversations with him. Rinpoché accordingly engaged Dongkong in discussion, and he therefore wondered aloud whether Dongkong should be included in his list of teachers. When asked later, Rinpoché replied that Dongkong was indeed to be included in the list.

19 | Appointment as Sharpa Chöjé

T HE INCUMBENT Sharpa Chöjé, Sera Jé Lawa Yeshé, had passed away, and in accordance with tradition, it was now the turn of Rinpoché to assume that title. Therefore, in 1949, the precious regent requested Rinpoché to immediately take on the duties of the Sharpa Chöjé. Accordingly, an appropriately auspicious date for the enthronement was quickly calculated by the Astro-Medical Institute. In the reception room at the labrang, Rinpoché ascended an east-facing throne, and the ceremony was performed. This was followed by the audience at the Potala that is customary when a new position is taken on.

Every year at Ganden during the summer retreat, the Sharpa Chöjé had to deliver a teaching based on Tsongkhapa's *Middle-Length Stages of the Path*. However, Rinpoché had not previously received a transmission of this text, so he began receiving the transmission of this text from the regent Takdrak Rinpoché. Furthermore, Rinpoché requested the precious regent to give the teachings on the intermediate-length guide to the *Guru Puja*[111] by Yongzin Yeshé Gyaltsen of Tsechokling Monastery, and the Guhyasamāja work *Five Stages Complete on One Seat* by Jé Tsongkhapa. He joyfully accepted this request, but because of his workload the teachings had to be postponed.

After this, during the summer retreat, Rinpoché went to Ganden, where he stayed on the top floor of Lhopa House. On the actual day of the Sharpa Chöjé enthronement, as Rinpoché was making his way from Lhopa House to the assembly, he encountered a water carrier on the path. A monk called Tashi from lower Gadong Kashi, a clerk from the government treasury office who was helping with the rituals, placed a top-quality ceremonial scarf over the full bucket of water that the man was carrying. The water carrier went directly to the residence of the Ganden Throneholder. Some remarked that this was an auspicious omen for Rinpoché's future ascension to the position of regent of Mañjunātha, the second Buddha.[112]

On that day Rinpoché made extensive donations and offerings to the Ganden assembly, the two colleges of Shartsé and Jangtsé, and affiliated houses. He made visits to the precious golden reliquary of Jé Tsongkhapa and other great beings and with extensive prayers made the thousand five-senses cloud offerings. The government, the monastic council of Ganden, the colleges, the houses, and so forth presented him with auspicious congratulatory scarves. For three days Rinpoché gave teachings from the beginning of Tsongkhapa's *Middle-Length Stages of the Path* to the Jangtsé Chöjé in the Shartsé residence, and the same teachings to the past and present abbots of Jangtsé and Shartsé colleges, lamas, tulkus, geshés, and many others in the area. In response to a request from Geshé Ngawang Tashi of Lhopa House, Rinpoché gave transmissions of the thirteen-deity Vajrabhairava sādhana and the *Eighteen-Step Guide to Vajrabhairava*, composed by the previous incarnation of Ling Rinpoché, Losang Lungtok Tenzin Trinlé, in the assembly hall of Lhopa House.

In the spring of 1950, in response to a request from the Nepalese owner of a glass business, Rinpoché gave the initiation of single-deity Vajrabhairava as well as extensive and detailed teachings on the generation and completion stages on this tantra in Shidé Monastery assembly hall to an audience of over a thousand. Before he returned to Nepal, this merchant bought from the Shöl printing press a complete set of the collected works of Jé Tsongkhapa and his two principal disciples. He asked Kyabjé Rinpoché to mark each volume with his personal seal as a blessing and took them to Nepal. After 1959, when these texts became scarce in India, he offered the complete set of these texts to Rinpoché. Previously in Tibet this Nepalese merchant had set up a trust with a sum of money as capital whose interest would fund Garpa Hermitage for its ritual offerings. During the invasion the hermitage was razed to the ground by the Chinese soldiers, and this Nepalese glass merchant returned the entire capital together with interest to the labrang in India. As the hermitage had been completely destroyed, Rinpoché used the capital to make offerings in India and Nepal. Later when Rinpoché heard that this merchant had suffered much because of a prolonged illness, he immediately sent a sum of money to Nepal to help him.

In recognition of Ling Rinpoché's excellent upholding of the title of tutor to the Dalai Lama, the government offered Chakbam estate in Kharek to the labrang as a monastic estate. Rinpoché's current attendant, Druklha,

Shidé Monastery

volunteered to go to the estate, and Thupten Tsering took up the duties of attendant.

The monk Chösang Thutop of Sera Monastery's Ngakpa House, popularly known as "the bearded one," was the hermitage resident monk. He spent most of his time attending on Rinpoché at the Norbulingka and the Potala and only stayed at the hermitage during the bimonthly confession ceremonies. Chösang Thutop was very skilled in making tormas, ornamenting them, and so on, as well as being learned in chanting. Consequently, he served Rinpoché as ritual assistant during initiation ceremonies.

In response to a request from Geshé Gyümé of Loseling's Nyakré House, Rinpoché gave the transmission of Tsongkhapa's *Great Stages of the Path to Enlightenment*. On another occasion, in response to a request from some monks who were engaged in a retreat on the deity Sitātapatrā, Rinpoché conferred the initiation of the seventeen-deity Sitātapatrā in his residence at the Norbulingka.

In 1950[113] a large Chinese force invaded areas of eastern Tibet and imprisoned the governor and his officials, thereby rendering the situation in Tibet dire. Therefore, in response to the wishes and hopes of the Tibetan people, lay and monastic, on the seventeenth of November of that year, in the great reception hall in the Potala Palace called the Glories of Samsara and Nirvana, I assumed the responsibilities of the spiritual and temporal leadership of Tibet. (plate 16) During that ceremony the precious tutor performed an extensive mandala recitation during the long-life prayers for me. The Tibetan national assembly unanimously requested that I should move to Dromo[114] at least temporarily to escape any danger. Accordingly, on the nineteenth of December I had to leave Lhasa, and on the same day the precious tutor, accompanied by the labrang manager Losang Lungrik, the attendant Thupten Tsering, and others, also left Lhasa. That evening arrangements had been made for Rinpoché to stay at Tashi Gang Monastery in Nyethang. Not having received any directions to the monastery, they missed it and traveled past. A guide from the monastery caught up with Rinpoché's party and escorted them back. To the attendants, having to turn around and travel back was an auspicious portent that they would soon return to Lhasa.

After Tashi Gang the party set out for Dromo. On the way they stayed at Sharsingma and reached their destination of Dungkar Monastery in Upper Dromo. There, in the Tashi Chöling assembly hall, Rinpoché bestowed the initiation of the single-deity Vajrabhairava and gave experiential instructions on the generation and completion stages. This was in response to a request from Khyenrap Wangchuk from Dompo, an acting monastic government official, who had made the request for the sake of the virtues of his late brother, the steward Gyalten Namgyal.

As preparation for my retreats on single-deity Vajrabhairava, Eleven-Face Avalokiteśvara, and the inner practice of protector Kālarūpa, Rinpoché kindly gave me the initiations again, as well as teachings on the visualization procedures and so on.

At that time there were conflicting opinions on whether we should proceed to India from Dromo or return to Lhasa. A dough-ball divination was performed suggesting that it would be better to return to Lhasa. Therefore the precious tutor advised that we should follow this advice, and accordingly it was decided to return to Lhasa. As the time to leave grew near, Rinpoché suddenly fell ill. The labrang manager, Losang Lungrik, said that in Dungkar Monastery there was an oracle of the peaceful and wrathful forms of the protector Gyalchen[115] and asked whether it would be proper to rely upon the peaceful form for a divination concerning Rinpoché's health. Rinpoché replied that to determine the suitability of Gyalchen, it would

At Dungkar Monastery in Dromo in 1951. The Dalai Lama is holding relics of the Buddha, brought from India. Ling Rinpoché stands in the foreground, right.

be best to perform a dough-ball divination in the presence of the statue of most revered goddess Tārā that was inside the neck amulet he carried with him at all times. He had great faith and trust in this amulet and regarded it as a treasure. The dough-ball divination was performed, and the result did not come out favorably for relying upon the peaceful aspect of Gyalchen. Therefore this idea was abandoned.

On July 20, 1951, the seventeenth of the fifth[116] Tibetan month of the iron-rabbit year, I set out from Dromo to return to the capital Lhasa. On the way, at Palkhor Chödé Monastery in Gyantsé, I gave the Avalokiteśvara initiation to many ordained and lay people. My great root lama was seated in the rows, and during the torma ritual to pacify the hindering spirits, I was throwing the grains when the vajra slipped out of my hand and disappeared. It had fallen into a fold in the upper garment of the precious tutor. Immediately he stood up and returned the vajra to me. Many present remarked that this was an extraordinary thing to happen and were convinced it was a very auspicious sign.

After Rinpoché reached Lhasa, he stayed at the Norbulingka for a few

The Dalai Lama giving his first Avalokiteśvara initiation
in Gyantsé. Ling Rinpoché is far left.

days and then spent about a week in Garpa Hermitage, where he rested and
recovered his strength.

I requested Rinpoché to grant me the Kālacakra initiation, a unique system of tantra that differs from other tantras in its mode of exposition. This
he joyfully accepted. Consequently, in his Losang Dunsa residence at the
Potala Palace, he completed a qualifying retreat on the mind mandala of
the blessed Kālacakra, followed by a fire offering at the Lhasa labrang. Then
in 1952, in the Tibetan water-dragon year, in the Potala's great reception
hall called Glories of Samsara and Nirvana, the complete mandala of body,
speech, and mind using colored sand was constructed. This was preceded
by the necessary preliminaries of the ritual of caring for the disciple, followed by the preparatory rites of the site consecration, the earth-goddess
ritual, and so on. Then, having performed the rites of self-generation and
making offerings, he conducted the self-empowerment ceremony by means
of entering into the mandala and took the four initiations. Then on the
special day of the full moon of the *caitra* month—which was the day that
Buddha Śākyamuni arose in the form of the primordial Buddha glorious
Kālacakra and turned the Dharma wheel of this king of tantras to King

The Fourteenth Dalai Lama wearing a ritual costume
for the Kālacakra initiation bestowed by Ling Rinpoché

Sucandra and other fortunate beings—for the following three days he
taught the procedures for entering the mandala and granted the seven initiations resembling the stages of childhood, the three higher initiations,
and the vajrācārya lord-and-master initiation together with concluding ceremonies. The Kālacakra tradition stemming from the great Jé Tsongkhapa
carries the thinking of *Stainless Light*, Puṇḍarīka's great commentary on the
Kālacakra tantra. It possesses numerous explanatory traditions from India
and Tibet, it is praised in the same way that King Sucandra was praised by

Kālacakra himself, and it was established by the glorious Khedrup Gelek Palsang in his extensive commentary on the Kālacakra tantra as well as in his manuals on the mandala rite and its ancillary materials. In a similar manner, Rinpoché gave detailed and extensive explanations on Kālacakra perfected through the threefold validation,[117] and the teachings on practice too were profound and extensive, without simplifications. Therefore, not only was just the understanding of the initiation conveyed to me, but every contamination of doubt stemming from ignorance and wrong conceptions with regard to all the essential points of the outer, inner, and other Kālacakra was dispelled, and he bestowed on me a complete understanding that would conclusively determine all points of the tantra for discerning scholars.

During the vajrācārya lord-and-master initiation, after teaching the pledges of the master, there is a verse that petitions the main deity:

> I give you this disciple,
> who will maintain the tantras.

On reciting this, Rinpoché looked a little sad. I also felt the same way.

Kyabjé Trijang Rinpoché had compared the notes taken by himself and others during the teaching from the master Phabongkha Dechen Nyingpo on the Cakrasaṃvara body mandala, and had compiled *Gateway to the Ocean of Great Bliss* on the generation stage of the body mandala in the Ghaṇṭapāda tradition. He gave this work to the precious tutor to look over and requested that he make any necessary corrections. This Rinpoché did with great dedication. At another time Phabongkha Rinpoché's secretary, Losang Dorjé, requested Rinpoché to look at and correct the notes taken on the generation and completion stages of the thirteen-deity Vajrabhairava, with the intention of including them in the collected works of Phabongkha. Rinpoché fulfilled his wishes. Rinpoché also complied with the request of the Takdrak administrator[118] to carefully go through the list of teachings received by the former regent because the administrator was planning to print the former regent's collected works.

Once when Rinpoché was giving teachings and transmissions on Khedrup Jé's Guhyasamāja generation-stage work *Ocean of Attainments* and Tsongkhapa's completion-stage work *Lamp to Illuminate the Five Stages*, the former Ganden Throneholder Lhundrup Tsöndrü of Sera Jé asked through Ratö Khyongla Tulku if he would be allowed to attend, stating that the precious tutor was a very special being like those great Kadampa masters of the past. Rinpoché replied, "How could I offer teachings to such a learned being?" When he asked again, Rinpoché said, "This is the Ganden Throneholder, and for him to receive teachings with many other people is unbecoming. Therefore I could offer him teachings in private." However, because of Rinpoché's busy schedule, there was not the time to give the teachings as Lhundrup Tsöndrü had wished. Therefore, it seems that Lhundrup Tsöndrü strongly advised former Sera Jé abbot Thapkhé and others that it was important for them to request teachings and transmissions on these great texts from this Vajradhara tutor.

At that time Kumbum Minyak Rinpoché was in Lhasa. He was a very learned master, and Rinpoché wondered if it would be beneficial for the Buddha's teaching if he were to receive from him transmissions of teachings he had not previously received. Therefore he sent Ratö Khyongla Tulku to the Lhasa main temple to perform a dough-ball divination in the presence of the Jowo Rinpoché statue. The divination was favorable. Therefore that winter in the Losang Dunsa residence in the Potala, with Kyabjé Trijang Rinpoché, Ratö Khyongla Tulku, and a few others, Rinpoché received teachings from Minyak Rinpoché. They included a transmission of *Instructions on the Guru Puja: Testament Carried on the Wind*.[119] This was followed by transmissions and teachings on Jé Tsongkhapa's *Clarifying the Intention: Explanation of Entering the Middle Way*, Jé Tsongkhapa's *Essence of Excellent Explanation: Differentiating the Definitive and the Provisional*, Khedrup Jé's *Dose of Emptiness: Opening the Eyes of the Fortunate*, the root text and commentary of Gungthang Tenpai Drönmé's *Praise of Jé Tsongkhapa: Meaningful to Behold*, and *Rays of the Sun: Training the Mind in Bodhicitta* by Hortön Namkha Pal. In the following year from the same master, Rinpoché listened to teachings on Haribhadra's *Clarification of the Meaning of the Ornament of Realization*, Akhu Sherap Gyatso's instructions on the generation and completion stages of Guhyasamāja, Cakrasaṃvara, and Vajrabhairava, a transmission of the annotations on the *Condensed Kālacakra Tantra* and *Root Kālacakra Tantra*, for which a few documents still needed to be compiled, and teachings on Langri Thangpa's *Eight Verses on Mind Training*, Dharmarakṣita's *Wheel of Sharp Weapons*, and others.

In response to a request from Minyak Rinpoché, the precious tutor gave transmission and teachings on Aśvaghoṣa's *Fifty Verses on the Guru*, Candragomin's *Twenty Verses on the Bodhisattva Vow*, and others. In this way these two masters became very close.

Later a scholar learned in grammar arrived in Lhasa. Rinpoché wondered if it would be beneficial to the doctrine if he were to receive teachings on grammar he had not heard before. He sent Ratö Khyongla Tulku to perform a dough-ball divination in the presence of the Jowo Rinpoché statue, but the divination was not favorable.

In response to a request from the shapdrung of Nakshö Driru, in the assembly hall of Lhasa's Shidé Monastery, Rinpoché gave the initiation of single-deity Vajrabhairava and experiential instructions on the generation and completion stages to an audience of over a thousand who had pledged to recite daily the Vajrabhairava sādhana.

20 | Appointment as Senior Tutor

FOLLOWING IN the footsteps of Phurchok Tulku Jampa Gyatso, senior tutor to the Great Thirteenth Dalai Lama, Rinpoché was now obliged to assume the role of senior tutor.[120] Therefore, in response to an official request from the council of ministers and the secretarial and revenue committee,[121] Rinpoché attended the ceremonial audience for assuming the new position of senior tutor at the beginning of October 1953. From then on, when staying in the Potala, Rinpoché lived in the Rikné Kunsal lower residence formerly occupied by Takdrak Rinpoché, and in the Norbulingka he moved from his residence above the outer area of the stables to new rooms above the Shapten temple.

Whether Rinpoché was staying in the Potala or the Norbulingka, he always took with him the texts of short, intermediate, and extensive *Stages of the Path* by Jé Tsongkhapa, the annotations on the stages of the path by Phabongkha Rinpoché, the presentations on the minds and mental factors by Yongzin Yeshé Gyaltsen entitled *Ornament for Those with Intelligent Minds: Clear Teachings on Mind and Mental Factors*, and its summary in verse called *Jewel Garland* by the same author. He would study these texts regularly. When people would visit, he would put the texts away shortly before they arrived. Whenever Rinpoché borrowed texts from the Druzin palace library at the Norbulingka, he always wrote a receipt, and when he returned them he would retrieve the receipt. He was very meticulous in this way.

There were many texts housed in the Lhasa labrang, and when they were to be brought to the Potala or the Norbulingka for Rinpoché to read, he sent servants or disciples to fetch them, and without hesitation could say exactly where they were, the size of the volume, the color of the cloth wrapping, and so on. His respect for texts was very high. When reading a text he would never put it on the table without its cloth wrapping or wooden covers. Usually the labrang manager, rather than Rinpoché, took care of the various affairs within the labrang. However, whenever someone asked to borrow a text, Rinpoché had to be consulted.

Rinpoché had already received the initiation of Cakrasaṃvara of the Lūipa tradition from Khangsar Rinpoché in his Jamyang Kyil chambers and had even taken notes. However, because he wanted to do the generation-stage retreat, he invited Kyabjé Trijang Rinpoché to the Lhasa labrang, where over two days he received on his own the preparation ceremonies and the actual initiation again. Rinpoché requested that there was no need to give explanation on the initiation verses, but he asked for a rough explanation of the text detailing the initiation procedure. Rinpoché said that such an explanation was probably not given, but he was confident he received the initiation.

Rinpoché then engaged in a strict retreat in his Rikné Kunsal residence at the Potala. Early in the morning he performed his usual recitations. After that, accompanied by Chösang Thutop, he began the self-generation of Cakrasaṃvara. Rinpoché spent a long time on the visualization processes, and it took three hours to reach the mantra recitation. In the evening up until seven o'clock, he did one session. In this way he accumulated the mantra count and in three weeks had completed the required amount for the retreat. He then moved to the labrang and, together with the Gyütö ritual monks, he perfectly performed the supplementary peaceful form of fire offering.

One winter, in response to my request, Rinpoché conferred the Akṣobhya Vajra Guhyasamāja and Lūipa Cakrasaṃvara initiations that I had not previously received from Takdrak Rinpoché. He also gave experience-based instructions on the generation and completion stages of Cakrasaṃvara, Guhyasamāja, and Vajrabhairava using Akhu Sherap Gyatso's instruction texts, a reading transmission of the *Kadam Father and Son Teachings* compiled by Dromtönpa, and a transmission and teaching on the Seventh Dalai Lama's guide to the *Hundred Deities of Tuṣita* guruyoga. Also, I clearly remember one summer receiving experiential instructions on the generation and completion stages of thirteen-deity Vajrabhairava using the works of Ngulchu Dharmabhadra in rooms above the Druzin Palace at the Norbulingka, and in the Jangchup Gakyil rooms instructions on the Vajrabhairava magical wheel and the sixty-four-part torma ritual, the shared and exclusive practices of the peaceful and wrathful forms combined, and explanation and transmission of Butön Rinchen Drup's *Annotations on the Kālacakra Stainless Light Great Commentary*. I received many other teaching from him, but I cannot list them here because the record of teachings received at that time was left behind in Tibet.

Around that time the labrang manager bought a fine-looking black mule. When he brought it to the Norbulingka for Rinpoché to look at, he took great delight in it. He knew for sure that this mule was destined to serve him on his journey to China the following year.

Amdo Jinpa Gyatso and two other disciples of Rinpoché suggested that it was important for the labrang to expand somewhat, and they offered to undertake some business toward that end. The manager also asked Rinpoché once whether it was appropriate to start up some business. In reply Rinpoché spoke of the importance of contentment and of having few desires. He himself never had the slightest desire for any kind of extravagance. However, he would not prevent the manager from regularly buying horses, mules, and so on but insisted that these animals be treated with affection.

In 1954, on the eighth day of the first Tibetan month of the wood-horse year, Rinpoché gave novice-monk vows in his residence in Lhasa to the ninth incarnation of Drakyap Hothokthu. For the two preceding years, leading up to the time when I was of age to take the full monastic ordination, Rinpoché gave novice and full-ordination vows to lamas and individual monks regardless of tradition, thereby performing a great service to the sacred Vinaya, which is the very foundation of the Buddha's teaching. However, I shall not elaborate on these here.

In order to proclaim the greatness of the Dharma, I was required to petition for full ordination three times in the previous year. Accordingly, on the fifteenth of the above month in the main Lhasa temple in the presence of the Jowo Śākyamuni, this sacred spiritual mentor, who is endowed with the twin qualities of knowledge and monastic discipline, the crown jewel of the upholders of the Vinaya in Tibet, performed gloriously and flawlessly the ceremony of making me into a fully ordained monk. He thus laid for me the complete foundation for spiritual practice, an act of immense kindness whose full worth cannot be measured until enlightenment.

In that month, and at the request of Amdo Geshé Losang Nyima of Gyütö, Trijang Rinpoché composed a supplication to the former incarnations of Rinpoché called *Precious Necklace of the Most Powerful Wish-Fulfilling Jewels.*[122] He presented it together with a mandala of the three representations to Rinpoché and petitioned that he live a long life. Ratö Khyongla Tulku asked Kyabjé Trijang Rinpoché what the source for the

Ling Rinpoché at Garpa Hermitage in 1955

accounts of the former incarnations was. He replied that a vision of these former lives had appeared to Rinpoché's predecessor, Venerable Losang Lungtok Tenzin Trinlé, and that these were depicted on the walls of Garpa Hermitage.

At another time Dokhang Losang Könchok, a geshé of Ganden Shartsé, presented Rinpoché with four bundles, each containing fifty *sang* coins, and requested that he compose a supplication to the former incarnations of Kyabjé Trijang Rinpoché. Rinpoché accepted the request and asked the geshé to take back the offering. The geshé replied, "Please accept the offering—unless it is too little." This made Rinpoché laugh. However, although he did not compose the supplication at that time, he did so after he set foot in India, as will be described.

In response to a request from Phuntsok Wangdü, the secretary of Chamdo philosophy college, Rinpoché gave the initiation of single-deity Vajrabhairava after the annual Great Prayer Festival of that year in the assembly rooms of Shidé Monastery, preceded by a preparation day, to an audience of over a thousand who had pledged to recite daily the extensive self-generation sādhana.

PART 3

First Visits Abroad, 1954–58

21 | Visit to China

CHINA WAS determining the creation of its constitution, and I had to attend the meeting of its national assembly. Therefore, on the eleventh of the fifth month I set out for China. I spent a few days at Ganden Monastery accompanied by the precious tutor. One day Adruk, a trader from Drakyap, sponsored the thousand butter-lamp offering in the Yangpachen temple with the entire monastic community of Ganden's Nyakré House. This was being done in connection with his offering of a brocade robe to the golden reliquary of Jé Tsongkhapa and a fine set of clothes to the oath-bound protector Kālarūpa. For this event the sponsor invited Rinpoché, who attended and made many prayers.

After this we left Ganden and traveled as far as Gönshöl by horse, then by motor until almost over the Kongpowa pass. After this point there were no motorable roads, and so the journey continued by mule. That year the rainfall had been unprecedented and the roads had been damaged, meaning that on the hills Rinpoché had to travel up and down on foot. His mule had developed sores on its back, all of which meant that the journey was a difficult one. However, as Rinpoché had developed the patience of taking on suffering, he was not bothered by the hardship. When the party reached Powo Tramo, except for manager Losang Lungrik, the attendant Thupten Tsering, and Lochö the cook, all other attendants, mule keepers, as well as the mules were sent back to Lhasa.

At that time some people who said they were from the birthplace of Ngawang Lungtok Yönten Gyatso, the predecessor of Rinpoché's predecessor, came for an audience. Rinpoché made them joyously happy with pleasing nectar in the form of gifts of blessed substances and so on.

Then we traveled to Chamdo by motor, where we stayed at Chamdo Tsenyi Dratsang Monastery. There Rinpoché received visits from disciples whom he had known from the past, such as Shiwa Lha and Gyara Tulku, as

Trijang Rinpoché and Ling Rinpoché visiting Beihai Park, Beijing, 1954

well as many other devoted monastics and laypeople. Finally, after passing through many places in Kham, we arrived in Chengdu in China. This was the first time Rinpoché had been to another country. Although Rinpoché had spent all day every day traveling in vehicles since leaving the Tibetan town of Powo Tramo, he showed no signs that it had adversely affected him in any way. From Chengdu Rinpoché traveled with me by plane to Xian. There Rinpoché visited the temple and the seat where the statue of Buddha now in the main temple at Lhasa was once placed. Rinpoché offered the butter he had been given in Chamdo.

The Tenth Panchen Lama, Mao, Ling Rinpoché,
and the Dalai Lama in Beijing, 1954

From Xian we traveled to Beijing by train, and we both stayed in the same place, called Yukha Jao. Together with me Rinpoché attended meetings, visited factories, attended films, and so on, but he never went sightseeing around the town. Secretly, he gave teachings to a few Chinese people who had requested them, including Yang Thankon, who had previously received the Kālacakra initiation from the all-knowing Panchen Rinpoché Chökyi Nyima. Geshé Sherap Gyatso would often visit.[123] Rinpoché would engage him in discussions of Buddhist and general sciences with great respect. I heard that Geshé Sherap Gyatso remarked to others that although Kyabjé Trijang Rinpoché was one of his disciples and the precious tutor Ling Rinpoché had not received teachings from him, Rinpoché had nevertheless

Guests at the Office of the Tibetan Representative in Beijing, New Year's Day, 1955. Front row from the left: Lord Chamberlain Phalha, Secretary General Ngawang Döndrup, Assistant Tutor Gyatso Ling, Deputy Minister Neshar, Minling Chung Rinpoché, Ngaphö Ngawang Jikmé, Ling Rinpoché, the Dalai Lama, Trijang Rinpoché, Karmapa Rinpoché, Minister Surkhang, the Dalai Lama's mother Diki Tsering, Ngari Rinpoché, the Dalai Lama's sister Tsering Drolma, Sakya Dakchen Rinpoché.

Group photo in Beijing, September 11, 1954, during the National People's Congress.
Front row: Li Wei Han, Huang Yan Pei, Zhang Lan, Song Ching Ling (Sun Yat Sen's
wife), Tenth Panchen Lama, Mao Zedong, Dalai Lama, Liu Shaoqi, Li Ji Shen,
Guo Mo Ruo, Chen Shu Tong. Back row: Bapa Phuntsok Wangyal, Diki Tsering
(the Dalai Lama's mother), Ngaphö Ngawang Jikmé, Karmapa Rinpoché, Fan Ming,
Trijang Rinpoché, Zhang Jing Wu, Ling Rinpoché, unknown, unknown,
Ngulchu Rinpoché, Phuntsok Wangyal Jikmé, unknown, unknown.

showed him so much respect and was clearly a well-disciplined and conscientious lama.

Once when Mao Zedong came to meet me, Rinpoché was among the
entourage, and when they were shaking hands, Mao remarked jokingly that
Rinpoché was not wearing a hat.

From an early age eating eggs had made Rinpoché ill. Consequently,
the labrang never served the dish that contained a mixture of fish, pork,
and eggs. As for chicken, Rinpoché said that it was not right for such a
small animal to be killed for our food, and he had no wish to eat it. Rinpoché liked tsampa, dried meat, and Tibetan tea. In the winter he liked
thukpa soup, momo dumplings, and fruits such as oranges and peaches.
He did not like Chinese food. Moreover, at that time in Beijing he was
sick with a fever and a cough and could not eat much. However, Rinpoché
suspected that if the Chinese were aware that he was unable to eat the
food, they might take him to a hospital for examination. Therefore he
gave a lot of the food the Chinese brought to him to Lochö the cook and
others. In the mornings Rinpoché ate the tsampa he had brought with
him from Tibet.

The Chinese insisted that Kyabjé Ling Rinpoché take on the responsibility of heading the Religious Affairs Office of the Tibetan government.
To this request Rinpoché replied that he did not possess the knowledge

Pilgrims visiting Kumbum Monastery, Amdo, mid-1950s

required to undertake such a role and that there were far more competent lamas present, thereby never making any promises. All these things contributed to his being unwell, losing weight, and never being completely at ease during his stay in China. He took Tibetan medicine from the entourage physician, but that did not cure him.

As soon as Rinpoché arrived in China, he had written letter to his labrang instructing them to give his former reading tutor Ngawang Lhundrup from Gyütö's Phu House whatever he required and needed. However, not long afterward, this tutor passed away. The labrang also said that in Lhasa the fine-looking black mule and a good riding horse belonging to the labrang had suddenly died, and because it had been the horse year, there had been great obstacles.

When I had a little free time during my stay in Beijing, I received teachings from the precious tutor a few times on the special insight section of Tsongkhapa's *Great Stages of the Path to Enlightenment*, but I was not able to receive the entire section.

The events in China came to an end, and we traveled to Kumbum Monastery. There, as arranged by the Chinese authorities, Rinpoché stayed in a house close to the monastery. Rinpoché visited the golden reliquary there[124] and made the thousand five-senses cloud offerings. In Kumbum Rinpoché met up and exchanged ceremonial scarves with Minyak Rinpoché, a lama with whom he had previously exchanged teachings. Then Rinpoché traveled to Labrang Tashi Khyil Monastery, where he gave novice-monk vows to the sixth incarnation of Jamyang Shépa and other young monks. In response to a request from the branch of Gyütö there, Rinpoché gave teachings on Tsongkhapa's *Foundation of All Good Qualities*. His reputation of being knowledgeable, of pure ethics, and of compassionate conduct was growing by the day. Consequently, many people came for audience daily, and in Kham and Amdo he gave teachings and so on without any reluctance, according to the wishes of the people.

He then traveled to Tau Nyetso Monastery in Trehor, Bari Monastery, Dargyé Monastery, the philosophy and tantric colleges in Karzé, Degé, Chamdo Tsenyi Dratsang, and elsewhere, where he gave teachings according to request. He always returned the offerings he was given. Rinpoché made offerings to monasteries of all traditions, big and small, even if not actually located on the road back to Lhasa. At the request of Gyara Tulku, Rinpoché visited Drugu Monastery, where he stayed for a few days and gave teachings as requested. Gyara Labrang presented Rinpoché with ten bags of Chinese silver coins, a variety of brocade, and a complete set of the twenty-one gold gilded statues of Tārā known as the Gyara Taras. Rinpoché did not accept the coins and the other gifts, but he accepted the Tārā statues with great joy. Later in Lhasa he placed these among the sacred objects in Garpa Hermitage.

On the June 30, 1955, we arrived back in Lhasa, and Rinpoché went to Garpa Hermitage to rest for a few weeks. While Rinpoché was in China, the labrang staff in Lhasa had built a small house for his relaxation behind the hermitage, and he happily spent those days there. Rinpoché always thoroughly enjoyed his visits to a the hermitage. He would tell others that when he stayed there, it was an excellent opportunity to engage solely in Dharma activities such as recitation or reading scripture.

During Rinpoché's stay in China, as mentioned previously, and again after he had returned to Lhasa, the Chinese authorities continually requested that he become the leader of the Religious Affairs Office. Rinpoché would reply that from an early age he had trained in the Dharma and had gained a little knowledge in that area, but other than that he had no knowledge of modern secular affairs. Therefore to assume that title in name only would be of no benefit at all. In this way, for many years he did not agree to the request. However, later the Bumthang chief secretary[125] repeatedly told Rinpoché that if he did not at least accept the title of head of the Religious Affairs Office, the Chinese would be suspicious of him. Therefore, until he left for exile in India, Rinpoché had to accept at least the title of head of this department. Whenever Rinpoché met with Chinese dignitaries, his discussions were always polite and agreeable, but he was adamant in stating that he knew nothing about politics. Whenever serious students would seek an audience, he always happily gave them advice on whatever they requested. To high lamas and important people he was respectful and to the point, but he never conversed much, thereby taking to heart the example set by Atiśa and the Kadampa masters of the past of having few distractions and few mundane activities.

In early summer of 1956, in response to the repeated requests made over many years by the renunciant Geshé Nyakré Gendun Tashi, who lived in the Draklha Luguk temple in Lhasa, Rinpoché gave very detailed teachings over a number of days in the assembly hall of Shidé Ganden Samten Ling Monastery on Khedrup Jé's *Great Exposition of the Vajrabhairava Generation Stage* and the notes on the generation and completion stages of Guhyasamāja, Cakrasaṃvara, and Vajrabhairava by Akhu Sherap Gyatso of Tashi Khyil Monastery. The audience numbered over a thousand and included lamas and tulkus such as Phakpa Lha Hothokthu from Chamdo, Drakyap Hothokthu, and Kyabjé Serkong Rinpoché, as well as geshés, monks from the three monastic seats and Gyütö and Gyümé, the court physician Khyenrap Norbu, and other teachers from the Astro-Medical Institute and lay men and women.

In the eighth Tibetan month of that year, when I visited Radreng Gephel Ling Monastery, I was accompanied by the precious tutor. There I gave novice-monk vows to the precious incarnation of the former regent, Radreng Rinpoché Thupten Jampal Yeshé Tenpai Gyaltsen, and the precious tutor assisted in the ceremony. In Yangön Hermitage, where the great being Tsongkhapa wrote the incomparable work the *Great Stages of the Path to Enlightenment* in the fourteenth century, we recited a few pages of this work and made prayers. Radreng, as a source of the Kadampa teachings, is a very special place, and so Rinpoché made many offerings there.

On the way back to Lhasa we visited Phuchu Miklung in Tölung, where the monks of the glorious Gyümé, preservers of the treasury that is the doctrine of secret tantra, were staying for their late summer retreat. Rinpoché made donations to the monks, offered the communal tea, gave audiences to the faithful, and fulfilled their hopes with teachings and so on.

The Dalai Lama and his two tutors inside the Mahabodhi shrine, Bodhgaya, 1956

22 | Pilgrimage to India and Nepal

THE FOLLOWING YEAR would mark twenty-five hundred years, according to the Theravada tradition, since our Teacher, the Buddha, who taught the way of peace and nonviolence, passed into nirvana. Consequently, I received an invitation from the Indian government and the Mahabodhi Society to attend the ceremonies of that very special commemoration. Therefore, in 1956, on the nineteenth of November, I set out from Lhasa accompanied by the precious tutor. We stopped at Tashi Lhunpo Monastery and the following day met with the all-knowing Panchen Rinpoché. After that we traveled to Gyantsé, where we were invited to stay at the Paljor Lhunpo estate of the Phalha family. Then we journeyed by motor to Dromo Sharsingma, and then by horse to Gangtok, the capital of Sikkim. The next day we journeyed by car to the Indian town of Siliguri, and then by air to New Delhi. We stayed at Hyderabad House, a guesthouse belonging to the Indian government, which as our host had made all the arrangements. Rinpoché accompanied me on the various religious ceremonies and pilgrimages, as well as visits to towns and factories. (plate 3)

Before returning to Tibet, the precious tutor and his entourage visited Nepal for pilgrimage. At the three great stupas[126] and other places in Nepal, Rinpoché made extensive offerings, prayers for the propagation of the Buddha's teachings and the happiness of all living beings, and so on. He then went to Kalimpong, where he stayed at the house of the Shakabpa family. During his stay in India and Nepal, Rinpoché gave teachings and received many visitors every day.

On the return journey we spent about ten days in Sikkim, and on the fourteenth of February 1957, we left Gangtok. At Gyantsé Rinpoché stayed in rooms above Riding College. Every day he gave audience to thousands and became quite tired. In response to a request from a college there, he gave teachings to the entire assembly. The labrang manager, Losang Lungrik, was

The Dalai Lama and the Tenth Panchen Lama,
followed by the two tutors, arriving at the Indian border, 1956

The Dalai Lama with his two tutors, entourage, and members of his family, right,
at Hyderabad House, New Delhi, 1956

unwell with flu-like symptoms for a few days. Rinpoché often came to him and asked how he was progressing. He suggested that if he did not recover soon, Ratö Khyongla Tulku should accompany him back to Lhasa ahead of time.

On arrival at Shigatsé, Rinpoché stayed in rooms at Samdruptsé fort. In the rooms was hanging a set of paintings depicting the wish-fulfilling tree of hundredfold lives.[127] Rinpoché was very familiar with the stories and events behind the paintings, and even though each life event was not accompanied by a caption, Rinpoché was able to explain to Ratö Khyongla Tulku which particular life of the Buddha each painting depicted.

In the reception rooms of the fort at Shigatsé, the monks, nuns, and laypeople of the thirteen counties of Tsang performed a long-life ritual for me,

The fort at Shigatsé

and Rinpoché performed the mandala-offering eulogy. While I was staying at Tashi Lhunpo, the precious tutor resided at the rooms of Lochen Rinpoché[128] as the guest of Tashi Lhunpo Monastery. Panchen Rinpoché came for an audience with me and both tutors. Rinpoché accompanied me to all the places I visited, such as Narthang, until finally he arrived back at the Norbulingka on the first of the second Tibetan month.

In the fifth Tibetan month of that year, in keeping with the wishes of Karmapa Rinpoché of Tsurphu Monastery, I visited Tsurphu accompanied by the precious tutor. Since the visit to China, Rinpoché had become very close to the Karmapa, and they met and conversed with each other often. In Tsurphu Rinpoché happily accompanied me for the opening of the sacred treasure box of Tsurphu and for the summer religious dances of the eight manifestations of Guru Rinpoché. After this, in response to an invitation, Rinpoché accompanied me to the monastery that was the seat of Nenang Pawo Rinpoché. We stayed there for one day before returning to Lhasa.

In the rooms of the Norbulingka's Shapten temple, Rinpoché gave teachings to Dagyab Rinpoché and a few other lamas and tulkus. These teachings included the root text of the practice of peaceful and wrathful aspects of Mañjuśrī combined, together with its commentary by the First Jamyang Shépa; a practice of the peaceful and wrathful aspects of Mañjuśrī combined in which the practices of the enlightened body, speech, and mind of the outer, inner, and secret Mañjuśrī are combined in a single work using the annotations by Geshé Köndar of Khagya; meditation instructions on the practice of the peaceful and wrathful aspects of Mañjuśrī combined composed by Takphu Yongzin, as well as various transmissions.

On another occasion, in the reception hall of the Norbulingka's Shapten temple, Rinpoché gave transmissions to Dagyab Rinpoché, the young incarnation of Phabongkha Rinpoché, and many assembled geshés. These included Shamar Pandita's *Stages of the Path* text, Gyalrong Chözé Losang Thokmé's *Kutsap Stages of the Path*, the collected works of Akhu Sherap Gyatso, *Instructions on the Guru Puja: Testament Carried on the Wind,*[129] the *Ra Lotsāwa Collection on Vajrabhairava*, the *Palzin Sangpo Collection on Vajrabhairava,*[130] and *Collected Rituals on Vaiśravaṇa*.

In the eighth Tibetan month on my return to Lhasa from Drak Yerpa, I visited Garpa Hermitage at the insistent request of the precious tutor. I was met on the road by a procession of the hermitage monks and by my root lama standing outside the hermitage holding sticks of incense. In the reception hall Rinpoché offered me the three representations and the mandala, and tea and sweet rice were served. The next day Rinpoché, together with the resident monks, performed the ritual for my long life. The precious tutor urged me to live long. Holding the mandala in his hands, he spoke on how the noble Avalokiteśvara generated the mind of enlightenment, on how the successive previous incarnations had worked for sentient beings, on the wretchedness of living beings, and so on. I was helplessly moved, and with tears filling my eyes I prayed that I would indeed, as my root lama was so fervently wishing, live a long life and accomplish great things for living beings and the Buddha's teachings.

One day I gave a discourse on the benefits of properly serving the lama and so forth to the manager and the labrang staff and told them that as they are doing now, they should continue to serve the Guru Vajradhara properly. I stayed at the labrang for four days and then returned to the Norbulingka. Rinpoché then requested that Kyabjé Trijang Rinpoché spend a few days at the labrang, which he accepted. The two tutors relaxed in each other's company and spent the time happily discussing the subtle points of sutra and tantra.

The former Trijang Rinpoché, the Ganden Throneholder Losang Tsultrim, and the former Ling Rinpoché, Losang Lungtok Tenzin Trinlé, were close friends. Likewise, my two great tutors were close from an early age. Moreover, they had received teachings together from Phabongkha Rinpoché and many other lamas. Later on they were bound together by being lama and disciple to each other, and many discerning individuals have heaped praise on how they always showed great respect and admiration for each other. As Kyabjé Trijang Rinpoché was about to leave Garpa Hermitage for Lhasa, he presented the manager, Losang Lungrik, with a gold coin and a ceremonial scarf. He expressed his delight at the well-organized manner in which the labrang was being run, and most importantly, he hoped that as manager he would continue to follow the wishes of Kyabjé Ling Rinpoché. He said that Rinpoché was always so happy at the hermitage, and therefore if it were possible to deal with the few places in need of repair it would be very good. Accordingly, the manager later renovated the hermitage.

In the past, when he was young, the precious tutor had asked Kyabjé Phabongkha Dechen Nyingpo with which wisdom deity and which meditation deity he had a strong connection. The reply came in the form of the verses cited earlier. Now Phabongkha Rinpoché's secretary, Losang Dorjé, intended to include this composition in the collected works of Phabongkha Rinpoché and had borrowed it once when Rinpoché was at the Norbulingka. On the way back he lost it on Chapgo Bridge near the Norbulingka. Later someone from Lhasa found it and brought it to the labrang. Losang Dorjé again came to Rinpoché and asked for the composition, and today this verse is among the collected works of Phabongkha Rinpoché.

Losang Dorjé requested Rinpoché to compose a supplement to Yongzin Yeshé Gyaltsen's *Biographies of the Lineage Masters of the Stages of the Path.* This would be in the form of extensive biographies of the lineage masters from Yeshé Gyaltsen up to Rinpoché's own root guru Phabongkha Rinpoché. Rinpoché replied, "I will decide on this later."

Ratö Khyongla Tulku asked Rinpoché if he would compose extensive and profound instructions on the generation and completion stages of single-deity Vajrabhairava and offered to serve as the scribe himself. Rinpoché declined, saying, "These days we are bereft of practitioners, not of practices to follow."

In 1958, in the sixth month of the earth-dog year, as part of my preparation for obtaining the title of "one who has completed the debate rounds," I went to that great seat of learning, glorious Drepung Monastery. There the precious tutor's labrang invited me to lead a prayer assembly. The entire assembly of monks was offered tea, excellent thukpa soup, and rice pudding. Each monk received fifteen *sang* and a ceremonial scarf. The labrang pledged to donate one *sang* to each monk every year. I too was presented with lavish gifts and offered a long-life ceremony to ripen as the indestructible life essence.

At the actual monastic debate I sat in the main assembly hall courtyard with my two tutors on thrones on each side. The length of the debates to be performed by the incumbent and former abbots and so on who were posing the questions was discussed with tutor Ling Rinpoché, and Trijang Rinpoché would give the signal for the debates to end. Not long after the debates had begun, the chief protector of the doctrine Dralha Öden Karpo[131] suddenly entered his medium. He offered me the representations of body, speech, and mind and scarves of congratulation to tutor Ling Rinpoché. Then the abbots of Gomang and Loseling sat as position defenders, and I began my debate with them with the *Individual Liberation Sutra* line "Banner of fame renowned throughout the three worlds." After about half

The Fourteenth Dalai Lama debating at Drepung Monastery during his
geshé examination in 1958

an hour, Yongzin Ling Rinpoché placed his palms together and gestured
for me to finish.

One day Kyabjé Trijang Rinpoché and his attendants were invited for
food at Ling House. There the two tutors spent the time happily in private
conversation.

When I traveled to Sera, the precious tutor stayed, as arranged, in Rigya
Labrang. There he went especially to the labrang of Phabongkha Rinpoché
to visit the young incarnation. He also met with Lhatsun Rinpoché, as they
had been lama to each other in giving each other teachings. He made donations and offerings to the great assembly and to all the affiliated houses such
as Trehor. During the ceremonies of the intermonastic debate, the abbots of
Sera Jé and Sera Mé sat as defenders. I cited the homage verse from Nāgārjuna's *Verses on the Fundamental Wisdom of the Middle Way*, which began
"He who taught that whatever arises through dependence . . ." and began
debating on the eight characteristics mentioned in that verse, such as cessation, that are lacking in dependently arisen phenomena. After about half an
hour, my root guru signaled for the debate to finish.

In the eighth month I traveled to that great seat of learning Ganden for
the monastic debate. My precious tutor, as he had done previously, stayed in

The Fourteenth Dalai Lama debating at Ganden Monastery during his
geshé examination in 1958

rooms above Lhopa House. In the courtyard outside the great assembly hall,
first of all the best scholars of that monastic center debated with me. Then
the abbots of Ganden Shartsé and Jangtsé sat down as defenders. I began my
debate with the lines from Vasubandhu's *Treasury of Abhidharma*:

> Seeing the three truths, one will have ethics,
> and knowing the Dharma, one will gain faith.

At an auspicious point in the debate I complied with the gesture to finish
the debate made by tutor Ling Rinpoché placing his palms together, as he
had done previously.

After the debates we went to the sacred reliquary of Jé Tsongkhapa and
other sacred objects and performed the consecration ceremony, during
which the precious tutor performed the merging of the *samaya* beings and
wisdom beings.

We then went up Enthronement Mount to perform an incense purification ceremony, and Rinpoché accompanied me riding on a yak. He looked

so happy. Without question he was offering prayers for happiness and prosperity for all beings both generally and specifically.

After the monastic debates in the three monasteries had finished, Rinpoché returned to Garpa Hermitage. He was immensely pleased with the repairs done to the hermitage and performed the very brief "horseback" consecration ceremony.[132] About two weeks later Rinpoché traveled to Drak Yerpa, where he gave extensive teachings, as had been previously requested, on the common and exclusive stages of the path using Paṇchen Losang Yeshé's *Swift Path Direct Instructions* in the college assembly hall to a large audience of monks, nuns, and laypeople. In the audience was a butcher who was able to understand the presentation on karma. He offered to the great Vajradhara all the sheep and goats that he had recently bought for slaughter as part of his livelihood. From that day on he gave his pledge not to engage in the act of killing again. To be able to recognize a wrong as a wrong and to declare and confess it is something worthy of praise. The sheep and goats were sent to the labrang's Garpa estate, where there were about four hundred sheep and goats that had been rescued from slaughter over the years.

Normally in his rooms at the hermitage were hung paintings of the three longevity deities[133] and a beautiful decorated canopy. However, that year as Rinpoché was about to leave the hermitage, he said that they should be taken down and stored so as to prevent deterioration. This was seen as a sign that this incarnation would not set foot in the hermitage again.

On the first of March 1959, the thirteenth day of the first Tibetan month of the earth-pig year, when I sat for the lharampa monastic debate sessions of the Great Prayer Festival during the month of the miraculous feats,[134] Rinpoché attended the morning communal tea assembly, the debate sessions in the discourse courtyard, the noon communal tea assembly, the afternoon debate sessions, the afternoon prayer and communal tea assembly, the great evening debate sessions, and the short-discourse debate session. There the cream of the scholars debated with me on the difficult points in the vast and profound classical texts.[135] Rinpoché observed with great attention. Afterward, the nectar of his words in expressing his pleasure with me developed in me a great youthful fountain of joy.

It was the tradition to offer gifts to the two tutors for taking on the great responsibility of my education and so forth. For this reason minister Surkhang came to the precious tutor in person and said that the government was offering him a large estate called Thökar. Rinpoché replied that no matter how much one gains, at no point is satisfaction found, and added that he had already been given the Chakbam estate in Kharek and there was no need to offer anything else. However, it was impressed on Rinpoché that it would not be proper not to accept something as recognition for the success of the geshé examination. In reply Rinpoché asked that instead of him accepting the estate would they please make repairs to Drigung Mangra Monastery and its branch monastery Gyalteng Monastery, both of which were affiliated to the labrang. However, it was again insisted that Rinpoché willingly accept an estate. Finally it was agreed that Rinpoché would be offered small working estates close to Kharek estate, that the repairs to the monasteries would be carried out as Rinpoché wished, and that without employing a separate supervisor, the labrang manager, Losang Lungrik, would oversee the renovation.

After the Great Prayer Festival had concluded, I returned to the Norbu-lingka in a grand procession as was the custom, and Rinpoché also returned to the Shapten temple.

PART 4

Exile in India, 1959–80

23 | Escape and Settling in Mussoorie

A s I wrote in the book *My Land and My People*, the confrontation between Tibet and China escalated a few days after the conclusion of the Great Prayer Festival. One afternoon a large convoy of Chinese vehicles was seen traveling from the Nortölingka[136] toward Lhasa. Everybody said they were probably heading for the Norbulingka. The situation had now become very dangerous, and some people were saying that it was vital for Rinpoché to secretly flee Lhasa for a while. Because of this, Rinpoché had picked up his bowl for drinking tea and was ready to leave. However, it was not deemed necessary to leave that day.

On the evening of March the seventeenth, the situation had become so serious that I was powerless to do anything other than to escape from the Norbulingka Palace in Lhasa. I told the precious tutor that he should accompany me. Consequently, in his rooms at the Shapten temple, he took off his robes and put on a lynx hide undergarment owned by his predecessor, a brown woolen *chupa*[137] belonging to the labrang manager, and a fox-fur hat. He carried with him in the pockets of his *chupa* a golden amulet box containing the photograph of Kyabjé Phabongkha impressed with his thumbprint on the back and a small ivory statue of Vajrabhairava carved by the Mongolian artist Dharma. He also sorted out and took some of his daily recitation texts. He told the monk Chösang Thutop to take good care of his pet dog Drölma. The manager told the other attendants that Rinpoché was going to the hermitage for a few days, thereby ensuring the secrecy of the situation.

At ten o'clock that evening, the precious tutor, his manager and attendant, Kyabjé Trijang Rinpoché and his attendants, the ministers Surkhang, Shenkha, and Neshar,[138] and my three household attendants emerged through a secret door on the veranda of the Kalsang Palace and climbed onto a tarpaulin-covered transport truck. At Chapgo bridge we left the truck and walked as far as the Ramagang ferry site. Having crossed the river, we continued on horseback. We traveled as far as Ushang, where in the ninth century the famous emperor Tri Ralpachen, one of the three ancestral Dharma kings of Tibet, stopped to take tea in its temple. The following evening we stayed at Kyishong Rawamé Monastery. We traveled through Chongyé Riwo Dechen and Yartö Drala, and then Rinpoché went ahead to Thösam Dargyé Ling Monastery, a great monastic center of Yarlung that was affiliated to the labrang.

When I finally arrived at Dargyé Ling, Guru Vajradhara greeted me with an incense-led procession, and as soon as I arrived in my rooms, he offered me the three representations. That evening the monastery cared for me and all the government officials and attendants with excellent hospitality, providing all that was needed. On the twenty-sixth of March, at Yulgyal Lhuntsé Dzong, the residence of the former rulers of Jayul, Tenzin Norbu and Miwang Tsokyé Dorjé, a new Tibetan administration in the manner of a temporary government was created. During the ceremonies for the auspiciousness of its declaration, Rinpoché kindly performed the mandala eulogy.

All the while we were escaping we wore the clothes of laymen, and this prompted Rinpoché to joke, "Today we have had to become Bodongpas."[139] As we were approaching Tsona, a plane flew overhead from southeast to northwest. Rinpoché was concerned that this was a spy plane and that we could be bombed. On horseback Rinpoché only recited prayers, and that night he slept very well.

On the thirty-first of March, we reached Chudangmo, the border of Tibet and India, and we felt very relieved to be free of Chinese oppression and danger. Eventually we arrived at Tawang in Mön, Arunachal Pradesh. Rinpoché stayed in a house below the monastery. Tsona Göntsé Rinpoché offered Rinpoché all provisions and invited him to stay in a small hermitage, where they engaged in private conversation. Göntsé Tulku had been a student at Drepung Monastery. While he was studying there and after he had left, he had been to discourses given by Phabongkha Rinpoché and had received teachings on Sanskrit grammar from him together with Ling Rinpoché. Therefore they were Dharma friends and they had exchanged texts and letters over time. He had received teachings from Phabongkha Rinpoché on peaceful and wrathful Mañjuśrī combined, and from his notes taken at those teachings, he offered to Rinpoché the notes on the practice of longevity and requested the Vajradhara tutor to live a long life.

Four days after leaving Tsona, having traveled through Tawang, we arrived at Bomdila. There, Kyabjé Trijang Rinpoché offered a spontaneous song in the form of a request for tutor Ling Rinpoché to remain in this world for a long time. Rinpoché wrote down the words to the song.

While we were traveling through Pangjen district, the horse belonging to Lochö the cook fell into a ravine and died. That evening Lochö offered butter lamps, and Rinpoché asked his attendant, the Amdo monk Jinpa Gyatso, to recite the five common aspiration prayers[140] in their entirety. Moreover, the Vajradhara tutor himself along with Trijang Rinpoché recited prayers and made their own fervent prayers for the horse. Clearly, that animal possessed fortunate karma.

At the request of Guru Rinpoché in Bomdila, who was the incarnation of the Merak Lama Lodrö Gyatso, founder of the Mön Tawang Monastery, Kyabjé Vajradhara gave him a transmission and a teaching of the Fifth Dalai Lama's *Oral Transmission of Mañjuśrī: Instructions on the Stages of the Path to Enlightenment*. At that time the horses and mules that had been brought from Tibet, the stable keeper, saddles, equipment, and so on were all entrusted to Guru Rinpoché. He in turn showed great attention to Rinpoché's horse and mule and took great care of them.

From Bomdila we traveled to Tezpur in Assam. Then, by train, we all arrived safely at Mussoorie in northern India in the middle of April. There the Indian government arranged for Rinpoché to stay in a house near to Birla House, where I was staying. At that time there were very few visitors seeking audiences, so Rinpoché spent much of his time in meditation.

Rinpoché's manager remarked that he was concerned as they had not been able to bring any belongings from the labrang. To which Rinpoché replied, "Now the most important thing is that we, and in particular the Dalai Lama, have managed to escape to safety. It is because of the kindness of the Dalai Lama that we have safely reached the freedom of India. If we had remained in Tibet, we would all have been separated by the Chinese and been subject to the oppression of harsh treatment in prison. What would that have been like? Think like this and put aside your material concerns. Be happy and content that we are alive. No matter how much wealth we have, we all know it all has to be left behind one day. Only for us, leaving behind our possessions has come a little early now. Because of our karmic debt, now we have to pay back the loan. It is good we had something to pay with."

On the twenty-third of April, the precious tutor and I, along with Trijang Rinpoché, performed the rituals to invoke the commitment of the Dharma protectors who had vowed to guard the teachings of the Buddha, in order to quickly pacify these troubling times in the world at large and specifically in the land of Tibet surrounded by snowy mountains.

The Dalai Lama greeting Nehru at Birla House, Mussoorie, April 24, 1959.
Kazi Sönam Topgyal interprets.

The next day the Indian prime minister, Pandit Nehru, came from Delhi to meet me. The Tibetan administration officials, along with the precious tutor, respectfully formed the line to welcome Prime Minister Nehru with ceremonial scarves. Likewise, the following day Rinpoché was among those who saw the prime minister off.

On the second of May, which was the fifth day of the third Tibetan month, we performed an extensive Guru Puja *tsok* ritual and made many prayers for those who had recently passed on to the great highway of future lives because of the conflict in Tibet. The precious tutor, as requested, kindly made prayers for those who had lost their lives to quickly find the good path of lasting happiness.

The twenty-second of May coincided with the great festival of the *vaiśākha* month. On the lawn in front of my residence, Buddhists from different parts of the world spoke in detail on the need to practice the essence of Buddhism. After this, the two tutors and I, along with others, recited various prayers, including the refuge prayer, the ablution ritual, and dedication verses. I gave a transmission of the six-syllable heart mantra of Avalokiteśvara to about one thousand people, including Tibetan residents of Mussoorie and foreign guests. Rinpoché also received the transmission. The next day Mr. Menon, the Indian government liaison officer, took

The Dalai Lama's first teaching in Mussoorie, 1959,
accompanied by his two tutors

photographs of me, the precious tutor, and others while we were engaging in religious discussions.

On the twenty-eighth of August, the monastic and lay members of administration in the form of the council of ministers performed a long-life ceremony for me by way of the Guru Puja ritual. Rinpoché led the rituals and kindly offered the prayers that "were to ripen into an indestructible life-force."[141]

24 | Visits to Ladakh, Dalhousie, Buxa, Sarnath, and Bodhgaya

I WAS ASKED BY the Buddhist Society of Ladakh to attend the opening ceremonies for a new Buddhist philosophy college in that region. However, I was unable to go because of the urgency created by the continuing arrival of many refugees from Tibet. So I asked the Vajradhara tutor if he would kindly go in my place. Consequently, on the third of September Rinpoché left Mussoorie by car for Pathankot. From there he flew to Srinagar in Kashmir, where he spent about five days as a guest of the state Buddhist society. The Ladakhi prince, Bakula Rinpoché,[142] took Rinpoché on a sightseeing tour of the area. The Kashmiri chief minister Bakshi Ghulam Muhammad and the raja of Kashmir, Karan Singh, invited Rinpoché for tea. Ladakh Kashmiri families in Srinagar that had fled Tibet extended invitations to Rinpoché and welcomed him joyfully with great hospitality and excellent meals.

Then on the eleventh of September, he flew to Leh. At the airport Rinpoché was given an elaborate welcome by the abbots, lamas, and monk officials of the various monasteries, local leaders, and Indian army officers. From the airport Rinpoché traveled by horse to Pethup Monastery, where he spent the night. The next day he traveled again by horse to Samkar Monastery. There, as requested, he conducted the ceremonies for the opening of the philosophy college and performed the textual recitation for the debate. In the town of Leh Rinpoché gave the initiation of the thirteen-deity Vajrabhairava, together with preparatory empowerment, to about four thousand people. A few days later, in response to a request from the local people, Rinpoché gave the Avalokiteśvara initiation.

Rinpoché was invited to Triksé Monastery, Lukhyil (Likhir) Monastery, Rizong Monastery, Hemis Monastery, Takna Monastery, and others. At these places, in response to the requests of the monks and laypeople, he gave teachings and transmissions of the *Hundred Deities of Tuṣita*, Tsongkhapa's

Ling Rinpoché, accompanied by Thupten Tsering and Losang Lungrik, right, in
Srinagar with Kashmiri hosts and Ladakhi prince Bakula Rinpoché, left, 1959

Foundation of All Good Qualities, the blessings of the four initiations of the
exalted Vajrayoginī of the Nāropa lineage, a long-life initiation, and a verbal
transmission of the *maṇi* mantra. He made tea offerings, donations, and
so on to monasteries of all affiliations, and made prayers for the Buddha's
teaching and living beings, both generally and specifically. Rinpoché traveled everywhere by horse in this region, but because he had recently journeyed from Tibet by horse, he showed no signs of tiredness.

After he had perfectly completed his activities of bringing benefit to the
teaching and sentient beings in Ladakh, on the fifth of November Rinpoché
traveled by air from Leh to Kashmir. From there the party journeyed by car
to Jammu, where they stayed one night at the house of Bakula Rinpoché.
There he also gave a long-life initiation. The next day he returned to Mussoorie, where he visited me and told me in detail about life in Ladakh, and
about his activities in bringing benefit to the Buddha's teaching and living
beings. Two days later, with a Guru Puja *tsok* ritual, I petitioned Rinpoché
to plant his lotus feet on this earth for a long time to come.

For some time, many lamas, tulkus, and monks and nuns from the various
monasteries, as well as laypeople, had been arriving as refugees from Tibet

and coming to the temporary Tibetan settlements in Dalhousie and Buxa Duar. I requested the precious tutor to go in my place to greet them and give them—especially the monks and nuns from the various traditions—advice on what to do in the short and long term. Consequently, on the fourteenth of December Rinpoché set out by car for Dalhousie, accompanied by the labrang manager and his attendant, by Phalha the lord chamberlain, a translator called Phursam, and others. There he stayed in a guesthouse arranged by the Indian government. On the following day, on open ground in response to requests, Rinpoché gave the initiation of the thirteen-deity Vajrabhairava, the great initiation of Eleven-Headed Avalokiteśvara, the permission empowerment of Avalokiteśvara Who Liberates All Beings from the Unfortunate Realms, a long-life initiation, and so on to a large audience that included the two tantric colleges, Trehor Kyorpön Tsewang Norbu, who was a spiritual friend that held aloft the standard of great learning, Pangnang Tulku, and others. He also gave advice on what to do in these new circumstances. He also visited the places in Dalhousie where monks of the three monastic universities (Ganden, Drepung, and Sera) were being housed.

Monks at the Buxa Duar refugee camp, West Bengal

The next day Khamtrul Tenpai Nyima Rinpoché came from Tashi Jong to visit Rinpoché in Dalhousie. He invited Kyabjé Rinpoché to visit his place of residence and to see the statue building and restoration workshop there. He also presented Rinpoché with a painting of White Tārā he had made himself, as well as an offering of the three representations together with a ceremonial scarf and a ritual request for Rinpoché to live a long life. Rinpoché spent a week there giving teachings, visiting places, sightseeing, and so on.

After this the party traveled to Pathankot in order to travel to the temporary settlement in Buxa Duar to see the lamas, tulkus, monks, and nuns who had set up monastic institutions there. Rinpoché had arrived rather late at Pathankot. Consequently, Rinpoché was unable to obtain a first or second-class ticket, and the compartment was very cramped and hot. However, Rinpoché adopted the attitude that if it is for the sake of others, then any hardship can be tolerated.

In Buxa Duar Rinpoché's living quarters were arranged by the Indian government. In response to requests from several monks from Namgyal Monastery, Rinpoché gave the Vajrayoginī blessing to those who pledged to perform the self-generation and recite the mantras daily. He also gave the great initiation of the noble Eleven-Faced Avalokiteśvara, the treasure of compassion, as well as a long-life initiation to over a thousand monks and nuns from all traditions and many laypeople. Among the ordained who had come from Tibet were many who had been forced by the troubles to give up their novice or full-ordination vows. Rinpoché bestowed on them again first their novice vows and then their full-ordination vows. Rinpoché was delighted to see that the monks were attending assembly and debate and taking on the responsibility of abiding in the four marks of contentment of an ārya. Some had requested the initiation of single-deity Vajrabhairava, but Rinpoché had no time. To the ordained of all traditions, Rinpoché gave extensive alms.

In Dalhousie and Buxa Duar, as well as giving teachings to the crowds that had gathered, Rinpoché also gave them advice, which included reminding them that the desperate situation unfolding in Tibet was like some great hindrance descending upon the Buddha's teaching and the living beings but primarily was, without doubt, the result of bad karma that we had collected. Therefore we should never develop hatred toward the enemy but, with love, compassion, and bodhicitta, make prayers that they will be able to destroy the causes they may have accumulated for rebirth in the tortuous realms of suffering. He advised the ordained to guard the vows and pledges they had taken as they would protect their own eyes and to make this the foundation of their practice. They should concentrate on studying, contemplating, and meditating in equal measure the texts of their respective traditions. The Sakya, Geluk, Kagyü, and Nyingma traditions of Tibet were all genuine Dharma lineages that follow the same founding Teacher, and it was important therefore to abandon sectarianism and to let the jewel light of pure perception shine.

On the first of January 1960, Rinpoché went by train to the pilgrimage site of Sarnath. As arranged, he stayed in an Indian house where the consumption of meat was forbidden. Rinpoché made a thousand offerings in front of the precious shrine built by Dharma King Aśoka. Among other places, he often visited the park known as the Deer Park Where the Sages Fell to Earth, the site where our compassionate Teacher first turned the wheel of Dharma with his teachings on the four noble truths. There Rinpoché made prayers that the teachings set forth by the supreme guide who taught the path of nonviolence, in its aspects of insight and scripture, would prosper and remain for a long time to come.

I also arrived in Sarnath at that time, and on the tenth of January at eleven o'clock in the morning, Rinpoché came to where I was staying and described to me in great detail the situation of the monastic and lay Tibetan refugees in Dalhousie and Buxa Duar, as well as the essentials of the teachings and advice he had given them. At five thirty on the morning of the thirteenth, in response to my request, Rinpoché bestowed on me the daylong Mahayana precepts. On the fifteenth at nine in the morning, a long-life ceremony, combined with the Guru Puja ritual sponsored by Thupten Jungné, the administrator of the Sarnath Tibetan monastery, was offered to me. Vajradhara sat at the head of the chanting monks, and the ritual unfolded into the glory of enhancing the longevity and good merits of all.

On the eighteenth I invited the precious tutor to my residence and offered him lunch, where we engaged in substantive conversation. Later on in the afternoon, Rinpoché gave novice vows to eighteen people. On the nineteenth, in keeping with the activities of the previous Dalai Lamas, I was to perform my first bestowing of the monastic vows. Before the ceremony Rinpoché very kindly gave me advice on the practices of the great Vinaya holders of the past. Furthermore, on the actual day, I was supposedly the preceptor bestowing full monastic vows on fifteen recipients, including Dagyab Rinpoché, while Rinpoché was the master of the ritual, ensuring a faultless execution of the ceremony and carrying out all the main and minor points like an instructor.

On the twenty-fourth at one o'clock in the afternoon, I asked Rinpoché a few questions on sutra and tantra, to which he gave detailed replies that greatly expanded my understanding. At four o'clock Rinpoché accompanied me on a visit to the Sarnath temple. There he recited Tsongkhapa's *Praise of Dependent Origination*, thereby kindly bringing to our minds how the compassionate Buddha taught emptiness by means of the truth of dependent origination.

On the second of February we went to Bodhgaya by train. On the third of February, in Ganden Phelgyé Ling, which was the Tibetan monastery in Bodhgaya, representatives from the three main provinces of Tibet performed a long-life ceremony for me that would "ripen into an indestructible life-force." During the ceremony the precious tutor presented me with the emblems of the eight auspicious substances.

On the fourth of February at nine in the morning in the temple of the sacred Bodhgaya shrine,[143] I bestowed full ordination on thirty-one recipients, and Rinpoché acted as the master of the rituals. In the evening in front of the sacred shrine, the Tibetan monks, nuns, and laypeople sponsored a Guru Puja *tsok* ritual and made extensive offerings in the presence of the Buddha and his spiritual sons. Rinpoché also attended and made extensive prayers.

On the twelfth of February, at nine in the morning, Rinpoché accompanied me to the sacred Bodhi Tree and we performed the bimonthly confession ceremony. At half past five in the evening, Rinpoché performed a Guru Puja *tsok* ritual to delight the objects of refuge. On the twenty-first Rinpoché and attendants returned to Mussoorie.

On the twenty-seventh of February 1960, the iron-rat new year, Rinpoché made the customary offering of a ceremonial scarf to the thangka painting of Palden Lhamo, which has been known to speak. He also presented me with a mandala and the three representations, and celebrated Tibetan New Year. On the twenty-ninth, the third day of the first Tibetan month, Rinpoché accompanied me at the customary offering ritual to Palden Lhamo — the mistress of the desire realm — in placing upon her head the vajra-crown decree that she must continue to perform without hesitation the activities of the four feats appropriate to the needs of people in order that disease, famine, and violent conflicts are pacified throughout the world and that all beings live in the glory of Dharma, prosperity, and happiness.

On the third of March, in response to a request by finance minister Shakabpa Wangchuk Deden, Rinpoché made prayers for those who had passed away, especially the minister's own wife, that they would purify their wrongs and broken vows and before too long reach the great city of the four enlightened bodies endowed with the five exalted wisdoms.

On the tenth of March, on a stage erected outside my residence, Rinpoché accompanied me in the commemoration of the first anniversary of the popular uprising by the Tibetan people against Communist China. The thirteenth of March was the fifteenth day of the first Tibetan month, and was the day that we traditionally commemorate our incomparable Buddha Śākyamuni's defeat of the six non-Buddhist teachers and their disciples, who were outside the perfect path, with a display of miraculous powers. Therefore a ceremony of offerings and requests was held in my residence. Rinpoché attended and he focused on making prayers that the good path taught by the genuine Teacher would remain a long time in this world and so forth.

For three days beginning on the fifteenth, a number of propitiation rituals to Mahākāla, Kālarūpa, and Palden Lhamo were performed for the sake of the Buddha's teaching and the temporal well-being of Tibet.

Inauguration of the first Tibetan school in Mussoorie, March 3, 1960

Rinpoché made fervent prayers embraced by wisdom that understands all three elements—the object of propitiation, the propitiation, and the agent performing the propitiation—to be empty of inherent existence. On the nineteenth of April, additional protector propitiation rituals for the benefit of the Buddha's teaching and the temporal well-being of Tibet were performed, which Rinpoché attended.

25 | Moving to Dharamsala

O N THE THIRTIETH of April 1960, my teachers, my attendants, and I all moved to Dharamsala in the north Indian state of Himachal Pradesh. The Indian government had organized a residence for Rinpoché called Chopra House, the eastern half of which was to be occupied by the Indian government liaison officer for the new Tibetan resettlement, and the western half was to be occupied by the precious tutor and his attendants. A few years later the liaison office moved elsewhere. Rinpoché renamed Chopra House Losang Chökyi Kyetsal, "Grove of Tsongkhapa's Teaching," and in keeping with that name, he spent his time in meditation on the very essence of the teachings of that great master and second Buddha, as well as giving teachings to others and so on, as will be related later.

On the third of May, the monastic community of the three monastic centers and the two tantric colleges, as well as the administration and the lay devotees, performed a long-life ceremony for me. Rinpoché sat as the head of the ceremony.

On the fourth of May, which was the eighth of the third Tibetan month, Rinpoché accompanied me in maintaining the continuity of the annual great ceremony of the eighth-day torma rite.[144] First the self-initiation of Vajrabhairava was performed, followed by invocation and propitiation rituals for various Dharma protectors, including Vajrapañjara Mahākāla and Four-Faced Mahākāla Robber of Strength.

Rinpoché had not been feeling well for a while. Doctor Yeshé Dönden arrived from Dalhousie on the first of June, and at seven in the morning he examined Rinpoché's urine and pulse and gave him medicine.

On the fourth of June, tulkus, lamas, geshés, and monks of the monastic community in Dharamsala assembled at Rinpoché's residence and offered him a long-life ceremony in conjunction with the Guru Puja *tsok* ritual, sponsored by the council of ministers. They fervently requested that all hindrance to the life of the Vajradhara tutor that appears to exist to the eyes of ordinary beings be removed and that the master keeps his feet planted a long time on this earth. On the next day a long-life ceremony sponsored by the former acting prime minister Dekhar[145] was offered to me, and the precious tutor led the ritual monks in prayer. On the nineteenth, in response to a request from Ratö Khyongla Tulku, Rinpoché gave the great initiation of single-deity Vajrabhairava, complete with a day of preparatory empowerment, to about fifty monastic and lay practitioners at his residence.

On the eighteenth of October, in response to my request, Rinpoché gave the preparation ceremonies for the Vajrabhairava initiation, and on the nineteenth he kindly gave its four initiations. On the twenty-fourth the staff of Ling Labrang offered a long-life ceremony to the precious tutor. The monastic councils of the three monastic seats, the two tantric colleges, and Namgyal Monastery prayed for his lotus feet to remain firmly on the earth for a long time.

On the twenty-ninth of October, Rinpoché gave the blessings of the four initiations of Vajrayoginī, which is the legacy of the great scholar practitioners of the Sakya and Geluk traditions that has not degenerated in the slightest, and which without doubt brings one face to face with the outer, inner, and secret venerable lady Vajrayoginī. This was in response to a request from cabinet minister Shenkhawa Gyurmé Topgyal and given to an audience of about forty who had promised to undertake the daily commitment of self-generation and mantra recitation.

26 | Visits to Calcutta and Darjeeling for Medical Treatment

ON THE SEVENTH of November, on my instructions, the Private Office invited the monastic community of Dharamsala to offer a long-life ceremony for the precious tutor, which he joyfully accepted. On the fifteenth Rinpoché gave novice-monk vows to eight people from Ladakh.

Rinpoché was still not feeling well, and it was decided that he would go to Calcutta for treatment. On the seventeenth of November, he came to my residence to say goodbye. We had an informal conversation, and I requested him to remain with us for a long time in order to benefit the Buddha's teaching and sentient beings by taking suitable medicine and so forth. On the eighteenth the home affairs minister Phalha Thupten Öden, the external affairs minister Neshar Thupten Tharpa, and other devoted disciples came to visit Rinpoché and request that this sun of the Buddha's teaching remain firmly and for a long time on this earth as a guide for all beings. On the nineteenth Rinpoché left Chopra House, and the council of ministers and administration officials assembled in McLeod Ganj to see him off.

He traveled to Pathankot by car and then by train to Calcutta, where he stayed in a guesthouse arranged by the minister Surkhang. A few days later he was examined by Dr. Hunter,[146] a well-known German doctor, in Woodland Nursing Home. He diagnosed a goiter and heart problems. Rinpoché was aware that his mother had had a goiter, and that during his six-month stay in Dromo in 1950 he had drunk local woodland water causing his goiter to swell, but he did not pay that much attention to it. However, the doctor said that it would be best to remain in the hospital for a while and that the illness was quite serious. Concurring with his advice, Rinpoché remained in Woodland Nursing Home in Calcutta. He was given several different medicines to take each day, but he was not able to eat much of the hospital food. His Calcutta residence planned to cook food there and bring it into the hospital for Rinpoché. However, Rinpoché did not approve of this idea because he thought it would upset the hospital staff. Consequently, Rinpoché became weaker each day, and the labrang manager attempted to bring him back to his residence, but the doctor said he could not take that responsibility and did not agree. Tsarong Rimshi, who was present as translator and assistant, insisted that whatever the outcome they would take on the responsibility, and finally the doctor agreed that Rinpoché could leave the hospital.

It was advised that for a while Rinpoché should refrain from walking long distances, uphill, upstairs, and so on. Therefore a ground-floor room was arranged in his residence to make things easier, and he was brought from the hospital. As well as taking medicine, Rinpoché was able to eat Tibetan food, which agreed with him, and consequently his health improved somewhat. At that time Karmapa Rinpoché came to visit the precious tutor in his residence and requested that he remain a long time on this earth. I sent a donation to the hospital and requested that the Vajradhara tutor live a long life. I also sent Rinpoché a letter suggesting that he might be more at ease staying in Darjeeling, as the weather was cooler and many Tibetans lived there. Consequently, Rinpoché decided to move to Darjeeling and told the doctor of his plans. The doctor objected, saying that traveling by air and moving to such a high region was not conducive to his health. However, Rinpoché said that we Tibetans were born at high altitude and that this would be no such problem.

Therefore Rinpoché left Calcutta and traveled by air to Bagdogra, and then by road to Ghoom Samten Chöling Monastery in Darjeeling. In keeping with the doctor's advice of not walking upstairs, the monastery constructed a new entrance that allowed Rinpoché easy access through the back of the monastery via a wooden bridge. In this and other ways they willingly made every possible arrangement to look after Rinpoché's health. The doctor, who had accompanied Rinpoché to Darjeeling, examined him after a week and was very surprised at how much Rinpoché had recovered. Before he returned to Calcutta, he instructed Dr. Penpa, a Tibetan living in Darjeeling trained in Western medicine, to look after Rinpoché.

At that time Trijang Rinpoché was in Sonada near Darjeeling, and one day Rinpoché traveled by train to visit him. They spent a few hours together discussing Rinpoché's health and so on. Later Trijang Rinpoché also came to Ghoom Monastery and made requests for the Vajradhara tutor's long life and so on.

Gyara Tulku of Drepung Loseling made a visit to Rinpoché. He addressed Rinpoché, saying that if a biography of Kyabjé Vajradhara were to be produced in the future it would be of immense benefit to the Buddha's teaching and sentient beings, and he requested Rinpoché to compassionately plant the seeds of his life story. Rinpoché replied saying that he was the child of an ordinary villager and had nothing to say about any illustrious lineage, and that he was an ordinary being and had nothing to say about any special qualities of learning and insight. At this reply, Gyara Rinpoché did not dare ask again.

In keeping with the results of divinations made through various deities, the labrang sponsored the monks of Tharpa Chöling Monastery in Kalimpong to perform the ceremony of a thousand *arura*[147] offerings in connection with the deity Amitāyus. Ghoom Monastery led by Gyara Tulku performed the iron-fortress ritual. The monastic communities of all traditions at Buxa Duar and elsewhere performed extensive rituals to bring about good fortune. Ghoom Monastery, Drepung Loseling, the Nepalese glass merchant, recently arrived from Lhasa, and many others, both private individuals and communities, petitioned Rinpoché to remain a long time on this earth through their ceremonies of long-life rituals. As a result Rinpoché recovered from his illness.

On the thirtieth of September 1961, in response to a request from Ghoom Samten Chöling Monastery, Rinpoché gave the permission ritual for the practice of the Three Wrathful Forms Combined to an assembly of over a thousand monks, nuns, and laypeople from Darjeeling and Kalimpong. On the twenty-fifth of October Rinpoché traveled to Kurseong, where he gave the Cittamani Tārā long-life initiation, at the request of the local people.

In Darjeeling Rinpoché had been successfully treated over the summer. At that time ten-year-old Lama Zopa Rinpoché, who was also known as the Laudo Lama, was studying in Ghoom Samten Chöling Monastery. While the Kyabjé Vajradhara tutor was staying at the monastery, he would often take Lama Zopa on walks with him. They would often eat together and so on, and Rinpoché liked him very much.

Picnic in the Darjeeling Botanical Gardens, 1961. Geshé Ngawang Jinpa,
Lama Zopa Rinpoché, Ling Rinpoché, Losang Lungrik, and Mingyur-la.

RETURN TO DHARAMSALA

On October 31, 1961, Rinpoché took the train from Siliguri back to Dharamsala. In those days there were no motorable roads from McLeod Ganj
to the labrang. Therefore, acting minister Shenkhawa Sönam Topgyal
arranged for Rinpoché to go by horse.

On the second of November the three monastic seats and the two tantric
colleges offered Rinpoché a long-life ceremony. Also, on the twenty-first
Rinpoché accepted the petitions to live a long life offered by former acting
prime minister Dekharwa. On the ninth of December, the Gadong Shingja
Chen Dharma protector was invoked by way of the oracle and was asked
about medicine, treatment, and other questions concerning the care of Rinpoché's health in the future. As well as giving answers to these questions, the
protector petitioned for Rinpoché to live a long time.

Three days later Rinpoché went to Penpo Nalendra Simok Rinpoché to request a long-life initiation. These two great lineage holders of the Sakya and Geluk traditions petitioned that each should live a long time for the sake of the Dharma and for living beings. The next day Rinpoché came to see me and told me of his plans to spend the winter in Sarnath. I also requested that he take great care of his health and requested that he remain a long time in this world. Three days later Rinpoché set out for Sarnath by train from Pathankot. In Sarnath he stayed at the Mahabodhi Society's guesthouse.

On the tenth of January 1962, at the request of the Sera Mé monk Tenzin Gyaltsen, Rinpoché gave Vajrabhairava initiation to about eighty recipients. On the next day he bestowed the Vajrayoginī blessing.

Previously, when Rinpoché had come to say goodbye in mid-December, I had fervently petitioned him to live a long life. However, all kinds of worrying thoughts now arose within me. If the Vajradhara tutor were not to remain with us, I would be left with much of the Buddha's teachings yet to be received, especially the transmitted teachings of Jé Tsongkhapa. At this difficult time for the doctrine and the country, I was still very young and would become like a baby bird left alone in the world. I at once wrote a letter to Rinpoché expressing these concerns. I also instructed Dagyab Rinpoché to convey these thoughts in person, which he did when he arrived at Rinpoché's residence in Sarnath, near Varanasi, on the twelfth of February.

On the nineteenth of February, a long-life ceremony was performed with the profound practice of the Guru Puja ritual. Dagyab Rinpoché led the assembly as agreed, and Trehor Kyorpön Rinpoché and his followers were invited as participants. Rinpoché's reply to my letter delivered on Dagyab Rinpoché's return read, "I am just an ordinary being and therefore have no control over life and death. However, I continue to pray that I will live a long life so as to perform my share of service. If you, great treasure of compassion, could do likewise . . ." and so forth.

On the seventh of March Rinpoché left Varanasi by train and was met at Pathankot by representatives of the Tibetan administration, who accompanied him to Chopra House by car. On the ninth he came to see me and told me of the medical treatment he had received during his stay in Varanasi over the past few months.

The tenth of March 1962 marked three years since the uprising against the Chinese in the struggle for Tibetan freedom, and Rinpoché accompanied me in prayers. On the seventeenth of April, the Tibetan people of the three provinces of Tibet presented me with a long-life ceremony by way of Guru Puja and the *tsok* ritual. The assembly was led by Rinpoché. On the twenty-fourth and over the next thirteen days Rinpoché gave an explanation to Dagyab Rinpoché and Ling Yiga Tulku on Palkhang Lotsāwa's *Lexicon Lamp of Speech*. As these classes had to be fitted into Rinpoché's busy schedule, the course was actually completed in 1964.

The eleventh of May was the annual great ceremony of the eighth-day torma. Rinpoché presented me with a ceremonial scarf, and we spent time in meaningful discussion until about five thirty in the afternoon. On the twelfth, with Serkong Rinpoché leading the assembly, the administration offered a long-life ceremony to the precious tutor. Every year from around this time onward, monasteries, lamas and tulkus, Tibetan road construction crews, the volunteer soldiers, and many other monks, nuns, and laypeople would offer long-life ceremonies to the great Vajradhara tutor. I will not take the trouble to write of all them here. Rinpoché would accept the offerings of the three representations and the scarves but would never take the actual offerings.

On the twenty-fifth of May, Tibetan representatives of the refugees living in Gangtok sponsored a long-life ceremony for me in which Rinpoché presided as vajra master.

On the twenty-fifth of August, Rinpoché gave full-ordination vows to fifty-one novice monks. Beginning on the third of September and continuing daily, Rinpoché joyfully gave me an explicit explanation and transmission of the *Great Exposition of Secret Mantra* by the great Tsongkhapa. I was indeed fortunate to receive these teachings.

Rinpoché composed the supplication to the former incarnations of Kyabjé Trijang Rinpoché entitled *Moon that Swells the Ocean of Faith*.[148] On the fifteenth of August he went down to the Trijang Labrang in Gangchen Kyishong in Dharamsala, where he presented the text of the supplication, together with the three representations and a ceremonial scarf, and requested Trijang Rinpoché to accept to live a long and healthy life. Trijang Rinpoché received the transmission of the supplication from Rinpoché. Rinpoché told Khyongla that the source for the inclusion of Vimalaśrī[149] in the supplication list was the visions that appeared to Takphu Rinpoché.

For six days beginning from the twenty-sixth of October sixteen geshés underwent a debate examination on tantra. The Vajradhara tutor joined me as debate monitor.

Eight abbots from the Thösam Thardö Ling College for the Preservation of Buddhist Culture in Buxa Duar came for their annual audience after being released from their summer rainy-season retreat commitments. Together with the Namgyal Monastery assembly, they offered me a long-life ceremony on the thirtieth of October by way of a Guru Puja ritual, and the great Vajradhara sat at the head of the assembly.

Kyabjé Trijang Rinpoché, the eight abbots, the sixteen geshés who sat the tantric exam, lamas, tulkus and geshés resident in Dharamsala, and the Namgyal Monastery monks joined me in my residence to perform the ceremony of making a hundred thousand offerings by way of a Guru Puja ritual. The Vajradhara tutor was also invited and invoked the compassion of the buddhas and bodhisattvas for the sake of the Buddha's teaching and the country of Tibet.

I asked that new life diagrams[150] be prepared for the Nechung and Gadong oracles to wear on their bodies. These were the life diagram of the five king emanations focused primarily on the king of enlightened activity and the life diagram focused primarily on the king of excellent qualities. Consequently, on the twenty-first of December, Rinpoché together with Trijang Rinpoché performed the necessary life diagram rituals. That day was also the commemoration of Tsongkhapa's passing known as the offerings of the twenty-fifth.[151] Therefore, Rinpoché accompanied me with the assistance of the Namgyal Monastery monks in performing the guru offering, the prayers of Guhyasamāja, Cakrasaṃvara, Vajrabhairava, and Kālacakra, as well as verses of auspiciousness and dedication.

On the seventh of January 1963, Rinpoché traveled to Varanasi, where he was welcomed by the Tibetan lamas, tulkus, and geshés who were studying at the Sanskrit university there. On the tenth he went to the precious shrine built by Dharma King Aśoka and performed an extensive thousand butter-lamp offering. He also went to other shrines and temples there and made prayers. On another day, he again went to the precious shrine and performed the thousandfold offering ceremony in response to an invitation from Trijang Rinpoché. At the request of Geshé Khyenrap Söpa of Drepung Monastery's Gowo House, Rinpoché gave on the twenty-fifth the preparation ceremonies of single-deity Vajrabhairava. On the following day he bestowed the initiation, concluding with a long-life initiation.

In response to an invitation from the monastic community at Ganden Phelgyé Ling in Bodhgaya, Rinpoché traveled to Bodhgaya on the third of

February, where he stayed on the top floor of the monastery. On the sixth he made offerings to the monks of that monastery and performed the thousand butter-lamp offering in front of the sacred shrine there. In response to a request from Ashé Yangkyi and the Phakri Serkhang family, over three days starting February 9, Rinpoché performed the ceremony of the bodhicitta vow, the preparation ceremonies for the Eleven-Faced Avalokiteśvara initiation, and finally the initiation itself in front of the sacred shrine. On the twenty-first the sponsors and the Religious Affairs Office from the Tibetan administration offered Rinpoché a long-life ceremony.

On the third of March Rinpoché made offerings to the assembly of the prayer festival and performed the thousandfold offering ceremony sitting at the head of the assembly. The next day he returned to Sarnath. On the tenth, at the request of Chamdo Gyara Tulku, Rinpoché performed the permission ceremony of the inseparability of the guru and Mahākāla to about thirty recipients. Four days later Rinpoché returned to Dharamsala and told me of the excellent deeds he had undertaken for the sake of the doctrine and living beings.

On the fourth of April, a long-life ceremony sponsored by the Tibetan monastic and lay refugees living in northern Ladakh was performed for me by the Namgyal Monastery monks and the lamas, tulkus, and geshés living in Dharamsala. Rinpoché attended along with Trijang Rinpoché and kindly made fervent prayers. Two days later, from two in the afternoon until eight in the evening, the monks of Namgyal Monastery and I performed the propitiation rituals of the host of Dharma protectors endowed with the power of the pledge to guard the teachings specifically and generally. We were joined in these prayers by the two tutors.

At the joint request of Shakor Khen Rinpoché Nyima Gyaltsen and Dagyab Rinpoché, from the ninth of April until the twentieth Rinpoché gave a transmission and explanation of Guṇaprabha's *Vinaya Sutra* to many scholars of philosophy. Along with the Home Affairs Office and the Religious Affairs Office, Rinpoché offered donations and tea to the recipients.

For seven days starting the twenty-ninth of April 1963, Rinpoché gave experiential teachings on the generation and completion stages of single-deity Vajrabhairava to many assembled practitioners. At the request of Ling Yiga Tulku, on the twelfth and thirteenth of May Rinpoché gave the life entrustment of the five king emanations to Yiga Tulku, Shakor Khen Rinpoché, and Dagyab Rinpoché. Over the next two days Rinpoché and I took part in Namgyal Monastery's Kālacakra practice and offering ritual, with Rinpoché leading the assembly.

The seventeenth of May marked the third anniversary of the founding of the Tibetan Children's Village, and Rinpoché and Trijang Rinpoché accompanied me as guests for lunch.

From May 30 until June 27, kindly fitting into my busy schedule, Rinpoché gave me a transmission and explanation of Guṇaprabha's *Vinaya Sutra*, a transmission of the Fifth Ling Rinpoché Losang Lungtok Tenzin Trinlé's *Eighteen-Step Guide to Vajrabhairava*, a profound and extensive combined explanation of the *Condensed Perfection of Wisdom Sutra*, Maitreya's *Ornament of Realization*, and Haribhadra's commentary *Clarification of the Meaning of the Ornament of Realization*.

On the evening of the seventh of June, Simok Rinpoché Jampa Ngawang Kunga Tenzin of Penpo Nālendra passed away to the celestial pure land. Rinpoché accompanied me in performing the Guru Puja ritual and the *Prayer of Samantabhadra* and made strong prayers that the aspirations this great being made for the Buddha's teachings and for living beings be realized.

In response to a request made by former acting prime minister Dekharwa, over a period of seven days beginning from the twenty-fifth of July, Rinpoché gave teachings on the root text of the *Guru Puja* by Panchen Losang Chökyi Gyaltsen to an audience of about three hundred.

On the fourth of August eighteen geshés from the three monastic centers were undergoing their geshé exams, and Rinpoché accompanied me to act as adjudicator. Around this time Rinpoché very kindly gave me transmissions and explanations of Tsongkhapa's *Essence of Excellent Explanation: Differentiating the Definitive and the Provisional* and Khedrup Jé's *Dose of Emptiness: Opening the Eyes of the Fortunate.*

At four o'clock in the morning on August 5, ninety-seven other monks and I took the pledges of the early-summer rainy retreat. In accordance with the instructions of the Nechung and Gadong oracles, during those three months on the fifteenth, thirtieth, and eighth days of the Tibetan month, and on the commemoration of the Buddha's return from the celestial realms in the ninth Tibetan month, the monks in the summer retreat had to perform the horseback consecration ritual and the ritual of making effective offerings from afar in order to avert any damage from humans or nonhumans to the statues and shrines in Tibet—especially the two main Buddha statues in Lhasa and the five-aspect self-arisen statue of Avalokiteśvara.[152] Therefore, on that day the Religious Affairs Office organized extensive offerings, and tutor Ling Rinpoché and I, together with the monks, began with the Vajrabhairava self-generation sādhana and continued with the ritual of offering ablutions to the buddhas and bodhisattvas, the horseback consecration, and finally made recitations of *Praise of Avalokiteśvara*, *Praise of Dependent Origination*, *Praise to the Twenty-One Tārās*, and *Prayer of the Words of Truth*.[153] This was done from nine in the morning until noon.

Beginning on the nineteenth, over a period of several days with breaks in between, Rinpoché gave teachings on the development of the visualization practices of the Guhyasamāja self-generation to Dagyab Rinpoché. These teachings were completed the following year. On the twenty-first of August, the entire Namgyal Monastery assembly and I performed by way of glorious Vajrabhairava the consecration ritual called Causing the Rain of Goodness to Fall. This was performed for all the shrines, which exist as a way for disciples to accumulate merit, in the land of Tibet enclosed within its surrounding snow-clad mountains. The precious tutor attended the ritual.

On the twenty-eighth, in keeping with the instructions from Nechung and Gadong, the lamas, tulkus, and geshés, together with the assistance of Namgyal Monastery, offered me a long-life ceremony known as Halting the Ḍākinīs' Escort, by way of the Guru Puja *tsok* ritual. The precious tutor acted as vajra master and offered me the support of the eight auspicious substances.

On the thirteenth of September, the precious tutor, myself, and all monks and nuns of Dharamsala made fervent prayers to Jinasāgara Avalokiteśvara,[154] the embodiment of the Three Jewels, for the righteous cause of the followers of the Buddha in South Vietnam to be accomplished.

For twenty days beginning on the seventh of October, I was fortunate to be able to enjoy the great feast of receiving from Rinpoché teachings on Candrakīrti's great treatise *Entering the Middle Way*, combined with Tsongkhapa's commentary *Clarifying the Intention*. Beginning on the sixteenth, in response to a request from Dagyab Rinpoché, the precious tutor gave teachings to a few recipients, including assistant tutor Serkong Rinpoché, on Tsongkhapa's *Essence of Excellent Explanation: Differentiating the Definitive and the Provisional*.

The protectors Nechung and Gadong urged that in order to avert any disaster occurring in the sacred place of Lhasa, the powerful nāga rituals of the hidden nāga vase and the nāga torma should be performed. Therefore, during the summer retreat, on those days that nāgas are deemed to appear above ground we regularly performed the nāga torma ritual and the nāga incense cleansing ritual. Also, for five days beginning on the twenty-second, we performed the ritual of creating the nāga vase with its contents, such as the six excellent medicines.[155] In all of these practices the two tutors were constant participants.

In accord with indications from Nechung and Gadong, over a hundred monks and I, including lamas and abbots from all Tibetan traditions, together with a rotation of staff from the various government departments, performed over eleven days an extensive Guru Puja *tsok* ritual, as well recitations of the prayers *All Wishes to Be Spontaneously Fulfilled*, *Removing Obstacles to the Path*, *Praise of Avalokiteśvara*, and *Prayer of the Words of Truth*. This was made possible through donations from Tibetans in the various settlements and with help from the Tibetan administration. The precious tutor attended the ceremony and raised to a new level the good omens for the teachings and living beings, both generally and specifically.

On the sixth and seventh of October, the Tibetan trainee soldiers at Dehradun and the Amdo community, respectively, offered me a long-life ceremony, at which Vajradhara served as the vajra master.

On the ninth of November a religious conference comprising delegates from the Sakya, Geluk, Kagyü, Nyingma, and Bön traditions of Tibet was convened. Rinpoché was among the fifty-seven delegates that included Sakya Trizin, who was the precious Sakya throneholder and illuminator of the teachings of the Khön family, as well as Düdjom Rinpoché. During the prayer sessions, Rinpoché along with the Namgyal Monastery monks chanted the various recitations, such as the long-life prayers. After this I gave a talk on the necessity of a strong and profound unity between the different Tibetan traditions. Rinpoché listened with evident joy. On the next day speeches were given by twelve lamas and tulkus, such as Sakya Trizin. The Vajradhara tutor also offered his thoughts, which would without doubt ripen into auspicious events for the teachings and living beings. On the morning of the eleventh, Rinpoché came to my rooms and gave me some Dharma advice. At noon Sakya Tri Rinpoché, Karmapa Rinpoché,

Attendees at a religious conference of all Tibetan Buddhist traditions, November 1963. In the front row are Düdjom Rinpoché, Karmapa Rinpoché, Sakya Trizin, the Dalai Lama, Ling Rinpoché, Trijang Rinpoché, and Bakula Rinpoché.

Düdjom Rinpoché, Dechen Chögön Rinpoché, the two tutors, and myself had lunch together, where we informally proffered ideas on how to maintain, protect, and develop the different Buddhist traditions of Tibet. After this Karmapa Rinpoché came to Chopra House to visit the precious tutor and to engage in informal and private conversation.

On the next day Rinpoché helped draft the conference's resolutions. Sakya Tri Rinpoché came to visit the precious tutor in his residence. It was an informal visit, and it was evident that they enjoyed each other's company immensely.

On the thirteenth the different traditions of Tibet offered me a long-life ceremony. Rinpoché joined the other great lamas in making prayers for my long life. On the morning of the next day Sakya Tri Rinpoché, the Vajradhara tutor, Karmapa Rinpoché, Düdjom Rinpoché, and I put our signatures to the proclamations and resolutions of the conference. I gave a concluding speech on the success of the conference. After this the *Prayer for the Teachings to Flourish* and dedications were chanted, the monks of Namgyal Monastery provided musical offerings, and the conference ended. The heads of the traditions visited Chopra House to petition the great Vajradhara to live a long life. Rinpoché said that he would pray to the Three

Jewels and try to live a long life and requested the great lamas present to do the same. The same day the labrang offered a banquet to the great lamas.

On the twenty-second Rinpoché gave a long-life initiation to the Gadong oracle and others.

On the fourth of December the precious tutor visited me as he was about to leave for Bodhgaya, where he would spend the winter for the sake of his health. In the afternoon at three-thirty, he traveled to Pathankot by jeep and then by train to Bodhgaya. On the nineteenth Rinpoché made donations to the monks of the Tibetan monastery in Bodhgaya, and in front of the sacred shrine he performed the thousandfold offering ceremony and made prayers for the spread of the doctrine, the happiness and welfare of living beings, and so on. Rinpoché was staying in new rooms built for him, and on the morning of the twenty-first, the Bodhgaya monks offered Rinpoché the three representations as well as tea and rice to mark the occasion. Rinpoché then began a longevity practice using Cittamaṇi Tārā. In the afternoon he bestowed full-ordination vows on twenty novice monks in the assembly hall.

Beginning on the twenty-sixth, in response to a request from Jampa Söpa from Nepal, Rinpoché gave the initiation of single-deity Vajrabhairava followed by experiential instructions on the generation and completion stages to about three hundred practitioners.

On the third of January 1964, in front of the sacred shrine, Rinpoché gave the bodhisattva vows followed by a White Tārā long-life initiation to over a thousand recipients, who included the resident monks and nuns and the monastics and laypeople there on pilgrimage. On the ninth Kyabjé Trijang Rinpoché invited the Vajradhara tutor to lead the monastic assembly, and by way of a Cakrasaṃvara guru-offering *tsok* ritual, he and the resident monks petitioned Rinpoché to plant his feet forever in the world. On the next day the two venerable tutors performed the offerings and practice of the mandala of Vajrayoginī from the Nāropa lineage.

For two days beginning on the twelfth, in the assembly hall of the Bodhgaya Tibetan monastery, Rinpoché gave the transmission of Tsongkhapa's *Essence of Excellent Explanation: Differentiating the Definitive and the Provisional* to several hundred recipients, pausing at the sentence breaks and so on to ensure that the meaning could be followed. For three days starting on the thirtieth, Rinpoché gave teachings on the Seventh Dalai Lama's *Hundred Deities of Tuṣita* in the assembly hall of the monastery.

Beginning on the sixth of February, in response to a request from the Mongolian lama Guru Dewachen, Rinpoché gave the single-deity Vajrabhairava initiation preceded by a separate preparation day. From the seventeenth to the twenty-seventh, during the Great Prayer Festival in Bodhgaya, Rinpoché gave teachings on Āryaśūra's *Garland of the Buddha's Birth Stories* in the mornings, thereby maintaining one of the traditions of the great Tsongkhapa. He also sat at the head of the festival assemblies.

On the first of March, the precious tutor gave the Cittamaṇi White Tārā long-life initiation to over a thousand monks, nuns, and laypeople. On the eighth of March in the Bodhgaya monastery, Rinpoché sat at the head of the assembly for the yearly consecration ritual known as Causing the Rain of Goodness to Fall and united the wisdom beings and samaya beings.

On the fourteenth Rinpoché left Bodhgaya by train to return to Dharamsala. On the day after he arrived, Rinpoché came to visit me to tell me how he carried out his deeds of liberating sentient beings, which was a source of great joy to me. On the seventeenth, the Tibetan Women's Association offered Rinpoché a long-life ceremony, which he joyfully accepted. In response to a request from the Religious Affairs Office the next day, Rinpoché began a longevity practice for my long life.

On the fourteenth of April, when the government staff offered a ceremony for my long life, Rinpoché acted as the master of the proceedings. The next day was the anniversary of the Tibetan Children's Village, and the two tutors and I performed the consecration of three new assembly rooms. Two days later Rinpoché bestowed on me a long-life initiation.

In response to my request, for seven days beginning on the eighteenth of May, Rinpoché performed an appropriate number of propitiation rituals of the Dharma protectors for the sake of the Buddha's teaching and the temporal well-being of Tibet. On the twenty-eighth Rinpoché attended a memorial service with me for Pandit Nehru, the Indian prime minister, who had just passed away. He listened with great respect as the liaison officer, Mr. Malik, and I gave short accounts of the deeds of Pandit Nehru. After this, as a mark of the grief for his passing, everyone observed a minute's silence. After the service had finished, Rinpoché participated with me in the Guru Puja ritual, and with the recitation of Tsongkhapa's *Prayer of Auspiciousness at the Beginning, Middle, and End* and *Prayer for Rebirth in Sukhāvatī*, he made extensive prayers dedicated to Prime Minister Nehru.

Around this time Losang Lungrik, the labrang manager, requested Kyabjé Trijang Rinpoché for a divination concerning the health of the Vajradhara tutor. That night Trijang Rinpoché said he dreamed of a great wind rising from Chushur.[156] In reality Rinpoché was renowned as an incarnation of Ra Lotsāwa Dorjé Drak, a personification of great power. This had been established by much scripture and reasoning. Consequently, there was no possibility of him being subject to the harms of the four types of māras. However, in the eyes of ordinary beings, Rinpoché's previous incarnation, Losang Lungtok Tenzin Trinlé, passed into the next life when he was thrown from his horse when returning from the great deity of Nyethang[157] in front of which he had been performing a wrathful fire offering at the request of the government. And now it seemed as if something left over from that time was happening to the present incarnation. It became clear that this would have to be averted through the Hayagrīva secret-accomplishment ritual. Consequently, Trijang Rinpoché himself engaged in this practice for seven days, after which, as Trijang Rinpoché has mentioned in his autobiography, there were signs that the threat to Rinpoché's health had been removed.

On the thirtieth of July, the monastic communities of Buxa Duar offered me a long-life ceremony, and Rinpoché acted as the vajra master. On the sixth of August the same group offered the great Vajradhara tutor a long-life ceremony, which he happily accepted. On the seventeenth Rinpoché was invited to the Dharamsala Teachers Training College to give a lecture. From the twenty-second of July to the tenth of August, in response to my request and whenever time was available, Rinpoché gave me teachings on Khedrup Jé's *Great Exposition of the Vajrabhairava Generation Stage*. On the twenty-second the Religious Affairs Office offered Kyabjé Vajradhara a long-life ceremony.

On the tenth of September the labrang invoked the Gadong and Nechung protectors through the oracles and requested them for practices to be performed in order to ensure Rinpoché's long life. At the request of the Dakpo Bamchö Tulku, Jampa Gyatso, Rinpoché gave teachings on Haribhadra's *Clarification of the Meaning of the Ornament of Realization* for several days beginning on the nineteenth to a few disciples at his residence.

Kyabjé Trijang Rinpoché performed the long-life accomplishment practice for the Vajradhara tutor, and on the third of October he presented Rinpoché with the longevity substances, which Rinpoché accepted. On the twelfth Rinpoché gave a White Tārā initiation to Tsechokling Tulku, and on the twenty-seventh Rinpoché had lunch with this tulku, during which Rinpoché advised him to study well. On the thirty-first, at the request of the head of the secretariat, Chokteng Thupten Norsang, Rinpoché gave the preparation rituals of single-deity Vajrabhairava to about three hundred recipients and the full initiation on the following day.

On the thirteenth, at the request of someone from Phakri, Rinpoché bestowed the White Tārā long-life initiation on about fifty monks, nuns, and laypeople. On the fourteenth, at the request of Tara Tulku from Tsul House of Drepung Monastery, he gave a transmission and teaching on Khedrup Jé's generation-stage work *Ocean of Attainments* for seven days to about two hundred devotees, including Dagyab Rinpoché. On the twenty-third of November, Tsering Drölma, my elder sister, passed into the next life, and at the request of those close to her, Rinpoché joined the Namgyal Monastery monks in offering prayers and reciting words of truth. On the twenty-fifth, just before he was to set out for Bodhgaya, Rinpoché came to see me, and we had an informal conversation based around topics related to the profound view and vast practices.

On the third of December Rinpoché was invited by Namgyal Monastery to lead the assembly. On the following day Rinpoché left Dharamsala for his winter stay in the pilgrimage place of Bodhgaya.

On the twelfth of December in Bodhgaya, Rinpoché ordained several people, including Drakgom Tulku. On the following day he gave a long-life initiation, and on the day after that, Rinpoché gave full-ordination vows to sixteen novice monks. On the twenty-fifth he gave teachings on the Vajrabhairava protector offering ritual to sixteen monks.

On the twelfth of January 1965, at the request of Chödrön, the mother of the king of Bhutan, Rinpoché gave transmissions of the *Prayer of Samant-abhadra* and so on. At the request of the Ratö storekeeper monk Tsewang Tashi, Tsawa Dampa Lodrö, Dotsé from Chamdo, the Phakri government office, and Thupten Chöjor of Drepung's Nyakré House, Rinpoché gave the initiation of single-deity Vajrabhairava to about four thousand recipients beginning on the tenth of February and followed that with an experiential guide to the generation and completion stages. Afterward the sponsors jointly offered Rinpoché a long-life ceremony. On the twenty-fourth Rinpoché performed for the same recipients the permission empowerment of Avalokiteśvara Who Liberates All Beings from the Unfortunate Realms and the bodhicitta ceremony. After this the Tibetan administration offered a long-life ceremony in order that this great master would remain for a long time on this earth. On the following day the labrang and the monastic community of Bodhgaya offered Rinpoché a long-life ceremony, which he kindly and happily accepted.

Plate 1. Kyabjé Ling Rinpoché

Plate 2. Ling Rinpoché giving an empowerment in 1974

Plate 3. The Fourteenth Dalai Lama flanked by his two tutors, India, 1956

Plate 4. A painting of the Fifth Ling Rinpoché based on original murals at Garpa Hermitage

Plate 5. The monastery of Ratsa, near the birthplace of the Sixth Ling Rinpoché. Visible on the mountainside is the Palace of Cakrasaṃvara.

Plate 6. The site of Garpa Hermitage

Plate 7. Drepung Monastery with Nechung Monastery in the foreground, 1936

Plate 8. Loseling College of Drepung Monastery, 1997

Plate 9. The Potala Palace, 1937

Plate 10. The Thirteenth Dalai Lama's reliquary in the Potala Palace

Plate 11. The main Buddha statue in the Ramoché temple

Plate 12. The reliquary of Tsongkhapa at Ganden Monastery

Plate 13. The Great Peacock Tent at Dögu Thang, 1939

Plate 14. The interior of the Great Peacock Tent, showing the throne where the young Fourteenth Dalai Lama met Ling Rinpoché for the first time

Plate 15. Ling Rinpoché sits on a horse in a ceremonial procession to the Norbulingka summer palace.

Plate 16. The installation of the fifteen-year-old Dalai Lama as spiritual and temporal leader of Tibet at the Norbulingka on November 17, 1950

Plate 17. Drigung Mangra Monastery, about fifty miles northeast of Lhasa, seat of the Kadam master Jayulwa Shönu Ö, 2007

Plate 18. Thösam Dargyé Ling Monastery, Yarlung, Lhokha region, Tibet, 2007

Plate 19. The Fourteenth Dalai Lama dressed in lay clothes arriving at the Indian border, March 1959. On the left is Phalha Thupten Öden, the lord chamberlain.

Plate 20. The Dalai Lama and Ling Rinpoché at the opening of Tibet House in New Delhi, 1965

Above: Plate 21. Ling Rinpoché
conducting a fire offering near his
Chopra House residence

Plate 22. The Mangyul
Kyirong statue, also
known as Wati Sangpo

Plate 23. Ling Rinpoché with Mr. Kühn and monks in the assembly hall at Rikon Monastery, Switzerland, 1968

Plate 24. Ling Rinpoché with schoolchildren, their teacher Rakra Tulku, and houseparents of the Tibetan children's village in Trogen, Switzerland, 1968

Plate 25. Ling Rinpoché and Trijang Rinpoché conducting the inauguration of Rikon Monastery

Plate 26. Ling Rinpoche visiting with Professor Schöllermann, curator at Bonn University's Cultural Studies Department

Plate 27. Ling Rinpoché with family members of the Fourteenth Dalai Lama, and Tibetan representative Phalha Thupten Öden, left, in Geneva, 1968

Plate 28. (above) Ling Rinpoché and Losang Lungrik with Dakpo Rinpoché on the Eiffel Tower, 1968

Plate 29. (right) The two tutors with Thubten Tsering, Losang Lungrik, Gyurmé Sadutshang, Palden Tsering, and Norbu Chöphel, France, 1968

Plate 30. Ling Rinpoché with schoolchildren and houseparents at the Tibetan children's village in Blenau, France, 1968

Plate 31. Ling Rinpoché, Bodhgaya, 1972

Plate 32. Ling Rinpoché relaxing with Losang Lungrik during a trip to Italy

Plate 33. Ling Rinpoché during a
visit to Italy in 1980

Plate 34. Ling Rinpoché arriving in New
York, greeted by Khyongla Rinpoché, 1980

Plate 35. Ling Rinpoché visiting the Mongolian lama Geshé Wangyal at Labsum Shedrup Ling Monastery in New Jersey, 1980. Gomang Khorpen Geshé and Geshé Wangyal, left, and Losang Lungrik and Dakpo Rinpoché, right.

Plate 36. The two tutors, Song Rinpoché, and labrang managers Losang Lungrik and Palden Tsering, 1980

Plate 37. Ling Rinpoché teaching foreigners at Tushita Meditation Centre,
Dharamsala, 1982

Plate 38. Tara Tulku, Serkong Rinpoché, the Dalai Lama, and Ling Rinpoché
at a ceremony at the Mahabodhi Temple, Bodhgaya, 1981

Plate 39. Ling Rinpoché greeted by Lama Thubten Yeshe at Tushita
Meditation Centre, Dharamsala, 1982

Plate 40. The procession of Ling Rinpoché's body on a palanquin from Kalsang Yeshé's house to Chopra House, 1983. Khyongla Rinpoché is in the foreground.

Plate 41. The embalmed body of the Sixth Ling Rinpoché at the Thekchen Chöling residence of the Dalai Lama, Dharamsala

Plate 42. The golden reliquary shrine of the Sixth Ling Rinpoché at Drepung Monastery, Mundgod, South India

Plate 43. His Holiness the Dalai Lama confirms the recognition of the Seventh Ling Rinpoché at Ling Labrang on October 5, 1987

Plate 44. The Seventh Ling Rinpoché making an offering to the Dalai Lama at Thekchen Chöling Temple, Dharamsala, 2004, upon receiving bhikṣu vows, fifty years after His Holiness received bhikṣu vows from the Sixth Ling Rinpoché

Plate 45. The Seventh Ling Rinpoché, 2016

Plate 46. The Seventh Ling Rinpoché at Drepung Loseling Monastery, Mundgod,
November 21, 2016, on the occasion of receiving his geshé degree

Plate 47. The Sixth Ling Rinpoché at his Chopra House residence, Dharamsala, 1979

Plate 48. The Seventh Ling Rinpoché at his Chopra House residence, Dharamsala, 1988

27 | Accepting the Title of Ganden Throneholder

THE NINETY-SIXTH Ganden Throneholder, Jedrung Thupten Kunga of Sera Jé Monastery's Hardong House, had passed away in Lhasa under the yoke of the Chinese occupation. It had been the custom that the throne alternated between the Sharpa Chöjé and the Jangtsé Chöjé. Therefore the present Sharpa incumbent, the great Vajradhara tutor, Kyabjé Ling Rinpoché, was to receive the title of the Ninety-Seventh Ganden Throneholder. At the same time the Religious Affairs Office of the Tibetan administration requested Rinpoché to become the abbot of the Bodhgaya Tibetan monastery, Ganden Phelgyé Ling. Consequently, on the sixth of March 1965, in the main hall of Ganden Phelgyé Ling, Rinpoché became the regent of the second Buddha Tsongkhapa and ascended the throne of the abbot of the Bodhgaya monastery as well. During the proceedings assistant tutor and assistant Religious Affairs minister Serkong Rinpoché, who represented the administration, recited the ritual offering of the eight auspicious substances. The assistant minister Dampa Lodrö, the former minister Thupten Norsang, representatives of the three monastic seats, and the abbots and monastic officials of the two tantric colleges, who had all come specially for the inauguration, presented ceremonial scarves. Kyabjé Trijang Rinpoché also sent one of his staff to present a ceremonial scarf, a mandala, and the three representations, the pandit hat, and so on. After the ceremony, in front of the Bodhi Tree Rinpoché gave a transmission and teaching on the first few pages of Tsongkhapa's *Great Stages of the Path to Enlightenment* to the special guests who had attended the ceremony, as well as local residents and a crowd who had spontaneously gathered. With this, the ceremonies for the inauguration of the ninety-seventh holder of the throne of the regent of the second Buddha Tsongkhapa and the acceptance of being the abbot of the Bodhgaya Tibetan monastery were complete. On the eighth Rinpoché left Bodhgaya by train and returned to Dharamsala. On the eleventh he came to see me.

On the sixteenth the Tibetan administration offered me a long-life ceremony by way of the ritual of Halting the Ḍākinīs' Escort. Before the actual ceremony, the Vajradhara tutor along with Trijang Rinpoché, the council of ministers, and representatives of the people offered me the three representations. The ministers read out a document of all the activities they had pledged to implement, in which they stated that everyone would carry out their duties sincerely and honestly without any contravention of my wishes and for which they asked that I should accept to live a long life. I replied that although I was doing what I could from my side, one person alone cannot do much. Therefore it was important that the officials and the people also share the responsibility, that their commitment was pure, and that they went about their work sincerely. If this were done, then in my opinion nothing bad would happen. During the actual long-life ceremony, the great Vajradhara tutor performed the mandala-offering recitation.

On the seventeenth of March, in response to a request from the Religious Affairs Office, Rinpoché conferred the one-day Mahayana vows to a large gathering.

Although the actual ceremony for assuming the title of Ninety-Seventh Ganden Throneholder had been performed in Bodhgaya previously, it was the custom to hold a new-appointment audience for those who ascend to the position of throneholder. Accordingly, on the eighteenth of March, which was a very auspicious day of the first Tibetan month, the Vajradhara tutor visited me in the reception room of Dharamsala Thekchen Chöling at eight in the morning wearing the pandit hat and the monastic robe. He performed three prostrations and presented me with the throneholder mandala offering. He also made presentations of the three representations, a ceremonial scarf, a symbolic wheel, a Dharma conch, and so on for the new-appointment audience of becoming the abbot of Ganden Phelgyé Ling in Bodhgaya. He then ascended the Ganden throne. Tea was served, and assistant tutor Serkong Rinpoché, who also was the Religious Affairs assistant minister, led the tea-offering recitation. Sweet rice was served, and Serkong Rinpoché again led the assembly in the rice-offering recitation.

The four ministers and the chair of the Assembly of Tibetan People's Deputies, together with representatives of the Tibetan religious traditions and the three provinces, presented ceremonial scarves to the precious throneholder. When they had returned to their seats, the abbot and monks of Namgyal Monastery and the chant masters stood up, and together we recited the long-life prayer for the precious tutor as well as Gungthangpa's *Prayer for the Flourishing of Tsongkhapa's Teachings*. After this everyone put on monastic pandit hats and recited the Vajrabhairava auspicious verses to the accompaniment of cymbals. I personally presented with the deepest respect a ceremonial scarf and knotted protection cords to my root guru and presented the ceremonial gifts to him. I also presented protection cords to the labrang staff.

All the Tibetan administration officials offered ceremonial scarves to the precious throneholder at his labrang. The same day Kyabjé Trijang Vajradhara came to the labrang and presented Rinpoché with a very long, high quality ceremonial scarf embroidered with representations symbolizing the spread of his enlightened activity, as well as the three representations, and a copy of Khedrup Jé's biography of Tsongkhapa entitled *Bridge of Faith*. Hundreds of other monastic and lay devotees came and presented gifts and offerings.

On the next day Rinpoché visited Trijang Rinpoché at his residence, where he offered him a ceremonial scarf and the three representations, and together they enjoyed a lengthy conversation. On the same day Rinpoché gave novice-monk vows to a small group of recipients in the reception room of the labrang.

On the seventh of April the precious throneholder was invited to the Halting the Ḍākinīs' Escort long-life ceremony, performed for me by way of the ritual of the five immortality deities of the Amitāyus inner attainment. The ceremony was attended by about two hundred people, including representatives of the three provinces and the religious traditions of Tibet and others. On the next day the same representatives offered a long-life ceremony to the great Vajradhara. On the twelfth, sponsored by the Religious Affairs Office, the whole assembly of Namgyal Monastery offered Rinpoché a long-life ceremony using the ritual of life-granting Cittamaṇi White Tārā. Rinpoché graciously accepted both ceremonies. Two days later Rinpoché was also invited to a long-life ceremony offered to me by the people of the Khampa organization Chushi Gangdruk ("four rivers and six ranges").

In response to a request from the incarnation of the great master Phabongkha Dechen Nyingpo, from the second of May to the eighteenth Rinpoché gave teachings and a transmission of Khedrup Jé's *Ocean of*

Attainments on the Guhyasamāja generation stage to a great number of lamas, tulkus, geshés, and so on. For several days beginning on the nineteenth, to an audience that included Denma Lochö Rinpoché and Gangchen Tulku of Sera Mé Monastery, he gave an explanation of the two stages of the exalted Vajrayoginī of the Nāropa lineage using the self-generation sādhana. On the twenty-sixth Rinpoché bestowed the Vajrasattva permission initiation on about eighty monastic and lay recipients.

On the first of June Rinpoché gave novice-monk vows to the American Robert Alexander Thurman.

When Rinpoché was the abbot of Gyütö, he undertook the generation-stage retreat of Guhyasamāja and supplemented it with a fire offering. He also had conferred the initiation several times. However, because he intended entering the retreat once more, Rinpoché again received the initiation complete with the preparation day from Kyabjé Trijang Rinpoché. On the fifteenth of June Rinpoché entered into the retreat of this supreme meditation deity.

While undertaking this retreat Rinpoché gave thirteen days of teaching, beginning on the tenth of July, on Tsongkhapa's *Lamp to Illuminate the Five Stages*, on the Guhyasamāja completion stage, at the request of Dagyab Rinpoché to a large audience of practitioners that included lamas, tulkus, geshés, and meditators.

On the early morning of the first of August, at the request of Dampa Lodrö, who was the assistant to the Religious Affairs minister, Rinpoché gave the one-day Mahayana vows in Mortimer Hall to many monastic and lay recipients of Dharamsala.

On the second of September at the beginning of the second teacher-training course, Rinpoché was invited to the college, where he gave pertinent advice on the choices they should make.

On the thirteenth, Nechung and Gadong, the protectors Rinpoché had mainly relied upon for a long time, were invoked through oracles, and questions were put to them concerning rituals and practices to be performed for Rinpoché's everyday health.

About ten days before the completion of the Guhyasamāja retreat, war broke out between Pakistan and India. Pakistan dropped bombs on Yol military camp near Dharamsala, killing two people and injuring several others. Because of the serious situation, the Indian government recommended that I should move temporarily to New Delhi to escape the danger. I asked the two tutors to accompany me. Nechung offered the sword of the great Dharmarājā to the two tutors. The tutors stayed in Tibet House in New Delhi, as arranged. As the conflict between the two countries had escalated, Rinpoché was very concerned for the danger to the lives of the people. However, a few days after they had arrived in Delhi, Rinpoché heard news of the ceasefire and was delighted.

28 | A Life Reflecting the Insights of the Four Noble Ones

THE TWO TUTORS were staying in Tibet House and so met each other often. One day while they were together, Trijang Rinpoché sang the following song as a plea to the great Vajradhara throneholder to live a long life and to turn the wheel of the vast and profound Dharma for a long time:

> Lotus petals of past prayers may have bloomed by the thousands,
> but the frost of wandering aimlessly without thought or purpose
> has destroyed the nourishment of the good honey of enlightenment.
> Therefore, please listen to the pleas of this stupid old lion.[158]

> Having understood flawlessly and pristinely the transmission
>   of Tsongkhapa,
> which is the very essence of the mighty Buddha's teachings,
> sing out across the eons the far-reaching song of your excellent
>   deeds,
> which will show disciples in their many forms the great path
>   of the Buddha.

> With a life reflecting the insights of the four noble ones,[159]
> built on the path of scripture and reasoning,
> and of teachings unassailable by opponents,
> the light of your perfected activities, which amaze all the buddhas,
> let it the shine as the path dispelling the darkness of destructive
>   forces.

After this Trijang Rinpoché recited the following verses to the labrang manager Losang Lungrik, stressing the importance of continuing to serve the great Vajradhara master:

Listen to me, my wise and broad-minded friend.
By continuing to live the life of the youth Sudhana,[160]
if you hold the ring of unshakable faith at your heart,
without doubt it will be held forever
by the hook of compassion of the master of the three families.

With a mind one-pointedly focused, and with pure thought
    and deed,
devote yourself untiringly to your kind lama,
and without searching amid the hills and valleys,
the wish-granting jewel will fall into your hands.

Tibet House had several old paintings and statues that remained uniden-
tified, and while Rinpoché was staying in Delhi, he looked at them and
was able to identify and speak knowledgeably on them. One day, at the
request of a lama from Ladakh called Losang, Rinpoché went to the Ladakh
Buddhist Temple accompanied by Trijang Rinpoché. There they performed
consecration rituals for the sacred objects housed there. Afterward Ladakhi
students presented them with a show of singing and dancing from Ladakhi
culture, which they thoroughly enjoyed. Also, at that time, at the request of
the incarnation of Phabongkha, Rinpoché gave teachings on Tsongkhapa's
Great Exposition of Secret Mantra for fifteen days beginning the thirteenth
of October. On the twenty-fifth of October, Rinpoché and I performed the
dedication prayers during the ceremonies for the official opening of Tibet
House.

On the first of December Rinpoché left for the pilgrimage place of Sarnath. There on the eighth, at the request of the monk Jinpa Gyatso, Rinpoché gave teachings on Tsongkhapa's *Three Principal Aspects of the Path* to
many hundreds of monastic and lay recipients. On the following day, at the
request of a Mongolian lama, he gave an explanation of Tsongkhapa's *Foundation of All Good Qualities*, and on the twelfth, at the request of Rizong
Tulku from Ladakh, he began a teaching on the generation and completion
stages of Guhyasamāja.

After visiting Sarnath, Rinpoché went to the pilgrimage place of Bodhgaya. There on the twenty-fifth he performed the thousand five-senses cloud
offerings in the presence of the sacred shrine, as well as making donations to
the monks of the Bodhgaya Tibetan monastery and praying that the good

Ling Rinpoché attending the inauguration of Tibet House, Delhi,
on October 26, 1965. Indira Gandhi sits to his right. Sitting next to
the Dalai Lama is M. C. Chagla, Union Minister of Education.

path of peace and nonviolence propagated by the peerless Buddha would
spread through the world. He completed his teaching on the generation
and completion stages of Guhyasamāja to Rizong Tulku.

On the twenty-sixth I arrived at the Bodhgaya Ganden Phelgyé Ling
Tibetan monastery, and immediately the precious throneholder offered me
the mandala and the three representations on behalf of the monastery. On

the twenty-seventh he offered me the three representations in my new quarters at the Bodhgaya Tibetan monastery. When Trijang Rinpoché arrived from Bhopal, the precious throneholder went at once to meet him. On the twenty-eighth Rinpoché accompanied me in a special vow-purification ceremony[161] and the consecration rituals to mark the completion of the restoration and expansion of the assembly hall of the Bodhgaya Tibetan monastery.

At three o'clock on the afternoon of the thirtieth, Rinpoché came to see me accompanied by the precious Sakya Trizin, Düdjom Rinpoché, Drukpa Thuksé Rinpoché, Kalu Rinpoché, Öser Gyaltsen, who was the Religious Affairs minister, and Tsewang Tamdrin, who was the chair of the Assembly of Tibetan People's Deputies. They told me of the progress on the research into the classical Indian Buddhist texts for the study program of the Central Institute of Higher Tibetan Studies.[162]

On the thirty-first the administration performed a vast offering ceremony in front of the sacred shrine for the religious and political situation in Tibet. Rinpoché and I attended and made prayers.

1966

On the fifteenth of January 1966, Rinpoché gave a permission initiation for the general accomplishment of the three Buddha families. On the next day he bestowed novice-monk vows on eight recipients from Kinnaur and Ladakh. After that he ordained fifteen novice monks with full-ordination vows.

On the fifth of February, at the request of the Namgyal Monastery ritual assistant, Rinpoché gave the one-day Mahayana vows to a large number of recipients.

On the sixteenth Rinpoché left Bodhgaya for Dharamsala, and on the way to his residence he visited Trijang Rinpoché. On the following day he visited me and told me of his time in Bodhgaya, where he had surely performed great deeds for the sake of the teachings and sentient beings. Some days later Trijang Rinpoché came to Ling Labrang, where he offered Rinpoché a silver statue of White Tārā and requested that the precious throneholder accept to remain for a long time on this earth.

Beginning on the twenty-second and lasting for a week, Rinpoché joined me in performing prosperity rituals for the Tibetans living in exile. Relying upon White Jambhala, White Mahākāla, and Vaiśravaṇa, we prayed for all the wealth of samsara and nirvana to fall like rain.

On the second of June, the monastic community of Buxa Duar offered a long-life ceremony to Rinpoché. On the afternoon of the fourth, Rinpoché and I watched a film made by a French filmmaker on the Tibetan religious traditions. The twenty-first of June, which was the fourth of the sixth Tibetan month, was the commemoration of the special day the Blessed Buddha first turned the wheel of Dharma by preaching the four noble truths in the Deer Park at Sarnath, Varanasi. On that day, at the request of the Religious Affairs Office, Rinpoché gave teachings on Tsongkhapa's *Three Principal Aspects of the Path* to a large audience at Mortimer Hall. On the twenty-fourth and twenty-fifth, at the request of Ratö Khyongla Tulku, Rinpoché gave the preparation day and the initiation of single-deity Vajrabhairava to about eighty recipients.

On the first of July[163] Rinpoché gave the White Tārā long-life initiation to the same recipients.

Around this time I was a recipient of Rinpoché's ultimate kindness when he gave me an explanation of Tsongkhapa's *Great Exposition of Secret Mantra*. This was an explicit teaching delivered in a relaxed manner. On the sixth of July, my birthday, Rinpoché attended the celebrations and presented me with a ceremonial scarf. On the eleventh Rinpoché gave teachings on how to practice the guruyoga of the *Hundred Deities of Tuṣita* to Pema Dechen from Lhasa and others.

Beginning on the twenty-fourth of September, and in consideration of my busy schedule, Rinpoché gave me regular teachings on the four Guhyasamāja commentaries combined. With the precious tutor's extraordinary explanation, and particularly after his teachings on the meanings of the forty syllables of the introduction in the *Guhyasamāja Root Tantra*, I developed faith in the Guhyasamāja tantra in general, and especially a strong belief and deep sense of amazement that the glorious Candrakīrti was an unbelievable master and practitioner. For many days afterward, I experienced a feeling of great fortune at this inconceivable kindness, which produced in me a newfound faith and joy that never left me. This was a moment of great fortune and extraordinary kindness. Recipients of this teaching included the Namgyal Monastery abbot Losang Döndrup of Ganden Jangtsé, Lati Tulku, and Geshé Rapten. Rinpoché finished the teachings on the combined four commentaries on the fourth of November.

On the twenty-seventh of September, Rinpoché gave the long-life initiation of White Tārā at the request of Lati Rinpoché. A few days later Nechung and Gadong were invoked via oracles, and questions were put to them concerning his health, activities, and so on.

On the twenty-fifth of October, Rinpoché gave a long-life initiation to about a hundred monastic and lay residents of Dharamsala, and on the twenty-eighth he bestowed full monastic ordination vows on, among others, Triksé Tulku from Ladakh.

On the fifth of November, which was the day commemorating the Buddha's return from the celestial realms, Rinpoché gave the one-day Mahayana vows to many monks, nuns, and laypeople, in response to a request by the Religious Affairs Office. On the same day Rinpoché accompanied me in performing the consecration for the newly built shrine in the middle of McLeod Ganj.

On the ninth of November, in response to an invitation by Gyütö Monastery, Rinpoché traveled by car to Dalhousie, where he was welcomed by a large number of resident monks, nuns, and laypeople. He stayed as arranged at Ambartara House. On the fifteenth, as requested by the Tibetan people of Dalhousie, Rinpoché gave teachings in a school playground on Tsongkhapa's *Three Principal Aspects of the Path* and the permission empowerment of Avalokiteśvara Who Liberates All Beings from the Unfortunate Realms. The teachings were accompanied by a long-life ceremony offered to Rinpoché. On the seventeenth, in response to a request from Geshé Jampa Tenzin of Gyütö, Rinpoché gave teachings on mind training to the general public. On the twentieth and twenty-first, he gave the thirteen-deity Vajrabhairava initiation complete with preparatory empowerment. On the twenty-second, in response to a request made by Shakor Khen Rinpoché Nyima Gyaltsen, Rinpoché gave the blessings of the four initiations of the exalted Vajrayoginī of the Nāropa lineage. On the twenty-third, at the request of the monastic communities of Gyütö and Gyümé, he bestowed the permission empowerment of Avalokiteśvara Who Liberates All Beings from the Unfortunate Realms and a long-life initiation to a large monastic and lay gathering. On the following day, Rinpoché was invited to Gyütö, where he gave for several hours a transmission on the Guhyasamāja commentary composed by Jetsun Kunga Döndrup. The transmission was completed on the eighteenth.[164]

On the twenty-fifth Rinpoché was invited to sit at the head of the Gyümé assembly. On the next day he was invited to the Dalhousie Tibetan government school, where he gave novice-monk vows to eighty students. On the twenty-seventh he bestowed novice-nun vows on ten female recipients and the lay vows on five men and women. Rinpoché attended the bimonthly vow purification ceremony held in the school playground with monks and nuns from all traditions. He also recited the *Individual Liberation Sutra* during the ceremony. The labrang made donations to the monastic practitioners.

For this particular time in Dalhousie, Rinpoché had completed his activities for the teachings and sentient beings, and he returned to Dharamsala.

On the seventh of December, in response to a request from Chogyé Trichen Rinpoché, he gave a long-life initiation to this lama and his entourage. Two days later Rinpoché came to see me and told me that he was about to leave for his winter stay in Bodhgaya. He left the next day.

In Bodhgaya, beginning on the fifteenth of December, in order to live a long life for the sake of the Buddha's teachings and sentient beings, each morning Rinpoché undertook one session of a special recitation retreat focused on strengthening, restoring, and lengthening his life using the ritual of life-granting Cittamaṇi White Tārā.

1967

On the sixteenth of February 1967, Rinpoché gave the full-ordination vows, which form the complete basis of practice, to twenty recipients. At the request of the monk Jinpa Gyatso, he gave a long-life initiation to the entire Tibetan monastic and lay community in Bodhgaya. In response to an invitation from Mr. Tsarong, a fourth-rank official, on the twenty-third Rinpoché traveled by car to visit Gayday Iron and Steel Company.[165] He was shown round the area, made prayers, and returned the same day to Bodhgaya.

On the twenty-fifth, Rinpoché was invited to sit at the head of the assembly in the Tibetan monastery for the consecration of newly built statues of Tsongkhapa and his two principal disciples, which had been sponsored by the Trehor Trungsar Labrang of Drepung Loseling. Rinpoché merged the wisdom beings with the *samaya* beings. Two days later, at the request of Sadu Gyurmé, Rinpoché left Bodhgaya by train for Bhopal, where on the third of March he performed the horseback consecration in a paper mill.[166] On the fourth Rinpoché gave the Vajrabhairava initiation, together with a day of ritual preparation, to about fifteen recipients consisting of the family

Ling Rinpoché at the Tibetan Children's Village, Dharamsala

of Sadu Gyurmé and the workers of the paper mill. On the next day he bestowed the permission empowerment of Avalokiteśvara Who Liberates All Beings from the Unfortunate Realms and a long-life initiation on about eighty Tibetans who had just arrived in Bhopal.

On the seventh Rinpoché left for a pilgrimage to the sacred shrine of Sanchi. On the ninth he left Bhopal and arrived back in Dharamsala on the eleventh.

Two days later Rinpoché came to see me and engaged me in meaningful conversation. On the same day the precious throneholder made offerings, as well as donations, in the presence of the central head and the wrathful head of the five-aspect self-arisen statue of Avalokiteśvara that was all but destroyed by the Communist Chinese. He said that I should attend, and I did as he asked.

In keeping with advice given by Nechung, I performed a five-day torma practice for the benefit of the Buddha's teaching and the country using the Phurba[167] practice called Innermost Essence Blade, which was revealed by Tertön Sögyal Lerap Lingpa. During this practice Rinpoché sat at the head of the assembly alongside other great beings from nine in the morning until eight in the evening, where he focused on pacifying forever the negative intentions of those humans and nonhumans who work to harm the teachings and living beings.

On the thirtieth of March, in response to a request from former abbot Gyalrong Jampal Samphel of Drepung Loseling, Rinpoché gave a transmission of Panchen Sönam Drakpa's work on the Guhyasamāja generation and completion stages to about a hundred disciples.

In response to a request made by the former steward of Ratö College Thupten Ngawang and Thupten Topjor, at the beginning of April Rinpoché gave the single-deity Vajrabhairava initiation, together with the preparation day, to about four hundred recipients in the assembly hall of the Dharamsala Tibetan Children's Village. On the seventh Rinpoché gave explicit instructions on the practice known as Recitation of the Neutral Letter *Ha* to an audience that included Chöze Yulgyal of the Sadu family and others, who had pledged to perform daily recitations of the *miktsema*. This Recitation of the Neutral Letter *Ha* was a practice Jé Tsongkhapa had received when he was suffering from back pain from someone well versed in the core practices of the Sakya tradition.

On the nineteenth of April the statue known as the lord of Mangyul Kyirong, or Noble Wati Sangpo,[168] which was one of the "four self-arisen noble ones," was brought to my residence from Nepal. The precious tutor and others were invited, and we made offerings and performed the consecration. (plate 22)

On the twenty-second of May Rinpoché bestowed full-ordination vows on seven monks from Kinnaur. The next day was the full moon day of the *vaiśākha*, or fourth Tibetan month, and the administration offered Rinpoché a long-life ceremony, which he happily accepted.

On the twentieth of July, the monastic community of Buxa Duar offered Rinpoché a long-life ceremony.

On the twenty-second of September, just before I was to leave for Japan, Rinpoché came to see me and gave me some advice. Previously, I had asked Rinpoché for the Guhyasamāja initiation again, and he had replied that he would grant my request after he had completed a semi-strict retreat on this deity. At that time, as previously mentioned, he had almost completed the retreat when war broke out between Pakistan and India, and he had to suspend the meditation. This year in the spring, he again entered a retreat on Guhyasamāja Akṣobhyavajra. Concerned that those who wanted to see him would feel disappointed if they were refused, he set the boundary of his retreat area only as far as his meditation seat. However, apart from the ritual to set outer boundaries of the retreat, Rinpoché performed all the other preliminaries. After his regular morning practices, such as the torma offering, at 6:30 he took tea and breakfast with his retreat assistant, Lati Rinpoché. From around seven, he began the recitations. He performed the seven-limbed preliminary practice and mandala offering in conjunction with the *Hundred Deities of Tuṣita* guruyoga meditation. Using Tsongkhapa's *Foundation of All Good Qualities*, he reviewed the complete path of sutra and tantra. After this he recited the *miktsema* mantra, and with the words "The glorious root guru . . ." he focused on bringing the guru to his heart. Then he began the main practice from the recitation of the lineage of the Guhyasamāja masters. He performed the instantaneous generation of the deity and initiated the protection-wheel practice. He recited the verses beginning "There being no phenomena, there is no meditation . . ." up to "each departs for their individual buddha realm." At all the important visualization processes, such as gathering into the body and taking the three enlightened forms as the path, Rinpoché would pause the recitation of the verses and focus for a long time. On the self-generation alone, Rinpoché would spend about two and a half hours.

Then he began the mantra repetition by counting the beads of his rosary with thumb and finger. He continued in this way until one o'clock, when he paused for lunch. Rinpoché spent five and a half months in this retreat. He made an initial hundred thousand mantras of the main deity, followed by another hundred thousand. He then performed ten thousand of the extensive mantra of Vighnāntaka, ten thousand of each of the attendant deities, and so on, as prescribed in the texts.

On the twenty-third of September, Rinpoché performed a one-tenth fire-offering[169] near Chopra House. This was done over two sessions, and even in the second session Rinpoché recited the entire ritual text. With the Namgyal Monastery chant master performing the count, about twenty thousand offerings were made. After the fire offering was complete, Rinpoché performed a *tsok* ritual with the ritual chanting assistants.

Rinpoché said that previously in Tibet, when he had performed the retreat, he had to hurry it, but this time he had managed a relaxed retreat. In all of Rinpoché's retreats, whenever he had to recite from texts and the power failed or the weather was bad, he was concerned that he was not fulfilling the requirements of the retreat and would not count the mantras of that day as part of the total count. He was very meticulous and honest in his practice.

On the twenty-sixth the regular invocation of the protectors Nechung and Gadong through the use of oracles was performed and advice was sought. I am not certain whether it was this year or at some other time, but Gadong advised Rinpoché to make offerings and prayers to his birth deity. From then on, Rinpoché would regularly recite a newly composed verse of supplication to this deity after the libation offerings.

On the thirtieth Rinpoché left Dharamsala for Pathankot and traveled to Bodhgaya.

On the fifth of October, he began a special long-life retreat of White Tārā. On the twenty-third Rinpoché gave teachings on the practices and visualizations of the *Hundred Deities of Tuṣita* guruyoga from the Sé tradition to Sharlhoi Ama from Kalimpong and about three hundred other devotees. In response to a request from Rigya Tulku, he gave the permission initiation of Amitāyus and Hayagrīva combined to about thirty recipients.

On the seventeenth and eighteenth of December, respectively, Rinpoché fulfilled the hopes of many recipients by bestowing upon them preliminary novice-monk vows and full-ordination vows, which form the basis of all practice.

1968

On the seventh of January 1968, in the assembly hall of the Tibetan monastery in Bodhgaya, Rinpoché gave the initiation of the Three Wrathful Forms Combined to about two hundred ordained and lay recipients at the request of Amdo Jinpa from Darjeeling and others. On the twenty-fourth, in response to a request from Jampa Norbu of Sera Jé Monastery, he gave the blessings of the four initiations of the exalted Vajrayoginī of the Nāropa lineage to about a hundred disciples who had pledged to practice the self-generation daily. On the following day, as requested by a person from Bhutan, Rinpoché gave the White Tārā initiation and the transmission of the praise and prostrations to the twenty-one Tārās to about 350 recipients.

On the twenty-seventh, in response to the persistent request of a husband and wife from Amdo, Rinpoché gave an accessible version of the Amitāyus long-life initiation to about fifteen family members in his residence.

In response to a request from four devotees from Bhutan, he bestowed the lay vows on the first of February. On the seventh Rinpoché traveled to the sacred site where the Buddha practiced austerities for six years, as he had been invited to perform a consecration of a newly built shrine. On the fifteenth Rinpoché gave full-ordination vows to one Bhutanese monk and seven monks from Ladakh.

On the second of March, in response to a request from the Bodhgaya monk Jinpa from Amdo, Rinpoché gave a White Tārā initiation in the assembly hall of the monastery to about 350 recipients.

The Bodhgaya monastery, Ling Labrang, the Mongolian lama Gurudeva, and the Mongolian monk Ngakchö, who lived in America, jointly requested Rinpoché to allow them to offer him a long-life ceremony. Rinpoché agreed. On that day the Mongolian lama offered a mandala and the three representations and requested that as Bodhgaya was the sacred place where the Bhagavan gained the highest enlightenment, would Rinpoché give teachings and a transmission on Tsongkhapa's *Great Stages of the Path to Enlightenment*. Rinpoché replied that he would see when the time was right.

On the eighteenth Rinpoché left Bodhgaya and arrived back in Dharamsala on the twentieth. On the way he stopped to visit Kyabjé Trijang Rinpoché at his residence. They exchanged New Year ceremonial scarves and cordial greetings. Two days later Rinpoché came to see me, and I experienced great joy to see his face, which was so meaningful to behold.

On the thirty-first Rinpoché ordained three nuns and five youths with novice vows.

From childhood I have always had a great interest in Guhyasamāja. I don't know why, but I always felt great joy and great faith for this deity. Later on it seems as if I developed a faith in Guhyasamāja based upon knowledge. Although I had received the initiation once before in Lhasa, a few years previous, I had respectfully requested the precious tutor to grant me the initiation once again. In consideration of my pursuit and special interest in this practice, the precious tutor took on the responsibility and announced that he would undertake a special retreat on Guhyasamāja and then offer me the initiation. As he had completed that retreat the previous year, I went to see him to request again on the first of May. He confirmed a date, and consequently on the eighth and ninth respectively in Chopra House, Rinpoché happily conferred the preparation rituals and the complete initiation on me alone. As his retreat was undertaken purely for my sake, his kindness is beyond compare. From that day onward I performed the regular recitations of the Guhyasamāja and preparatory rituals focusing on the long life and health of the precious tutor.

On the following day Rinpoché ordained two men from the volunteer army force. In response to a request from a monk from Ganden Jangtsé Monastery, Rinpoché gave the permission initiations of Hayagrīva, Vajrapāṇi, and Garuḍa to about 250 ordained and lay recipients on the sixteenth of May. On the thirty-first he gave novice-monk vows to Namgyal the tailor and others, and the celibate lay vows to someone from Gyalthang.

On the second of June, the protector Nechung was invoked. Rinpoché had been invited to Rikon in Switzerland to consecrate a monastery that had just been built there, and Nechung was asked for advice. His reply was that it would be good to go. On the tenth of June, in response to a request from former abbot Gyalrong Jampal Samphel of Drepung Loseling, Rinpoché gave the daylong Mahayana vow to about four hundred devotees. On the next day, at the request of Trehor Losang Namgyal, he gave the permission initiation of Avalokiteśvara Who Liberates All Beings from the Unfortunate Realms and the permission initiation of the general accomplishment of the three buddha families to a large monastic and lay gathering. On the following day Rinpoché gave full-ordination vows to nine novice monks from Ladakh. After that, for the next three days, he gave teachings on the *Hundred Deities of Tuṣita* guruyoga together with the visualizations for increasing wisdom to Tsechokling Tulku and others.

In response to a joint request from monks from Dalhousie belonging to the three monastic seats and monks from Dzongkar Chödé Monastery, on the twenty-first and twenty-second Rinpoché gave the preparation rituals and the actual initiation of Vajrabhairava, thereby definitively creating the seeds of the four enlightened forms and fulfilling completely the hopes of those disciples.

Rinpoché had received in their entirety the lineage teachings and explanation of Tsongkhapa's *Great Stages of the Path to Enlightenment* from the Great Thirteenth Dalai Lama. However, at that time he had been young, and so he thought it important to receive the teachings contained in the lineage coming from Phabongkha Dechen Nyingpo. Therefore, on the twenty-eighth, Rinpoché sent the labrang manager to Kyabjé Trijang Rinpoché, where after offering a mandala and the three representations, he requested him to give the precious tutor transmissions of the *Great Stages of the Path*. Trijang Rinpoché immediately and happily agreed to comply with this request.

On the second of July, the monastic community of Buxa Duar offered me a long-life ceremony, and Rinpoché was invited to be the master of the assembly. Three days later, the same monastic delegation offered a long-life ceremony to Rinpoché at Chopra House. On the sixth of July, Rinpoché came to see me on the birthday for my thirty-fourth year[170] and offered a celebratory offering scarf. On the next day, after the regular monastic vow purification ceremony, Rinpoché spent some time with me and spoke on the various difficult points of sutra and tantra.

On the twenty-ninth, Rinpoché kindly bestowed novice vows on Lochen Tulku of Tashi Lhunpo Monastery and on four women from the Tibetan Children's Village and celibate lay vows on two devotees.

On the first of August, at the Tibetan Children's Village, Rinpoché gave the White Tārā initiation to an audience of about a thousand teachers, staff members, and pupils. He also gave them advice and gave sweets to the

The Dalai Lama with young Tibetan orphans at his first residence
in Dharamsala, Swarg Ashram, 1960

The Thekchen Chöling temple, Dharamsala, in the early 1960s

children. On the second, at the request of Kachen Drukgyal from Spiti, he bestowed the blessings of the four initiations of Vajrayoginī to thirty-two people who had pledged to perform the self-generation daily. On the thirty-first of August, ceremonies were held for moving my residence from Swarg Ashram to a newly purchased piece of land named Kapurthala Thekchen Chöling. A photograph of the five-aspect self-arisen statue of Avalokiteśvara and the statue known as the lord of Mangyul Kyirong, or Noble Wati Sangpo, was escorted with an incense procession to their new residences.

The two tutors and I were invited to the Thekchen Chöling reception rooms, where we initiated the bathing and consecration rituals, performed a special auspicious purification ceremony, and recited the sutra *Perfection of Wisdom in Twenty-Five Thousand Lines*.

On the fourth of September, in the assembly hall, ten monks from the two tantric colleges, including the abbots and chant masters, along with eight monks from Namgyal Dratsang performed the actual consecration ceremony called Causing the Rain of Goodness to Fall using the ritual of Guhyasamāja. The Vajradhara tutor officiated as vajra master for the rite. On the ninth and tenth Rinpoché bestowed on me the preparation rituals and actual initiation of single-deity Vajrabhairava.

29 | First Visit to Europe

SWITZERLAND

IN 1968 a new Tibetan monastery, Chökhor Ling,[171] had been completed in Rikon, Switzerland, and its sponsor Mr. Kuhn, a kitchen utensil manufacturer, had invited Rinpoché to perform the opening ceremonies and the consecration. Rinpoché had decided to go, and he came to see me to say goodbye. We spent some time in pleasant conversation. A few days later Rinpoché's party traveled to Pathankot, and together with Trijang Rinpoché's party, they traveled by train to Delhi. The next morning they arrived at the Old Delhi railway station, where they were met by my elder brother Gyalo Thondup, Tibetan administration officials, and Tibet House officials. Rinpoché spent two nights at Tibet House.

On the twentieth of September,[172] at ten in the evening, the precious tutor, manager Losang Lungrik, and attendant Thupten Tsering, together with Trijang Rinpoché's party, left Delhi by Air France for Paris. From there they flew to Zurich by Swissair. There they were welcomed by many lay and monastic Tibetans and Swiss people. The Tibetan administration representative in Switzerland, Phalha Thupten Öden, the sponsor of the monastery, Mr. Kuhn, the abbot of the monastery, Orgyen Tseten, and others presented ceremonial scarves with an elaborate welcoming ceremony.

They traveled by car to the Rikon monastery and on arrival were afforded a ceremony that was drawn from Tibetan tradition but was adapted to the time and place. Then Rinpoché retired to his rooms. One day the sponsor invited the two tutors for a pleasant cable-car excursion on the slopes of Mount Rigi and treated them to a lunch in a hotel. Afterward they did some sightseeing around the area at the base of the mountain, looking at the island formations in the lake and so on. Then they were taken by car to the Christian monastery of Einsiedeln. There the congregation were in prayer, and the two tutors stayed a short time and made prayers.

The seventh day of the eighth Tibetan month saw the actual opening ceremonies of Chökhor Ling Tibetan monastery. (plates 23 and 25) On that day the two tutors came the short distance from the monastery and were again welcomed by a large gathering of Tibetans and Swiss people holding flags and playing musical instruments. The lamas and monks wore the three monastic robes and amid the procession walked serenely up to the door of the temple. Verses of the auspiciousness of the Three Jewels, beginning "Replete with all perfection, like a golden mountain . . . ," were recited, and the Vajradhara tutor cut the ribbon and opened the door. In the assembly hall the tutors blessed the place and the offering substances and chanted the bathing ritual, the seven-limb prayer, and so on. Rinpoché offered a ceremonial scarf to the main statue of the Buddha and made prayers, followed by Trijang Rinpoché and all the other monks. Later, together with the monks, the two tutors performed the ritual over the written mantras to be placed inside the main statue of the Buddha, and afterward they placed the mantras by hand inside the statue.

The next morning Rinpoché gave a White Tārā long-life initiation to a large lay and monastic audience. In the afternoon, the Swiss office of the Tibetan administration hosted a banquet for the sponsor of the monastery and others. Rinpoché shook hands with all the non-Tibetan guests, as was the Western custom.

During his stay there, Rinpoché, whenever he had free time, would take teachings on the *Great Stages of the Path* from Trijang Rinpoché, as he had requested previously. Whenever Trijang Rinpoché came to give these teachings, Rinpoché would escort him into the house with incense, alongside other measures of respect and devotion, in accordance with practices described in Aśvaghoṣa's *Fifty Verses on the Guru*. Through listening to and studying all the essential points concerning the stages of the path to enlightenment, tutor Ling Rinpoché had eliminated all wrong conceptions and uncertainties related to this topic. Moreover, he had developed both effort-based and effortless experiences and was teaching these to others. Therefore these teachings were for the purposes of receiving the transmission of the teachings. There was no extensive explanation. Nevertheless, Rinpoché made handwritten notes on what he heard.

On the thirteenth of October, Rinpoché was invited by Rakra Tulku, and the administration, teachers, and pupils of Yumbu Lagang, to the Tibetan children's village in the town of Trogen. (plate 24) Consequently, on the twenty-third of October, the two tutors traveled from Rikon by car to the town, where they were welcomed by the children holding flowers, incense, and other offerings. The two tutors showed their delight at this reception with beaming smiles. They were invited into the temple and seated on thrones. There they were served Tibetan tea and sweet rice. Everyone offered ceremonial scarves, which the Rinpochés returned with hand blessings.

On the second day of their visit to the children's village, Rinpoché was invited to the home of Arthur Bill, the director of the village. There both tutors offered ceremonial scarves and gifts to him and thanked him for showing so much kindness and affection to the Tibetan children. On the third day, at the request of Rakra Tulku and Phalha Thupten Öden, Rinpoché gave the permission initiations of the secret and inner accomplishments of Mañjuśrī from the Mañjuśrī literature to a few recipients. On the following day, he gave the permission initiations of Mañjuśrī Arapatsa and Green Tārā taken from the Rinjung Cycle of initiations to the whole school. Afterward Rinpoché was invited to see the classrooms and facilities of the school, in which he took a keen interest.

On the thirtieth, together with Trijang Rinpoché, he visited the village's temple, where they made offerings, prayers, and performed consecrations. After this they returned to the Yumbu Lagang Tibetan children's village for lunch. In the afternoon they returned to the Rikon monastery.

On the fourth of November a gathering of the sixty or so Tibetan children who had been placed in Swiss families were invited together with their foster parents to a party arranged for the tutors. The precious tutor thanked the foster mothers and fathers for showing the Tibetan children the same love and affection they give to their own children. He advised the children not to be lazy in pursuing the education they needed and stressed the importance of not forgetting their own language and of working hard to learn the Dharma and their own culture. The two tutors donated a thousand Swiss francs so that, beginning from the following year, the Tibetan children could come together once a year for the birthday celebrations of the Dalai Lama.

On the following day the two tutors hosted a Tibetan-style banquet. Guests included important officials connected with the Tibetans in Switzerland, such as Mr. Kuhn, the sponsor of the monastery, his staff, the director of the Red Cross, the heads of the Tibetan settlements, and others, as well as the representative and staff of the Swiss office of the Tibetan administration. The tutors thanked the guests for giving assistance to Tibetans and urged them to continue to do so in the future.

On the next day the two tutors and the monks of the Rikon monastery performed a consecration of the site and of the sacred objects in the monastery temple. They used the intermediate consecration ritual, *Sheaves of Auspiciousness*,[173] performed in conjunction with single-deity Vajrabhairava, as the basic ritual, and supplemented it with the ordinary and supreme bathing rituals from the Causing the Rain of Goodness to Fall consecration ceremony. During the ceremony of honoring of the patrons, the tutors presented the sponsor of the monastery and others with elaborate representations of the eight auspicious substances and so on, and all those present were filled with delight.

On the eighth of November, at one o'clock, in response to an invitation from Dagyab Rinpoché, Shakor Khentrul Yeshé Palden, and Ling Yiga Tulku Losang Tenzin, Rinpoché left by car for a three-day visit to the town of Lanquart. There he was invited by the owner of a paper mill where many Tibetans worked to view the factory. Rinpoché presented gifts to the owner and thanked him for giving sympathetic support to the Tibetan people.

On the tenth, Rinpoché returned to the Rikon monastery. In response to a request from Chöphel of Tsāri, Rinpoché gave the permission initiation of the Three Wrathful Forms Combined to about 180 Tibetan and Western devotees. That day was also the religious holiday commemorating the day that the Buddha returned to this world from the celestial realm.[174] Therefore, as requested by the sponsors of the teachings and the people of the Tibetan settlements in Rikon, Rinpoché came to the temple, where with Trijang Rinpoché and resident monks and nuns, they performed the Guru Puja *tsok* ritual.

The following day Rinpoché gave the single-deity Vajrabhairava initiation, together with preparation rituals, to about fifteen recipients, including Geshé Orgyen Tseten and Phalha Thupten Öden. He also gave a donation of 1,800 Swiss francs for the supply of monastic offerings.

On the fifteenth Rinpoché traveled to Ebnat-Kappel at the invitation of the Dzarong household, where he stayed for two days. Then he journeyed by car to Zurich and then by air to Geneva, where he stayed at the home of Mr. Phalha, the Tibetan representative. (plate 27) He was taken to see various United Nations offices, the lake, parks, and so on. My elder brother Losang Samten invited Rinpoché for a meal, and at that time my mother was also staying in Geneva. Therefore she cooked the meal herself and served it to Rinpoché, who enjoyed it. They exchanged old stories of Amdo, Lhasa, and so on.

GERMANY

Rinpoché spent about two weeks in Geneva. Then, at the request of the Mongolian monk Achunor and others of the Mongolian Dharma center in Munich, Germany, on the eighth of December he flew to Munich, where he was welcomed by members of the Mongolian community as well as by tulkus, geshés, and so on who lived in Munich. He was driven by car to the Mongolian monastery, Thekchen Chöphel Ling. Two days later he gave a talk to about thirty people, mostly Mongolians, on how to hold the Buddha as the teacher of refuge, the Dharma as the actual refuge, and the Sangha as companions who help in the accomplishment of that refuge. He also consecrated the representations of the enlightened body, speech, and mind in the temple at the request of the sponsors.

In response to a request from Dagyab Rinpoché, at half past twelve on the afternoon of the twelfth, Rinpoché flew to Bonn, then the capital of Germany, with Phalha, the Tibetan administration representative. There he was welcomed by Dagyab Rinpoché and the Phukhang Khentrul of Ganden Shartsé. He was taken by car to the guesthouse of the Christian St. Augustine Monastery, where arrangements had been made for him to stay. The next day Rinpoché was invited to the Central Asian Cultural Studies Department of Bonn University, where he took a keen interest in the Tibetan Cultural Research section. Rinpoché was invited to a lunch hosted by the department and attended by the director and the staff. Afterward, he stayed a short while at Dagyab Rinpoché's house.

Later on he was invited for afternoon tea by Professor Schöllerman, curator of the Cultural Studies Department. Rinpoché gave him words of encouragement for his efforts in taking care of the Tibetan artifacts he had collected. (plate 26)

ENGLAND

At 3:35 the next afternoon, Rinpoché flew to London. He was welcomed at the airport with ceremonial scarves by the staff of the UK Tibet Society, the former administration official Ngawang who was now a housefather at the Pestalozzi children's village, the Buddhist teacher Geshé Tsultrim Gyaltsen, and others. Rinpoché was driven to the Trisong Ngönga children's village in Sussex, where the children turned out to welcome him with offering scarves and flowers. On the twenty-second Rinpoché gave the permission initiation of White Mañjuśrī, the transmission of the *Guru Puja* and the *Hundred Deities of Tuṣita* guruyoga, together with words of advice to Geshé Tsultrim Gyaltsen, the head of the Tibetan school, and to the pupils themselves.

In response to the insistence from the teachers and the pupils to be allowed to offer Rinpoché a long-life ceremony, on January 5, 1969, Rinpoché acceded to their requests and fulfilled their wishes. On the same day Tibetan students who were living in Sweden came specially to attend the ceremony, and with the nectar of his words he satisfied their minds.

FRANCE

Dakpo Bamchö Tulku and others had repeatedly suggested that now Rinpoché was in the West, it was very important that he have a full medical checkup. In response Rinpoché asked Kyabjé Trijang Rinpoché to perform a divination to determine whether France or Switzerland would provide the more suitable treatment. The result came out for France. Therefore, Rinpoché flew on the sixth to Paris, where he was welcomed by Dakpo Bamchö Tulku and others. Yvonne Laurence, a French national, took Rinpoché in her own car. However, she took a wrong turn on the way from the airport. Normally the journey from the airport to Dakpo Tulku's house takes no more than twenty minutes, but on that day Rinpoché took more than two hours to arrive, and those waiting for him at the house said that they were becoming increasingly concerned. Yvonne said that just seeing Rinpoché's face she was lost in joy and just wanted to follow his every word. Later she became a nun, receiving the name Thupten Drölkar.

On the eleventh of January, Rinpoché was invited to a Tibetan children's village in Blenau, where he was welcomed by the children in Tibetan fashion. This home for Tibetan children was set up and supported by the French department of education. (plate 30) It housed twenty children, and Norgyé and his wife had been specially sent from Dharamsala to be the houseparents. The next day Rinpoché gave to an audience of mostly Tibetans a transmission of the refuge prayer, the *Hundred Deities of Tuṣita* guruyoga, the *miktsema* mantra, and so on, together with advice on how to accomplish both the temporary and ultimate aims of life. Afterward the children put on a show of singing and dancing to the delight of Rinpoché.

On the sixteenth, Rinpoché returned to the home of Dakpo Bamchö Tulku, where he went to the American Hospital of Paris for treatment. Previously, Chinese doctors had diagnosed that the precious tutor suffered from thyroid problems, and Dakpo Bamchö Tulku translated this information to the doctor. Rinpoché was examined with the help of X-rays, and it was discovered that a goiter in his neck was hindering the proper operation of the thyroid gland. Therefore the goiter had to be treated. Radioactive iodine therapy or an operation was recommended. Because of Rinpoché's age, it was suggested that the iodine therapy would be better. Also, Rinpoché had to attend three other clinics to undergo further tests.

On the twentieth Rinpoché attended a liver clinic, and two blood samples were taken for analysis. On the twenty-second he attended a clinic specializing in goiters, where X-rays and blood samples were taken. He was told he would have to attend again, and so on the following day he came to the same clinic for two further X-rays and another blood sample. Rinpoché returned to the hospital to receive the results of the tests made at the clinics, and the original diagnosis of the doctor was confirmed. Consequently, Rinpoché had to attend the goiter clinic for five afternoons to receive injections and occasionally to be given oral medicine. On the thirtieth he again attended the clinic for an X-ray at ten in the morning and another at four in the afternoon. On the thirtieth, at eleven o'clock, he undertook one long and one short scan and was given a blood test.

Beginning on the third of February, Rinpoché took three tablets every day with lunch.

Rinpoché suffered from a chronic knee problem, and on the sixth he attended an arthritis clinic, where his hands and legs were X-rayed and blood samples taken. The knee ailment was a result of being overweight, and Rinpoché was advised to avoid flour, potatoes, and butter.

The seventeenth of February was the first day of the Tibetan earth-bird year, and Dakpo Bamchö Rinpoché, the labrang manager, and others offered Rinpoché a ceremonial scarf, the three representations, tsampa, sweet rice, Tibetan tea, and so on, in keeping with Tibetan tradition. Later, on the fifteenth of the first Tibetan month, at the request of Dakpo Bamchö Rinpoché, Rinpoché began a transmission of the two great works on the stages of the paths of sutra and tantra by the Dharma master of the three realms, Jé Tsongkhapa, by reading a couple of pages from each.

On the nineteenth Rinpoché attended the goiter clinic, where he was given radioactive iodine. On the twentieth the clinic gave Rinpoché a small bottle of the same medicine and was told that the ailment should clear up in about five or six months, and if it did not, Rinpoché was to return to the clinic.

Rinpoché rested until the ninth of March, as advised by the doctors. After only fifteen days of taking the medicine his appetite improved greatly. Previously, he had not been able to eat much. Also, when he walked uphill or upstairs, he would get out of breath. These too improved.

During his stay in Paris, Rinpoché enjoyed being taken to museums and public parks with gardens. (plates 28 and 29) Whenever Westerners he had not met before came to see him, he would always stand up and shake hands. Those who had faith in Buddhism he would satisfy with advice on Dharma, and others he delighted by engaging them in conversation they found agreeable.

After finishing his daily meditation practice, he would mainly read scriptures. Sometimes he would go for a walk. He always had a happy, relaxed disposition and never displayed any anxiety.

When Kyabjé Trijang Rinpoché came from London to Dakpo Bamchö Rinpoché's house in Paris, the two tutors met, and they talked about Rinpoché's medical treatment and recent events. They also decided on the time to return to India. On Mongolian New Year, the Mongolian community in Paris invited the two tutors to a grand restaurant. Rinpoché advised the elder Mongolians to recite the *maṇi* mantra and the younger to place their faith in the Dharma and to preserve the good traditions of their forefathers.

On the tenth of March 1969, at the invitation of Phalha Öden, the Tibetan representative in Switzerland, Rinpoché and his two attendants flew to Geneva. At the airport he was welcomed with ceremonial scarves presented by Phalha Öden and the staff of the Tibet Office. He was driven to the Tibet Office, where arrangements had been made for his stay. During his stay he was sometimes taken by Phalha into the city for sightseeing. On the thirty-first Rinpoché returned to the Paris clinic, where he was examined by the doctors.

30 | Return to India

URING HIS STAY in Europe, Rinpoché had carried out his religious duties as well as completing a course of medical treatment, and at nine in the evening of the seventh of April 1969, he flew from Paris to India with Trijang Rinpoché and attendants. The next morning, about ten hours later, he arrived at the Delhi airport. He was welcomed by the staff of the Delhi Tibet Office and Tibet House, Bakula Rinpoché from Ladakh, Nyakré Khentrul, and others. They were taken to Tibet House, where arrangements had been made for their stay.

On the eleventh Rinpoché returned to Dharamsala. On the thirteenth at ten in the morning, he visited me and presented me with a ceremonial scarf, the three representations, and gifts. He then proceeded to tell me of his activities in the West, which clearly had brought great benefit to living beings and the Buddha's teaching, and about his medical treatment and how much it had benefitted him. This brought my joy to fulfillment.

On the twenty-second of May, Nechung and Gadong were invoked. Gratitude was expressed for the success of Rinpoché's medical treatment in the West, his activities, and so on. Their assistance was sought for the successful accomplishment of Rinpoché's work for the Buddha's teaching and sentient beings in the future, in keeping with his wishes.

For three days beginning on the twenty-fifth, the first conference for the Association for the Preservation of the Geluk Tradition was held in the reception rooms of Rinpoché's residence. It was attended by the abbots of the three monastic seats and the two tantric colleges, the Tibetan People's Deputies, Samdhong Tulku, and others. It opened with the Vajradhara tutor giving a speech followed by a speech from Trijang Rinpoché. Discussions focused on what important practices should be implemented, and conference resolutions on proposals were issued. Throughout the three days, Ling Labrang offered tea and food to the delegates.

Conference of the Association for the Preservation of the Geluk Tradition
at Chopra House, 1969

After the conference, at the request of the nun Tenzin Sangmo from the
Tibetan Children's Village, Rinpoché gave the single-deity Vajrabhairava
initiation, together with a day of preparation, to about eighty recipients.

On the eleventh of June, Rinpoché bestowed novice-monk vows on
seven youths. On the thirteenth he gave teachings on the sixty-four-part
torma-offering ritual to about sixty monks from Gyütö. On the following
day he gave the permission initiation of the Vajrabhairava mantra formulation to twenty-eight monks from Gyümé. On the fifteenth the monks of
the two tantric colleges offered Rinpoché a long-life ceremony, which he
accepted. On the nineteenth the monastic community of Buxa Duar and
about 180 monks offered Rinpoché a long-life ceremony. He accepted and
returned the offerings to the monks.

I was soon to give teachings on Tsongkhapa's *Great Exposition of Secret
Mantra*. Therefore, on the twenty-second at ten in the morning, I invited
the precious tutor and requested him to explain some of the more difficult
points of the text. In doing so he untied whatever knots of doubts I had.

After this he gave teachings on the sixty-four-part torma-offering ritual to four monks from Sera Mé Monastery.

On the sixth of July Rinpoché came to the ceremonies for the birthday of my thirty-fifth year. He presented me with a ceremonial scarf and the three representations, and we spent the time in conversation. On the thirteenth the monks and abbots of the two tantric colleges in Dharamsala and of Namgyal Monastery, as well as others, took part in three days of rituals for the Buddha's teaching and the temporal well-being of the Tibetan people, sponsored by the Tibetan administration. Rinpoché acted as vajra master in the assembly.

On the twenty-fourth, Lochö from the labrang sponsored a long-life ceremony for Rinpoché by way of the Guru Puja *tsok* ritual. On the twenty-eighth, Rinpoché bestowed the complete lay vows, consisting of the four root vows and the vow to abstain from alcohol, to the lady Nyinglak from Gangtok and one other member of her family.

On the fourth of August, at the request of Serkong Rinpoché, Rinpoché gave teachings on the Vajrabhairava protector offering ritual to eight monks. From the seventh of August onward, again at the request of Serkong Rinpoché, he gave one session each day of teachings and a transmission of Khedrup Jé's work on the Guhyasamāja generation stage, *Ocean of Attainments*, and from the fourteenth to the twenty-third similar teachings on Tsongkhapa's work on the Guhyasamāja completion stage, *Lamp to Illuminate the Five Stages*. These he gave to Serkong Rinpoché, Dakpo Bamchö Tulku, and others. On the last day a Guhyasamāja *tsok* ritual together with the guru-offering ceremony was performed.

On the twenty-first, the private secretary of the Tibetan administration visited Rinpoché and requested Rinpoché to undertake a longevity meditation practice so that I might live a long life. With great kindness Rinpoché accepted.

The precious tutor had received transmissions and teachings on Tsongkhapa's *Great Stages of the Path to Enlightenment* from the Great Thirteenth Dalai Lama. Therefore I thought it would be good to receive this lineage, and I requested it from Rinpoché. Consequently, for thirteen days from the first of September, he gave me detailed teachings on this work. On the twenty-second, at the request of the wife of the former acting prime minister Dekharwa, Rinpoché gave a White Tārā long-life initiation to about fifty monastic and lay recipients. On the thirtieth, Rinpoché was visited by the Religious Affairs minister, who requested Rinpoché to undertake a longevity meditation practice for my long life. This he joyfully accepted.

The newly constructed Thekchen Chöling temple hosted three main statues: a gilded Śākyamuni Buddha, a thousand-armed, thousand-eyed Avalokiteśvara made of silver, and a gilded Guru Rinpoché in the form of "he who subjugates all that appears and exists."[175] On the tenth of November at nine in the morning, Rinpoché accompanied me in the temple for the ritual of preparing the mantras to be placed inside the statues.

Rinpoché planned to spend the winter in Bodhgaya, and at two o'clock that day he left my residence, and he arrived in Bodhgaya Tibetan monastery on the twelfth. On the seventeenth in response to a request from a Mongolian lama, Rinpoché began a teaching on the *Great Stages of the Path* to about eight hundred disciples, including assistant tutor Serkong Rinpoché and other lamas, tulkus, and geshés. Three times Rinpoché recited from the beginning of the text from memory up to the passage ending "and so his [Atiśa's] fame spread everywhere. This the great translator Drolungpa has said." After this, Serkong Rinpoché repeated the recitation once from memory. Then Rinpoché recited the verses beginning "This human life of opportunity is more precious than a wish-granting jewel." In this way the preliminaries were followed in great detail. Then Rinpoché began the actual transmission and teachings.

The next day Rinpoché began giving a session in the morning and afternoon, with a break once a week. On the twentieth of November, the twelfth of December, and the thirteenth of December, Drepung Loseling Monastery, the Ganden Monastery governing body, and the Chatreng Chözé,[176] respectively, made offerings to the assembly and offered a long-life ceremony to Rinpoché. Also, at the request of a monk, Rinpoché gave during the teachings a transmission of Dakpo Losang Jinpa's *Review Meditation on the Stages of the Path*.

1970

At the request of Chatreng Losang Gyaltsen, on the seventh of January 1970, early in the morning when the lines on the hand are still not visible, Rinpoché gave the daylong Mahayana vows to all those taking the *Great*

Stages of the Path teachings in the monastery assembly hall. On the next day, following my instructions, the private office offered a long-life ceremony to the great Vajradhara tutor, which he graciously accepted. On the tenth the teachings were concluded and were followed by the bodhicitta ceremony. On the eleventh, in response to a request by the sponsors of the teaching, Rinpoché gave a White Tārā long-life initiation to around a thousand people and, as requested by Tsarong Achen, a permission initiation of Avalokiteśvara Who Liberates All Beings from the Unfortunate Realms. On the next day he gave novice-monk vows to eight recipients. On the twenty-seventh Rinpoché gave the permission initiation of the Three Wrathful Forms Combined and a long-life initiation to Rigya Tulku, the abbot of Tawang Monastery in Arunachal Pradesh.

The seventh of February was the first day of the iron-dog year. As part of the New Year celebrations, Kyabjé Rinpoché was invited to sit as the master of the Bodhgaya monastery assembly. Tea, sweet rice, and so on were offered. Tenzin Gyaltsen Khunu Lama Rinpoché, supreme teacher and bearer of the banner of much learning, as well as the many monks of the monastery offered Rinpoché the three representations and ceremonial scarves. This was followed by Tibetan pilgrims in Bodhgaya seeking an audience with Rinpoché.

Beginning on the sixth, as part of the Great Prayer Festival, Rinpoché taught from Āryaśūra's *Garland of the Buddha's Birth Stories* and attended the dry assembly session,[177] as was customary. On the twenty-sixth, the Bodhgaya monastery and the labrang jointly offered Rinpoché a long-life ceremony. On the twenty-first Rinpoché gave lay vows to Yvonne from France.

On the sixth Rinpoché left Bodhgaya and returned to Dharamsala. On the way up to Chopra House, he stopped at Trijang Rinpoché's residence in Gangchen Kyishong. They exchanged New Year greetings with ceremonial scarves and talked about recent events. On the ninth at two o'clock, Rinpoché came to see me. He told me about his teaching of the *Great Stages of the Path* in Bodhgaya and presented me with the three representations and a ceremonial scarf as auspicious greetings for the new year.

Eight days later Rinpoché conferred novice-monk vows on thirty-four aspirants, novice nun vows on nine girls, and full-ordination vows on fifty-two monks from the three monastic seats.

On the twenty-fifth, after I had given the Kālacakra initiation in the Thekchen Chöling temple, Rinpoché gave the permission initiation of

Avalokiteśvara Who Liberates All Beings from the Unfortunate Realms, at the request of the merchant Thupten and Jinpa Gyatso from Amdo. Tibetans from the three provinces of Tibet who were living in Gangtok offered me a long-life ceremony, and Rinpoché was invited to sit at the head of the assembly as vajra master. The next day representatives from the Gangtok delegation visited Rinpoché at the labrang and asked that he place his lotus feet for a long time on this earth for the sake of the teachings and living beings. Rinpoché replied that he would pray to the Three Jewels for that to happen.

On the seventeenth of April, Rinpoché gave novice-monk vows to eighteen aspirants. On the twenty-second, the former manager of Gyütö and others invited Rinpoché along with Trijang Rinpoché to the Nyungné temple[178] and offered them a long-life ceremony, which they graciously accepted.

In the same temple on the first of May, at the request of Kundor Tulku from Chamdo, Rinpoché gave the preparation rituals for the initiation of single-deity Vajrabhairava to about 380 lay and monastic recipients, who had promised to recite the self-generation sādhana daily. On the following day he bestowed the actual initiation.

On the seventh, representatives of the three provinces of Tibet came to see Rinpoché and requested him to perform a longevity meditation practice for my long life, which he joyfully agreed to do. The twenty-first of May was the full-moon day of *vaiśākha*, the fourth month, and in response to a request from several nuns from Mount Michung Nunnery, Rinpoché conferred the daylong Mahayana vows to about five hundred people in the Nyungné temple.

From the fifteenth of May, Rinpoché kindly began giving me teachings on the *Cakrasaṃvara Root Tantra* combined with Tsongkhapa's *Elucidation of All Hidden Points* commentary. He completed these teachings on the twenty-fifth. Serkong Rinpoché, the abbot of Namgyal Monastery, Lati Rinpoché, and Geshé Rapten also attended these teachings. Sometimes the precious tutor would ask questions to those around him to settle doubts about critical points. The Namgyal abbot was someone who could both respond to the questions as well as also put questions in return. He later remarked, "The precious tutor would engage in debate like those young monks undergoing philosophical training at the monasteries these days. This was extraordinary!"

On the eleventh of June, Rinpoché came to Gangchen Kyishong at the

Ceremonial prayers for laying the foundation stone of the Library of Tibetan Works and Archives, Dharamsala, 1970. Ling Rinpoché is on the throne on the left.

site where the new library was to be built. A special vow purification ceremony was performed, and in the presence of fully ordained monks whose minds were restrained by the training in ethics, I recited from the *Individual Liberation Sutra* as a ground-purifying ritual.

On the fourth of July, just before he returned to France, Dakpo Bamchö Tulku came to visit Rinpoché and beseeched him to live a long life. On the next day the Gadong and Nechung oracles were invoked and asked for advice. The following day was the birthday for my thirty-sixth year, and as always, at eleven o'clock Rinpoché presented me with a ceremonial scarf. Afterward, with the great Vajradhara, Kyabjé Trijang Rinpoché, and my mother, we had lunch.

On the sixth of August Rinpoché bestowed vows upon nine novice monks and one layman.

The lineage of the Abhisambodhi Vairocana initiation, the principal deity of the performance tantra class, is very rare. Therefore I fervently requested Rinpoché to undertake the retreat of this deity and to confer on me the initiation. Consequently, with Chamdo geshé Gelek Losang as recitation assistant, Rinpoché entered into a retreat on this deity.

Rinpoché completed the retreat on the thirteenth of September and performed the supplementary fire offering.

Beginning the nineteenth Rinpoché gave teachings on the Vajrabhairava great-approach retreat to four monks of both Dharamsala tantric colleges who were in retreat and to Lati Rinpoché.

On the fifteenth of October, at half past twelve, Rinpoché came to see me on my request in order to remove some doubts I had on a discourse I was about to give. He gave answers that completely dispelled all doubts.

In response to a request from Barshi Phuntsok Wangyal and others, Rinpoché gave the White Tārā long-life initiation in his residence on the fourteenth of October. On the twenty-seventh, at the request of Amdo Jikmé, he gave the permission initiation of the Three Wrathful Forms Combined, thereby fulfilling the spiritual aspirations of the disciples.

Around that time the minister for home affairs visited Rinpoché and requested him to undertake a longevity meditation practice for my long life.

On the ninth of November, in the upper chapel of the Thekchen Chöling temple, Rinpoché bestowed on me the preparatory rituals for initiation of Abhisambodhi Vairocana, and on the following day he conferred the actual initiation. At five o'clock, after the teachings, he very kindly engaged with me in conversation on vast and profound topics of the Dharma. Others at the initiation included Kyabjé Trijang Rinpoché, the abbot and senior monks of Namgyal Monastery, and about fifty other monks. Beginning on the seventeenth, Rinpoché gave me detailed teachings on the generation and completion stages of Vajrabhairava, based on the lineage of these teachings he had received from the Mongolian Palden Sangpo.

On the twenty-seventh Rinpoché left Dharamsala for his winter stay in Bodhgaya.

On the fifth of December, in the assembly hall of the Bodhgaya monastery, Ling Labrang sponsored a long-life ceremony by way of a Guru Puja *tsok* ritual for Vajradhara Kyabjé Trijang Rinpoché. Rinpoché offered the eight auspicious substances and other longevity supports for him to remain for a long time on earth. On the next day and for the following eleven days, Rinpoché gave one session of teachings and a transmission of Tsongkhapa's *Great Exposition of Secret Mantra* to Trijang Rinpoché alone. On the twelfth the labrang prepared a vast thousand-offering ceremony in front of the sacred shrine, and for living beings in general and in particular for Tibetans in exile or in Tibet, whether living or passed away, Rinpoché brought about a rain of prayers based upon the unfailing truth of the Three Jewels, who embody the greatest virtue and happiness now and at all times.

Sometime later, Kyabjé Trijang Rinpoché performed a vast thousand butter-lamp offering in front of the sacred shrine, and Rinpoché was invited to sit at the head of the assembly. On the fifteenth of December, with the intention to undertake the retreat again, Rinpoché received from Kyabjé Trijang Rinpoché the preparation rituals and the actual initiation of single-deity Vajrabhairava in the Kangyur temple of the Bodhgaya monastery. On the following day he received the initiation of thirteen-deity Vajrabhairava. Later when he was doing the retreat of these two deities, Rinpoché added a verse to the guru-lineage supplication prayer. This was a name-interwoven praise[179] to Trijang Rinpoché and came just after the name of Kyabjé Phabongkha Dechen Nyingpo, from whom he had first received the initiations. This is clear from his handwritten notes.

On the seventeenth of December, Trijang Rinpoché invited Rinpoché to the assembly hall of the monastery, and together with the assembly monks, he made prayers for Rinpoché to plant his feet firmly until the end of samsara by way of a Guru Puja *tsok* ritual. He also sponsored the offering of the eight auspicious substances and other tokens of longevity. Rinpoché requested Trijang Rinpoché to give teachings and a transmission of the *Hundred Deities of Tuṣita* guruyoga and Tsongkhapa's *Foundation of All Good Qualities* to the monks of the Bodhgaya monastery so that they might establish a Dharma connection with him. Consequently, Trijang Rinpoché complied with the request on the eighteenth of December in the assembly hall.

Bakula Rinpoché of Ladakh had previously requested Rinpoché to attend the ceremonies of the offerings of the twenty-fifth at Ladakh Vihara in Delhi. Therefore, on the twenty-first, Rinpoché left Bodhgaya for Delhi, where he stayed at Tibet House. On the twenty-fifth, at Ladakh Vihara, Rinpoché gave a talk and an account of the deeds of Jé Tsongkhapa and sat at the head of the assembly during the offering ceremony. The next day he returned to Bodhgaya.

1971

On the second of January 1971, the Chögyal of Sikkim came to visit Rinpoché. The Chögyal told Rinpoché that this year was his obstacle year and requested Rinpoché to make prayers for the rest of his life to be fruitful. In response to a request from Jampa Söpa from Nepal, Rinpoché gave the single-deity Vajrabhairava initiation and teachings on the generation and completion stages to about three hundred lay and monastic devotees beginning on the seventh of January and lasting until the twentieth. On the twenty-second he gave a long-life initiation to about seven hundred people in response to a request from the businessman Rapten from Trehor. Three days later Rinpoché ordained fifteen novice monks.

On the sixth of February, Rinpoché was invited by the Tibetan Bodhgaya monastery to visit the place where the Buddha undertook six years of ascetic practices. On the tenth he gave the daylong Mahayana vows to about three hundred people. Three days later, at the request of Chamdo Gyara Tulku, Rinpoché gave a transmission and a teaching on the *Hundred Deities of Tuṣita* guruyoga.

The twenty-sixth of February was the first day of the iron-pig year. On that morning Rinpoché was requested to sit at the head of the assembly of the Tibetan monastery. The labrang and the monks offered him tea, sweet rice, and the three representations. Many lay and monastic Tibetans in Bodhgaya at that time came for an audience, and Rinpoché gave them hand blessings and protection cords.

On the fourth of March, the labrang and the Bodhgaya monastery jointly offered Rinpoché a long-life ceremony in conjunction with a Guru Puja *tsok* ritual. Rinpoché attended the prayer festival sessions as was customary.

On the twenty-fifth, Rinpoché left Bodhgaya and arrived in Dharamsala on the twenty-seventh. On the way to his residence, he visited Kyabjé Trijang Rinpoché. The two tutors exchanged New Year ceremonial scarves and spent some time in each other's company. On the next day Rinpoché visited me and told me of his activities in Bodhgaya, which were of great benefit in developing and preserving the teachings.

As a way of gathering a store of merit, I planned to offer this supreme master an extensive meal every ninth, nineteenth, and twenty-ninth of each Tibetan month for a period of three years and three fortnights. Therefore, on the fourteenth of April, I offered Rinpoché money for this, which he graciously accepted. This year was my thirty-seventh year, which is considered an obstacle year. Therefore the Association for the Preservation of the Geluk Tradition sponsored a three-day ritual for long life using Amitāyus of the Niguma tradition, attended by the whole Namgyal Monastery assembly. On the twenty-eighth, a Niguma long-life ritual together with a Guru Puja *tsok* ritual was performed, and the precious tutor sat at the head of the assembly. Assistant tutor Serkong Rinpoché gave the mandala discourse, offered the eight auspicious substances, and so on. The tutor Kyabjé Trijang Rinpoché offered me a mandala and the three representations as well as commencing the recitations. These were very auspicious events.

On the third of May, the Association for the Preservation of the Geluk Tradition brought the two tutors together and offered them a long-life ceremony by way of the Guru Puja *tsok* ritual, which they both happily accepted. The seventeenth of May was the eleventh commemoration of the opening of the Tibetan Children's Village in Dharamsala. After the ceremonies for the opening of the infant home and home number 8, Rinpoché and I spent the day in the marquee discussing Dharma.

On the twenty-seventh Rinpoché conferred a long-life initiation on Dorjé from Kalimpong and fourteen others.

On the first of June, he conferred the daylong Mahayana vows on many people at the request of Dolep Tulku from Mön in Arunachal Pradesh. On the following day, the Assembly of the Tibetan People's Deputies requested Rinpoché to undertake a longevity meditation practice for my long life, which he accepted with great delight.

Two days later the precious Sakya Trizin came to Chopra House to visit the great Vajradhara. Rinpoché welcomed him with great respect, and they spent the time engaged in Dharma discussions.

On the sixth of July, I reached my thirty-seventh year of this life, and as commemoration, Rinpoché arrived with Trijang Rinpoché at twelve o'clock. They presented me with ceremonial scarves and delighted me with their Dharma conversations. On the nineteenth the annual ritual of invocation of the protectors Nechung and Gadong through oracles was performed.

Every other day from the thirty-first of July to the twenty-sixth of August, Rinpoché gave me various transmissions, which included the works of Ra Lotsāwa, various charms associated with Vajrabhairava, and the root text of the sixty-four-part torma ritual from the Shalu tradition. Assistant tutor Serkong Rinpoché was also present at these transmissions. Afterward, Rinpoché entered a single-deity Vajrabhairava retreat. On the fifteenth of August he performed the supplementary fire offering.

I had requested Rinpoché to grant the glorious Guhyasamāja initiation by way of the sand mandala. Consequently, on the twentieth of September, Rinpoché came to the Thekchen Chöling temple in the morning to perform the site rituals. At noon I invited him to lunch. On the twenty-third, before an audience comprised of myself and about four hundred monks, including those from the two tantric colleges, as well as about forty laypeople, including two young Americans, Rinpoché gave the preparatory rituals. On the next day he conferred the vase initiation, and the following day the higher initiations, which consisted of the secret initiation, the wisdom initiation, and the word initiation. The initiation concluded with a thanksgiving *tsok* ritual.

The accompanying explanation of the initiation was so extensive that although each session began at one in the afternoon, it would last until about half past eight in the evening. At nine in the morning on the final day of the teachings, the entire congregation offered Rinpoché a long-life ceremony together with a thanksgiving *tsok* ritual. This was followed by the Guhyasamāja prayers and dedication, the prayer for the flourishing of the Geluk teachings, and many other prayers.

On the sixth of October, the two tutors increased the length of my life with a long-life ceremony. On the next day Kyabjé Trijang Rinpoché came to Ling Labrang and engaged in general conversation with Rinpoché for some time.

For a few days beginning on the fourteenth, Rinpoché gave instructions on how to perform a single-deity Vajrabhairava great-approach retreat to five people, including the abbot of Nārkaṇṭa Monastery in Simla. On the twenty-third and twenty-fourth of October, in response to my request, Rinpoché bestowed the preparatory rituals and actual initiation of single-deity Vajrabhairava on about six hundred monastic and lay recipients in the Thekchen Chöling temple. This planted without doubt the seeds of the four buddha bodies of enlightenment. Two days later in the Nyungné temple, Rinpoché sat at the head of the assembly of the Gyütö monks to perform a consecration.

Rinpoché was soon to be leaving for Bodhgaya, and so at eleven o'clock on the thirty-first of October, I invited him to come to visit me. For four and a half hours he conversed on many difficult points of sutra and tantra, thereby fulfilling all my hopes.

On the fourth of November, Rinpoché arrived in Bodhgaya and rested a few days. In response to a longstanding request by Dagyab Rinpoché, Rinpoché gave teachings and transmission of one session each day of Tsongkhapa's *Great Exposition of Secret Mantra* to Dagyab Rinpoché as sponsor and to Trehor Sikgyap Tulku of Tashi Lhunpo Monastery from the twenty-sixth of November to the fifth of December.

After these teachings had concluded, Rinpoché gave novice-monk vows to nine devotees and full-ordination vows to eight novice monks. On the seventeenth he bestowed lay vows on a Tibetan man and woman from the

Bhutanese settlement. On the twenty-fifth the ex-abbot of Gyümé, Geshé Orgyen Tseten, visited Rinpoché to ask questions on certain matters of practice. Rinpoché was able to clear up his doubts.

1972

On the morning of the sixth of January 1972, in the temple of the sacred Bodhgaya shrine, Rinpoché with great delight gave me the transmission and teaching on the Seventh Dalai Lama's *Guide to the View: A Song of the Four Recollections.* January 10 was the twenty-fifth of the eleventh month, and as was the wish of Guru Vajradhara, I came to the assembly hall of the Bodhgaya monastery to preside over the assembly. As I sat on the throne, the supreme guru first offered the mandala and the three representations with prostrations and then performed an extensive *tsok* ritual beginning from the line "In the vast space of emptiness and bliss united . . ." Thus I partook in the great feast enriched by the six types of fulfillment.[180]

From the thirteenth to the twenty-fourth, Rinpoché gave teachings in his rooms to Trulshik Rinpoché and his entourage. On the seventeenth, when I was sitting as head of the assembly, Rinpoché attended the assembly in keeping with the wishes of Trulshik Rinpoché. On the twenty-fifth Rinpoché made a pilgrimage by car to Vultures' Peak, where the Blessed Buddha taught the Perfection of Wisdom sutras, and to the site of Nālandā Monastery, the source of many a great being who gained the rank of learned practitioner, such as the glorious guide Nāgārjuna, renowned as being like a second Buddha.

On the thirtieth, in response to the great spiritual friend Rikzin Tenpa, Rinpoché attended an auspicious vow-purification ceremony with the other monks.

The fifteenth of February was the water-bird new year. As was customary, Rinpoché performed the first-day commemorations in the assembly hall of the Bodhgaya Monastery, and from the nineteenth he sat as head of the prayer festival. On the twentieth, Rinpoché bestowed the permission initiation of the Three Wrathful Forms Combined on about fifteen recipients, including the queen of the third king of Bhutan. (plate 31)

On the fourth of March, Rinpoché left Bodhgaya, arriving on the morning of the sixth in Dharamsala, where he first went to pay his New Year greetings to Kyabjé Trijang Rinpoché. On the following day he visited me and told me in great detail of his stay in Bodhgaya. At eleven o'clock on the twenty-first, I invited Rinpoché to visit so that I could ask for advice on teachings I was shortly to give. On the twentieth, in the Thekchen Chöling temple, Rinpoché gave the permission initiation of Three Wrathful Forms Combined to about thirty-five hundred monastic and lay recipients. On the following day he gave a transmission and teaching on the *Seven-Chapter Vajrabhairava Root Tantra* using the annotated explanations known as the *Precious Garland of the Oral Transmission* to about four hundred monks.

In response to a request made by the monks of the two tantric colleges, who are the supreme community of vajra-holding tantric practitioners possessing all three vows, Rinpoché gave several teachings, including explanations of the Vajrabhairava generation and completion stages, to about 150 monks in the labrang from the sixth of April to the twenty-fifth. The Tibetan Religious Affairs Office made donations to the assembled recipients of the teachings, and Rinpoché gave a talk on the importance of ensuring the development and flourishing of all religious traditions of Tibet regardless of their sectarian affiliations.

On the morning of the twenty-second, the two tantric colleges jointly offered a long-life ceremony to Rinpoché, which he happily accepted. On the following day, toward the end of the teachings, Rinpoché gave profound and extensive advice stressing how important it was for the two tantric colleges to follow the example of the great tantric practitioners of the past and to engage in the study, contemplation, and meditation on the meditation deities of Guhyasamāja, Cakrasaṃvara, and Vajrabhairava equally and without partiality. When the American monk Ngawang Chödrak sponsored a thousand butter-lamp offering performed by the Namgyal Monastery monks, Rinpoché attended the assembly and made prayers that the sponsor and all those connected with him be able in all future lives to devote themselves to making offerings to the Three Jewels and so on.

On the twenty-first, Rinpoché accompanied me to the Thekchen Chöling temple to perform the consecration of treasure vases using the White Mahākāla ritual. On the following day Rinpoché gave novice-nun vows to the wife of the former acting prime minister Dekharwa. On the next day he gave teachings on the iron-fortress ritual to nineteen monks of Gyütö, including the ritual assistants and geshés. On the twenty-seventh, from eight in the morning until eleven thirty, Rinpoché sat at the head of the assembly in Thekchen Chöling temple for the last day of the treasure-vase consecrations. After that I invited both tutors for lunch.

On the sixteenth of June, the cabinet of the Tibetan administration requested Rinpoché to undertake a longevity meditation practice for my long life. This he accepted with great delight and began the practice right away. On the twenty-first, Rinpoché was invited to the hundred-thousand butter-lamp offering held in the Thekchen Chöling temple. There he prayed for an increase in virtuous activity that brings benefit and well-being to living beings and the teachings in Tibet.

On the eighth of August, at the request of Trethong Rakra Tulku, Rinpoché gave the permission initiation of the Heap of Blessings of the General Accomplishment of the Three Buddha Families That Enter the Heart, based upon the writings of Pashö Lama Jampa Gelek and Sharchen Ngawang Tsultrim, as well as the long-life initiation of Tsongkhapa in the form of a longevity deity from the visions of Dragom Tulku, Lodrö Palden Öser.

On the eighth of August, in response to an invitation from the Tibetan Astro-Medical Institute, Rinpoché visited the institute and performed the consecration. At the request of Rizong Tulku from Ladakh, Rinpoché gave teachings on how to conduct the great-approach retreat of Vajrabhairava for three sessions over three days beginning on the nineteenth,

Having completed a retreat on the thirteen-deity Vajrabhairava, Rinpoché performed the supplementary fire offering on the twenty-second.

At my request, Rinpoché undertook a retreat on Vajrabhairava Surrounded by a Retinue of Eight Vetala beginning on the thirtieth and lasting until the eighth of October. The following day he performed the fire offering, and during it a Westerner offered him an Indian curved knife. Rinpoché regarded this as very auspicious and happily accepted it.

I invited both tutors to lunch at twelve o'clock on the ninth, and we enjoyed conversations on the vast and profound aspects of the Dharma.

On the eleventh of November, Rinpoché visited Kyabjé Trijang Rinpoché at Gangchen Kyishong. There they exchanged accounts of their recent retreats and other activities. Two days later the Nechung protector was invoked and advice sought. Beginning on the fifteenth for three days, Rinpoché bestowed upon me initiations, including a very special Cittamani Tārā initiation.

Drepung Loseling Monastery, Mundgod, Karnataka State, India, 1971

31 | The Throneholder Returns to the Three Seats

IN RESPONSE to requests from the three great monastic seats in South India, from Tashi Lhunpo, the two tantric colleges, from other traditions, and from many lay and monastic residents of the settlements in the south, Rinpoché left Dharamsala for Delhi on the twenty-second of November and flew from there to Bangalore. From there he traveled by car to Mundgod.[181] This was the first time Rinpoché had been to the three monasteries since assuming the title of Ganden Throneholder, and as an auspicious omen he was first requested by the Ganden Monastery council to visit the Ganden monastic settlement. Walking within a monastic procession, Rinpoché ascended a throne in Ganden Shartsé's assembly hall. There he was served tea, sweet rice, and biscuits, while the monastic council and officials from each college offered the mandala and the three representations. From there he traveled by car to his special residence in the settlement.

On the third day, in a large open space outside, Rinpoché gave the permission initiation of Avalokiteśvara Who Liberates All Beings from the Unfortunate Realms and a long-life initiation to all monastic and lay residents of the Mundgod settlement. On the next day he was invited to visit the school, where he gave a speech to the students stressing the importance of attending to hygiene and health, respecting school regulations, and working hard in their education.

On the first of December, as requested by the monastic governing body of Ganden, and in keeping with tradition, Rinpoché went to the main assembly hall for the ceremonial procedures of a Ganden Throneholder. There he was served tea, sweet rice, and biscuits and presented with the three representations and so on. Audiences were granted to the monastery council, the tulkus, officials, and so forth.

Next, he journeyed to Drepung Monastery, where he was welcomed by the monks and escorted in a procession. Drepung Loseling had just constructed a new debating courtyard, and in response to a request from the college, and as an auspicious omen for its inauguration, Rinpoché gave the initial textual recitation from the monastic textbook *Analysis of the Perfection of Wisdom* composed by Panchen Sönam Drakpa. Then he read and taught a few passages from the beginning of the root texts of the five great classical subjects[182] and with great kindness prayed that the precious tradition of study and practice be disseminated widely on this earth and remain for a long time to come.

Again, in response to a request from Drepung Loseling, Rinpoché gave three days of teachings on Tsongkhapa's *Stages of the Path: A Song of Experience* to the abbots, lamas, and monks from Ganden, Drepung, and other traditions and to the general public. To a number of practitioners he conferred the blessings of the exalted Vajrayoginī. At Ganden Monastery, at the request of the Ganden Monastery governing body, he bestowed the single-deity Vajrabhairava initiation and the permission initiation of the outer, inner, and secret accomplishments of protector Kālarūpa on the monks of the two monasteries and many other monastic and lay devotees.

Up to 1959 it was the tradition in Ganden Namgyal Ling Monastery that during the summer rainy-season retreat, the incumbent Ganden Throneholder would give annual classes on Tsongkhapa's *Great Stages of the Path to Enlightenment*. Consequently, the great Vajradhara throneholder, in order to mark that tradition, read for one session from the beginning of the *Great Stages of the Path*. On the site for the new assembly hall, Rinpoché held an auspicious vow-purification ceremony with the other monks and brought forth a rain of prayers for its success. He also went to the Lingsé[183] debating ground, where he remained for a long time watching with great delight the fresh young minds examining and analyzing the meaning of the Buddha's words using the perfect path of reasoning and logic, as was the tradition. On the sixth and seventh, in the debate courtyard of Drepung Loseling, Rinpoché gave the preparation rituals and the actual initiation of the seventeen-deity Sitātapatrā to a large monastic and lay assembly.

In response to an invitation by the Bylakuppe Tibetan settlement, Rinpoché left by car the next day for the settlement. On arrival he was given an extensive welcome by the officials and people of the settlement and escorted to his residence. On the tenth he bestowed the permission initiation of Avalokiteśvara Who Liberates All Beings from the Unfortunate

Realms and a long-life initiation on all the lamas, tulkus, monks, and lay-people of the settlement. The following day, Rinpoché was invited to the local Tibetan school and gave a talk to the children. On the next day, to an audience of around twenty dedicated lamas and tulkus, Rinpoché gave teachings on the practice known as Recitation of the Neutral Letter *Ha* and the sixty-four-part torma-offering ritual. On the thirteenth he bestowed novice-monk vows on fifty-two new entrants to Sera Monastery.

On the following day, in response to an invitation, Rinpoché traveled by car to Tashi Lhunpo. There the monks of that monastery and the Mongolian Guru Deva offered Rinpoché a long-life ceremony, which he happily accepted. On the fifteenth of December, he gave teachings on the *Hundred Deities of Tuṣita* guruyoga. After this he went to Thekchen Chöling, the monastery of Dagyab Rinpoché, in Camp 2 of the settlement. There he performed a consecration. After this he rested for a while.

On the next day all the monastic and lay Tibetans of the area offered Rinpoché a long-life ceremony. On the seventeenth, at the site of the new Sera Monastery assembly hall, Rinpoché held an auspicious vow-purification ceremony with the monks. In the afternoon he gave a transmission and teaching on Tsongkhapa's *Three Principal Aspects of the Path*. On the following day he gave the preparation rituals and the actual initiation of Sitātapatrā.

On the nineteenth, in response to a joint invitation from the Rapgyé Ling Tibetan settlement in Hunsur and Gyümé, at the community temple for Camps 5 and 6 on the way to Hunsur, Rinpoché gave the transmission of the *Guru Puja* to about two hundred monastic and lay residents. On the morning of the next day, in the assembly hall of Gyümé, Rinpoché gave a transmission and teachings on Tsongkhapa's *Foundation of All Good Qualities* and permission initiations of Hayagrīva, Vajrapāṇi, and Garuḍa to all the monastic and lay residents, thereby completely fulfilling the wishes of the faithful.

On the next day Rinpoché flew from Bangalore to Delhi, where he stayed for two days before going to Bodhgaya. In Bodhgaya Rinpoché performed the haircutting ceremony of the young incarnation of Phabongkha Rinpoché, Losang Thupten Trinlé Kunkhyap. Kyabjé Trijang Vajradhara was also staying in Bodhgaya at that time, and the two tutors met up.

On the twenty-fifth, Ling Labrang sponsored a long-life ceremony for Kyabjé Trijang Rinpoché by way of a Guru Puja *tsok* ritual in the assembly hall of the Tibetan Bodhgaya monastery, attended by the resident Bodhgaya monks and those from elsewhere. Rinpoché recited the verses for the offering of the eight auspicious substances and other aids to longevity.

When Rinpoché was young, he had received teachings on the *Guru Puja*, combined with Yongzin Yeshé Gyaltsen's *Instructions on the Guru Puja*, from Kyabjé Phabongkha Jampa Tenzin Trinlé Gyatso. However, the teachings did not go beyond the section on the single-pointed prayers. Later, he received teachings on the root text of the *Guru Puja* from Kyabjé Lhatsun Rinpoché. He had fully practiced this ritual and taught it to others. However, he wished to receive a transmission and teachings on the *Instructions* in its entirety. Therefore, beginning on the twenty-third, Rinpoché received experiential instructions each day from Trijang Vajradhara on the *Guru Puja* root text combined with Yeshé Gyaltsen's *Instructions on the Guru Puja*. As was the practice, Rinpoché performed the visualizations during the instructions.

On the twenty-fifth, Trijang Labrang sponsored a long-life ceremony performed by the monks for the Vajradhara tutor by way of a Guru Puja *tsok* ritual in the assembly hall of the Tibetan Bodhgaya monastery. Trijang Rinpoché performed the offering of the eight auspicious substances and other tokens of longevity. On the thirtieth, the Bodhgaya monk Tsöndrü Gyaltsen sponsored a long-life ceremony for the two tutors by way of a Guru Puja ritual, which they happily accepted.

1973

Beginning January 1, 1973, Rinpoché gave teachings to Trijang Rinpoché alone. These teachings were the recitation ritual of the sixteen-side iron-fortress according to the practice of Gyütö, profound teachings on the iron fortress as the magical wheel of Vajrabhairava using *Three Chapters* composed by the Fifth Ling Rinpoché, Losang Lungtok Tenzin Trinlé, as well as supplementary teachings on the earth ritual. Not only had Trijang Rinpoché previously received and fully understood the magical-wheel teachings, he had taught it to others. Therefore Rinpoché only gave explanations of drawing the mandala, mantra formulation, and so on and did not describe the actual practices.

The precious tutor, when he was young, had received the complete teachings on the accomplishment of the peaceful and wrathful forms of Mañjuśrī combined and had continued to practice them. Nevertheless, again in Bodhgaya, he received from Kyabjé Trijang Rinpoché the root text *Great Vajra Words on the Exclusive Practice of Combining of the Peaceful and Wrathful Forms of Mañjuśrī* together with the commentary, *Peaceful and Wrathful Forms of Mañjuśrī Combined: Fulfilling the Hopes of the Fortunate*, by Jamyang Shepa Dorjé Ngawang Tsöndrü.

On the fourth of January, Rinpoché gave an Amitāyus initiation, sponsored by Ashé Yangkyi, to about seven hundred recipients. From the sixth to the twenty-fifth, in response to a request from Drakyap Thupten Chöjor, Rinpoché bestowed the single-deity Vajrabhairava initiation together with its day of preparation, as well as experiential teachings of the root text of the *Guru Puja* together with an extensive exposition of the *Instructions* by the Tséchokling tutor Yeshé Gyaltsen to about 450 monastic and lay recipients. Among the audience was Tromthok Tulku from Sera Jé Monastery, who would often visit Rinpoché to act as his scribe. On the last day of the teachings, at the request of Geshé Tenzin Bakdro from the Tibetan Khasakha settlement in Bhutan, Rinpoché gave the permission initiation of the general accomplishment of the three buddha families. After the teachings had concluded, the recipients offered Rinpoché a long-life ceremony. During the ceremony Ngawang Norbu, a Gyümé artist from Darjeeling, offered Rinpoché a large painting of White Tārā. Rinpoché remarked that this was very auspicious and accepted it happily.

On the seventh of February, Rinpoché gave practical instructions on the *Torma Offering Rites* to Geshé Tenzin Bakdro and fourteen others.

There is one method of taking the bodhicitta vows that is followed at the time of taking an initiation belonging to any of the four classes of tantra. There is also a tradition, known as the tradition of taking together the pledges of both bodhisattva aspiration and bodhisattva engagement[184] by way of two verses in Śāntideva's *Guide to the Bodhisattva's Way of Life* that begin "Just as the sugatas of the past developed the mind of enlightenment. . . ." However, the meaning of the words "taking together" is something to be investigated. Moreover Jé Tsongkhapa, in both his *Middle-Length Stages of the Path* and *Great Stages of the Path*, speaks of the bodhisattva aspiration being initiated on the basis of its own ritual. For taking the bodhisattva vows of engagement, he refers to the Ethics chapter in Asaṅga's *Stages of the Bodhisattva*, as stated in his *Highway to Enlightenment: An Exposition of Bodhisattva Ethics*. The lineage of receiving and bestowing bodhisattva vows using this particular ritual was present up to the time of Changkya Rölpai Dorjé and others. However, in recent times it has not been that well known in central Tibet, and the practice has declined. In order to revive it, in Dharamsala I presented Rinpoché with a copy of *Highway to Enlightenment* and at the same time requested him to confer on me a lineage of the vows by way of this ritual. With great delight and compassion he agreed to this.

It is the position of many authentic scriptural traditions that when a qualified guru cannot be found, it is possible to generate the bodhisattva vows in your mind by taking them in front of a sacred object. Therefore, on the tenth of February, Rinpoché first took the vows in the presence of the precious Buddha in the temple of the great Bodhgaya shrine. Then, using the rite found in *Highway to Enlightenment*, Rinpoché conferred the bodhisattva vows on me and assistant tutor Serkong Rinpoché. This was a truly blessed moment. From then on, in order to restore this tradition, I have often bestowed the bodhisattva vows using this method.

The fifth of March marked the first day of the water-ox year. Rinpoché sat at the head of the assembly in the Bodhgaya monastery and received a procession of visitors, including the monks of the monastery, the labrang staff, and the general public, who offered ceremonial scarves and the three representations as auspicious tokens for the new year. On the eighth, the labrang and monastery jointly offered Rinpoché a long-life ceremony, which he accepted. On the ninth, he sat at the head of the prayer festival assembly and so on, as he had done in previous years.

On the thirteenth of March, Rinpoché left Bodhgaya and arrived back in Dharamsala on the fifteenth. On the way up he stopped to visit Trijang Rinpoché, and the two tutors engaged in conversation on Dharma topics. Later he came to visit me and told me of news and events that had occurred since we last met. At my request he sat as the master of the prayer festival assembly in Thekchen Chöling. The entire monastic community of Gyütö had come from Dalhousie to attend the Great Prayer Festival in this month of miraculous feats, and on the twenty-fourth, in the Nyungné temple, the tantric college offered the precious tutor a long-life ceremony by way of a Guru Puja *tsok* ritual together with the ritual of Halting the Ḍākinīs' Escort. Rinpoché happily accepted the ceremony.

On the ninth of April, Rinpoché bestowed the life entrustment of the five king emanations to nine monks, including Drepung Loseling former abbot Pema Gyaltsen. On that day Dilgo Khyentsé Rinpoché came to

Chopra House to visit the precious tutor and to offer prayers for his long life. At the same time, as a way of establishing a Dharma connection, Rinpoché received from Dilgo Khyentsé Rinpoché a transmission of the fasting ritual composed by the Great Seventh Dalai Lama.

On the twentieth of May, I invited the precious tutor together with Trijang Rinpoché to my residence, and we engaged in vast and profound Dharma conversations.

On the twenty-second of June, Rinpoché gave the permission initiation of Avalokiteśvara Who Liberates All Beings from the Unfortunate Realms to around thirty people, including Chamdo Gendun Losang of Loseling.

According to divinations received from lamas and deities, it was clear that this year there were one or two obstacles to the life of the precious tutor. Therefore ten monks from Namgyal Monastery, including the abbot, performed a week-long longevity accomplishment ritual.

On the fifth of July, in Thekchen Chöling, two hundred monks performed the long-life ceremony Halting the Ḍākinīs' Escort for the Vajradhara throneholder. This consisted of a Guru Puja *tsok* ritual and a longevity ritual and was jointly sponsored by the administration officials, Drepung, Sera, Ganden, and Tashi Lhunpo monasteries, and the two tantric colleges. The mandala discourse, the eight auspicious substances, and other tokens of longevity were presented by assistant tutor Serkong Rinpoché. After the long-life ceremony had finished, I invited Rinpoché to my residence for conversation.

The next day was my birthday, and as was customary Rinpoché came to visit me and offered me a ceremonial scarf. At ten o'clock on the seventh, I invited the precious throneholder to my residence and earnestly requested that he remain with us for many years to come. On the eleventh, Rinpoché gave the permission initiation of the outer accomplishment of the oath-bound protector Kālarūpa to eight Westerners who had previously received the Vajrabhairava initiation. On the following day the labrang invoked the Nechung and Gadong protectors and asked them if there were a need for any additional rituals on top of those long-life rituals already performed and those being performed at the present. The reply was that it was still necessary to perform more long-life rituals, and they both pledged to work single-pointedly on initiating the four types of activities for the sake of the long life of the great Vajradhara.

In order to remove the obstacles to Rinpoché's life and ensure his long-life, officials from the Bodhgaya monastery came to Dharamsala and offered a long-life ceremony on the eighth of August.

On the third, Rinpoché bestowed novice-nun vows on three devotees. Previously I had requested Kyabjé Trijang Rinpoché to perform a longevity meditation practice for Rinpoché. Consequently, he undertook a seventeen-day long-life retreat on Cittamaṇi White Tārā. On the sixteenth he visited Rinpoché in Chopra House, where he offered him the auspicious substances of longevity and requested that he plant his lotus feet on the earth for a long time.

On the seventeenth, Rinpoché gave teachings to Norgyé and his wife— the houseparents of the home for Tibetan children in France—and to the children. The teachings on refuge in the Three Jewels—the best gateway into the Buddha's teaching—concerned the reasons one should go for refuge, the way to go for refuge, and having gone for refuge, how to keep the commitments of refuge.

On the thirty-first, in response to a request from a Western nun, Rinpoché gave a transmission of the single-deity Vajrabhairava extensive sādhana from the works of Phabongkha Dechen Nyingpo.

Khetsun Sangpo, the Dharamsala Tibetan Library research scholar, was compiling a history of the four great traditions of Tibetan Buddhism. He visited Rinpoché and earnestly requested him to compose an autobiography so that he could include it in the biographies of the line of Ganden Throneholders. In response Rinpoché wrote a very brief autobiography.

Four geshés from the two tantric colleges who had completed the great-approach retreat of Vajrabhairava had finished the accomplishment of a Vajrabhairava magical wheel, and on the afternoon of the nineteenth I joined Rinpoché in performing the thanksgiving ritual of pleasing the deity and his oath-bound protector with a *tsok* ritual. On the twenty-third Rinpoché kindly gave me a teaching that I had requested.

On the eleventh of November, Rinpoché performed a fire offering as a supplement to a retreat on a particular deity he had recently completed.

The Communist Chinese had dismantled the statue of Buddha Akṣobhyavajra that was housed in the Ramoché Temple in Lhasa and transported it to China. Therefore Gyütö commissioned a new statue in Nepal and brought it to the Thekchen Chöling temple. Consequently, on the fourteenth, with the Vajradhara tutor as vajra master, Trijang Rinpoché and forty monks from the tantric college performed the mantra-accomplishment ritual using the Vajrabhairava self-generation ritual. This was followed by the ceremony of placing the mantras in the statue using the practices of Changkya Ngawang Chokden. That day I offered lunch to the two tutors, which they happily accepted, and we spent a pleasant time in conversation.

The next day saw the annual invocation of the Nechung and Gadong protectors. In response to a request from Geshé Rapten, Rinpoché bestowed on him and a few others a long-life initiation. On the seventeenth, which was the day commemorating the Buddha's return from the celestial realms, the extensive consecration called Making the Rains of Goodness to Fall was performed by the entire Gyütö assembly, using the Vajrabhairava ritual, for the newly constructed Akṣobhyavajra statue in Thekchen Chöling. Rinpoché attended this ceremony on the main day of the rite and participated in the ritual from the section on the yoga of self- and front-generation of the deity up to the concluding rituals and performed the role of vajra master. I also attended the ceremony from the invitation of the wisdom beings up to the initiation of the deities. In the assembly breaks, Rinpoché visited me and told me of his plans to go to Bodhgaya for the winter. Three days later he left Dharamsala.

In Bodhgaya, beginning in December, Rinpoché did one morning session each day of a special longevity practice using Cittamaṇi Tārā. On the twenty-fifth I arrived in Bodhgaya, where Rinpoché welcomed me with an incense-led procession and presented me with a mandala and the three representations.

32 | New Residence

IN JANUARY 1974, I gave the Kālacakra initiation in Bodhgaya, and each day I came to the precious tutor for advice and for help in ensuring that all would become virtuous activity bringing benefit to living beings and the doctrine. On the tenth, the day after I finished conferring the Kālacakra initiation, Rinpoché gave the permission initiation of the Three Wrathful Forms Combined and transmissions of the Seventh Dalai Lama's *Praise of Avalokiteśvara*, Tārā prayers, and the six-syllable mantra to those who had attended the initiation. On the sixteenth he bestowed novice-monk vows on fifty-two devotees. On the seventeenth, the recipients of the teachings sponsored a long-life ceremony for the great Vajradhara tutor, which was performed by the resident and visiting lamas, tulkus, and monks. On the following day Rinpoché bestowed full-ordination vows on twenty-eight novice monks. On the twenty-eighth he bestowed the five lifelong lay vows on Mrs. Dekhang Noryang Norbu of Kalimpong and a person from Gyalthang.

In response to an invitation from a branch of the Bodhgaya monastery at the site where the Buddha engaged in ascetic practices for six years, Rinpoché visited this place on the ninth of February to perform a consecration, make prayers, and so on. On the fourteenth, at the fervent request of twelve Westerners who had a single-pointed devotion for the teachings of the Vinaya, the very root of the teachings, Rinpoché enriched their minds with the bestowal of the novice monastic vows.

The twenty-second marked the wood-tiger new year, and Rinpoché attended the customary ceremonies. On the twenty-fourth the labrang and the monastery offered him a long-life ceremony.

On the twenty-fifth Rinpoché traveled to Delhi by train, where he stayed for two days. On the twenty-seventh he left by plane for the south of India. At Belgaum Airport he was met by officials of the Mundgod settlements, abbots and officials of the monasteries, and so on, who offered Rinpoché ceremonial scarves, which he returned, as was the custom. That day he stayed at Hubli, and the following day he traveled by car to the home of Trehor Sangra Tulku in Mundgod. There the governing body of Drepung Monastery as well as Loseling College offered Rinpoché ceremonial scarves and the three representations.

Previously, the manager of the labrang had asked the great Dharma king Nechung if it were appropriate for the labrang to buy a residence for Rinpoché in Dharamsala. The reply came that it would be better to build a new residence on the monastery land in Mundgod. Consequently, the current and former abbots and officials of Drepung Loseling had approached Rinpoché with the offer to construct a new residence on the land given to them by the Indian government for the purpose of building a monastery. The Vajradhara tutor had replied that it should be a simple building, not elaborate, and designed solely for living in. The residence was built accordingly. Therefore, on the second of March, the lamas and tulkus, present and former abbots of Drepung and Ganden, the Nechung and Ganden oracles, and many others escorted the Vajradhara tutor in an incense-led procession to the new residence, called Gelek Palbar, where he was seated on a throne in the reception room. There, someone born in an auspicious year offered him *tsampa*, tea, and sweet rice. Then the labrang, the monasteries, the tantric colleges, representatives from other traditions, and many other lay and monastic devotees lined up to present him with ceremonial scarves, mandalas, and the three representations, all of which he joyfully received. Eight monks from Nechung Monastery performed an incense purification ritual as well as the *Praise of the Warrior Protectors*[185] and the rites propitiating the Dharma protectors in general. Afterward, in the courtyard of Drepung Loseling, the monastery assembly offered Rinpoché a long-life ceremony, which he happily accepted.

On the morning of the third, while I was performing the ceremony to open the new assembly hall of Gomang College, the precious throneholder also attended. In the afternoon during the opening of the new Ganden Monastery's assembly hall, the great Vajradhara throneholder and tutor presented the mandala and the three representations. After that he was served tea and sweet rice. I took on the role of sutra reciter and together with the monks performed an auspicious vow-purification ceremony.

Three days later, the Association for the Preservation of the Geluk Tradition convened a special meeting in the Ganden assembly hall to present me with a certificate of merit conferring the degree of lharampa and ngakrampa on me. During this ceremony the great Vajradhara throneholder gave the introductory discourse and presented me with a certificate of completion of extensive studies in the sutra and tantra scriptures, a gold medal, and a high-quality ceremonial silk scarf. In the morning the Nechung and Gadong protectors were invoked and offered thanks for the successful completion of Rinpoché's residence. The two protectors also consecrated the rooms of the residence.

The great Vajradhara said that I should come to the new labrang residence to perform a consecration. Therefore I visited on the eighth of March. The house was a simple one-story building, not too big and not too small, in which he would be very happy. I also requested him to live a long life and fulfilled his wish by consecrating the sacred representations of the Buddha's body, speech, and mind in the labrang.

Two days later in the great assembly hall at Ganden, the governing bodies of Drepung and Ganden monasteries offered Rinpoché a sutra-tradition long-life ceremony. On the next day Rinpoché bestowed novice-monk vows on thirty-eight recipients. On the morning of the thirteenth, in the debate courtyard of Drepung Loseling, Rinpoché gave a transmission of the fasting ritual and explanation of its practice to a lay and monastic audience of four hundred. In the afternoon, in the same courtyard he gave teachings on the sixty-four-part torma-offering ritual to about fifty lamas, tulkus, and geshés.

Two days later Rinpoché flew to Delhi, and on the eighteenth he gave lay vows to a Westerner called Pema and to Mrs. Taring and Mrs. Surkhang. On the evening of the twenty-first, Rinpoché left Delhi by train and arrived back in Dharamsala on the morning of the twenty-second. On the way to his residence he called on Kyabjé Trijang Rinpoché at his Tashi Rapten residence.[186] The two tutors exchanged New Year ceremonial scarves and enjoyed a short conversation.

On the fifth of April, at the request of Rigya Tulku, Rinpoché bestowed a White Tārā long-life initiation on him and his entourage. At the request of an American monk, Rinpoché conferred the single-deity Vajrabhairava initiation on about thirty recipients on the thirtieth, with the preparatory rituals given the day before.

Three days later, at the request of Denma Lochö Rinpoché, the Vajra-dhara tutor gave for six days to a lay and monastic audience of about three hundred a transmission and teachings on the mind-training text *Rays of the Sun* composed by Hortön Namkha Pal, a direct disciple of Jé Tsongkhapa.

Beginning on the ninth of May, and during his free time, Rinpoché gave an explanation of Anubhūti's *Sarasvatī Grammar Treatise* up to and including the section on the five types of sandhi, using Ngawang Phuntsok Lhundrup's *Illuminating Treatise* commentary, to Geshé Ngawang Dargyey, Khamlung Tulku, Sharpa Tulku, and others, thereby fulfilling their wishes.

On the third of June, at the request of the teachers and students of the Astro-Medical Institute, Rinpoché gave the transmission of the *Gangloma* prayer to Mañjuśrī—personification of the wisdom of all the buddhas—the permission initiations of the goddess of language White Sarasvatī and of the wealth goddess Vasudhārā. On the next day he bestowed the daylong Mahayana vows on eight devotees. On the twenty-second of June, at the request of the minister Tsewang Tamdrin, Rinpoché gave the permission initiation of Cittamaṇi White Mahākāla.

On the sixth of July, I entered my fortieth year, and in commemoration Rinpoché accompanied by Trijang Rinpoché came to the Private Office reception room at three o'clock and offered me ceremonial scarves and so on. On the afternoon of the eighteenth of July, I invited the precious throneholder and assistant tutor Serkong Rinpoché to my residence rooms for conversations on Dharma.

Rinpoché had recently completed a meditation retreat on a particular deity, and on the twelfth of September, he performed the supplementary pacifying fire offering. On the twenty-second, at the invitation of a Western monk, Rinpoché joined Western Dharma practitioners at Tushita Meditation Centre to perform the Guru Puja ritual.

On the seventeenth of October, the annual invocation of the Gadong and Nechung protectors was performed. On the thirtieth, Rinpoché was invited to the celebrations for the fourteenth anniversary of the founding of the Tibetan Children's Village. We met in the marquee that had been set up for us, and he told me of his plans to go to Mundgod and Bodhgaya that winter.

On the seventh of November Rinpoché left Dharamsala and spent two days in Delhi. On the eleventh, he traveled by plane to Mundgod. On the way to Drepung he was invited to the great assembly hall of Ganden, where the monastery council, lamas, tulkus, and officials sought an audience with him. Then he traveled to his labrang residence in Drepung Monastery. There the Drepung monastic governing body and the past and present abbots of Loseling came to visit him. On the fourteenth, as requested by Drepung Loseling and the Chamdo geshé Losang Dargyé, who lived in Bomdila, Rinpoché began a transmission and teaching of Tsongkhapa's *Great Stages of the Path* to a monastic and lay audience of around eighteen hundred.

On the morning of the thirtieth of November, Rinpoché was invited to the great assembly hall of Ganden, where the entire assembly offered him a long-life ceremony by way of the Guru Puja sponsored by Trijang Labrang. The great Vajradhara Trijang Rinpoché presented tokens of longevity such as the eight auspicious substances. After the ceremony Rinpoché went to Trijang Labrang, where he offered Trijang Rinpoché a ceremonial scarf as an omen for the success of his new residence, and the two tutors spent the time in private conversation.

Ling Labrang sponsored a long-life ceremony for Vajradhara Trijang Rinpoché held in the Loseling debate courtyard. The precious throneholder presented tokens of longevity such as the eight auspicious substances and requested that he remain a long time on this earth. Trijang Rinpoché and his labrang staff were invited to Ling Labrang, where he was offered food and drink of the best quality. Trijang Rinpoché offered Rinpoché a ceremonial scarf and the three representations as auspicious tokens of the successful completion of Ling Rinpoché's new residence the previous year.

On the twenty-first of December, Drepung and Ganden monasteries, a Sakya college, a Nyingma college, and the general public, all of which make up the Mundgod Dögu Ling Tibetan settlement, jointly sponsored a long-life ceremony for the two tutors in the Loseling debate courtyard, which they happily accepted. On the nineteenth, Rinpoché performed the bodhicitta ceremony and bestowed a long-life initiation. The sponsors of these teachings offered Rinpoché the long-life ceremony Halting the Ḍākinīs' Escort, during which the Drepung council, the heads of Loseling, Shephel Ling, Thoding Monastery, and the Sakya monastery offered the three representations and prayed that Rinpoché firmly plant his lotus feet on the earth for a long time. On the thirty-first, the two sponsors of the stages of the path teaching offered the two tutors a long-life ceremony in the Drepung Loseling debate courtyard.

1975

On the morning of the fifth of January 1975, in the Ganden great assembly hall, the monastery governing council offered the two tutors a long-life ceremony in the sutra tradition. In the afternoon, the precious tutor together with Trijang Rinpoché cast the flowers of consecration of the Ganden great assembly hall and its sacred objects by way of the short horseback consecration. On the ninth, Lochen Tulku invited Rinpoché to sit as the head of the great assembly of Drepung. Rinpoché complied with their wishes. On the thirteenth, the Association for the Preservation of the Geluk Tradition invited Rinpoché to the Ganden great assembly hall. Among the monastic community, consisting primarily of the three monastic seats, Samdhong Tulku of Loseling opened the meeting, and the abbot of Namgyal gave the introductory speech. The precious throneholder was presented with a lharampa geshé certificate, a gold medal, and a high-quality ceremonial silk scarf. Kyabjé Trijang Rinpoché was also presented with the same award. It was customary to award certificates and to present garlands of flowers and so on to those geshés who had passed the lharampa and ngakrampa debate examinations in the past in Lhasa or later in India. Therefore the monastic community and representatives of the residents of the settlements presented the two tutors with gifts in recognition of their achievements. On the fifteenth, in the Ganden great assembly hall, the Association for the Preservation of the Geluk Tradition offered the two tutors a long-life ceremony in accordance with the sutra tradition.

On the following day, in the Drepung Loseling courtyard, Rinpoché kindly bestowed novice-monk vows on twenty devotees and novice-nun vows on seven women. On the morning of the twentieth, Rinpoché went to Gomang College, where with Trijang Rinpoché he consecrated the assembly hall and its sacred objects. In the afternoon, in an open space in front of Rinpoché's residence, a dance and drama group from the Mundgod settlement gave a performance for two hours mainly on the life of the devout King Sudhana. Rinpoché enjoyed this greatly, thereby fulfilling the wishes of the participants. On the twenty-third, in the Drepung Loseling courtyard, the labrang sponsored the long-life ceremony Halting the Ḍākinīs' Escort for the great Vajradhara protector preceded by a longevity accomplishment ritual performed by the resident monks.

On the morning of the twenty-eighth, Rinpoché traveled by car to Belgaum, and then by air to Delhi, where he stayed for three days before traveling to Bodhgaya.

Rinpoché arrived in Bodhgaya on the first of February and was welcomed by the Bodhgaya monastery officials and many monks. On the eleventh, Rinpoché performed the celebratory rituals of the wood-rabbit new year. On the fifteenth, the monastery and the labrang jointly offered Rinpoché a long-life ceremony. On that day Rinpoché began the customary rituals and ceremonies of the Great Prayer Festival.

Rinpoché spent the winter happily in this special place.

33 | Master of the Five Sciences

O N THE THIRTEENTH of March 1975, Rinpoché left by train for Pathankot and then traveled by car to Dharamsala, arriving on the fifteenth. On the way up to his residence, Rinpoché called on Trijang Rinpoché, where the two tutors exchanged New Year ceremonial scarves. On the next day Rinpoché visited me and told me in detail of his recent activities, including the transmission and teaching of the *Great Stages of the Path*, the sole lamp for the three worlds, that he gave in Drepung.

Beginning on the third of May Rinpoché gave me teachings on Hortön Namkha Pal's *Rays of the Sun: Training the Mind in Bodhicitta*, an explanation from the great oral tradition, and on the eleventh, he gave me instructions on the *Torma Offering Rites*.

Rinpoché then spent seven days undertaking a longevity meditation practice for the health and well-being of Kyabjé Trijang Rinpoché, and on the eighteenth he went to Tashi Rapten, the residence of Trijang Rinpoché, to offer him the auspicious substances of longevity. The twenty-fifth of May was the full moon of *vaiśākha*, and Rinpoché was invited to the Tibetan Library at Gangchen Kyishong by dedicated Westerners who were studying and meditating on Buddhism. There he participated in a Guru Puja *tsok* ritual. At the same time, he visited Trijang Rinpoché, and the two tutors engaged in wide-ranging and profound conversations on the Dharma.

On the nineteenth, Rinpoché gave a simplified initiation of Vajrabhairava, together with the preparatory rituals, to eighteen Westerners and Tibetans.

On the eighteenth of June, Rinpoché led the assembly at the ritual of a hundred thousand *tsok* offerings made to Guru Rinpoché for the sake of the spiritual and temporal well-being of the people of Tibet performed in the Thekchen Chöling temple. He made prayers for the spread of the Buddha's teaching, for the happiness of living beings, and especially for the fulfillment of the immediate and long-term wishes of the people of Tibet. On the following day, Gadong and Nechung, who were the main protectors on whom Rinpoché had a long-term relationship, were invoked through oracles, and questions were put to them. After this, Rinpoché gave teachings on the sixty-four-part torma-offering ritual to two Western monks.

On the eighteenth of July, Drigung Tsetsang Rinpoché visited Chopra House and requested Rinpoché to live a life that followed the great practitioners of the past in learning, contemplation, preserving, disseminating, and so on. On the following day, at the request of the Swiss nun Tenzin Lophel, Rinpoché gave a long-life initiation.

On the third of August, Rinpoché gave the permission initiation of oath-bound Kālarūpa to five ordained Westerners, thereby fulfilling their wishes.

Recently, Rinpoché had undertaken a retreat on single-deity Vajra-bhairava, and on the fourteenth he performed the supplementary fire offering. On the eighteenth, Rinpoché gave me the initiation into the corpus of the five king emanations from the cycle of Gyalpo Jeché.[187] On the twenty-fifth he gave me the initiations of the forty-nine-deity Vajrabhairava, complete with preceding preparation rituals and, on the following day, the initiation of Vajrabhairava Surrounded by a Retinue of Eight Vetala, thereby maintaining the practice of previous masters.

On the third of September, Rinpoché gave lay vows to three male and female members of the staff of the Tibetan Children's Village.

On the third of November, Rinpoché gave novice-nun vows to three women. On the eighteenth, Trijang Rinpoché came to Chopra House, and for a few hours the two tutors enjoyed pleasant conversation. On the tenth of November, Rinpoché came to see me and told me of his planned winter visit to Bodhgaya. On the same day he bestowed a long-life initiation on Denma Lochö Rinpoché and others. On the following day Rinpoché went down to Gangchen Kyishong to spend some time with Trijang Rinpoché. Two days later he gave teachings to Serkong Rinpoché, and the following day he bestowed lay vows on a French woman called Dekyi.

On the twenty-third Rinpoché arrived at the Tibetan monastery in the holy place of Bodhgaya, where he was welcomed by many monks. At the request of Mrs. Dekhang Noryang Norbu of Kalimpong, beginning on the thirtieth of November, Rinpoché gave teachings for eight days on Hortön's *Rays of the Sun: Training the Mind in Bodhicitta* to a lay and monastic audience of about eight hundred.

1976

From the fifth of January 1976 to the seventeenth, at the request of Mrs. Dekhar, the nun and widow of the former acting prime minister Dekharwa, Rinpoché gave the initiation of single-deity Vajrabhairava preceded by a day for the preparatory rituals, as well as teachings on its generation and completion stages. On the fourteenth, Drepung Loseling offered Rinpoché a long-life ceremony and made donations to those receiving the teachings. On the eighteenth, at the request of Mrs. Dekhang Noryang Norbu of Kalimpong and the businessman Rapten from Trehor, Rinpoché conferred a long-life initiation and the permission initiation of Avalokiteśvara Who Liberates All Beings from the Unfortunate Realms.

On the twenty-fourth, Rinpoché bestowed novice-monk vows on nineteen recipients.

On the fifteenth of February, on my instructions, assistant tutor Serkong Rinpoché traveled to Bodhgaya and, with the whole assembly of the Tibetan monastery, offered the precious throneholder a long-life ceremony, in conjunction with a thousandfold offering ceremony of the Guru Puja ritual, which he kindly accepted.

The first of March was the first day of the fire-dragon year, and Rinpoché took part in all the celebratory rituals as usual. Moreover, as he did every year, when he first arrived in Bodhgaya he performed the thousand five-senses offerings in front of the sacred shrine, made donations to the monks, and during the Great Prayer Festival made similar offerings at the shrine and donations to the monastic community.

At my request, Serkong Rinpoché, Geshé Rikzin Tenpa Rinpoché of Gomang's Jadral House, and about thirty others again offered the precious tutor a long-life ceremony by way of blessed Cittamaṇi White Tārā, which he joyfully accepted. During this ceremony Ling Labrang offered extensive food and drink to the lamas and monks performing the ritual. On the seventh, the labrang and the Bodhgaya monastery jointly offered Rinpoché a long-life ceremony. From that day on Rinpoché sat at the head of the prayer festival assembly for its duration, as usual.

On the tenth, Rinpoché returned to Dharamsala. On the thirteenth he visited me and we spent a relaxing time in my residence. After that he visited Trijang Rinpoché. On the fifteenth Rinpoché was invited to sit at the head of the prayer festival assembly. In the morning he came to the discourse on

Āryaśūra's *Garland of the Buddha's Birth Stories*, and on the next day he was head of the afternoon assembly and attended the afternoon prayer sessions. I invited both Vajradhara tutors to the rooms above the temple and served them lunch.

On the twenty-third, the precious throneholder accompanied by Trijang Rinpoché came to my residence. They requested that I should strive to live a long life for the sake of the teachings and sentient beings, as had been requested by the representatives of the people and the end-of-year general assembly, and recently expressed by the senior administration officials. In this connection the great Dharma king Nechung had been consulted, and the reply indicated that something had upset the mind of Palden Lhamo. This was something that was beyond the comprehension of the Tibetan people, and so on the following day it was decided that it would be right to perform an effective *tsok* ritual propitiation of Palden Lhamo and the five king emanations, to be followed by an invitation of Nechung by way of an oracle, during which confessions and apologies would be made to Lhamo and Nechung would be asked to clarify what we had done wrong.

The next day the Tibetan people sponsored a long-life ceremony for the two tutors in the Thekchen Chöling temple performed by resident and visiting monks and nuns. On the following day, the great Vajradhara, Trijang Rinpoché, assistant tutor Serkong Rinpoché, and all the monks of Namgyal Monastery and Nechung Monastery performed a *tsok* ritual propitiation of Palden Lhamo and the five-emanation Dharma king. Nechung was invoked through an oracle and asked for guidance on what should be done. The protector replied that in order to relieve the concerns of the mistress of the desire realm, Dharma practitioners of all traditions should behave correctly and so on.

On the twenty-ninth Rinpoché conferred the Vajrabhairava initiation on me.

On the fourteenth of April, Rinpoché was invited to be head of a Guru Puja assembly at the Tibetan Library in Gangchen Kyishong. There with Western and Tibetan Dharma practitioners, he made vast offerings to please the buddhas and bodhisattvas.

On the seventh of May, Rinpoché bestowed the great fortune of the novice-nun vows on five devotees. On the twenty-seventh, with Chamdo Geshé, he began a generation-stage retreat on a particular deity. On the twelfth of July, Rinpoché went to a room in Nechung Monastery, where the great protector was invoked through an oracle and advice was sought.

On the twentieth of August, at half past eight in the morning, I stopped for a short time at the residence of assistant tutor Serkong Rinpoché and then went on to Chopra House to visit the great Vajradhara tutor, to offer him a new set of robes and to request that he keep his lotus feet planted on this earth for a long time.

Kyabjé Trijang Rinpoché undertook a special longevity meditation practice for the sake of the great Vajradhara tutor. On the twenty-fourth, he offered the auspicious substances of longevity to Rinpoché in Chopra House and urged that Rinpoché not relax his desire to set his lotus feet a long time on this earth for the sake of the teachings and living beings. On the twenty-sixth of August, Rinpoché performed a supplementary fire offering at the completion of a retreat on a particular deity. On the following day, Chogyé Trichen Rinpoché, who was working at the Religious Affairs Office, heard that the precious teacher was giving teachings on the generation and completion stages of single-deity Vajrabhairava and asked if he might be allowed to attend. Rinpoché asked him if he had previously received the single-deity Vajrabhairava initiation, to which he replied that he had not received it within the Geluk tradition but had received it within the Sakya *Compendium of All Tantras*.[188] Rinpoché questioned him on the ritual used for the initiation. Chogyé Trichen Rinpoché replied that it was the Changkya initiation ritual, to which Rinpoché responded by saying that such an initiation was acceptable, and therefore he attended the teachings.

In the perception of Chogyé Trichen Rinpoché the precious tutor had appeared with a head, nose, and so forth that was extraordinarily bright, and behind his ears were two small horns radiating blue light and with decorations like small tongue-like wall hangings. He told me that he had not spoken of this vision to anyone until now. I think this reveals the extraordinary qualities of both these lamas. Chogyé Trichen Rinpoché would often meet with the Vajradhara tutor and engage in Dharma conversations.

On the eighteenth of September, Rinpoché was invited by the Western retreaters in Tushita Meditation Centre. There he led a *tsok* ritual performed with the Guru Puja to please the buddhas and bodhisattvas.

On the twenty-seventh, at half past two, Rinpoché came to visit me and told me he would soon be going to Kullu district. I offered the suggestion that if possible it would be good to give the proposed initiations using sand mandalas. Rinpoché stayed until half past three, joyfully and compassionately answering my questions and resolving all my doubts on various difficult points of sutra and tantra. Afterward, Rinpoché visited Trijang Rinpoché, and they exchanged accounts of their recent activities.

On the first of October, the Trehor Dzarong household made donations and offerings to the whole Namgyal assembly, and Rinpoché attended as head of the assembly at the request of the sponsor. He prayed that the sponsor and all those connected with him be free of all harm, and that through an uninterrupted succession of lives of leisure and opportunity, they soon attain the four enlightened bodies endowed with the five wisdoms.

In response to an invitation from the Tibetan Ganden Chökhor Ling Monastery in Kullu, on the third of October, Rinpoché left for Kullu by car. First he visited a Tibetan school there, where he was lavishly welcomed by the students. He gave an audience and words of advice to about a hundred people, comprising staff, pupils, and parents. Two days later, at the request of the Tibetan monastery, Rinpoché conferred the seventeen-deity initiation of Sitātapatrā, together with the preparatory rituals, to about five hundred recipients. On the following day, to around fifteen hundred lay and monastic Tibetan and Kinnauri followers, Rinpoché gave a long-life initiation and a speech on the importance of taking the Three Jewels to the crown of your head and of acting correctly with regard to the law of karma.

On the eighth, over a period of three days, Rinpoché conferred initiations, complete with preparatory rituals, of thirteen-deity and forty-nine-deity Vajrabhairava, and Vajrabhairava Surrounded by a Retinue of Eight Vetala, thereby planting the seeds of the four enlightened bodies for a lay and monastic audience of about four hundred people. Although Rinpoché had wanted to bestow these initiations using sand mandalas, lack of resources dictated that cloth mandalas were used instead. On the following day, in response to a request from Gyalsé Tulku of Drepung Loseling and Rigya Tulku, Rinpoché gave a transmission and teachings of Tsongkhapa's *Abridged Stages of the Path*, thereby fulfilling the wishes of the people.

On the sixteenth, Rinpoché went by invitation to the Tibetan Sangyé Chöling Monastery in Shimla. On the eighteenth, he was invited to sit at the head of its assembly. On the twenty-first, as requested by administrator Gé Jinpa Gyatso, Rinpoché kindly gave teachings on all the paths of sutra and tantra using Tsongkhapa's *Foundation of All Good Qualities* as the base text, to about thirteen hundred lay and monastic residents of the area, as well as the permission initiation of Avalokiteśvara Who Liberates All Beings from the Unfortunate Realms and a long-life initiation. Administrator Jinpa Gyatso and Chöphel, who was a former member of the labrang, jointly offered Rinpoché a long-life ceremony together with a Guru Puja *tsok* ritual. The general public and the children of the local Tibetan school who were present at the ceremony offered the three representations and lined up to offer ceremonial scarves. Afterward in the temple, Rinpoché merged the wisdom beings and the samaya beings by way of the horseback consecration.

On the morning of the sixth, in response to a request by the local Tibetan school, Rinpoché gave the permission initiation of the Three Wrathful Forms Combined, an explanation of the Fourteenth Dalai Lama's *Prayer of the Words of Truth*, and general words of advice to an audience of about five hundred lay and monastic recipients drawn from the general public and the staff and students of the school. All offerings that he received that day, he returned to the presenters.

The following day Rinpoché returned to Dharamsala, and two days later he visited me and told me of his activities in Kullu, Manali, and Shimla, which were acts of great kindness bringing benefit to living beings and the doctrine.

The fourteenth was the twenty-second of the ninth Tibetan month, the day commemorating the Buddha's descent from the celestial realms. Rinpoché came to the Thekchen Chöling temple to preside over a consecration.

On the seventh of November, Rinpoché conferred on me the preparatory rituals for the Sitātapatrā initiation, and on the following day he bestowed the actual initiation. Afterward he gave me the permission initiations for Four-Faced Mahākāla and Palden Lhamo. On the following day, Rinpoché bestowed the life entrustment of the five king emanations on the new incarnation of Dzokchen Pema Rikzin,[189] assistant tutor Serkong Rinpoché, the Nechung oracle, and fifteen monks from Nechung Monastery. On the twentieth Rinpoché performed an exorcism ritual by way of Sitātapatrā for the nun Kalden from the Tibetan Children's Village, among others.

For five days beginning from the twenty-third, and in accordance with my schedule, Rinpoché kindly gave me many teachings that I had requested. On the last day he came to see me because he was leaving for Mundgod.

On the third of December he left for Delhi, where he gave a long-life initiation to Adar from Lithang and about thirty other Delhi residents.

Rinpoché flew from Delhi to Belgaum on the sixth, and from there he traveled by car to his labrang residence in Drepung Monastery. The Drepung council, Drepung Loseling, and others presented him with the mandala and the three representations.

The twenty-fifth of the Tibetan tenth month commemorates the day that the great Mañjunātha lama, Tsongkhapa, left for the Tuṣita buddha realm.[190] Rinpoché was invited by the Trehor Trungsar Labrang to preside over the assembly in the morning and by Drepung Loseling in the afternoon. On the twenty-fourth of December, at the request of Gomang College, Rinpoché gave the permission initiation of Six-Armed Mahākāla to the entire monastic community of Ganden and Drepung. On the twenty-ninth, Sakya Trizin, the precious Sakya throneholder and illuminator of the doctrine of the Khön family, came to visit Ling Vajradhara, the precious tutor and throneholder of Ganden. They presented each other with ceremonial scarves and the three representations and spent an informal time together engaging in Dharma conversations on sutra and tantra. Sakya Rinpoché also visited Kyabjé Trijang Rinpoché that day.

1977

On the first of January 1977, Rinpoché visited Trijang Rinpoché in Ganden, and the two tutors spent a relaxing day together. Four days later, Rinpoché presided over the Drepung Loseling assembly during a wealth-generating ritual. On the sixteenth, Losang Lungrik, the labrang manager, suffered something like a mild stroke. This caused Rinpoché great concern, and beginning from the fifteenth of the Tibetan month, he performed a cleansing ritual using the deity Vajravidāraṇa.

On the eighteenth, in Ganden Shartsé, Rinpoché began a transmission and teachings on Hortön's *Rays of the Sun: Training the Mind in Bodhicitta* to an audience of about five hundred. The teaching was completed on the twenty-ninth. All offerings Rinpoché received during the teachings were returned. On the following day, at the request of Chatreng Gé Losang Chözin, Rinpoché bestowed the permission initiation of Avalokiteśvara Who Liberates All Beings from the Unfortunate Realms on the recipients of the teachings. On the thirty-first, Drepung Loseling offered a long-life ceremony with a Guru Puja ritual to both tutors. On the same day the Drepung Monastery governing body and representatives of the Mundgod settlements offered Rinpoché the three representations and requested that he set his lotus feet upon the earth for a long time.

On the second of February, the Ganden Monastery governing body invited Rinpoché to sit at the head of the assembly with Trijang Rinpoché and offered them a long-life ceremony according to the sutra tradition. Afterward Rinpoché visited Trijang Rinpoché's residence, where they took lunch.

The following day, in the Drepung Loseling assembly hall, the Trijang Labrang sponsored the long-life ceremony Halting the Ḍākinīs' Escort with a Guru Puja ritual for the precious throneholder. Trijang Rinpoché offered the eight auspicious substances and other tokens of longevity. The following day Rinpoché received from Kyabjé Trijang Rinpoché a long-life initiation in the Niguma tradition. The labrang manager, Losang Lungrik, also attended. Beginning on the sixth of February, Rinpoché gave four days of teachings in the Drepung Loseling debate courtyard to around forty lamas, tulkus, and geshés on undertaking the great-approach retreat of single-deity Vajrabhairava. On the tenth, Rinpoché was invited to perform a consecration preparation at Ganden Shartsé. While there he visited Trijang Labrang, where Trijang Rinpoché specially performed for Losang Lungrik the Cleansing Ritual Expelling Poison. Rinpoché also sat in with his manager.

The nineteenth of February was the first day of the fire-snake year. In the labrang, all the usual ceremonies were followed, after which Rinpoché was invited to sit as head of the assembly, where he was offered tsampa, tea, sweet rice, and so on. After this, he granted audience to the abbot, lamas, and officials and distributed protection cords.

On the twenty-first, Rinpoché went to Ganden. While there, he visited Trijang Rinpoché and offered him longevity pills consecrated during a long-life meditation practice and a ceremonial scarf as a New Year greeting. The two tutors spent some time together in relaxed conversation.

On the morning of the twenty-fourth, Rinpoché was invited to the great assembly at Drepung, where he held an auspicious vow-purification ceremony with the monks. Afterward, Drepung Loseling invited him to their assembly hall, and the assembled monks offered him a long-life ceremony. The monastery council, the various houses, and the Sakya and Nyingma monasteries offered him the three representations and ceremonial scarves. Beginning on the twenty-sixth, Rinpoché sat at the head of the joint Ganden and Drepung prayer festival assembly in the Drepung great assembly hall. On the first day, during the morning tea session, the assembled monks offered the two tutors a long-life ceremony according to the sutra tradition. Afterward, Trijang Rinpoché visited Rinpoché in his rooms at the labrang, where he offered him a ceremonial scarf as a New Year greeting, and the two tutors spent some time together in conversation.

On the first of March, Rinpoché bestowed novice-monk vows on forty-five recipients in the Drepung Loseling debate courtyard, and on the third of March he gave full-ordination vows to twenty novice monks. On the seventh, as requested by the governing bodies of Drepung and Ganden and by Gowo Chözé,[191] Rinpoché conferred a long-life initiation to a lay and monastic audience of several thousand people. He satisfied them with the nectar of advice that stressed how important it was for the ordained to apply themselves equally to study, contemplation, and meditation, and for the lay community to strive to leave behind wrong actions and develop good actions.

On the fourteenth of March, the great Vajradhara and his two attendants left for Delhi by air. On the morning of the eighteenth, he gave a long-life initiation to a Western woman called Pema and others. In the afternoon he left for Dharamsala. On the twenty-second, Rinpoché came to visit me, and I spent a pleasant time with the Vajradhara tutor and Trijang Rinpoché. On the thirtieth, Rinpoché was invited to Tushita Meditation Centre, where he conferred full monastic vows on some Westerners and novice vows on others. Six days later, on my instructions, the Private Office sponsored a long-life ceremony for Rinpoché in his room at the labrang. After this, at my suggestion, Rinpoché conferred novice monk vows on an Indian.

On the sixth of June, the Nechung Dharma-king protector was invoked through an oracle and asked for prediction and advice. On the thirteenth Rinpoché and I engaged in a meaningful discussion. On the thirtieth, about twenty people, including Western practitioners of Buddhism, Geshé Ngawang Dargyey, and other participating monks joyfully performed the Guru Puja ceremony, together with a *tsok* ritual, in Rinpoché's room at the labrang. It was sponsored by the Western novice monk Thupten Chödar.

On the sixth of July, I reached my forty-third year, and the great root lama, accompanied by Trijang Rinpoché, visited me and offered ceremonial scarves. On the twenty-sixth, Rinpoché gave a long-life initiation to Mrs. Dekhar, the nun who is the widow of the former acting prime minister Dekharwa.

On the eighteenth of August, Gyütö Monastery offered Rinpoché a long-life ceremony. During the ceremony, Trijang Rinpoché presented a written request asking that the great Vajradhara remain forever as a permanent entity on this earth, to be the powerful guide and protector for the Dharma and living beings, and presented him with long-life substances consecrated in a longevity meditation practice. On the thirtieth of August, Rinpoché came to see me at my invitation, and I told him of the teachings I had given to various monasteries on my recent visit to South India. He replied to these accounts with heartfelt delight.

On the third of September, Rinpoché gave teachings on the *Torma Offering Rites* and the initiation of the Master as Longevity Deity to Thubten Zopa and seven other lamas, tulkus, and geshés. On the eighth, he gave teachings on the *Hundred Deities of Tuṣita* guruyoga to an American by way of an interpreter. On the twenty-second of September, Rinpoché came to visit me at my invitation. In a very relaxed manner, he cut many knots of doubt I had regarding the difficult points of the profound and vast teachings.

On the thirteenth of October, the Religious Affairs Office requested Rinpoché to perform a longevity meditation practice for my long life. This he kindly accepted to do. Four days later Nechung was consulted.

At that time, the labrang manager, Losang Lungrik, was seriously ill with heart and edema complications. Consequently, Kyabjé Trijang Rinpoché came especially to the labrang and gave him some precious relic pills, performed a ritual command to the obstruction to leave, using Hayagrīva, and gave advice on treatment. The great Vajradhara showed great concern, and every evening just before going to bed, he would give Losang Lungrik relic pills and perform ritual commands for him.

On the eighteenth of October, Tibetans who lived in Canada requested the precious tutor to remain a long time on this earth. On the twenty-eighth, Rinpoché performed an exorcism ritual using the female deity Bhagavatī Ārya Sitātapatrā for Jampa Söpa and his family. Two days later, the Gyütö monks performed a long-life ceremony for Rinpoché, which he kindly accepted. It was sponsored by Jacqueline, the French nurse who cared for Rinpoché when he attended the hospital in France.

On the twenty-second of the ninth Tibetan month, I had presented a request to the precious tutor in which I asked him for teachings on Sanskrit grammar. Rinpoché replied that he had the transmission of Anubhūti's

Sarasvatī Grammar Treatise and Sarvavarmā's *Kalāpa Sutra* and asked me to consider which would be more appropriate. I performed a divination, and the *Kalāpa Sutra* was deemed more appropriate. I passed this information on to Rinpoché, who replied that he had received teachings a few times on the *Sarasvatī Grammar Treatise* but had not received teachings on the *Kalāpa Sutra*. Moreover, he had not looked at the text. So that Rinpoché might study the commentary, I offered him a copy kept in my residence. Consequently, beginning on the fourteenth of October, and fitting into my engagement schedule, Rinpoché gave me teachings on the *Kalāpa Sutra* up to and including the chapter on the five types of sandhi.

The precious tutor had received the *Kalāpa Sutra* from Khunu Lama Tenzin Gyaltsen before I was born. The commentary used in the transmission was composed by the early scholar Sasang Maṭi Panchen. In the intervening forty years or so, he had not found time to look at the text, and yet now having looked at the text just once, when giving the commentary he was able to recite freely from memory its explanations based on the *Kalāpa Sutra* root text. I thought to myself with a sense of real wonder that he must truly be a master pandit of the five sciences, and a deep and extraordinary respect and faith was born in me. Whenever I stumbled over some of the Sanskrit pronunciation, it caused the precious tutor much mirth. For me it was a wonderful and fortunate occasion.

Sometime later Rinpoché gave me teachings on poetics using the Fifth Dalai Lama's *Melody to Delight Sarasvatī*. These were not fully completed.

34 | The Greatest Accomplishment We Could Wish For

O N THE SIXTH of November 1977, the great Vajradhara came to see me before leaving to spend the winter in Sarnath and Bodhgaya. He left Dharamsala on the tenth. Arriving in Sarnath at the invitation of the Geluk Students' Welfare Committee, he was welcomed by Samdhong Rinpoché, who was the principal of the Tibetan Institute of Higher Studies, as well as Indian and Tibetan teachers and students. He stayed, as was arranged, in the Chinese temple.

On the fourteenth, Rinpoché gave a long-life initiation to Bakula Rinpoché from Ladakh and others. On the following day, the great Vajradhara and his attendants, accompanied by the French nun Thupten Drölkar and the French nurse Jacqueline, visited Śrāvastī, the sacred place where the Blessed Buddha spent many years with his disciples. There he stayed in the guesthouse of the Mahabodhi Society. Beside the guesthouse a shrine was being built for the descendants of a mother who used to own a shop in Shigatsé, and at the family's request Rinpoché performed a consecration of the mantras to be placed inside the shrine and made prayers. The labrang also made extensive offerings. Rinpoché spent a relaxing and very enjoyable time at this sacred spot.

At the request of Neshar Thupten Tharpa, the former external affairs minister, Rinpoché gave a transmission of *Praise of Dependent Origination*, which was composed by Tsongkhapa in acknowledgment of how the Buddha taught emptiness in terms of dependent origination. Rinpoché also gave a discourse on the greatness of this sacred place. On the seventeenth, Rinpoché traveled to Kuśinagarī, where the Buddha exhibited the act of passing into nirvana. He stayed in the newly constructed Tibetan monastery, as arranged by the Namgyal monk Tsangpa, and made many offerings and prayers.

After this visit he returned to Sarnath. As previously requested by the

Geluk Students' Welfare Committee, Rinpoché gave the initiation of glorious Vajrabhairava and teachings on *Guru Puja* to about 450 devotees beginning on the twenty-first of November in the Tibetan monastery. After these teachings, at the request of the administration monk official Pema from the Tibetan settlement in Switzerland and others, Rinpoché gave teachings on the Kālacakra guruyoga he himself had composed. The labrang gave tea, food, and donations to the recipients of the teaching and performed the thousand five-senses offerings in front of the great shrine. Drepung Loseling sponsored a long-life ceremony and made donations to the recipients.

On the fourth of December, the Geluk Students' Welfare Committee offered a long-life ceremony to Rinpoché, which he happily accepted. The principal, Samdhong Rinpoché, performed the mandala offering and discourse. On the following day, at the request of the monk Losang Tenzin from Tau and Tenzin Phuntsok from the labrang, Rinpoché gave the permission initiation of Avalokiteśvara Who Liberates All Beings from the Unfortunate Realms and a long-life initiation. As part of the ceremonies on the day of the offerings of the twenty-fifth, Rinpoché gave a discourse and imparted advice, as requested.

On the seventh Rinpoché left for Bodhgaya. On top of his usual longevity meditation using Cittamaṇi White Tārā, Rinpoché performed morning sessions of a special longevity meditation beginning on the thirteenth. On the thirty-first, Rinpoché gave teachings for a few days on the great-approach retreat of Vajrabhairava to Jamyang Tulku of Sera Jé, and others.

1978

On the first of January 1978, Rinpoché bestowed novice-monk vows on ten recipients. I arrived in Bodhgaya at half past seven on the morning of the fourteenth, and Rinpoché welcomed me with an incense-led procession and offered me a mandala and the three representations. On the same day Rinpoché kindly bestowed lay vows on a French woman.

On the twenty-sixth, at the request of the artist Ngawang Norbu from Darjeeling, the Bodhgaya monk Tsöndrü Gyaltsen, and Drakgyap Ngaktsé, Rinpoché gave the oral transmission of the mantras of Tārā and Śākyamuni and a long-life initiation of White Tārā to an audience of about ten thousand. On the morning of the following day, Rinpoché attended the horseback consecration in the main temple of the sacred shrine, which I presided over with monks from both tantric colleges.

The eighth of February was the first day of the earth-horse year, and Rinpoché took part in the ceremonies as usual. From the thirteenth, Rinpoché was head of the assembly for the prayer festival. At the request of Mrs. Dekhang Noryang Norbu of Kalimpong, Rinpoché attended an auspicious vow-purification ceremony with all the monks. On the sixteenth, the labrang and the monastery jointly sponsored a long-life ceremony by way of the Guru Puja ritual and an elaborate *tsok* ritual. On the twenty-eighth, as requested by Gojo Gyurmé from the Tibetan settlement in Switzerland, Rinpoché conferred the White Tārā long-life initiation on about two hundred monastic and lay devotees.

On the tenth of March, Rinpoché brought a host of blessings to the newly renovated protector chapel of the Bodhgaya Tibetan monastery by performing the horseback consecration.

On the thirteenth, Rinpoché left for Dharamsala and came to visit me on the fifteenth. On the twenty-seventh, Kyabjé Trijang Rinpoché visited the labrang and offered Rinpoché the three volumes of his collected works, which Rinpoché joyfully accepted.

On the first of April, Rinpoché was invited to sit as head of the Namgyal Monastery assembly in the Thekchen Chöling temple. On the third, he gave novice-monk vows to two Westerners and five Tibetans. On the thirteenth, at the request of some Tibetans who had settled in Canada, Rinpoché conferred a long-life initiation. Afterward he gave novice-monk vows to a Westerner followed by the permission initiation of the Three Wrathful Forms Combined to Chamdo Gelek Losang and others.

On the twenty-fifth of April, I invited Rinpoché to my residence, where he gave me advice and resolved my doubts concerning a retreat on a particular meditation deity I was about to undertake and other topics.

On the fourth of June, Rinpoché was invited to Tushita Meditation Centre to perform single-deity Vajrabhairava self-initiation with those who had completed the generation-stage retreat. On the seventeenth, Nechung was invoked. On the twenty-first, Rinpoché gave a long-life initiation to twelve people in his residence.

On the nineteenth, at the request of Dakpo Bamchö Tulku, Rinpoché gave a permission initiation of Vajrasattva.

On the eighth of August, Rinpoché was invited to Geden Choeling Nunnery to give teachings on Tsongkhapa's *Foundation of All Good Qualities.* He remained for a few hours at the nunnery in relaxing conversation.

On the twelfth, Rinpoché gave teachings on the topic of refuge to about fifteen Westerners in his room, thereby fulfilling their wishes. These included the cause of refuge, the objects of refuge, and the commitments of taking refuge. On the twenty-sixth, Rinpoché visited Kyabjé Trijang Rinpoché in his residence in Gangchen Kyishong. Two days later I invited Rinpoché to my residence and asked his guidance on various matters.

On the tenth of September, Mongolian Geshé Wangyal, who was resident in America, visited Rinpoché and showed him slides of Mongolian monasteries in America. Rinpoché enjoyed the presentation, and they talked a lot about America.

From the fifth to the fourteenth of October, Rinpoché happily gave the initiation and explanations of single-deity Vajrabhairava to the Western monk Jampa Söpa[192] and about forty others. On the sixteenth, I invited Rinpoché for lunch and sought his advice to resolve certain doubts. On the twenty-sixth, Rinpoché gave novice-monk vows to twelve people.

On the eighth of November, Rinpoché gave teachings on the *Torma Offering Rites* to the monk Dönyö from the Tibetan Children's Village and others. The following day, in response to a request from some Westerners, Rinpoché gave teachings on refuge.

Some time ago the protector Nechung had announced through the oracle that it would be excellent if the Dalai Lama, as the head of the entire doctrine, could receive as many initiations, transmissions, and core teachings as possible from all Tibetan traditions. It had not been convenient to implement this immediately. Therefore, on the thirteenth of November, I invited the precious tutor to the room where Nechung is invoked, in front of the statue known as the lord of Mangyul Kyirong. Rinpoché is not only my root guru in this life, but in life after life he will be my root guru necessarily caring for me with compassion until I attain enlightenment. The protector is a warrior deity that has a special connection with the incarnations of the Dalai Lamas and with the Ganden Phodrang, the government of Tibet. Mangyul Kyirong, or Noble Wati Sangpo, is a statue of Avalokiteśvara, the patron deity of Tibet and recognized by the Great Fifth Dalai Lama as one of the "two noble brothers." Also in the room was a scroll painting of Palden Lhamo, which had served as the vehicle for meditational divination for the Dalai Lamas since the omniscient Gendun Gyatso, the Second Dalai Lama. A gathering of high lamas also attended.

Up to that time, except for the initiations from the Fifth Dalai Lama's *Pure Visions: The Sealed Secrets*, I had received no other Phurba initiations and transmissions. A Phurba practice from the Nyingma tradition called Innermost Essence Blade had been revealed by Tertön Sögyal Lerap Lingpa and was a treasure practice performed at appropriate times by the previous Dalai Lama. It had continued to be a regular practice followed by Namgyal Monastery, and at the urging of Nechung, I had performed the torma casting of this practice a few times together with the monastery, with evidential results. Nevertheless, in the presence of these deities and high lamas, I declared that I would perform a divination to see if I should seek to receive another Phurba initiation or not. The divination came out that I should again request the initiation, transmission, and core teachings on Phurba.

Afterward, the precious tutor said with great certainty, "The extensive development of His Holiness's enlightened activities is the greatest accomplishment we could wish for. As a means to fulfill that, no one with any intelligence would have the slightest doubt of the necessity of His Holiness receiving the Phurba initiation." In no uncertain terms, therefore, he gave me his approval. Kyabjé Trijang Rinpoché was not in Dharamsala at that time. Therefore later, when both tutors were together, I informed him of the above.

Incidentally, aside from determining whether I should seek out this Phurba initiation or not, we had made no divination to discover who I should request it from. Therefore Nechung was later consulted, and the names of several lamas were put forward for divination also. The name of Dilgo Khyentsé Rinpoché unanimously appeared. That morning, when Nechung was invoked and the divination made, the Vajradhara tutor was present.

A few days later Rinpoché visited me to announce that he was leaving for Bodhgaya. On the sixteenth he left Dharamsala and on the eighteenth arrived in Bodhgaya, where he was greeted by the monastic community. On the thirtieth and thirty-first, the two tutors offered each other long-life ceremonies.

Beginning on the fifteenth of December, Rinpoché performed special sessions of the White Tārā longevity meditations.

1979

On the second of January 1979, Rinpoché gave a long-life initiation to Mrs. Dekyi Surkhang. On the twenty-sixth, he gave a long-life initiation to the fully ordained Italian monk Thubten Dönyö and about twenty-five others. On the thirty-first, at the request of the monk Tsöndrü Gyaltsen, Rinpoché gave the preparatory rituals for the initiation of thirteen-deity Vajrabhairava, followed by the actual initiation, to around two hundred monastic and lay recipients.

On the second of February, at the request of a Tibetan living in Gangtok, Rinpoché gave a long-life initiation to about three hundred recipients. On the following day, to about two hundred recipients, Rinpoché kindly gave permission initiations of Mahākāla, Palden Lhamo, and the outer, inner, and secret Kālarūpa. This was followed by the permission initiation of Medicine Buddha and a discourse. Beginning on the seventh, the three-day consecration ritual known as Causing the Rain of Goodness to Fall was performed for the Tibetan monastery temple and its sacred objects, and Rinpoché sat as head of the assembly. It was sponsored by the monk Tsöndrü Gyaltsen. After this, Rinpoché gave instructions on the great-approach retreat of Vajrabhairava to four monks from Gyümé.

On the next day I arrived in Bodhgaya, and Rinpoché, as abbot of the monastery, presented me with the mandala and a ceremonial scarf. On the sixteenth he gave teachings on the sixty-four-part torma-offering ritual to the four monks from Gyümé. The following day was the first day of the earth-sheep year, and Rinpoché performed the customary ceremonies.

On the fifteenth of March Rinpoché traveled by train to Delhi, where he stayed at the house of Thupten Tsering. In response to a request made earlier, Rinpoché opened the new assembly hall of the Drepung tantric college in Delhi. On the eighteenth, he gave a permission initiation of the Three Wrathful Forms Combined at the request of the Tibetans living in Delhi and a long-life initiation at the request of Ama Chözom, owner of the York Restaurant. On the twentieth, Rinpoché gave a transmission of the *Praises to the Twenty-One Tārās* to Sadu Rinchen and others.[193] From the twenty-sixth, Rinpoché spent six days at the All India Medical Institute, where he received a complete physical checkup by Dr. Bhatia and others. On the afternoon of the thirty-first, Rinpoché performed a consecration ritual at Tibet House.

On the next day, the first of April, Rinpoché arrived back in Dharamsala. On the third, he visited me and informed me of his medical examination, and other matters. On the tenth at seven in the morning, the Tibetan government, representatives of the people, and the Amdo Association offered me a long-life ceremony by way of the ritual of the five immortality deities of the Amitāyus inner accomplishment, during which the precious tutor kindly performed the mandala-offering discourse. On the following day, at the request of Gelek Losang of Drepung Loseling, Rinpoché gave the permission initiation of Medicine Buddha in the Thekchen Chöling temple. On the twenty-second, at the request of Gyalsé Tulku, abbot of Tawang Monastery, Rinpoché conferred the permission initiation of White Mañjuśrī. Also, on the twenty-fourth, Rinpoché gave teachings on the *Torma Offering Rites* to Gyalsé Tulku, Geshé Sönam Rinchen, and others. On the thirtieth, Rinpoché gave a long-life initiation and a Tārā transmission to Drölma Yudrön, who lived in the United States, and her relatives.

On the sixth of May, Rinpoché gave the permission initiation of the Three Wrathful Forms Combined to Gomo Tulku and others.

Kyabjé Trijang Rinpoché was not feeling well around this time, and so on the eighth of May, Rinpoché went to his Tashi Rapten residence and made the request that he plant his lotus feet a long time upon this earth. Trijang Rinpoché expressed great joy with this visit, saying, "This unarranged and spontaneous auspicious event is without doubt wonderful proof of our connection that is bound by mutual faith, commitment, and purity." On the twentieth, at the request of two Italian monks, Rinpoché gave the permission initiation of oath-bound Kālarūpa. On the twenty-fourth, he gave a transmission of the *Guru Puja* to Chokdrup Gelek from Switzerland and others. On the twenty-eighth, the Religious Affairs Office sponsored an earth-treasure vase ritual in the Thekchen Chöling temple, for which the Vajradhara tutor attended as the head of the ritual monks. That afternoon I invited Rinpoché to my residence, where I requested Rinpoché to perform the propitiation of Palden Lhamo, the main government protector, so that my forthcoming visit to Outer Mongolia would be of benefit to the Buddha's teaching and living beings. Consequently, he performed the propitiation for a week beginning on the seventeenth of June. On the twenty-eighth, Rinpoché performed the summer invocation of the great Dharma king protector Nechung.

On the sixth of July, Rinpoché offered me a ceremonial scarf, and so on, on the occasion of the celebration of my birthday. On the twenty-second, Rinpoché performed an exorcism ritual by way of Sitātapatrā for the Children's Village nun Kalden and others. Rinpoché was invited to the Tibetan Library, where a new three-dimensional Avalokiteśvara mandala had been constructed. There with Trijang Rinpoché, he performed the cleansing

The two tutors and director Geshé Ngawang Dargyey, foreground, consecrating a three-dimensional mandala of Avalokiteśvara at the Library of Tibetan Works and Archives, Dharamsala

and consecration ritual. Afterward the tutors were invited by the Dharma teacher Geshé Ngawang Dargyey of Sera Jé Monastery to his residence, where he satisfied them with refreshment.

On the fourteenth, the eighteenth, and the twenty-first, rituals were performed in Thekchen Chöling temple for the benefit of the Buddha's teaching and the people of Tibet, and Rinpoché was invited to sit as head of the assembly. At the request of Dakpo Bamchö Tulku, from the sixteenth to the twenty-third Rinpoché gave a daily session of teachings on Tsongkhapa's *Essence of the Excellent Explanation: Differentiating the Definitive and the Provisional.* On the twenty-eighth, he gave the permission initiation of the Vajrabhairava mantra formulation to Bakula Rinpoché and others.

From the sixth to the eighth of September, Rinpoché gave the single-deity Vajrabhairava initiation, the permission initiation of Kālarūpa, and teachings on the *Hundred Deities of Tuṣita* guruyoga to Bob from Australia and about twenty other Westerners. On the twenty-seventh, Rinpoché gave a long-life initiation to the incarnation of Simok Rinpoché, his family, and members of the labrang.

The Western monk Jampa Söpa, together with the Gyütö monks, offered Rinpoché a long-life ceremony on the first of October. On the fifth Rinpoché kindly gave the permission initiation of the three wrathful Vajrapāṇi forms to Rap Yangchen and other monks from Namgyal Monastery. On the morning of the twenty-fourth, Rinpoché performed the summer invocation of Nechung. On the same day he visited me. On the twenty-seventh, Rinpoché was invited to the Tibetan Children's Village. On the thirtieth he gave a transmission of Chekawa's *Seven-Point Mind Training* and Atiśa's *Lamp on the Path to Enlightenment* to Drigung Chetsang Rinpoché.

At half past ten on the morning of the second of November, I came to the labrang to ask for some advice. Rinpoché more than exceeded my expectations with the answers that he happily and compassionately provided. On the third Rinpoché gave the permission initiation of the Three Wrathful Forms Combined to the monk Tenzin, a member of staff from the Children's Village, and others. At half past ten on the morning of the seventh, Rinpoché came to my residence, where he informed me of his regular winter departure to Bodhgaya and happily bestowed on me the purification ritual using Vajrabhairava that I had requested earlier.

Rinpoché left Dharamsala on the afternoon of the ninth and arrived in Delhi the next morning, where he stayed at the house of Thupten Tsering. There, on the morning of the thirteenth, Rinpoché gave the permission initiation of the Three Wrathful Forms Combined to Nyakré Khentrul and about fifteen others. On the following day Rinpoché was invited to the Tushita Mahayana Meditation Centre in Delhi, where he participated in a Guru Puja *tsok* ritual with Westerners.[194] He also gave, in accord with their wishes, a short discourse.

On the morning of the sixteenth, Rinpoché flew to Mundgod. That evening he stayed in Hubli. The following morning he traveled to his residence in the labrang at Drepung Monastery, where the monastery governing body, the colleges, and so on offered him the three representations and ceremonial scarves. On the twenty-first, Rinpoché performed the opening ceremony of the new assembly hall of Ling House. Afterward, representatives of Drepung and Ganden Monasteries and the abbots of the various colleges offered Rinpoché ceremonial scarves. The following day, Drepung's monastic governing body sponsored a long-life ceremony performed by the Drepung monks in the assembly hall using the Guru Puja for the purpose of the Vajradhara tutor remaining a long time on this earth to benefit the Dharma and living beings.

In response to the long-standing requests of Drepung Loseling and the monk Tsöndrü of the Bodhgaya monastery, Rinpoché gave the Vajrabhairava initiation and experiential instructions on its two stages in the Drepung Loseling assembly hall to about eleven hundred monks and around 150 lay recipients from the twenty-ninth of November to the seventh of December. This was followed by teachings and a transmission on Tsongkhapa's stages of the path text *Song of Experience* given at the request of Trungsar Labrang.

On the tenth, at the request of the Drepung governing body, in the great assembly hall of Drepung, Rinpoché gave the permission initiation of the Master as Longevity Deity to a monastic and lay audience of about thirty-seven hundred. This teaching was supplemented by a discourse in which Rinpoché urged the ordained members of the audience to maintain the fundamental basis of pure ethics and to engage in equal study, contemplation, and meditation on the meaning of the words of the Buddha. He urged the lay community to strive to abandon nonvirtuous deeds and cultivate good as much as possible. On the next day, in the Gomang assembly hall, to an audience of two thousand monastic and lay devotees, Rinpoché gave to great effect the transmission and teachings on Jé Tsongkhapa's *Three Principal Aspects of the Path*.

At the request of Ganden Monastery's governing body, Rinpoché gave teachings on the *Hundred Deities of Tuṣita* guruyoga to an audience of around two thousand in Ganden's great assembly hall. On that day Trijang Rinpoché came to the labrang for a visit. In the Drepung Loseling courtyard, Rinpoché gave novice-monk ordination to eighty-seven recipients, including tulkus, and full ordination to eighteen novice monks. On the twenty-second, Rinpoché went to Ganden, and in the Shartsé assembly hall he offered a long-life ceremony to Trijang Rinpoché, thereby inaugurating auspicious omens for his long life. On the twenty-sixth Rinpoché gave explanations on undertaking the Vajrabhairava approach retreat to thirteen monks from the two tantric colleges. On the morning of the twenty-eighth, he conducted the opening ceremonies of the new assembly hall of Drepung's Trehor House. In the afternoon, he gave the permission initiation of Palden Lhamo to about six hundred recipients. On the thirty-first Rinpoché presided over the prosperity rituals at Gomang College.

The abbot of Gomang at that time, the Mongolian Ngawang Nyima, mentioned to Rinpoché that not only had the Vajradhara tutor previously given novice-monk vows to the sixth incarnation of Jamyang Shepa, and had sent teachers to Tashi Khyil Monastery in Amdo to set up various ritual practices there in connection with the establishment of a branch of Gyütö, but now he was attending the Gomang prosperity rituals. He was showing great kindness to Gomang College! Rinpoché joked, "Not only that. I am a monk of Gomang. I am the incarnation of the Mongolian Döndrup Gyatso, the Fifty-Sixth Ganden Throneholder." The abbot also told of the time Rinpoché was receiving teachings from Buldü Rinpoché of Gomang. In the audience was the fourth incarnation of Takphu Garwang with his consort. Rinpoché remarked that the former Mokchok Tulku, Yeshé Tenpai Gyaltsen, had seen Takphu's consort as having one eye, and so Rinpoché was sure she was a manifestation of the one-eyed goddess Ekajaṭī.

On the same day Rinpoché performed a horseback consecration at Gowo House.

1980

On the morning of the second of January 1980, Rinpoché and Trijang Rinpoché were invited by Ganden Monastery to the great assembly hall, where the entire Ganden assembly offered the tutors a long-life ceremony. In the afternoon a similar long-life ceremony was performed at Ganden's Shartsé College. On the following day Trijang Labrang sponsored a long-life ceremony for the Vajradhara tutor in the Shartsé assembly hall. Trijang Rinpoché offered the auspicious substances and other tokens of longevity and made prayers for his longevity. At the invitation of Drepung Loseling, Rinpoché presided over a prosperity ritual in conjunction with prayers for spiritual and secular wealth to flow continually like a river.

On the eighth, Rinpoché was invited to preside over the proceedings of the third meeting of the Association for the Preservation of the Geluk Tradition in the main assembly hall of Drepung Monastery, during which certificates of scholarship and awards were presented to lharampa geshés. He also gave a speech in which he called for the implementation of what had been learned at the conference. On the thirteenth, Rinpoché was invited to the residence of Phukhang Song Rinpoché at Ganden. There with Trijang Rinpoché he was served lunch. In the presence of the two tutors, Song Rinpoché offered a long-life ceremony by way of the Guru Puja ritual. Afterward the two tutors, Song Rinpoché, and labrang managers Losang Lungrik and Palden had a group photograph taken. On the eighteenth Rinpoché visited Trijang Rinpoché at his residence, and the two tutors offered each other ceremonial scarves and the three representations.

On the twentieth Rinpoché left Mundgod by train for Hunsur, and from there he traveled by car to Sera Monastery. As he drew near, he was welcomed by the monks, who escorted him in a procession to his residence above Sera Jé. In response to a long-standing request from Trehor House, for five days from the twenty-second, Rinpoché gave a transmission and teachings on Tsongkhapa's *Essence of Excellent Explanation: Differentiating the Definitive and the Provisional* to almost a thousand monks and about fifty lay Tibetans and Westerners. On the following day Trehor House, the Sera monastic governing body, and the public gathered in the main assembly hall to offer Rinpoché a long-life ceremony. The next day, to a monastic and lay audience of forty-five hundred, Rinpoché gave the permission initiation of Avalokiteśvara Who Liberates All Beings from the Unfortunate Realms, the initiations of Hayagrīva, Vajrapāṇi, and Garuḍa, and a long-life initiation. Afterward, the recipients presented offering scarves and received protection cords from Rinpoché. All offerings were returned by Rinpoché.

On the twenty-eighth, in response to a request from Sera Mé, Rinpoché gave the permission initiation of the general accomplishment of the three Buddha families and a transmission of Tsongkhapa's *Praise of Dependent Origination* to a monastic and lay audience of around a thousand. On the morning of the following day, in the Sera Jé assembly hall, Rinpoché gave the permission initiation of White Mañjuśrī and a transmission of *Speaking the Names of Mañjuśrī*. Over the next two days, in the main assembly hall, Rinpoché gave novice-monk vows to 224 recipients. On the morning of the thirty-first, Rinpoché was invited to Trehor House, where he gave a transmission of the *Hundred Deities of Tuṣita* guruyoga to about a 150 recipients. In the afternoon Rinpoché was invited to Tashi Lhunpo Monastery and Drakyap Monastery to perform consecrations. Since his younger days Dagyab Rinpoché had been a Dharma friend of Rinpoché, and they had attended many teachings together. Therefore, the two now spent a pleasant time together and talked about current events.

Rinpoché was also invited to the Phabongkha Labrang, where he spent a pleasant time. He urged the incarnation to engage as much as possible in study, contemplation, and meditation, as well as teaching, debating, and composing, thereby emulating the life of his predecessor Kyabjé Dechen Nyingpo.

On the second of February, Rinpoché left Sera Monastery. He went first to the Tenth Day Association[195] temple, where he gave a transmission of the *Hundred Deities of Tuṣita* guruyoga and Tsongkhapa's *Foundation of All Good Qualities*. From there he went to Chakur Tibetan settlement, where he gave the initiations of Hayagrīva, Vajrapāṇi, and Garuḍa and a long-life initiation to about 450 monastic and lay recipients. When being presented with ceremonial scarves, he gave all offerings to the settlement.

As invited, Rinpoché next traveled to Gyumé Monastery near Hunsur. There, on the morning of the third, the tantric college and Dzongkar Chödé Monastery jointly offered Rinpoché a long-life ceremony. In the afternoon he gave the permission initiation of Avalokiteśvara Who Liberates All Beings from the Unfortunate Realms to about five thousand lay and monastic recipients. The next day, at the request of Gyumé, he gave the permission initiation of the outer, inner, and secret accomplishment of Kālarūpa and the transmission of the *Guhyasamāja Root Tantra* to about 350 recipients. On the following day Rinpoché went to Dzongkar Chödé to perform the horseback consecration. On the sixth he went to my residence in Kollegal, where the settlement representatives offered Rinpoché the three representations and ceremonial scarves. On the morning of the following day, Rinpoché conferred a long-life initiation and granted audience to about four thousand recipients. In the afternoon, Rinpoché along with the Gyumé abbot and the ritual monks performed the Guru Puja *tsok* ritual in the protector temple.

On the ninth of February, Rinpoché left Bangalore by air for Delhi, and on the eleventh traveled to Bodhgaya. On the seventeenth he performed the celebratory commemoration of the iron-monkey new year. On the twenty-first, the Tibetan monastery and Ling Labrang, together with a few learned masters and dedicated practitioners such as Geshé Rikzin Tenpa Rinpoché and Pangnang Rinpoché, offered Rinpoché a long-life ceremony, which he happily accepted. From the twenty-fifth to the first of March, Rinpoché, as was customary, presided over the Great Prayer Festival.

On the second of March, Rinpoché gave novice-monk vows to twelve recipients, and on the fifth, he presided over a consecration at the Tibetan monastery. On the eighth, Rinpoché left for Delhi and stayed at Bakula Rinpoché's residence. On the following day Trijang Rinpoché came to visit Rinpoché, and they exchanged New Year ceremonial scarves and enjoyed pleasant conversation. On the fifteenth, Rinpoché gave a long-life initiation to Nyakré Khentrul and about forty others. Rinpoché spent the sixteenth to the twenty-second in the hospital for a medical examination. On the twenty-ninth I arrived in Delhi, and Rinpoché came to visit me in the Ashok Hotel.

On the second of April Rinpoché left for Dharamsala. On the fifteenth, members from the first Tibetan delegation from India to Tibet showed film footage of Tibet, which Rinpoché and I attended. On the twenty-second, Rinpoché visited Kyabjé Trijang Rinpoché at Gangchen Kyishong. On the twenty-seventh at the labrang, the Private Office sponsored a long-life ceremony by way of the Guru Puja ceremony for Rinpoché, performed by the Namgyal Monastery abbot and twelve monks.

At four o'clock on the following day Rinpoché came by invitation to my residence. We talked about the time, as described earlier, when in the presence of the two tutors Nechung was consulted concerning Phurba practice, divination was sought before the Mangyul Kyirong statue and a scroll painting of Palden Lhamo, with the result that it was unanimously determined that Dilgo Khyentsé Rinpoché should be requested for the initiation of the Phurba practice revealed by Tertön Sögyal Lerap Lingpa. Rinpoché said that all Tibetans wish for happiness and that the source of that happiness is the activities of His Holiness. Therefore, if such a practice contributes to that, I should certainly seek out this teaching.

Rinpoché gave a transmission of Tsongkhapa's *Foundation of All Good Qualities* and a permission initiation of Medicine Buddha to the Italian monk Thubten Dönyö and about eighty-seven other Westerners. On the twenty-fifth, Nechung was consulted in connection with Rinpoché's forthcoming visit to several Western countries and urged to act in order to remove any hindering circumstances to the visit and to ensure that all his activities designed to bring benefit to living beings and the doctrine would be effortlessly accomplished. The great protector pledged to do so.

On the fifth of June, Trijang Rinpoché visited Ling Rinpoché, where he presented him with a ceremonial scarf and farewell gifts, and prayed that in the West Rinpoché would eagerly seek out the best doctors for medical examinations and treatment, and that he would tirelessly turn the vast and profound wheel of Dharma for those who are ready.

On the nineteenth, Rinpoché established eight devotees in the way of the Buddha by way of monastic ordination.

PART 5

The Final Years, 1980–83

35 | Visits to Europe and North America

FRANCE

ON THE TWENTY-NINTH of June 1980,[196] Rinpoché flew to Paris by Air France. At the airport he was welcomed by Dakpo Bamchö Tulku and people from the various Dharma centers. He traveled to Bamchö Tulku's home, where he was to stay. Those who had welcomed him at the airport and many others who had connections with Rinpoché offered him ceremonial scarves, and Rinpoché took tea and sweet rice with them.

On the ninth and twelfth of July, as arranged by the Gephel Jangchup Ling Dharma Center, Rinpoché gave teachings to an audience of around 250 people, which included a few Tibetans and many French and other Western devotees. The teachings were based around Kadampa Geshé Langri Thangpa's work, *Eight Verses on Mind Training*, and included extensive teachings on developing the mind of enlightenment as taught in Śāntideva's *Guide to the Bodhisattva's Way of Life*, such as the faults of self-cherishing, the benefits of cherishing others, that self and others are alike in not wanting the slightest suffering and in never being satisfied by our happiness, and the practice of exchanging self with others.

On the thirteenth Rinpoché was invited to a Vietnamese temple, where he gave a Dharma discourse to around two hundred people as well as making offerings and reciting prayers. Afterward he was given lunch and had talks with the administrators about the center. A group photograph was taken, and Rinpoché was presented with a statue of the venerable Tārā made of porcelain, about fourteen inches tall and holding a vase in her hand. Rinpoché was very pleased with this gift and later placed it in his rooms among his most precious sacred objects.

On the fifteenth, he was invited by Sögyal Tulku to the Dorjé Nyingpo Nyingma Dharma Center. As requested he gave a Dharma teaching, followed by essential advice on the importance of following in the footsteps of great beings of the past, such as the great yogi and master of the Nyingma teaching Tsokyé Dorjé,[197] his twenty-five disciples, and others, as well as engaging thoroughly in the study, contemplation, and meditation of the paths of sutra and tantra. The following day was the special day that the unexcelled teacher Śākyamuni turned the first wheel of Dharma on the four truths in the Deer Park in Sarnath. Therefore, at the invitation of Gephel Jangchup Ling, Rinpoché attended a *tsok* ritual and Guru Puja ceremony with the members of the center. Afterward, Rinpoché gave a talk about the commemoration of this special day.

On the twenty-sixth, at the invitation of Mrs. Dewakyi, Rinpoché flew to Nimes on the coast and spent five days relaxing for his health. Every day he went for a walk on the beach. Sometimes he sat under a large parasol and observed the vacationers. He joyfully remarked, "This country is a place for work and play. When they work, they work hard, and when they play, they play well! Looking at these people, they all seem so happy!" Rinpoché did not go into the sea, but at the urging of others he walked into the water up to his knees.

ITALY

On the first of August, at the longstanding invitation of the Dharma centers in Italy, Rinpoché flew to Milan, where he stayed for five days at the home of Mirela Bastoni. At the Ghe Pel Ling Dharma center, Rinpoché taught *Eight Verses on Mind Training* and conferred a long-life initiation. Elio was the translator. Rinpoché went by air to Pisa and then by car to the Istituto Lama Tzong Khapa in Pomaia. About sixty Westerners and Tibetans welcomed him in the Tibetan way with ceremonial scarves. On the eighth and ninth Rinpoché gave the preparatory rituals for the single-deity Vajrabhairava followed by actual initiation to about seventy recipients from within and without the center, including Dagyab Rinpoché, thereby planting without doubt the seeds for the attainment of the four enlightened forms. In the discourse on the day of preparation for the initiation, Rinpoché talked extensively about training in the paths common to sutra and tantra, as well as briefly on the differences between sutra and tantra, the features of tantra, and the four classes of tantra. Nevertheless, in response to a request from the recipients, he also gave an explanation of the complete paths of sutra and tantra based on Tsongkhapa's *Foundation of All Good Qualities*. Orgyen Tseten, the former abbot of Gyümé, was among the recipients, and at Vajradhara's request he presided over the chanting for the commentary torma, the mandala offering, the prayers, and so on during the discourse. Luca Corona translated the discourse into Italian, and his brother Massimo translated it into English. The discourse of the precious lama was profound and vast, and some of the Westerners had difficulty comprehending it. Therefore, when it came to the topic of the completion stage, Rinpoché only gave the outlines and did not elaborate. On the last day of the discourse, the recipients offered Rinpoché a long-life ceremony by way of the Guru Puja *tsok* ritual, which he happily accepted.

Each day after the teachings had finished, Rinpoché would relax in casual clothes on the veranda of labrang manager Losang Lungrik's room. There he would occasionally meet Dagyab Rinpoché and former abbot Orgyen Tseten and answer their questions on Dharma. (plates 32 and 33)

On the twentieth, Rinpoché kindly gave complete lay vows to some Westerners and novice monastic vows to others. Rinpoché presented a painting of the hundred deities of Tuṣita to the center as an object for their faith. Later that day, he received a telegram from the Mongolian Chöjé Lama in the United States requesting that the Vajradhara tutor bestow the single-deity Vajrabhairava initiation when he came to New York. Rinpoché accepted.

SWITZERLAND

On the following day Rinpoché flew to Geneva, where he was welcomed by Phalha Thupten Öden, Geshé Rapten, and many other Tibetans and Westerners. From Geneva he traveled by car to the Tharpa Chöling Dharma center.[198] On the twenty-fourth, with Gönsar Tulku translating, Rinpoché gave a White Mañjuśrī permission initiation and a White Tārā long-life initiation to about two hundred recipients. On the next day he began a three-day transmission and teaching on Choné Geshé's *Interwoven Praise* based upon Tsongkhapa's *Praise of Dependent Origination*. On the twenty-eighth, the Dharma center offered Rinpoché a long-life ceremony, and at the request of Losang Jamyang, the former disciplinarian of Ratö Monastery, Rinpoché performed the self-initiation of Vajrayoginī and a *tsok* ritual together with a group who had completed the generation-stage retreat of this deity.

On the twenty-ninth Rinpoché bestowed novice monastic ordination on a few recipients.

On the first of September, at the invitation of Kamé Losam and the Dzarong family, Rinpoché traveled to Horgen. On the third, to an audience of around a hundred Tibetans, Rinpoché gave a transmission of *Praises to the Twenty-One Tārās*, the Seventh Dalai Lama's *Praise of Avalokiteśvara*, and the mantra of Avalokiteśvara, as well as a long-life initiation.

On the seventh, Rinpoché went to Rikon Chökhor Monastery, where he was welcomed by the abbot and local Tibetans. There he gave a permission initiation of Avalokiteśvara, the Three Wrathful Forms Combined, a long-life initiation, and the transmissions of my long-life prayer and the Tārā prayer to a mostly Tibetan audience of about nine hundred. Afterward, Rinpoché gave some advice to the young Tibetans there. He told them that they should be strong and work hard in developing a modern Western education. At the same time they should strive to learn their own culture, such as the Tibetan language, and they should take an interest in ensuring that their faith in the Three Jewels and the law of karma remains strong. It was essential that in the future they support their own country through their good education. They should be able to preserve and maintain their religion, culture, and good customs, and they should know how Western education can be used to further the good aspects of this cultural heritage. He reminded them that now we have to live in other people's countries, and "if we drink a country's water we must obey that country's laws." Moreover, we should be mindful that we conform to standards of conduct and behavior that is not unseemly in the eyes of others.

On the ninth Rinpoché went to Zurich. At the Yiga Chözin Dharma center, Rinpoché brought satisfaction to an audience of about two hundred with a talk that centered on training oneself in the precious mind of enlightenment.

On the eighteenth Rinpoché returned to France. The doctors who had previously diagnosed a thyroid problem came to see Rinpoché at his residence and gave him another medical examination. He was asked to come to the clinic for an injection for the thyroid. While at the clinic for the injection, his knees were also examined.

When he had free time, Rinpoché would often go for walks.

United States and Canada

Ten days later, Rinpoché left for America at the invitation of Geshé Wangyal. On the afternoon of the twenty-eighth, Rinpoché arrived at Kennedy Airport in New York, where he was welcomed by the Tibetan administration representative, the Mongolian Geshé Wangyal, Ratö Khyongla Tulku, and others, as well as the directors of various Dharma centers and the abbots of the Mongolian monasteries. (plate 34) Rinpoché was presented with ceremonial scarves, which he accepted and returned. He was then driven to the home of the Mongolian Chöjé Lama, where Khyongla Tulku had made arrangements for him to stay.

The next day Rinpoché went to the Labsum Shedrub Ling Monastery in New Jersey. The resident monks in their yellow robes and pandit hats escorted Rinpoché in an incense-led procession to his room. (plate 35) After lunch Geshé Wangyal told him the story of the construction of the new monastery. The next day, with the American scholar Jeffrey Hopkins translating, Rinpoché gave a single-deity, single-vase Amitāyus long-life initiation from the Niguma tradition to around 250 Mongolians, Tibetans, and Westerners. On the next day a Mongolian called Dorjé requested Rinpoché for a teaching that would ensure that in his next life he would not fall into one of the lower realms, such as the hells, but would instead gain birth in a higher realm. Rinpoché laughed and asked his manager, "How can I give such a teaching?" At the manager's suggestion, Rinpoché kindly gave him the permission initiation of Avalokiteśvara Who Liberates All Beings from the Unfortunate Realms.

On the first of October,[199] Rinpoché was invited to the Mongolian Tashi Gephel Ling Monastery. There he gave an explanation of the *Hundred Deities of Tuṣita* guruyoga and a long-life initiation to around one hundred recipients, who included the abbot, Mongolian Geshé Yarphel, and Geshé Losang Tharchin of Sera Mé. Geshé Yarphel's eyes were failing him, and because of his advanced age, he wondered if he would ever see Rinpoché again. Therefore the next day as Rinpoché was leaving, he chanted out loud:

> May the lama, the glory of the teachings, live long;
> may the earth be filled with great upholders of the teachings.[200]

Rinpoché listened and offered prayers.

After this, Rinpoché went to the Mongolian Jangchup Chöling Monastery. There he kindly gave a long-life initiation to Yönten Gyatso and about a hundred others. On the following day Rinpoché visited the Mongolian Tashi Lhunpo Temple. There he gave the refuge vows, teachings on the benefits of reciting Avalokiteśvara's mantra, and a transmission of the first chapter of the *Guhyasamāja Root Tantra* to Dzogé Tulku and about a hundred other Mongolians. On the fourth he traveled to the city of Philadelphia, where he visited the new Mongolian monastery Ganden Dargyé Ling. There he gave an Avalokiteśvara permission initiation to around fifty recipients. Then he returned to New York in a car belonging to a Mongolian family. The car broke down on the way, and because no taxis were immediately available, Rinpoché was late returning to New York, and I heard that those who were waiting for him did so in some anxiety.

At their invitation, Rinpoché attended a gathering of the New York Tibetan Association, where in keeping with Tibetan customs he was offered tea and sweet rice, and presented with the three representations and so forth. Rinpoché gave an extensive and profound talk in which he said that if the Tibetan people remain united in friendship, then whatever common goal they had to achieve would be accomplished with a lot less difficulty, and any trouble and disturbance made by others would not affect them. This friendship and harmony should not be restricted to a few individuals or small communities but should apply to the different religious traditions, and to everyone of the three main Tibetan regions. There may well be a few differences in the assertions of the great lamas of the four main religious traditions of Tibet. There are also differences in chanting styles, and minor differences in practice and ritual, but apart from that they are all followers of the same teacher, the Buddha. They should remember this and not fall under the sway of the prejudices of resentment and attachment. They should strive to see as much as possible how all the teachings are noncontradictory, how all scriptures are instruction, and thereby radiate on each other the jewel light of a mutual admiration. The three provinces of Tibet are called "provinces" because they all share the same language, the same customs, and are the same in being under the dominion of Avalokiteśvara. Quarrelling and resentment on the basis of being from different regions should be given up completely, and with an attitude of cooperation they should never loosen the ties of mutual friendship.

On the next day Rinpoché was invited to Khyongla Tulku's Dharma center. There he gave teachings on the *Hundred Deities of Tuṣita* guruyoga and a Niguma-tradition Amitāyus long-life initiation to about 250 lay and monastic recipients. He named the center Kunkhyab Thardo Ling. On the back of a scroll of the Buddha he wrote in Tibetan, "Offered to Kunkhyab Thardo Ling Dharma center as an object for their faith by the one who bears the name of the Ling tutor, the ninety-seventh holder of the Ganden throne." An English translation was also inscribed. Rinpoché gave similar inscribed scrolls to all the monasteries and Dharma centers he visited.

After the teachings Rinpoché gave a speech in which he said that all the unwanted troubles in the world these days, such as wars, have come about due to the untamed mind. By abandoning the prejudice of resentment and attachment toward enemies, friends, and neutrals, and cherishing all living beings as wish-granting jewels that bring about all that is good in the world, it is very important that we continually develop the attitude of helping them in both thought and deed. Doing that depends upon studying and contemplating the Dharma. Merely knowing about it is of no use; we have to make use of it to tame our minds.

Not only had no one given the Vajrabhairava initiation in New York City before, but because, like someone tormented by thirst seeking for water, he longed to receive teachings in the presence of the great Vajradhara, and for many other reasons also, the Mongolian Chöjé Lama had previously requested the initiation. Accordingly, on the ninth and tenth of October, in Kunkhyab Thardo Ling Rinpoché gave the single-deity Vajrabhairava initiation together with the preparatory rituals to an audience of about thirty. Rinpoché emphasized the importance of reciting the six-session guruyoga six times a day and of performing the self-generation sādhana daily. Some in the audience were already reciting the self-generation of the thirteen-deity Vajrabhairava daily, and they asked Rinpoché to be excused from performing a separate single-deity self-generation, to which Rinpoché agreed. The translator at the various discourses in New York was the American Art Engle.

On the following day, Chöjé Lama, Bamchö Dakpo Tulku, Khyongla Tulku, and the other recipients of the initiation offered Rinpoché a long-life ceremony by way of a Guru Puja and *tsok* ritual. During the teachings Rinpoché was offered lunch at the apartment of a young Chinese Buddhist from Hong Kong called Max who lived above the Dharma center. At his recommendation Rinpoché received a few acupuncture treatments for his knees from a Chinese doctor.

Sometime later Rinpoché was invited by Philip Hemley to visit his Dharma center. There through the translator, the Ladakhi Jampal, Rinpoché talked about nirvana and gave valuable advice. One day, Marjorie, the Kunkhyab Thardo Ling secretary, invited Rinpoché to visit the World Trade Center with its 120 floors. From its top Rinpoché looked over the city through binoculars. Rinpoché relaxed in the restaurant for a while, where he was offered tea and snacks. Rinpoché expressed the wish to buy some artificial flowers as offering materials. He was taken to Chinatown, but the shop in question did not stock the kind of flowers he had in mind. Instead, Rinpoché bought a fine porcelain Hashang.[201]

On the next day, Nick, Tony, and Eric—three disciples of Khyongla Tulku—and others took Rinpoché for a brief visit to a museum affiliated with the United Nations. Rinpoché was particularly fascinated by a piece of moon rock on display. Afterward, Rinpoché was taken to Macy's, one of the largest stores in the world. There Losang Lungrik bought a fine pair of shoes for Rinpoché. While Losang and the others went to look at other departments of the store, Rinpoché rested in the shoe department. There he told Khyongla how Vajradhara Phabongkha actually saw Kyabjé Takdrak Rinpoché as Vajrabhairava. Rinpoché also recounted how Takdrak Rinpoché told him that the former Ling Tulku, Losang Lungtok Tenzin Trinlé, only served seven years as tutor to the Thirteenth Dalai Lama and that he should work to continue his legacy. This now seemed like such instruction came from a clear vision of the future.

Later, Marjorie took Rinpoché to see the Star Wars film *The Empire Strikes Back*. Rinpoché enjoyed the film very much and asked many questions about it. Students and staff of Kunkhyab Thardo Ling willingly did whatever they could to serve Rinpoché during his stay in New York, such as providing meals for him and so on.

On the morning of the twelfth, Rinpoché and his party flew to Montreal, Canada. At the airport the directors of various Dharma centers, resident Tibetans, and Western devotees assembled to welcome him and offered ceremonial scarves. He was driven by car to Jangchup Chöling Monastery. There he was offered tea and sweet rice. The directors of the Dharma centers, all the resident Tibetans, and the Western devotees came to seek audience.

On the next day, Karmapa Rinpoché and the Vajradhara tutor were invited for lunch at a Kagyü Dharma center. When Rinpoché arrived, Karmapa Rinpoché was already there, but because of his poor health, he waited

The Sixth Ling Rinpoché with the Sixteenth Karmapa Rinpoché in Montreal

by the door of his room and was unable to come outside to greet Rinpoché. He explained this to Rinpoché. Rinpoché had found it a little difficult to climb the steep stairs and requested of Karmapa Rinpoché, "Because of my age it is hard to climb stairs. You younger people should remain long on this earth in order to benefit living beings and the Buddha's teaching." Then they exchanged ceremonial scarves and touched foreheads.

The two guests enjoyed lunch in the residence. Then Karmapa Rinpoché took four hundred US dollars from under his cushion, offered them to the Vajradhara tutor, and requested that he perform an effective longevity ritual for his long life. Moreover, through Geshé Khyenrap from Ganden Jangtsé Monastery, he requested that Rinpoché put his seal on the longevity substances. Complying with these requests, Rinpoché carried out the longevity ritual and offered the longevity substances to Karmapa Rinpoché.

On the next day Rinpoché was invited to go shopping. From one shop he bought a pair of handmade, good-quality porcelain leopard cubs.

Around that time I arrived in Canada. Rinpoché came to visit me in the hotel where I was staying and was greeted at the main entrance by my younger brother Ngari Tulku. Inside we chatted, and I told Vajradhara what I had been doing for the sake of the teaching and sentient beings. In return he told me of his deeds to spread the teachings of the Buddha in Europe and the United States as well as an account of his health. On the following morning I was invited to perform the opening ceremony and the consecration of Jangchup Chöling Monastery. Kyabjé Rinpoché also attended and made prayers. Afterward I was invited to Rinpoché's residence. I noticed the porcelain leopard cubs on the table and remarked how beautiful they were, and Rinpoché at once offered them to me as a gift.

On the sixteenth, in response to a request from the local Tibetans and Western devotees, Rinpoché gave the permission initiation for the general accomplishment of the three buddha families and a talk on the essential practices for this and future lives. On the seventeenth the local Tibetan residents offered Rinpoché a long-life ceremony.

On the twenty-first, at the invitation of the Tibetan residents of Toronto, Rinpoché flew from Montreal to Lindsay Airport, where he was welcomed by many Tibetans and Westerners and taken into Toronto by car. On the following morning, he gave teachings to the resident community on Tsongkhapa's *Abridged Stages of the Path*, a White Tārā long-life initiation, and advice on how to increase the good and avert the bad in this and future lives. At the request of Dzasep Tulku, Giré Sidhar, and others, Rinpoché opened the Ganden Chöling Dharma center and, at their urging, agreed to accept the title of center director.

On the twenty-third, Rinpoché gave teachings on the *Eight Verses of Mind Training* in a Kagyü Dharma center at the request of Lama Karma Trinlé to about eighty recipients. Afterward Rinpoché was invited to view the entire city from the top of the CNN tower, the tallest building in the city. On the morning of the twenty-fourth Rinpoché was invited by Losang Paldrön, or Rosemary Patton, a student of Dakpo Rinpoché, to stay for three days at the home of her mother Kathleen in the town of Sutton. There he gave teachings and advice according to their wishes.

On the morning of the twenty-sixth, Rinpoché left Canada for the United States. The resident Tibetans and other Canadian residents came to the airport to see him off. At New York's La Guardia Airport, he was greeted by Ratö Khyongla and students and staff of Kunkhyab Thardo Ling. He was driven to his previous residence, where he rested for a while. The next day Rinpoché was leaving for Europe and was driven to Kennedy Airport. Because of the weather, he had to wait for an hour or so in the airport lounge. During that time Rinpoché took photos of Khyongla and Max

Doni, remarking that he used to develop and process photographs when he was younger.

Rinpoché arrived in Paris, where he was housed at the home of Bamchö Tulku. On the thirty-first, at the invitation of Geshé Ngawang Khyenrap from Drepung Loseling, the secretary of the Dharma center at Digne-les-Bains, and the city of Digne itself, Rinpoché flew to Digne, where he visited the home of Alexandra David-Néel, the French woman who had visited Tibet.[202]

On the first of November, Rinpoché gave a talk together with a question-and-answer session at the local Dharma center to about 125 devotees. On the following day he gave a teaching and a transmission on the *Eight Verses of Mind Training*. On the third, at the request of the Dharma center secretary, Rinpoché gave teachings on refuge. At the reception hosted by the city for Rinpoché, the mayor expressed his delight that Rinpoché had visited the city and had given teachings on Buddhism, and presented him with a flag of the city and a medallion. In return Rinpoché presented the mayor with a high-quality ceremonial scarf and a gift of three Tibetan coins. Rinpoché praised Alexandra David-Néel, saying that she had traveled to many places in Tibet and met with great lamas such as the Thirteenth Dalai Lama and the previous Panchen Rinpoché, Chökyi Nyima. She had photographed places and monasteries and published many books on Tibet. He added that it was important to support the foundation she had established.

Rinpoché stayed for three days in Digne. Many people came to take photographs of him, and the reports of his visit were shown on television screens across Europe.

On the fifth, Rinpoché returned to Paris. At the request of Gephel Jang-chup Ling Dharma Center, Rinpoché gave a talk to about three hundred devotees on the commemoration of the Buddha returning from teaching in the celestial realms. Afterward Rinpoché took part in the offering ceremonies. Also at the request of the Dharma center, and to the same three hundred devotees, Rinpoché gave teachings and a transmission over the next four days on Tsongkhapa's stages of the path text *Song of Experience* as well as permission initiations of White Mañjuśrī and Green Tārā.

On the thirteenth a Sri Lankan monk invited Rinpoché to lunch at the International Cultural Association, which he happily attended. Later, at the request of Geshé Lungrik Namgyal of Ganden Shartsé Monastery, Rinpoché gave an explanation of refuge to about eighty people at the Thardö

Ling Dharma Center. On the fifteenth he gave teachings on the *Hundred Deities of Tuṣita* guruyoga to about thirty Mongolians resident in France, thereby fulfilling their hopes and wishes.

RETURN TO INDIA

On the sixteenth of November Rinpoché left France for India. At the airport Bamchö Tulku, staff of the Dharma centers, and resident Tibetans and other devotees came to see him off. He arrived in Delhi on the morning of the seventeenth and was greeted at the airport by the Tibetan administration's representative Sadu Rinchen, the director of Tibet House Bakula Rinpoché of Ladakh, and others. In Delhi Rinpoché stayed at the home of Thupten Tsering. On the next day, at the request of Ashé Yangkyi, Rinpoché gave a White Tārā long-life initiation to about fifty people. On the twenty-first he left by train for Dharamsala.

The twenty-third was the fifteenth of the tenth Tibetan month and was a special day for Palden Lhamo. Therefore on that day, the entire assembly of Namgyal Monastery and I made offerings to and propitiated the protectors, both generally and specifically—including the black and red Dharma protectors[203]—for the benefit of the Buddha's teaching and the people of Tibet. Rinpoché visited me on that day and recounted in detail his activities in the West and his deeds to spread and preserve the teaching of the Buddha. In the afternoon he came with me to the propitiation ceremony.

On the twenty-seventh, the annual winter summoning of Nechung through the oracle was performed. Rinpoché offered thanks to Nechung for his undistracted work in ensuring that Rinpoché's activities in the West carried out for the sake of the Buddha's teaching and beings were successful.

On the first of December the precious tutor came to me to say his goodbyes as he was soon to leave for Bodhgaya. In the afternoon we went to Thekchen Chöling temple, where, with the Namgyal Monastery monks, he presided over the ceremonies for the commemoration known as the offerings of the twenty-fifth. These included a *tsok* ritual by way of a Guru Puja ceremony, prayers to Vajrabhairava, Cakrasaṃvara, Guhyasamāja, Kālacakra, and so on.

On the sixth Rinpoché left Dharamsala and arrived in Bodhgaya on the eighth. On the fifteenth he began a special long-life meditation practice. At the request of a Bhutanese monk, on the twenty-ninth Rinpoché gave teachings on the way to practice the generation stage of Vajrabhairava based on the self-generation sādhana practice.

1981

On the first of January 1981, Rinpoché bestowed full-ordination vows on twenty devotees. On the fifth he gave teachings to two Bhutanese monks on *Preparatory Practices: Necklace for the Fortunate*, which teaches the way to practice the six preparatory practices as a preliminary to entering the meditations on the graded path to enlightenment. On the morning of the eleventh I arrived in Bodhgaya, and the great Vajradhara came to my rooms and offered a mandala and the three representations. On the afternoon of the fourteenth, I received, as previously requested, the initiation of Vajrabhairava from Rinpoché in a room above the temple by the precious shrine of this sacred place of Bodhgaya. The role of ritual assistant was performed by Serkong Rinpoché. He was finding it tiring to be standing so much, and when Guru Vajradhara noticed this he laughed. I was very blessed to see his joy amid such a profound teaching.

At the place of the initiation, I received a sealed envelope. Opening it I saw that it contained the news that my mother had passed away. The government ministers had intended that the news be conveyed to me by the precious tutor so that he might console me. However, I had opened the letter first, and so I conveyed the news to Rinpoché. I asked both Rinpochés to offer prayers. The Vajradhara tutor gave me words of comfort, and I was both happy and sad.

On the eighteenth I was due to return to Dharamsala, and so Rinpoché came to see me for an informal conversation. On the next day, in front of the sacred Bodhgaya shrine, in response to a request from Kyizom who ran the York Restaurant in Delhi, Rinpoché gave a long-life initiation and words of advice on the importance of properly developing virtuous actions and reducing nonvirtuous actions to an audience of over a thousand monks, nuns, and laypeople.

The fifth of February was the iron-bird new year. Rinpoché performed the New Year ceremonies in his rooms and then attended the *tsok* ritual in the Tibetan Monastery. From the ninth onward he presided over the prayer festival as usual.

On the sixteenth of March, Rinpoché left Bodhgaya, and he arrived in

Dharamsala on the eighteenth. On the way up he stopped off at Trijang Rinpoché's residence to exchange New Year greetings. On the twenty-second he came to visit me.

At the request of Topden from Lithang and others, Rinpoché gave permission initiations of Hayagrīva, Vajrapāṇi, and Garuḍa to twenty recipients.

I was approaching an obstacle year, and in order to remove any hindrances that might befall me, on the nineteenth of April, the Tibetan administration and the people sponsored a long-life ceremony by way of the five-deity immortality mandala of Amitāyus. Among the leaders of the main religious traditions who attended were the precious throneholder and tutor, the precious Sakya Trizin, Drukchen Rinpoché, Minling Trichen, and the Bön abbot Lungtok Tenyi. Rinpoché sat at the head of the rows with Kyabjé Trijang Rinpoché and Serkong Rinpoché. This event did much to strengthen the pillar of the indestructible life force.

On the twenty-fifth of May, in response to a request from Dr. Yeshé Dönden, Rinpoché gave the permission initiations of Three Wrathful Forms Combined. I was about to fly to the United States to confer the Kālacakra initiation, and so on the twenty-seventh Rinpoché came with Trijang Rinpoché to visit me. They offered me ceremonial scarves and the three representations, and we had conversations on a number of topics.

On the twelfth of July the Gadong and Nechung protectors were summoned through the oracles, and predictions were sought. On the thirtieth Rinpoché gave novice nun vows to two Western women.

From the first of August, in response to a request from Dakpo Bamchö Tulku, Rinpoché gave a teaching each day on Tsongkhapa's *Essence of Excellent Explanation: Differentiating the Definitive and the Provisional*. During these teachings he resolved the differences between the standpoints of the textbooks of Gomang and Loseling colleges of Drepung Monastery.

On the twentieth I invited the precious tutor and Trijang Rinpoché to visit me. I told them of the Kālacakra initiation and other events during my recent visit to the United States.[204] In response they offered comforting words of praise. At the request of Ratö Khyongla Tulku, Rinpoché gave extensive teachings on Tsongkhapa's *Fire Offering Rituals: An Ocean of Attainments* and Gungthang Tenpai Drönmé's *Powerful Weapon Wheel: Protecting Circle and Repelling Torma Ritual of the Ten Wrathful Protectors* to Khyongla and Bamchö Rinpoché.

Ling Rinpoché, Sakya Trizin, and Minling Trichen offer prayers for the long life of the Dalai Lama in Dharamsala, April 19, 1981.

On the third of September, as Dakpo Bamchö Tulku was about to return to France, Rinpoché presented him with the complete Collected Works of Phabongkha. On the sixth, at the request of Barshi Phuntsok Wangyal, Rinpoché gave a transmission and short teaching of Tsongkhapa's *Praise of Dependent Origination.*

On the tenth of October, at the request of Tsethang Anan and others, Rinpoché conferred the long-life initiation of White Tārā.

Kyabjé Trijang Rinpoché had not been well, and on the thirty-first Rinpoché visited him at his Tashi Rapten residence in Gangchen Kyishong, where he requested Trijang Rinpoché to live a long life. As their forthcoming visits to Mundgod coincided, they talked about meeting each other in Ganden Monastery. This, I think, was a sign that in the future their reincarnations would be together in the monasteries in the south.

36 | The Passing of Trijang Rinpoché

O<small>N THE EIGHTH</small> of November, Rinpoché summoned the Nechung and Gadong protectors through the oracles. On the morning of the next day, Dr. Yeshé Dönden came to Chopra House for the regular examination of Rinpoché's pulse and reported that Trijang Rinpoché's pulse was very weak. Rinpoché immediately left for Tashi Rapten in Dr. Yeshé Dönden's car. He offered the three representations and a ceremonial scarf to Trijang Rinpoché and requested that he live a long time. Alternatively, if he had already decided to turn his mind elsewhere, Rinpoché urged that his unmistaken incarnation would soon appear. However, it seemed that by then he was already exhibiting the act of passing away.

As soon as I heard the news that Kyabjé Trijang Rinpoché's pulse was very weak, I left for the labrang. The precious tutor had already left. When I arrived, Trijang Rinpoché's breathing had almost disappeared. There was nothing to be done. I placed my head below the mattress of the bed on which Kyabjé Trijang Rinpoché lay and made fervent prayers. With Lati Rinpoché and Ratö Chubar Tulku, we performed the Guru Puja ceremony and recited the Cakrasaṃvara prayer. I had known Kyabjé Trijang Rinpoché since I was a child. He used to give me presents. Whatever the situation, he would give me skillful advice with great compassion and showed exceptional kindness to me. In the afternoon the precious tutor came to see me. I presented him with a statue of Guru Rinpoché and requested that he live a long life.

On the twelfth the precious tutor went to the Tashi Rapten residence. In the presence of the body of Trijang Rinpoché, he performed the thousand five-senses cloud offerings, and together with the funeral assistants recited three times a prayer for his speedy return that the precious tutor himself had composed.

On the fifteenth Rinpoché visited me to tell me of his impending visit to Mundgod. On the nineteenth he left for Pathankot and traveled to Bombay by train. There, as arranged, he stayed for two days at the home of an old lady from Kham. From there he traveled to Belgaum by air and to Mundgod by car. He had been invited to stop at Ganden on the way to his labrang and was escorted to the Ganden great assembly hall, where he was served tea and sweet rice. Afterward, officials of the monastic council and the colleges, lamas, tulkus, and others presented Rinpoché with ceremonial scarves.

He continued his journey to Ling Labrang, and as soon as he arrived, the officials of Drepung monastic council, its colleges, houses, lamas, tulkus, and so on came for an audience.

On the sixth of December the entire assembly of Drepung Loseling performed a long-life ceremony for the precious tutor by way of a *tsok* ritual and the Guru Puja offering ceremony. The monastic governing body, Gomang College, officials of the Sakya monastery, and representatives of the people offered the three representations and requested that he live a long life.

In response to a request made previously by Drepung Loseling, Ganden Shartsé, and the monk Tsöndrü Gyaltsen from the Bodhgaya monastery, Rinpoché conferred the thirteen-deity Vajrabhairava initiation in the Loseling courtyard to about eighteen hundred monks from the three monastic seats, Tashi Lhunpo Monastery, the two tantric colleges, and elsewhere, and about eighty laypeople. Afterward he began teachings on Panchen Losang Chökyi Gyaltsen's *Guru Puja*. On the nineteenth, the monasteries of Drepung, Sera, and Ganden, the two tantric colleges, Tashi Lhunpo Monastery, Amdo Tashi Khyil Monastery, and the Tibetan settlements of Mundgod jointly offered Rinpoché a long-life ceremony.

The twentieth of December was the day of the offerings of the twenty-fifth and coincided with the sixth week after Trijang Vajradhara's passing. Therefore, at the invitation of the Trijang Labrang, Rinpoché went to the main Ganden assembly hall in the morning. Together with the monks he prayed that Trijang Rinpoché's pure aspirations to bring about the welfare of living beings and the Buddha's teachings be actualized in their entirety and that his unmistaken incarnation soon return.

On the morning of the twenty-third at Drepung Monastery, Rinpoché bestowed the long-life initiation of Tsongkhapa as longevity deity to about twenty-five hundred monastics and laypeople. On the twenty-fourth

Rinpoché completed the teachings on the *Guru Puja*, and two of the sponsors and the Mongolian Guru Deva jointly offered a long-life ceremony by way of a *tsok* ritual and the Guru Puja ceremony, which Rinpoché happily accepted. On the twenty-seventh, Yiga Tulku and Ling House jointly offered Rinpoché a long-life ceremony in the Ling House assembly hall. On the twenty-ninth, he conferred novice-monk vows on seventy-five recipients. On the morning of the thirty-first, in the main Drepung assembly hall, the monastic governing body offered Rinpoché a long-life ceremony. In the afternoon he conferred full-ordination vows, the complete foundation of practice, on twenty novice monks.

That year Ling Labrang had sponsored the following for Drepung Loseling: an expansion to the Loseling debate courtyard; a life-size gilded statue of Tsongkhapa as longevity deity flanked by two seventeen-inch statues of his two main disciples in the courtyard; 115 statues of Tsongkhapa, each twelve inches high and attired in robes; altar cabinets to house these statues; scroll paintings of the sixteen elders; the handles for these paintings made from Chinese silver; a set of seven silver offering bowls; and a silver embossed butter lamp. The labrang also sponsored an elaborate day-long offering of donations, food, and drink to the assembly and, as it did each year, provided the funding for the *tsok* ritual, communal tea, food, and donations on the day of the offerings of the twenty-fifth.

1982

On the third of January 1982, at the request of the people of Tsahreng and Mundgod, Rinpoché gave the permission initiations of the Three Wrathful Forms Combined, a long-life initiation, and words of advice to a few thousand monastics and laypeople at the Mundgod Tibetan settlement.

On the following day Rinpoché received a letter from the Private Office asking him to undertake a longevity meditation practice for me. He happily agreed and began the practice straight away. Later, in Tsul House, Rinpoché gave the life entrustment of the five king emanations to over twenty tulkus, lamas, and monks. On the ninth Rinpoché was invited to preside over the Loseling prosperity rituals, where he prayed that all the good in samsara and nirvana should increase like the rain in summer. In response to an invitation by the Ganden monastic council, on the tenth Rinpoché went to the main assembly hall, where the assembly performed a long-life ritual. On the seventeenth he went to Trijang Labrang, where he performed the cleansing ritual over Kyabjé Rinpoché's bones, ashes, and hair and a bone ritual by way of Vajrayoginī practice.

On the twenty-fifth, in response to a request from Ganden Shartsé, Rinpoché gave the permission initiation of White Mañjuśrī and a transmission of the Mañjuśrī *Gangloma* prayer to the entire assembly of the two colleges in the Ganden Shartsé assembly hall. Afterward the monastery offered Rinpoché a long-life ceremony, which he happily accepted.

On the fourth of February Rinpoché flew from Belgaum to Delhi, where he was seen off by the Tibetan administration representative and Drepung Loseling. On the seventh he visited me at the Ashok Hotel in Delhi. Afterward, he went to Tushita Mahayana Meditation Centre in New Delhi, where he gave a long-life initiation to about four hundred lay and monastic recipients. On the eleventh Rinpoché presided over the ceremonies for opening of the Drepung tantric college in Delhi.

On the next day Rinpoché left Delhi for Bodhgaya and arrived on the thirteenth. From the fifteenth he began a special long-life meditation practice. The twenty-fourth was the first day of the water-dog year, and Rinpoché conducted the usual celebrations. From the twenty-eighth, during the Great Prayer Festival, he conducted the reading of Āryaśūra's *Garland of the Buddha's Birth Stories* in the morning and presided over the prayer gathering in the afternoon.

Previously, when Vajradhara was visiting New York and giving teachings at Kunkhyab Thardo Ling, he was looked after and served by an American called Rod Priece. Rod had just arrived in Bodhgaya and was welcomed as a guest of the labrang. When he visited sacred places such as Nālandā, Rinpoché would send his attendant Tenpa with him. Rinpoché also gave him a blessed rosary and a signed photo of himself. In front of the Bodhgaya shrine, Rod performed the thousandfold offering for the benefit of his parents, and the Vajradhara tutor presided over the ceremony. Rinpoché had a photo of the parents on his table and focused on it repeatedly while making prayers. I heard that Rod told others he could never forget this and other kindnesses Rinpoché had shown to him.

Also, Rinpoché heard of a crazy woman who would pick up paper in the streets with Tibetan lettering on it and burn it to prevent people walking over it. Rinpoché remarked that she was far from being crazy, and that the instruction to regard and respect even a single letter as the Jewel of the

Dharma should be followed like this. Rinpoché said that this should not only apply to Tibetan lettering and would give instructions to remove all English lettering from the soles of socks and shoes. Also, he said that it was not appropriate to use newspapers in other languages to wrap things and so on. In this way he showed reverence for all languages.

On the morning of the eighth of March, Rinpoché performed the hair-cutting ceremony for Chamdo Gyara Tulku and Sangbum Tulku and conferred the transmission of the *Hundred Deities of Tuṣita* guruyoga. On the eleventh, in response to their invitation, Rinpoché visited the Tibetan monastery at the sacred place where the Bhagavan Buddha spent six years practicing austerities. There he conferred novice-monk vows on eight recipients.

On the twenty-fourth Rinpoché returned to Dharamsala, and on the twenty-seventh I met with him in Thekchen Chöling.

On the twelfth of April, Rinpoché completed the longevity meditation practice he performed for me at the request of the administration and later presented me with the long-life substances. On the twenty-fourth and twenty-fifth, at the request of Lama Thubten Yeshe, and others, Rinpoché bestowed the preparatory rituals followed by the actual initiation of single-deity Vajrabhairava at Tushita Meditation Centre to around four hundred Western and Tibetan lay and monastic recipients. (plates 37 and 39)

On the twenty-third of May, Rinpoché gave a long-life initiation to the Tibetan Druphok family from Switzerland. On the morning of the thirtieth he gave the day-long vows to a large gathering of monks, nuns, and laypeople in Thekchen Chöling. On the same day he also presided over the *maṇi* recitations at the temple.

On the twenty-second of June, I went to the labrang and together with Serkong Rinpoché received from Rinpoché the long-life initiation of Yellow Vajrabhairava.

On the fifth of July the Tibetan people, monastic and lay, sponsored a long-life ceremony for me using the ritual Halting the Ḍākinīs' Escort by way of Cittamaṇi White Tārā practice. At this ceremony the great Vajradhara tutor served as vajra master and performed the mandala-offering discourse. Three days later the Tibetan people made requests for the great Vajradhara to live a long life.

My obstacle year was approaching. Therefore, on the twenty-fifth, Ling Labrang made extensive donations to monks and nuns of all traditions who lived in Dharamsala, such as those of Namgyal Monastery, the Institute of

Buddhist Dialectics, Tsechokling Monastery, and so on. The labrang also sponsored the ritual of *Offerings and Homage to the Sixteen Elders* composed by the Second Dalai Lama, the long-life rituals of Tārā and Amitāyus, the rituals of the propitiations of the host of oath-bound protectors of the teachings as exemplified by the black and red Dharma protectors, the practice of accumulating repetitions of my long-life prayer composed by the former regent Radreng Rinpoché, as well as sponsoring a lavish meal for me and my staff. The great Vajradhara offered a mandala and the three representations and spoke of why it is necessary for me to live a long life for the sake of the doctrine and living beings. Rinpoché also took lunch with me.

On the twenty-ninth Rinpoché performed the hair-cutting ceremony on the reincarnation of Gyalrong Tulku, the former abbot of Sera Mé.

Beginning on the third of August, Rinpoché undertook a special longevity meditation practice for a few weeks. Rinpoché visited me on the twenty-sixth, and we had a long discussion on many aspects of the Dharma. On the same day Rinpoché was invited to Tushita Meditation Centre by the Western students, where he participated in the recitations, such as the Guru Puja ritual. Afterward he gave some words of advice.

On the eighth of September, just before I was about to leave for a visit abroad, Rinpoché visited me and presented me with a ceremonial scarf.

On the tenth Rinpoché gave teachings on the *Hundred Deities of Tuṣita* guruyoga and the permission initiation of Kālarūpa to the Italian monk Jampa Thokmé and others. On the nineteenth he bestowed a White Tārā long-life initiation on Taklha Phuntsok Tashi, the commander of the bodyguard detachment, and his family. On the following day, he bestowed the permission initiations of Hayagrīva, Vajrapāṇi, and Garuḍa on Ngari Tulku. In this way he fulfilled the hopes and wishes of the recipients.

37 | Kindness Beyond Measure

ON THE NINETEENTH of October 1982, Rinpoché invoked the protector Nechung through the oracle. He asked the protector about his forthcoming teaching and transmission of Tsongkhapa's *Great Stages of the Path to Enlightenment* at Sera Monastery. Nechung replied that this was an excellent undertaking and urged Rinpoché with his great kindness to take on this profound teaching in keeping with considerations of his health.

Two days later Rinpoché performed an exorcism ritual by way of Sītātapatrā for the family of Dr. Losang Drölma of Kyirong.[205]

On the twenty-eighth Rinpoché left Dharamsala and traveled to Bodhgaya via Pathankot.

On the morning of the fourteenth of November, he began a special longevity meditation practice. On the twenty-second the Bodhgaya monastery and Ling Labrang jointly sponsored a long-life ceremony, which was presided over by the Shakor Monastery abbot Geshé Nyima Gyaltsen.

On the sixteenth of December, Rinpoché gave a public long-life initiation to many lay and monastic recipients.

On the eighteenth Rinpoché left Bodhgaya for Delhi, and on the nineteenth he stayed at the house of Bakula Rinpoché. He flew from Delhi to Bangalore on the twenty-third. There he stayed for three days, as had been previously requested, at a guesthouse belonging to Samten Chadzötsang and the Sadu family.

On the morning of the twenty-sixth, the abbots of Sera Mé and Sera Jé, the monastic governing body, representatives of the Tibetan settlements in South India, and others arrived to escort Rinpoché to Sera Monastery. On arrival he was led to the Sera Jé assembly hall in a procession formed by the monks. Inside he sat upon a throne, and the lamas, tulkus, and past and present abbots offered the mandala and the three representations, as well as food and drink. After the ceremonies Rinpoché was escorted to his rooms

Ling Rinpoché in Bodhgaya

above the college. On the next day Rinpoché was invited by the monk Norbu Dorjé of Trehor House to preside over the Sera Jé assembly.

On the thirtieth of December, as previously requested by Sera Jé College, Rinpoché began his teaching and transmission of the *Great Stages of the Path* in the assembly hall to the entire monastic community of the great monastic seat of Sera Thekchen Ling, as well as monks from other monasteries, several Westerners from the United States and elsewhere, and about three hundred Tibetan lay men and women. First, Rinpoché recited from memory a few passages from the beginning of the text three times. The abbot Denma Lekden then repeated these, thereby preserving the tradition of the great lineage-holding masters of the past. Rinpoché remarked that previously when the Great Thirteenth Dalai Lama taught the *Great Stages of the Path* in the Norbulingka Palace in Lhasa, there were no microphones and speakers, unlike today. However, it was said that as soon as you entered the main gate of Norbulingka you could clearly hear the Dalai Lama's voice. He cited Tsongkhapa's *Praise of Mañjuśrī* in the section praising his speech where it says, "When close, not too loud; when far away, not too faint." This, he said, could be understood as being an inconceivable quality of an enlightened being.

1983

On the eighteenth of January 1983, at the request of Trehor House, Rinpoché gave a transmission and teaching of Tsongkhapa's *Three Principal Aspects of the Path*. On the nineteenth Rinpoché completed the *Great Stages of the Path* teachings and conducted a bodhicitta-generation ceremony. On my instructions the Private Office sponsored a long-life ceremony for the Vajradhara tutor by way of a Guru Puja and *tsok* ritual, which was undertaken on the twentieth by the recipients of the teachings. On the thirtieth the two colleges of Sera Monastery and the monastic council offered Rinpoché a long-life ceremony, during which the heads of Drepung colleges Loseling and Gomang, the Ganden colleges Shartsé and Jangtsé, the monasteries of Tashi Lhunpo and Namdröl Ling, the Drigung Kagyü Monastery, and representatives of the administration and the people offered the three representations and prayed for his long life.

On the thirty-first in the assembly hall of Sera Mé, to an audience of about four thousand, Rinpoché gave the preparatory rituals of the seventeen-deity Sitātapatrā initiation. On the following day he conferred the actual initiation.

On the first of February, in response to a request from the monk Thupten Tsering who lived in Bomdila, Rinpoché gave the permission initiation of Avalokiteśvara Who Liberates All Beings from the Unfortunate Realms and a White Tārā long-life initiation. Afterward he granted an audience to the public. Around this time Dilgo Khyentsé Rinpoché came to visit the Vajradhara tutor. Rinpoché also gave lay vows to Tenzin Chökyi, a lady from Nepal. The labrang sponsored a Guru Puja *tsok* ritual for the recipients of the teachings and served tea and bread and made donations. It also made donations to the Sera monastic assembly, the two colleges, and Trehor House.

On the fifth, Rinpoché left for Hunsur Tibetan settlement. On the way he stopped at the Tibetan Children's Village, where he gave a transmission of the *Gangloma* Mañjuśrī praise and the mantra of Avalokiteśvara as well as words of advice to about three hundred staff and pupils. After this he traveled to Tashi Lhunpo Monastery, where he gave a Tārā transmission to a public gathering. He was also invited to Chatreng Monastery, where he was served tea and food. On the sixth Rinpoché visited Gyümé. There he conferred a long-life initiation on the monks and laypeople and gave words of advice on practice. The people offered him a long-life ceremony, after which he granted a public audience. On the seventh he visited Dzongkar Chödé Monastery, and on the following day he greatly enjoyed a ritual dance performance the monastery put on for him. Rinpoché made extensive offerings and donations to Dzongkar Chödé and Gyümé.

On the ninth Rinpoché left for Mundgod. On the tenth, on the way to the labrang, he was invited to Ganden Monastery, where past and present abbots, lamas, tulkus, and administration representatives sought audiences. On the eleventh I arrived in Mundgod, and I invited Rinpoché to visit me in my rooms above Drepung assembly hall.

The thirteenth of February began the water-pig year. In the morning Rinpoché sat on the throne in the labrang reception rooms and conducted the auspicious New Year rituals, after which the entire Drepung Loseling monastic community came for an audience. At nine o'clock I sat on the throne in the Drepung main assembly hall for the official administration-sponsored New Year celebration. The Namgyal Monastery choir recited the verses of offering the eight auspicious signs, the eight auspicious substances, and the seven royal emblems, followed by the verses of dedication and *Prayer for the Teachings to Flourish*. Then the senior minister offered me the three representations on behalf of the administration, and the Vajradhara tutor offered me the mandala and the three representations as well as the longevity substances from the long meditation practice he had undertaken earlier. These I experienced as blessed elixir.

As soon as the ceremonies were over, I invited the Vajradhara tutor to my rooms above the main assembly hall. Together with Serkong Rinpoché, I offered him a long-life ceremony by way of the Guru Puja *tsok* ritual and made requests for him to live a long life. On the following day Gyütö offered him a long-life ceremony. On the sixteenth Rinpoché accompanied me to perform the consecration for the opening of the new assembly hall of Ganden Jangtsé. Two days later, at ten in the morning, in response to the invitation from Trijang Labrang, Rinpoché accompanied me to the labrang for the Cakrasaṃvara consecration ritual performed by eighty monks of Gyütö for the silver reliquary containing votive images made from the bones of the body of Kyabjé Trijang Rinpoché.

At two o'clock in the afternoon, in the Ganden main assembly hall, in an event arranged by the Institute of Geluk Classical Studies,[206] the precious throneholder presented certificates to ninety geshés who had passed their karampa, lharampa, and master examinations in 1980, 1981, and 1982. I gave prizes to those who gained the top three places. On the twenty-second Ling Labrang sponsored a long-life ceremony for me at Drepung Loseling by way of a Guru Puja *tsok* ritual and the ceremony of Halting the Ḍākinīs' Escort. My supreme root guru, sitting on the throne wearing the yellow pandit hat, recited the mandala offering discourse and presented me the eight substances and other aids to longevity. I also prayed that in keeping with my guru's instruction, I would live a long life in order to serve the teachings of the Buddha and my temporal responsibilities. Afterward the precious tutor joined me and Serkong Rinpoché for lunch at his rooms in Ling Labrang. That day the labrang also offered a lavish lunch to all the officials who were there. During the lunch, assistant tutor Serkong Rinpoché made this moving request with tears rolling down his cheeks, "These days, in times such as these, the immense religious and temporal responsibility is being borne by His Holiness the Dalai Lama alone. Except for the precious tutor, there is no one he can turn to. How could the precious tutor not live long and leave His Holiness behind. So please, precious tutor, do remain with us for a long time." Rinpoché too was moved by this request, and I also shed tears, my heart aching.

Serkong Rinpoché was at all times a perfect example of someone with the faith of guru devotion. When we three would meet, he would say something in an emotional state of mind and cry. Then immediately he would make a joke and burst into uncontrollable laughter.

In this water-pig year, sixty years had passed since the Vajradhara gained his geshé degree in the last wood-pig year and twenty-five years had passed since I gained my geshé lharampa degree. The commemoration of these two events coincidentally occurred in the same year and took place on the twenty-fifth of February in the main Drepung assembly hall, presided over by my precious guru, the Vajradhara throneholder and tutor Ling Rinpoché. It was attended by all the administration officials, the monks of the monasteries, and Western guests. I began by quoting from Tsongkhapa's *Testimony of Aspirations Well Realized*:

> In particular, the Buddha has said that to take great joy,
> without conceit, in one's virtuous deeds of the past
> is to increase the virtue of those deeds.
> Therefore, to accomplish that, and for many other reasons,
> it is right, mind, for you to generate such joy.

I continued by giving a rough account of my life up to the present time primarily from a spiritual perspective. I said that as far as my studies were concerned, they were pursued up till the age of fifteen or thereabouts through the efforts of others, and from then on through the efforts of others and myself. Once I became a geshé, I put much effort into my studies without being urged to do so by others. From an early age I had a sharp mind, but because of laziness I did not always have a liking for study. The precious tutor would come to me every day, twice a day, month after month, year after year, to give me lessons. The great kindness of the Vajradhara tutor is difficult to measure, and will ever be so, even up to my enlightenment. I concluded by saying that now he is advanced in age but fundamentally is in good health and his mind is content. I reminded Vajradhara that he had already agreed to the request to remain with us until he reaches a hundred.

That year around thirty-five hundred monks had gathered for the eight days of the Great Prayer Festival. Phendé Lekshé Ling tantric college performed the instant entrusting of Dharmarājā to action, Gyümé performed the iron-fortress torma ritual, Gyütö performed Mahākāla rituals, the Sakya monastery performed the Tārā Thread-Cross Ritual That Repels Attacks, and the Nyingma monastery performed the Phurba torma ritual from the Northern Treasure tradition. Quarter past two on the afternoon of the eighth was the time for the annual throwing of the torma. Therefore, at twelve o'clock, together with assistant tutor Serkong Rinpoché and the Vajradhara tutor, we performed the sixty-four-part torma-offering ritual and made prayers for the benefit of the Buddha's teaching and the temporal well-being of Tibet.

At that time Ling Labrang made offerings in the prayer festival assembly, and made offerings of tea, thukpa soup, sweet rice, and money. It made similar offerings to the individual colleges and the Sakya and Nyingma monasteries.

One morning in the reception rooms of the labrang, Rinpoché invoked Nechung and Gadong via the oracle. Nechung made a somewhat oblique statement: "If the great Vajradhara accepts to live for a long time, I, the one without form, will provide assistance throughout the six periods of the day and night."

Previously, when the Nechung monk Phelgyé went to the United States, Rinpoché instructed him to present to Khyongla a set of the five root treatises[207] and a copy of *Vinaya Summary* composed by Sharchen Ngawang

Tsultrim of Sera Mé. Khyongla noticed that among these works, Guṇaprabha's *Vinaya Sutra* was annotated in Rinpoché's own hand from beginning to end, and he requested Rinpoché to give him the transmission of these annotations. Rinpoché replied, saying that if Khyongla would write out the notes, he would give him the transmission. The first print of these annotations was presented to Rinpoché in person by the former Home Affairs minister Phalha Thupten Öden. On that occasion he earnestly requested Rinpoché to live a long time. Rinpoché replied that he would definitely pray to the Three Jewels to live a long time but that he had no control over life and death, thereby not completely acceding to the request.

Phalha Thupten Öden told the labrang manager that when he held the post of lord chamberlain in Tibet, the assistant tutor Ngödrup Tsoknyi made a trip to Barma Mountain[208] specifically to seek divination from the protector Gesar concerning the good and bad that might befall the health and activities of myself and the two tutors, as well as the doctrine of the Buddha and the government of Tibet. The reply from the protector was that there would be a turbulent time for the doctrine and Tibet, with obstacles and great upheaval, but that Ling Rinpoché would ascend the throne of Ganden and greatly illuminate the teachings of sutra and tantra. At that time, with all the obstacles to the religious and political situation in Tibet, Phalha Thupten Öden thought it would be very difficult for Rinpoché to ascend the throne. But in India he did exactly that, which was truly amazing.

Many publishers of various texts in India and Nepal would present the first copies to Rinpoché. Those that were surplus Rinpoché gave to the Drepung Loseling library, saying that they would be useful for students. Rinpoché himself had received from the college the complete collection of the Drepung Loseling textbooks. He told Jampa Tulku that there was some good-quality Tibetan paper in the labrang, and that it should be used to print a clear copy of the stages of the path text *Liberation in the Palm of Your Hand* in Ganden Monastery, saying that it would be useful for a certain child. He also told him that he should come immediately if Rinpoché sent him an urgent telegram from Dharamsala. These and other occurrences seemed like clear predictions that he would soon be leaving us, and that his supreme and precious incarnation would engage in studies in the monastery.

On the eleventh of March, when Rinpoché left Mundgod by car, Loseling officials and administration representatives accompanied him to Belgaum Airport. When Rinpoché was about to board the plane for Delhi, he turned and looked again and again at those who had come to see him off, something he had never done before. Jampa Tulku felt that Rinpoché would not return to Mundgod again and said that he felt so sad.

In Delhi Rinpoché stayed at the house of Bakula Rinpoché. The director of Tibet House, Doboom Tulku, was in the process of inviting the various heads of the Tibetan traditions to come and give teachings. In this connection, Tibet House requested the great Vajradhara for teachings on behalf of Westerners. Consequently, on the fourteenth Rinpoché went to Tibet House. There, from the sixteenth to the twentieth, to an audience of a hundred Western devotees, he gave one session a day of teachings on the Seventh Dalai Lama's *Guide to the View: A Song of the Four Recollections*. The interpreter was Sharpa Tulku. After the teachings Tibet House offered Rinpoché a long-life ceremony by way of the Guru Puja *tsok* ritual. Among the offerings made to Rinpoché at that time were several texts published by Tibet House, including the complete works of Yongzin Yeshé Gyaltsen. Apart from these texts, Rinpoché returned all other offerings. Among the audience were Nyakré Khentrul and the Indian official Ravindra Verma.

Later, in response to a request from Tibet House, Rinpoché gave the permission initiation of Avalokiteśvara Who Liberates All Beings from the Unfortunate Realms, and the single-deity, single-vase Amitāyus long-life initiation to about a thousand Tibetans and Westerners. This was followed by words of advice on the importance of engaging in virtuous deeds to the best of one's abilities.

On the twenty-third, at the invitation of Thupten Tsering, Rinpoché left Tibet House and rested for a few days at his house. On the twenty-fifth Rinpoché spent five days at the All India Medical Institute with his labrang manager, Losang Lungrik, for a thorough medical check-up. During this time food and drink were brought daily from Thupten Tsering's house. The doctors concluded that he had no particular health problems. However, Rinpoché told Losang Lungrik that he did not wish to return to the hospital next year for a medical examination. This seemed to be a sign that Rinpoché would not come to Delhi again.

On the first of April Rinpoché left for Dharamsala. He was accompanied to the station by the Tibet House director, the Tibetan administration representative, Bakula Rinpoché, and others. On the following morning he was met at Pathankot Station by the senior minister and the chair of the

Assembly of Tibetan People's Deputies. After Rinpoché had arrived at the labrang in Dharamsala, they presented Rinpoché with the three representations and ceremonial scarves.

On the twenty-fourth the Religious Affairs Office sponsored the long-life ceremony Halting the Ḍākinīs' Escort for Rinpoché in the Thekchen Chöling temple by way of the single-deity, single-vase Amitāyus long-life ritual. This was attended by the entire assembly of Namgyal Monastery and members of the local monastic communities. On the twenty-eighth the labrang sponsored a longevity ritual with the long-life ritual of the deity Vijayā performed by the monks of Tsechokling Monastery. When the longevity substances were being offered to Rinpoché by the Tsechokling monk Tashi Gyaltsen, he requested Rinpoché to live for tens of thousands of years. Rinpoché joked, "Don't I need to live for *more* than tens of thousands of years?"

Khyongla was about to return to United States. When he went to say goodbye to Rinpoché, Khyongla said that he would come to see Rinpoché when the great Vajradhara made his annual visit to Bodhgaya that year. He also asked Rinpoché to compose an extensive version of his biography and asked if he could be allowed to serve as the scribe. Rinpoché was very pleased with this. He gave Khyongla teachings on *Guide to the View: A Song of the Four Recollections*. He presented Khyongla with his original copy of the text and gave him words of advice. He also asked Khyongla to do some research on the statue of Vajrayoginī at his birthplace in Ratsa.

On the eleventh of May at two o'clock, I invited the throneholder and tutor to my rooms along with Serkong Rinpoché. The visit lasted until half past three, and the conversation covered a number of topics. On the fifteenth Rinpoché gave a long-life initiation to Geshé Kayang of Sera Jé and others. On the nineteenth the Tibetan people offered me a long-life ceremony over which the great Vajradhara presided. On the twenty-second, former monastic and lay officials offered Rinpoché a long-life ceremony by way of a Guru Puja *tsok* ritual.

On the eleventh of June, Rinpoché gave explanations of the six-session guruyoga and the Vajrabhairava prayer to Sallie (Dawa)[209] and five other Westerners. Sharpa Tulku was the interpreter. On the twenty-third Rinpoché performed the usual invocation of Nechung and Gadong. Around this time, a French nun, Nadia, who regularly stayed at Trijang Labrang on her visits to India, came to visit Rinpoché. Rinpoché told her that the two previous Trijang and Ling Rinpochés were very close and in the labrangs they even had the same design of lids for the tea bowls! The French nun requested Rinpoché to live a long time, and he replied, "Trijang Rinpoché was eighty-one when he exhibited the act of passing away, and this year I too will be eighty-one." This seemed like an indication that this year he would pass away.

On the seventeenth of July, the lay and monastic people of central Tibet jointly sponsored a long-life ceremony for Rinpoché using the ritual Halting the Ḍākinīs' Escort together with a thousandfold Guru Puja and *tsok* ritual. It took place in Thekchen Chöling temple and was attended by local residents and by monks and nuns who had arrived in Dharamsala. On the twenty-fifth at two o'clock, I invited the great Vajradhara and assistant tutor Serkong Rinpoché for an informal visit, which lasted three and a half hours.

Among the initiations, transmissions, and core teachings that I had yet to receive from Rinpoché were those initiations from Abhayākaragupta's *Vajra Garland Mandala Procedures*, on whose deities Rinpoché had been unable to undertake a retreat. However, apart from those, I have received most of the initiations I requested from Rinpoché.

Basically my thinking is that I am keen to give transmissions, explanations, and teachings on texts as extensively as I am able and believe that it is excellent to do so. This is because I see no danger in doing so. With initiations, if both guru and disciple are not qualified, if there is no effective focusing on the meaning with single-pointed concentration and you are merely reciting the ritual, then you are turning secret mantra into a shadow of itself. There is a real danger for those giving such initiations. As for explanations and teachings on various texts, if you don't know something, there is nothing you can do; just say "I don't know this" and leave it. Other than that, if you teach what you know with a good motivation, then I think it can be of some benefit.

Therefore I received over time from the precious tutor the explanations of texts and teachings I had requested. The record of the teachings that the precious tutor himself received never reached India, but except for the transmission of one or two minor teachings, he joyfully told me that he had passed on all the teachings.

38 | The Passing of Serkong Rinpoché and the Onset of Illness

O N THE FOURTH of September 1983, in Spiti,[210] assistant tutor Serkong Rinpoché suddenly enacted the deed of passing away. The Ling Labrang manager was unable to break the news to the Vajradhara tutor. However, two monks from Namgyal Monastery arrived at the labrang to request Rinpoché for divination and advice on whether they should go to Spiti to help with Serkong Rinpoché's funeral arrangements. Therefore the manager had to inform Rinpoché of the news of Serkong Rinpoché's passing. The precious tutor was very concerned and told the monks they should go at once to Spiti. He also advised that some monks in Dharamsala from Ganden Shartsé should also go.

The next morning at five o'clock, when the manager as usual went to assist Rinpoché in getting up, it appeared as if Rinpoché had suffered a kind of stroke. A member of the labrang was immediately sent to fetch Dr. Yeshé Dönden and Gelek Dargyé from the Private Office. Yeshé Dönden gave Rinpoché medicine and performed the procedure of the golden needle. Gelek Dargyé went to Nechung Drayang Ling Monastery to consult the protector Nechung. The reply was, "As I, the formless one, have indicated previously, this seems to be an obstacle to His Holiness, but if rituals are performed promptly, there will be no great danger." The labrang immediately set about arranging long-life rituals such as commissioning the painting of White Tārā in a single day.

I was in Switzerland when I received the telegram informing me about Serkong Rinpoché's passing away in Spiti and of the precious tutor falling ill. This was clearly a serious illness, and I became very sad. I had known Serkong Rinpoché since I was a child. He was someone who would always willingly take on with the purest of intentions any responsibility for the sake of the Buddha's teaching and his country. How could it be that he died suddenly, leaving no time to do anything? On top of that, the precious tutor had come down with a serious illness. What was happening? I felt sad and troubled.

A few days later I received a more detailed letter from the Private Office. At first I thought to return at once to India. On reflection, Serkong Rinpoché had already passed away, and there was nothing I could immediately do for the precious tutor's illness. So I instructed the Private Office to take all immediate and necessary measures. For my part I made very strong prayers for the precious tutor to recover from this illness and decided to fulfill my schedule in the West as much as I could and then return to India.

The Religious Affairs Office, the three monastic seats, the two tantric colleges, and other monasteries as well as individuals and organizations, lay and monastic, and the labrang itself all sponsored and performed rituals for Rinpoché's well-being. Dr. Yeshé Dönden, when he was not attending to patients in his clinic, spent most of his time at the labrang, dedicating an enormous amount of effort to treating Rinpoché. Kalsang Yeshé sent a telegram to Drepung Loseling asking Sangra Jampa Tulku to come to Dharamsala. When he arrived, he served Rinpoché by performing his regular recitations. Thupten Tsering came from Delhi to help. Khyongla came from the United States, and when he arrived at the labrang, Rinpoché welcomed him warmly. Khyongla took on the duty of reciting Rinpoché's daily prayers. Rinpoché told him to recite them slowly and would occasionally mimic Khyongla's accent and laugh.

In the evenings Sangra Jampa Tulku, Khyongla, Dakpo Bamchö Tulku, the Gyütö monk Könchok Tenzin, and others performed the self-generation of Vajrabhairava in the presence of Rinpoché, as well as the sixty-four-part torma ritual, ransom rituals, and so on. All of Rinpoché's attendants assembled and recited long-life prayers, which were probably heard by Rinpoché. Dakpo Bamchö Tulku, Lama Thubten Yeshe, Lama Zopa, and others offered long-life ceremonies, which the ritual monks performed on the veranda outside Rinpoché's room. At breaks in the rituals, the sponsors would enter the room to offer Rinpoché the three representations and make requests for his long life. In response Rinpoché would make prayers to the Three Jewels and say that they too must make prayers.

Later a French disciple of Rinpoché called Jean Pierre, whom the Tibetans called Jampal, came to offer his help to Rinpoché. Each day he massaged Rinpoché's shoulders and left leg. He emphasized the importance of working on the enunciation of vowels such as *a* and *u* in order to improve his speech. Vajradhara asked Khyongla to recite the vowels with him. Jampal's wife Isabelle came to visit Rinpoché and asked him to bless her rosary. Rinpoché took the rosary, repeated the *maṇi* mantra on it twenty-one times, and handed it back.

On the morning of the nineteenth of September, while Khyongla was reciting *Speaking the Names of Mañjuśrī* as part of the recitation schedule, Rinpoché called him over. At first Khyongla could not make out what Rinpoché was saying, and he had to repeat it a few times. Finally, he understood Rinpoché to say that the mantra *Oṃ vajra tīkṣṇa duḥkha ccheda* meant "Vajratīkṣṇa cuts away the torment," that Vajra Tīkṣṇa was an epithet of Mañjuśrī, and that Puṇḍarīka's *Stainless Light* Kālacakra commentary was the main commentary to *Speaking the Names of Mañjuśrī*.

Once when Tenzin Phuntsok from the labrang was attending Rinpoché, Rinpoché asked Tenzin to put on him the knitted hat that he always wore. At the time Rinpoché was sitting with his right hand in the teaching mudrā and his left hand in the meditation mudrā. This seemed like a clear indication of the pose his precious embalmed body was to be in.

At twelve o'clock on the twenty-fifth of September, I arrived back in Dharamsala. At two o'clock I went to see the precious tutor at the labrang. Seeing him so ill I was very saddened, but there was nothing I could do. I prayed from my heart that he would recover and live a long life. On the morning of the twenty-sixth I visited again. I offered the mandala and the three representations and fervently requested that he recover from his illness. Nechung had indicated that we should offer the poison-extraction and impurity-removing ritual, but that was not convenient. Therefore I instead did a three-day retreat of the pacification goddess from among the goddesses of the four feats, which is a practice found in the volumes of *Pure Visions: The Sealed Secrets* by the Great Fifth Dalai Lama. I brought a bottle of the purified water created in this retreat to Rinpoché for him to drink daily.

The seventh of October was the first day of the ninth Tibetan month, and at eight in the morning I went again to the labrang to offer Rinpoché more of the blessed water from the retreat and to request he recover from the illness he was exhibiting. On the sixteenth I went again to the labrang at eight. He was slightly better, and I offered him more of the water.

On the third of November at ten o'clock, I visited Rinpoché at the labrang. I inquired about his illness and told him of what I had been recently doing for the sake of the Buddha's teaching and so on. At nine o'clock on the nineteenth, I again went for an audience and talked to the manager about Rinpoché's care. On the twentieth Nechung was invoked through the oracle. The protector performed a ritual dance in the presence of Rinpoché and then presented him with the three representations. Nechung then knelt in front of Rinpoché and implored the great Vajradhara tutor to recover from his illness and prayed to be cared for by him unceasingly in all future lives. Nechung had tears in his eyes and for a while could not speak. The protector then said, "As I said in Mundgod, if Rinpoché promises to live long, I will work for him without distraction throughout the six periods of the day and night." The protector then rubbed Rinpoché's hands and feet and performed a consecration of the room. He left the room and vacated the oracle's body.

Previously I had offered to Rinpoché a copy of the *Sutra of Immeasurable Wisdom and Life* and its mantra, written in gold ink, and asked the labrang manager to have it recited a set number of times. Consequently, Khyongla Tulku, who was helping Rinpoché with his recitations, and Sangra Jampa Tulku were reciting this sutra many times every day. Rinpoché specially asked Khyongla to do the repetition of the mantra.

One afternoon Rinpoché asked for the concluding verses of the Cakra-samvara body-mandala prayer to be recited. Rinpoché recited these verses with Khyongla:

> If in this lifetime I do not attain the supreme state,
> I pray that at the time of death
> I am welcomed by the deity, consort, and entourage
> accompanied by beautiful offerings, sweet sounds of music,
> and wonderful auspicious events.
>
> Then, at the conclusion of the clear light of death,
> I pray that I be led to the land of the pure ḍākinīs,
> where tantric knowledge holders practice the supreme path,
> and that I quickly complete this profound path.

On the afternoon of the twenty-first, although all the recitations had been completed, Rinpoché asked Khyongla to make two torma offerings for the Cakrasaṃvara body mandala, three recitations of the prayer, the dedication verses, and the Cakrasaṃvara body-mandala prayer again. Khyongla did as instructed as Rinpoché listened.

Chopra House, where Rinpoché lived, was high in the hills and was very cold in the winter. Therefore, for health reasons, Kalsang Yeshé[211] invited Rinpoché to his house in Gangchen Kyishong, and early in the morning of December the first Rinpoché was taken down by car. On arrival the host offered Rinpoché tea and sweet rice and presented him with the three representations and so on. Rinpoché received these with delight and thanked Kalsang Yeshé for the use of his house. Khyongla, the director and staff of the Astro-Medical Institute, and other disciples, as well as Kalsang Yeshé and his family, invited ritual monks to the house to offer a long-life ceremony, which Rinpoché happily accepted. Rinpoché was taken for outings on the veranda in a wheelchair. On one such occasion, Rinpoché saw Tashi, the man who had looked after the mules on his escape from Tibet. Right now he was helping in the kitchen. Rinpoché immediately called him over and gave him a blessing. "Do your duties well," Rinpoché instructed him.

At nine o'clock on the evening of the tenth of December, I heard that Rinpoché's condition had gotten worse. I went to him immediately. Although my grief was immeasurable, I was convinced that whatever a great and genuine yogi does, he does for a reason, and so I made prayers that his wishes would be fulfilled, and I recited his name mantra one thousand times in conjunction with focusing on the blessings of the four initiations. I visited again on the following day at nine o'clock. We had reached the point where giving medicine was no longer of much benefit. We now had to think very carefully whether Rinpoché should be taken to major hospital in India for treatment. After consultation with the doctors, it was decided he should remain where he was. Consequently, Rinpoché was examined by the Tibetan doctor Tsetan Dorji Sadutshang and given medicine. Sangra Jampa Tulku made a request to Rinpoché to please remain with us if possible for three years, and if that was not possible, then three months, or at the very least for two weeks. At this request Rinpoché showed small signs of recovery.

One time Rinpoché said to Sangra Jampa Tulku, "If I die, you should help manager Losang Lungrik." He replied that until the incarnation was discovered, as before, he would definitely be a worthy attendant, as others had been before him. Rinpoché was pleased. Rinpoché asked Denma Lochö Tulku to read to him Tsongkhapa's *Great Stages of the Path* and *Essence of Excellent Explanation: Differentiating the Definitive and the Provisional.*

Gradually Rinpoché's condition showed signs of worsening, and at eight o'clock on the morning of the twenty-second, I visited him. I made prayers, but it was clear that he would not remain for much longer. I said to Losang Lungrik that if Rinpoché showed the act of passing into the realm of peace, to please offer him a ceremonial scarf. I also gave him advice on what to do.

On the same day I gave the preparatory rituals and the actual initiation of the thirteen-deity Vajrabhairava to over a thousand monastic and lay recipients, after which there was a *tsok* offering ceremony based on this deity. This initiation was in response to several factors: it had been a request from Thupten Tenpa, the labrang manager's assistant; I had been intending to give teachings to Tibetans who had come from Tibet to see their relatives; it was also a way of remembering the great kindness of my tutor who, with enormous compassion, had fulfilled all my wishes by giving me initiations, transmissions, and core teachings; and by performing the offering of practice, it fulfilled his own profound wishes. I told the gathered assembly, among other things, that they should pray that the profound wishes of the Vajradhara tutor be completely fulfilled and that it was no use to feel upset. Whether a guru lives or passes away, it is all for the sake of the teachings and sentient beings, and the most important thing is that we practice according to the guru's teachings.

39 | The Passing of Ling Rinpoché

R INPOCHÉ'S CONDITION worsened and I heard the news that he had passed into the realm of peace at eleven o'clock on the morning of the twenty-fifth of December. Immediately I prayed to the best of my ability that this kind tutor's wishes for the teachings and living beings be perfectly fulfilled, that his unmistaken incarnation be quickly discovered, and that through his knowledge, pure ethics, and excellent conduct, as well as his teachings, compositions, and debating skills, the new incarnation emulates the life of his great predecessor.

On that day, as a mark of respect and to remember this great tutor's kindness, all Tibetan administration offices were closed. On the same day the labrang arranged a day-and-night performance of the Vajrabhairava self-initiation and so on in the presence of the precious body, headed by Denma Lochö Rinpoché with eight[212] ritual monks. From the twenty-sixth to the twenty-eighth, the Private Office sponsored the self-initiations of single-deity and thirteen-deity Vajrabhairava undertaken by Denma Lochö Rinpoché and fourteen ritual monks. December 29 was the twenty-fifth of the tenth Tibetan month and the day of the offerings of the twenty-fifth. In the Thekchen Chöling temple the labrang sponsored the offerings for a thousand five-senses cloud offerings and a *tsok* offering. A congregation of monks, headed by the entire assembly of Namgyal Monastery, as well as those monks, nuns, and laypeople who had completed the retreat, performed the thirteen-deity Vajrabhairava self-initiation. The public made a strong contribution reciting *Praise of Avalokiteśvara* and repeating the *maṇi* mantra. I joined the assembly at half past seven for the whole day, praying that the wishes of my root lama for living beings to be liberated be completely fulfilled, and that his supreme incarnation be unmistakably and quickly discovered.

For six days beginning on the thirtieth, the Private Office sponsored a reading of the Kangyur (the canonical teachings of the Buddha translated into Tibetan) and the Tengyur (their Indian commentaries and treatises) as well as the works of Tsongkhapa and his two main disciples. This was undertaken by monks and those laypeople who could read texts gathered together in Thekchen Chöling temple. I joined them on the first day.

Monks from the three monastic seats of learning, the two tantric colleges, and elsewhere, Westerners, and Tibetans made huge offerings, both real and visualized, in the presence of the precious body and prayed that life after life they would be joyfully cared for by that great being and that they would soon behold the golden face of his supreme incarnation.

The labrang manager, Losang Lungrik, requested me for divination to decide whether the body of the great being should be cremated or embalmed. The result was that embalming would be preferable for the preservation of the teachings of the Buddha in general, for those of Mañjunātha Tsongkhapa in particular, as well as for the huge benefit it would be for many living beings. I also advised him that for auspicious reasons, the body be placed in the pose of Tsongkhapa as Longevity Deity. However, unlike Tibet, India has a warm climate, and it was necessary to see if there existed in India a method of drying the body quickly. To this end Thupten Tsering and Dr. Tsetan Dorji Sadutshang were sent to Chandigarh to make inquiries at a medical college there. Also, through the Indian Ministry of External Affairs, three doctors from Delhi came up to Dharamsala. They and the medical college all agreed that there was no method to prevent the body from decomposing after one or two weeks. Therefore it was decided to follow the Tibetan ways of embalming.

The year 1983 had been one of powerful obstacles. Back while I was in the Ashok Hotel in Delhi about to travel to the West, Minling Trichen Rinpoché had come to see me. He was unwell and had to be supported on both arms. As soon as he arrived, he told me earnestly that this year was very dangerous, that I should take great care, and that such and such rituals should be performed at once. I responded by asking Rinpoché to take on the responsibility of arranging these rituals and that much effort be expended to make them effective. I said that I would offer whatever money was needed for offerings and donations.

It would appear that Serkong Rinpoché and the precious tutor both passing away that year were indications of those obstacles. When I returned from Switzerland, I looked into the details of Serkong Rinpoché's sudden passing. However, I look at it—what he said at that time, his movements at that time, how he passed away in just a few hours, and so on—it is clear that this was the action of a great Dharma practitioner, and it seems that he decided to deliberately pass away.

The Vajradhara throneholder showed signs of suffering a serious stroke, but it is difficult for us to know with any certainty the definitive reality of his inconceivable mysteries. When he was young he pursued his studies properly. Whatever he learned he put into practice and spent his whole life solely for the great purpose of the teachings and living beings. Therefore, even from an ordinary perspective, he was an inconceivably great being. As someone who spent a considerable number of years in his presence, I have complete conviction about this.

Generally, whatever great beings do, it is definitely done solely for the benefit of others. Concerning the precious tutor, regardless of how it might appear to others, I am convinced that taking on this illness and staying with us for more than three months was an act of unique compassion and special skillful means. Why? Because as I said earlier, my mind was tormented with the fear that I would not be able to bear it if the precious tutor showed the act of entering nirvana. That of course is just a foolish thought. Sooner or later I would have to face this situation. Nevertheless, these thoughts stayed in my mind. It was while I was in that state of mind that the precious tutor exhibited the serious illness. Over the next three months, sometimes he showed signs of improvement, and sometimes the illness appeared to get worse. During that period I had the opportunity to visit him a lot and make many requests. This led to me almost becoming used to this awful situation, and so finally when he actually showed his passing into nirvana, the earlier fear of not being able to bear the separation was not so strong. I have total conviction that this was Guru Vajradhara showing compassionate skillful means for my own sake. The kindness of this act alone is something I will find difficult to repay even over many lives.

On the fourth of January 1984, while the great being was engaged in death meditation (*thukdam*), his left hand moved a few inches on the bed where he lay. In many sutras and tantras of the Buddha it states that in those disciples who had gained the attainments of the path, the sense organs are clear, and the luster of the body does not disappear. Before he passed away

Rinpoché's body had lost some of his natural hue because of the hardships of the illness. However, when the coarse winds flowing through his nose had withdrawn inside, like a youthful Mañjuśrī casting off his external adornments and internally entering into meditation, Rinpoché's face was bright, glowing, and wore a slight smile. Denma Lochö Rinpoché, Sangra Jampa Tulku, and others who were attending on the body clearly heard the sounds of bell and *ḍamaru* drum. These and other extraordinary signs were evident during the fourteen days he dwelled in *thukdam* meditation.

At half past six in the morning of the sixth of January, there was a snow-storm with snowflakes that were shaped like flowers, and a lot of thunder was heard. It was during that time he left the meditation. As a sign of this, a little urine seeped from his vajra, and his complexion changed. However, there was still some warmth on his vest around the chest area, and so the ceremonial washing of the body was postponed for that day. On the seventh at around eleven o'clock, more urine was emitted, and a few tears came from his eyes. At four o'clock the washing ceremony was performed on his entire body, during which the position of his head remained unchanged. After the washing ceremony the salting ritual began.

On the seventeenth I came before the precious body to look at the embalming process. I also recited three times the prayer for his swift return that I had composed and made fervent requests. On the twenty-third, while teaching Śāntideva's *Guide to the Bodhisattva's Way of Life* in Bodhgaya, I gave a transmission of the prayer for his swift return and gave a talk to the audience urging them to make prayers for his stainless wishes to be completely fulfilled and for his unmistaken incarnation to be discovered quickly.

On the eighteenth of March, an incense-led procession of monks from Dharamsala and elsewhere, headed by the abbots of the various monasteries, the heads of the Religious Affairs Office, and so on, escorted the precious body on a palanquin from Kalsang Yeshé's house in Gangchen Kyishong to Ling Labrang at Chopra House. (plate 40) There I prostrated to the embalmed body, offered a ceremonial scarf, and made prayers. Afterward, the new Ganden Throneholder Jampal Shenphen, the Shartsé and Jangtsé Chöjés, past and present abbots of the monasteries, administration officials, and the Tibetans living in Dharamsala, as well as Westerners, all came to pay homage.

A few days later, in order to fulfill requests made by other devotees, and primarily to fulfill the wishes of the Vajradhara tutor, I gave combined teachings on the eight great works on the stages of the path[213] to a large gathering of monks, nuns, and laypeople. This was a vast cloud-like offering of practice made to please the lama and honor him.

The staff of the labrang, as exemplified by the manager Losang Lungrik, paid no attention to the hardships put upon them and shouldered the responsibility for the whole process from beginning to end with service that was both sincere and willing. Denma Lochö Tulku, who was the abbot of Namgyal Monastery, ritual monks from the two tantric colleges, and helpers Thupten Jikmé and Thupten Damchö from Nechung Drayang Ling Monastery worked tirelessly on the washing and salting rituals. Lisa Heath was an American who had received teachings from the precious tutor and who was a skilled sculptor. At her own suggestion, she happily and with single-pointed faith worked meticulously with modern techniques for three long years based on a photograph to produce a sculptured likeness of Rinpoché that was to cover the whole of the precious embalmed body. During that time, the American Tica Broch, who was a disciple of the precious tutor, was motivated by a joyful faith to provide for all expenses involved in Lisa's work. The embalmed body now stands in a room at the Thekchen Chöling residence as a shrine for reverence. (plate 41)

On the twelfth of March 1984, a day of a supremely virtuous planetary combination, I performed the effective ritual of the consecration of the precious body by way of single-deity Vajrabhairava. I performed a *tsok* offering and made many other real and visualized offerings, praying that the unmistaken incarnation be discovered.

In Drepung Monastery the labrang constructed a bodhi stupa made from gold and copper, more than eight feet high, containing at its heart Rinpoché's teeth and rare and very special substances, as described in the stupa inventory. It stands in the main Drepung assembly hall as the central sacred object. (plate 42)

On December 23, 1984, together with the Ganden Throneholder, the ritual monks from the two tantric colleges, and past and present abbots of the monasteries, I performed the consecration ritual known as Causing the Rain of Goodness to Fall, by way of glorious Guhyasamāja. I dedicated the virtue of all connected with this ceremony to be joyfully cared for by this great spiritual friend in all future lives, through which we will quickly travel the paths and levels, attaining the stage of the conqueror Vajradhara endowed with the seven features of union.[214]

The Guru Vajradhara had deliberately, and with a particular purpose in mind, placed a bookmark between pages fourteen and fifteen of the biography of the Tenth Dalai Lama Tsultrim Gyatso,[215] in the part describing the deed of his birth. There was found the following passage:

> On the ninth day of the ninth month of the fire-ox year (1817), a cuckoo sang sweetly on the east side of the mountain. In this world the sound of the cuckoo is said to be beautiful and regarded as auspicious. This was a clear sign that, likewise, the glory and renown of the extraordinary and wonderful deeds of the body, speech, and mind of this great being will again radiate far, far in all directions. All beings will think, "Now we have our guide and protector." Their joy and delight will multiply again and again. With devotion they will make prayers, they will praise his qualities, and they will cast their flowers of joy.

40 | A Summary of Rinpoché's Life

In keeping with the biographies of the great beings of the past, and so that the reader will be able to easily remember it, I will summarize the life of the precious tutor.

This great being relied upon thirty spiritual teachers. However, when he was very young the labrang would investigate and decide who would come to Rinpoché regularly to teach him texts. But after he became an adult, Rinpoché himself would examine very carefully to see if someone had the right qualifications of a teacher worthy of devotion, no matter which of the three vehicles (the Lesser, the Great, and the Vajra) they were teaching. He would never rush to judgment. This can be understood from the following examples. Rinpoché asked Phabongkha Rinpoché whether it were important to receive teachings from Choné Geshé Rinpoché Losang Gyatso, the wish-fulfilling cloud of Dharma. Later, he performed a dough-ball divination in front of the Jowo Rinpoché statue to see if he should take teachings from Kumbum Minyak Rinpoché.

Generally, all the lamas that Rinpoché received teachings from were completely qualified. However, even if their knowledge and realizations were equal to or lower than that of Rinpoché, because he had received teachings from them, he only talked of their excellent qualities of body, speech, and mind; he would never show them any disrespect or criticize them. He told Khyongla that he had learned from Guru Vajradhara Phabongkha Rinpoché in his teachings on guru devotion, as taught in the stages of the path, that there can be no certainty in your perception. Therefore whatever ordinary sides his lamas revealed, it never caused him any concern.

One time, after Rinpoché had become fully engaged in the activity of teaching others, Ngakrampa Losang Nyima from Gyütö, the teacher who taught him how to draw mandalas, mentioned how important it was to recite *Remembering the Three Jewels Sutra* each time before meals. Rinpoché

The Sixth Ling Rinpoché

immediately followed this advice, thereby showing that whether with a lama or a simple monk, he did not just ignore what they said but pleased them by making an offering of acting in accordance with their words.

In his youth Rinpoché received initiations into single-deity and thirteen-deity Vajrabhairava and teachings on their generation and completion stages from Phabongkha Rinpoché and others. Practicing these he then continued to confer and teach these practices extensively. Nevertheless, in the latter part of his life, Rinpoché again wished to do a generation-stage retreat on this deity, and in Bodhgaya he again took the initiation from Kyabjé Trijang Rinpoché. From that day onward, after the name-praise of Phabongkha Rinpoché, the first lama he had received the initiation from, he inserted and recited his own handwritten name-praise verse to Trijang Rinpoché. His devotion can be illustrated by the fact that he wrote name-praise requests for all his lamas and recited them daily, not only for Trijang Rinpoché. He regarded all those from whom he heard only one verse of teachings as actual buddhas and devoted himself to them by remembering their kindness.

Rinpoché did not receive many transmissions, but he did receive many initiations and explanatory teachings in particular. Moreover, he received all these teachings with the strong desire to practice them. He said, "Whenever I listened to teachings, I would always think, 'How can someone like me teach these to others?' Therefore, later I would always discuss matters, such as which initiation text can be used for a particular initiation, with my Dharma friends Drakri Rinpoché and others."

When listening to teachings Rinpoché would pay great attention to what to concentrate on, the visualizations, and so on. This can be understood from the following example. He had previously received the Lūipa Cakrasaṃvara initiation from Kyabjé Khangsar Rinpoché and had even taken notes on the teachings. However, he could not recollect the exact visualization process. Therefore, close to the time of undertaking the retreat on this deity, he again received the initiation from Kyabjé Trijang Rinpoché.

His Quality of Scholarly Learning

When he was studying at the monastery, Rinpoché was respected as having reached the level of an excellent debater. Many scholars of those times have recounted stories of Rinpoché shattering the confidence of his opponents when putting points or answering questions. Even after receiving his geshé degree, when he was not doing his practices or receiving guests, Rinpoché would always be studying texts. Because of this, he developed a supreme and self-reliant confidence in the sutras, tantras, and the sciences, and was a master orator.

However, he never wore the mantle of being learned in scripture, and when disciples would ask questions on points of scripture or on their practice, Rinpoché would first discuss the question with those lamas and geshés present. Should they not come up with a conclusive answer, this great being would give the answer clearly. Sometimes when relaxing with close disciples, Rinpoché would say that in such and such a text it says this and this, down to giving the correct page and line number. Even at an advanced age, knowledgeable scholars would come to visit Rinpoché, and they said that he would talk on the profound points of sutra and tantra while they had to maintain the practice of silence! Rinpoché still had the same great certainty on the topics of the classical texts as he did when he was in the debating courtyard. With some texts, even if he had not looked at them for many years, he could still recite them at will. This seemed to be a sign that he had attained the *dhāraṇī* (power of retention) of not forgetting.

HIS QUALITY OF PURE ETHICAL DISCIPLINE

For Rinpoché, taking the vows was not an act of mere resolve. He eliminated wrong notions about all aspects of the commitments and fully understood them. Nevertheless, he still kept a copy of Gungthang Tenpai Drönmé's *Summary of Advice on the Three Vows* in his box of regular recitation texts. He also treasured Yeshé Gyaltsen's root text and commentary on mind and mental factors. Rinpoché held the view that examining the mind during meditation sessions and post-meditation sessions, and applying the appropriate antidote to any mental affliction as soon as it arises, was the most important and greatest virtuous practice, and he counseled others to do likewise.

On the tenth and twenty-fifth respectively of each lunar month, Rinpoché undertook the self-initiation sādhana ritual of single-deity Vajrabhairava and Vajrayoginī. Each day he did the Vajrasattva practice with the hundred-syllable mantra and the extensive form of the rite of the blessings of the four initiations of single-deity Vajrabhairava. If a minor infraction of a vow occurred occasionally, he took on the practice of the great beings of the past of not letting it stay with him for more than a day.

HIS QUALITY OF EXCELLENT CONDUCT

Rinpoché had a great wish to live in a solitary hermitage, but when he became my tutor, most of the time he had to stay, except during breaks and so forth, at my residences at Norbulingka or the Potala. However, this did not displease him, and when there were no visitors, he would spend his time in recitation, reading texts, and so on. When reciting he would not rush but would focus on keeping the visualization process on track with each word of the ritual. Sometimes, to bring out the clarity of the visualization, he would repeat that section of the rite, or a particular mantra, four or five times.

As mentioned previously, when Rinpoché was doing the Lūipa Cakrasaṃvara generation-stage retreat in the Potala in Tibet, he would take about three hours just to recite the self-generation sādhana. Rinpoché was someone who was very meticulous in such practices. When he was young he completed a hundred thousand full-length prostrations, and even in advanced age when his body had become heavy, he made three prostrations every morning and night. When making mandala offerings during the six-session yoga practice and so forth, he would build the mandala there and then. He extended great efforts in these practices of purification and accumulation. On that foundation he put continuous effort in the task of study, contemplation, and meditation combined, like the stream of a great river. In this way, he developed in his mind the great qualities of compassion and so forth, whose clear signs I described above.

There was another sign of Rinpoché's clairvoyance. About a month before he passed away, at about eleven o'clock in the evening, he suddenly said to Könchok Tenzin, a Gyütö monk who was part of the labrang, "Go and see if your room has been burglarized." He at once went to his room, only to find that someone had broken in, stolen a tape recorder and other things, and fled. This was witnessed by a few members of the labrang.

By the infallibility of cause and effect, it can be established that someone who had practiced in the way that Rinpoché did must have developed profound tantric realizations. With such special inner qualities, he was able to use the Dharma protectors as his servants. Once there was a sign of that ability. In Garpa Hermitage in Tibet, Rinpoché was performing prosperity rituals, which were attended by the ritual monk Ngawang Lhundrup and his assistant Tsultrim. On the day that the rituals ended, during the act of brushing the dust off the costumes of an extraordinary-looking oracle statue of Nechung, it seemed as if Rinpoché had replaced the apron of Nechung a little too high. Tsultrim pointed this out to Rinpoché, who replied jokingly, "He will visit you this evening!" Just after midnight Tsultrim awoke in great fright when there was a loud cracking sound on an incense stand by his bed. However, he immediately remembered what Rinpoché had said and thought that he must have sent the protector. He was at once relieved, and his faith in Rinpoché was even greater than before. Tsultrim himself told this story.

I have also seen that even Palden Lhamo, mistress of the desire realm, could not compete with this great master and had to comply with his wishes, but here is not the place to talk about that.

Rinpoché held to the pure tradition of Tsongkhapa, the Mañjunātha Dharma king, and passed it on to others. However, he never showed disrespect or contempt toward other Tibetan traditions and their teachers. Whoever came to visit, he would always greet them with a smile and a welcome and would answer their questions fully. He never ignored or looked down on anybody. If you visited him a lot, your respect for his qualities of body, speech, and mind grew year after year. Everyone saw that Guru Vajradhara, like a great mountain, never changed toward those he had placed his trust in, regardless of their changing circumstances. Because of familiarity over many lifetimes with the four marks of contentment of an ārya, Rinpoché happily accepted whatever food, clothing, and so on was provided for him by his attendants and never said "I want this" or "I want that." In short, no one among those disciples or attendants who had been close to him for many years ever said that he showed any attachment for possessions or bias toward those he was close to.

To those who requested him to compose new works, he would reply, "These days we are short of those who study and contemplate. We are not short of texts to study and contemplate." He would therefore mostly decline such requests. Consequently, his body of written work is not large. Nevertheless, those works that he did compose are perfect in their explanations and are excellent compositions that delight the wise.

When giving transmissions he would read with good pronunciation, enunciate each word clearly and correctly, and never rush the text. When giving personal and experiential teachings and so on, he would primarily follow the practice and tradition of the masters of the past by following the fourfold-explanation practice and so on. When giving textual explanations he would give wide-ranging and profound explanations by way of reason and scriptural citations on the most difficult points of the classical texts. These captivated the minds of scholars. Except when he was of advanced age, whenever Rinpoché gave initiations, he would always hand out the initiation substances himself and would never cut corners. He always explained fully the entire initiation process from the preliminary of setting of the motivation up to the explanation of how the initiations were arranged into the path.

In Tibet once he gave a teaching and transmission of Tsongkhapa's *Great Stages of the Path to Enlightenment* to a single monk. Later, to me and others he gave very extensive teachings on the *Great Stages of the Path* four times and teachings on Panchen Losang Yeshé's *Swift Path Direct Instructions* six times. Because he was renowned as an unmistaken incarnation of Ra Lotsāwa, he would fulfill the desires of the many devotees who almost every year would ask him to confer the single-deity Vajrabhairava initiation and to give teachings on its generation and completion stages. He also gave the *Vairocana Enlightenment* initiation, whose lineage was very rare, as well as explanations on the classic treatises whose teaching lineages were rare in central Tibet. These and many more he gave to others throughout his life.

Saying Prayers for the Recently Deceased

As soon as someone arrived with a request for prayers to be said, Rinpoché would say a prayer immediately. Moreover, he would keep the paper containing the names and every month or every fortnight would make prayers in order to lead the deceased to the path of liberation. For this he would recite on his own or with others Tsongkhapa's *Prayer for Rebirth in Sukhāvatī*. Afterward he would burn the paper as was customary. This was another example of the inconceivable deeds of this great being and leader of living beings.

Disciples

Spiritual friends in the lineage of the Buddha with whom he alternated the role of teacher and student include: the tutor and regent Takdrak Vajradhara, master of the ocean of mandalas; the tutor Kyabjé Trijang Rinpoché, great illuminator of the doctrine of Tsongkhapa; and Khunu Lama Rin-poché Tenzin Gyaltsen, great illuminator of the Buddha's teaching. Other disciples include Dilgo Khyentsé Rinpoché, illuminator of the Nyingma teaching; and Sakya Trizin of the Tārā Palace and illuminator of the Khön family doctrine. Once he became the Dharma throneholder of the Geluk tradition, there was almost no one among the Geluk tradition who was not an actual disciple of this great protector. I too, through the force of good karma and prayers from previous lives, have been happily cared for by this protector from an early age. I enjoyed the fortune of receiving all the instructions that he possessed like a vase being filled to the brim. I hold these teachings primarily with the resolve to practice them and also to prop-agate them widely to others. I continue to hope and pray that for as long as the teachings of the Buddha remain, the nectar stream that issued from the lotus mouth of this great protector never ceases, and that it brings satisfac-tion to the swarms of fortunate bee-like disciples.

41 | The New Incarnation

THE DIRECT DISCIPLES of Guru Vajradhara, such as myself and others, as well as many others who possessed pure aspiration for the well-being of living beings and the Buddha's teaching with no discrimination of sectarian affiliations, longed for the unmistaken incarnation of this great guide and crown jewel of the "five and hundred"[216] to speedily and unequivocally return, possessed of the deeds and qualities of his great predecessor. To this end we continually made words-of-truth prayers[217] to the Three Jewels. Also, the labrang manager Losang Lungrik, who never lacked perseverance and a pure intention when it came to the practice of serving the guru, arranged numerous prayers and rituals to be performed a certain number of times according to the clearly divined instructions of the deities. These were never rushed, and no expense or difficulty was spared. He also made extensive offerings to the Three Jewels and donations to the monastic communities for the same purpose.

I was also requested to perform a divination concerning the whereabouts of the precious incarnation. Accordingly, in the fire-tiger year (1986) I performed a divination by way of requests to Jinasāgara Avalokiteśvara, the embodiment of the Three Jewels. The result clearly indicated that the incarnation had been born in the wood-ox year (1985), but his place of birth was not clearly divined. Therefore I issued instructions to undertake a thorough search for all children born in that year irrespective of whether they exhibited any special signs. Consequently, two groups consisting of Ling Gungbar Tulku, representing the abbot of Drepung Loseling, with an attendant, and Loseling Sangra Jampa Tulku from the labrang with Tenzin Phuntsok went out to the various Tibetan settlements in India to produce a list of all children born in the wood-ox year without regard to any special signs that might have occurred. They came up with a list of about 690 names. With these results I did a further divination in the first month of the fire-rabbit year (1987). The indication was that it would be better to wait a while before making the actual identification. Later I went to the shrine that held the body of the Guru Vajradhara, where I performed dough-ball divinations asking if the time was suitable for making identification. If it were, was the name included in the list? If it were included, under which of the three main location groupings, labeled *ka*, *ca*, and *ta* in the list, would his birthplace be found?[218] Not only did the results indicate that the time was ripe for making an identification, but they also indicated that we should search for the birthplace in the *ca* group. A few days later, in the presence of the Kyirong Wati Sangpo statue at Thekchen Chöling temple, I made a further divination asking from which of the *ca*, *cha*, *ja*, and *nya* groups, which were the four subgroups of the *ca* group, would the birthplace be found. The result came out strongly for the town of Bir[219] in the *ca* group. I asked that the list of names of children born in the wood-ox year be looked at again. There were eleven children born in Bir that year. Of these, ten were examined by Losang Lungrik and Jampa Tulku. None of them showed any remarkable signs.

The eleventh child was Tenzin Choephag, who had been entrusted to the Tibetan Children's Village after his mother died.[220] On the twenty-sixth of August 1987, which was the second day of the seventh Tibetan month of the fire-rabbit year, in the seventeenth sixty-year cycle, Sangra Jampa Tulku, Tenzin Phuntsok, who was an attendant of the predecessor, and Thupten Gelek all went to the Children's Village to examine him. They asked one of the housemothers where they could find the child Tenzin Choephag. While she looked among the children, a twenty-month-old child voluntarily took hold of Tenzin Phuntsok's hand. The housemother looked at him and said, "That is Tenzin Choephag." Tenzin Phuntsok took the child on his lap, where he sat smiling. "Do you recognize him?" he was asked, and the little boy nodded his head. Jampa Tulku showed the child four similar rosaries, one of which belonged to the predecessor. The boy took the correct rosary in his hand and counted off about twenty-one beads. Jampa Tulku was visibly overwhelmed with joy.

The next day the labrang manager went to the Children's Village to conduct further tests. Snacks had been arranged, and the child handed out food to the staff and members of the labrang. He gave hand blessings, touched heads, and so on, all of which were clearly inner signs of a great being. Moreover, the predecessor was left-handed when he was young, and it was noticed that Tenzin Choephag mainly used his left hand. The labrang manager reported all these details to me, and I asked that the child be brought to me for examination. The next day the boy arrived at the labrang and immediately sat for a long time very happily on the manager's lap. He was then brought to my residence at Thekchen Chöling, where I offered him a protection cord and some snacks, which he respectfully accepted. Judging from all he did and his mannerisms, he seemed to be the genuine incarnation. Nevertheless, as an indication of the importance of this matter, I received from Ling Labrang a request for divination on the names of three other boys from Bir who had been born in the wood-ox year along with Tenzin Choephag. Through the infallible Three Jewels, I performed thorough divinations one after the other to determine the truth. I found with complete certainty that Tenzin Choephag, whose father was Labukpa Sangpo from Tö Porong and whose mother was Kalsang Chödrön from Dranak, was the incarnation of the kind Guru Vajradhara. Thus it was conclusively decided. (plate 43)

Previously the labrang had requested the Tibetan Medical and Astrological Institute to perform an astrological observation known as the Arising of Vowels concerning the incarnation of the Vajradhara Guru. The result was as follows:

> The supreme incarnation is born, and in good health,
> perfect like the jewels that abide in the ocean.
> But the mother is gravely ill,
> the household is small, and without resources.
> To ensure that obstacles to his coming are removed,
> it is advisable to perform extensive rituals.
> Soon after one year, eight months, and seven days,
> a sure sign will appear.

These verses were very prescient. His mother had passed away, and at this time of meeting the supreme incarnation, one year and nine months had passed since his birth.

In response to a request from Ling Labrang, I bestowed upon him the name Tenzin Lungtok Trinley Choephag. At the same time, I composed a long-life prayer. This contained fervent wishes that all his activities, both public and private, ripen in order to nourish the Buddha's teaching and sentient beings.

The thirteenth of the eighth Tibetan month of the fire-rabbit year, or Monday the fifth of October 1987, was the day of the enthronement. It was performed upon the high Dharma Throne of Fearlessness that was used by his predecessor. From a young age I had been one of the disciples of the Guru Vajradhara, whom he had cared for greatly as he would his own eyes. I attended the enthronement at the labrang at twelve o'clock that day. The precious incarnation presented me with the mandala and the three representations with great respect. In turn I offered him a ceremonial scarf, and as an auspicious portent that he would become like a second Buddha, I presented him with a bronze statue of the Buddha and a protection cord together with prayers. Now that the incarnation had been recognized and was actually here, I felt a great joy in the residence of the Guru Vajradhara. I had lunch with Rinpoché, during which he took the food with his hand and happily offered it to me. After lunch when I was leaving, we touched heads as I sat in the car, and he took hold of my robe and wanted to come with me. This was a sign that produced in me a hair-tingling joyous faith that my root guru would unceasingly and happily care for me in all my lives.

If I may mention a few of the extraordinary activities the young precious incarnation has performed: When Rinpoché's incarnation had been confirmed, the Children's Village rented a guesthouse in which he was invited to stay. During a ceremony held by the labrang, he took a grape from a plate of sweet rice and offered it to labrang manager Losang Lungrik. He presented five rupees given to him as an offering together with a ceremonial scarf to his housemother Samdrup Drölma. On the evening of that first day, he was put to bed in the guesthouse using the bedding of his predecessor, and for about five minutes he was sad and cried. Before that, when the labrang manager was about to leave, he wanted to leave with him and threw his arms around his neck. The housemother had to use various methods to bring him into the room. When Palden, the manager of Trijang Labrang came to visit, he immediately jumped happily onto his lap. Palden asked the precious incarnation to say prayers over a scarf he was going to offer to the shrine that housed the body of the former Kyabjé Trijang Rinpoché. The precious incarnation took the scarf in his hands, placed it on his head for a long time, and made prayers.

Denma Lochö Rinpoché came to visit, and when tea was being served, the precious incarnation made it clear he wanted to take tea with him, and so tea was offered to him. The precious incarnation took the biscuits, broke them up, filled a bowl with them, and offered it to Denma Lochö Rinpoché. Ratö Chubar Rinpoché came to visit and stayed with him for some time. The precious incarnation picked up the walking stick that the previous Trijang Rinpoché had given Chubar Rinpoché. An old lady came with a rosary in her hand. The precious incarnation took the rosary and, with the stick in one hand and the rosary in the other, walked back and forth. Lati Rinpoché, former abbot of Ganden Shartsé, came to visit, and Rinpoché displayed many signs of a past familiarity, which were indications of the great compassionate regard the previous incarnation held for others.

After the precious incarnation had been brought to the labrang, during a hundred thousand Tārā practice, Losang Lungrik began the hundred butter-lamp offerings with the incense, and the precious incarnation took the incense and performed the incense circumambulation of the ritual monks. At that time, Topgyal, the abbot of the local nunnery, came to visit and gave the precious incarnation a gift of some towels. He gave them to the manager and then said "Ani,"[221] as though knowing Topgyal was abbot of the nunnery. When the precious incarnation came to visit me, a personal attendant of mine called Losang Gawa, who had been sick for a time and had not seen the precious incarnation before, began attending to me. The precious incarnation immediately took a ceremonial scarf from Sangra Jampa Tulku and presented it to Losang Gawa.

When he arrived at his rooms above the monastery at Bodhgaya, he took Kalsang, a caretaker monk, by the hand and urged him to open a cupboard beneath the altar. He took out a ceremonial scarf and offered it to a picture of Mañjuśrī on the Astro-Medical Institute's calendar. When he went inside his room, he took a high-quality ceremonial scarf from a table drawer and offered it to a photograph of me. There was a life-like statue of the previous Vajradhara in the room. "Who is this?" asked Losang Lungrik. The precious incarnation smiled, turned away, and sat down. Kamé Losang Samten, who belonged to the labrang, came from Switzerland to Bodhgaya. When Rinpoché saw him, he gave him a marigold as if he immediately recognized him. Losang Samten had offered Rinpoché a silver mandala, which included a badge of the ten-part stacked Kālacakra mantra with a photo of me at its top and a circular badge of Mañjuśrī. Rinpoché took these two items and urged that the Kālacakra badge be pinned on his right breast and the Mañjuśrī on his left. These examples evidently indicate a recollection of his previous existence.

After his mother had passed away, the child was entrusted to the Tibetan Children's Village in Dharamsala, and one day his father, Labukpa Sangpo, came to visit him. During this trip Labukpa Sangpo also went to Ling Labrang to visit the precious body. Then he went to Nechung Drayang Ling Monastery to seek the assistance of the protector. As he prayed by the door of the assembly hall, he saw a life-size photo of the predecessor on the altar, although in reality only the usual normal-size photo was there. This was evidently the Dharma protector, on whom the succession of predecessors had relied as their main deity, indicating that this was indeed the true incarnation.

I will continue to pray that this incarnation of the great Guru Vajradhara live a long life, that he completes well his studies, contemplations, and meditations on the great ocean of scripture, and in the teachings of the Buddha that he carries out deeds like a second Buddha.

42 | Dedication and Colophon

The body adorned with enlightened signs and features,
fashioned by the manifold refinement of supreme patience,
and upon whose sight all disharmony vanishes,
has clearly appeared in the skies of the good karma
that we of the snowy land have created.

To bring to blossom the lotus grove of <u>scripture</u> and <u>realizations</u>
of the <u>Buddha's teachings</u> in general, and those of Tsongkhapa,
you assumed the form of the <u>enlightened deeds</u> of every <u>conqueror</u>.
Again I remember you, mighty sun-like orator.[222]

Having walked a long time on the golden staircase
of learning, contemplation, and meditation,
now as one with all other buddhas,
you play in the palace of unified enlightened body and mind.

Nevertheless, in order to show the ford-like path
of what is to be developed and what is to be discarded
to those who strive for freedom,
you took on the endeavors of listening, contemplation,
    and meditation
as an illusion-like manifestation of great noble beings.

You devoted yourself to over twenty-nine spiritual mentors,
who were matchless and supreme navigators,
and on the boat of devoted and constant perseverance,
you reached the far shore of the ocean of learning.

Using the arrows of much scripture and reasoning,
you were victorious in the battle against ignorance,
and by beating the drum of victory,
you proclaimed the two truths throughout the world,
thereby revealing the true meaning of omniscience.

From the magical refinement of analytical and absorptive meditations,
you revealed the wish-granting jewel of experience and realization.
By its brilliant light of the higher paths and levels,
you produced a beautiful song to please all the buddhas.

From the vast expanse of rain clouds of love and compassion
come the great rains of the vast and profound sutra and tantra,
and the regions of this beautiful woman-like earth who grants all desires
are packed with the green groves of a golden age of the Buddha's teachings.

And you have hung around the necks of those with fresh minds
precious white lotus garlands of excellent teachings,
with their thousand fully blossomed petals of poetic elegance
and their vibrant flower eyes of beautiful meaning.

From the heap of precious jewels
of your spontaneous and unceasing enlightened activities,
I have taken a few and threaded them upon
the string of easy-to-understand words
to produce this *Jewel Pendant* biography.

By the virtue of my efforts in this composition,
I pray that all beings, who are as extensive as space itself,
be swiftly delivered from the wars of the two obscurations,
which is the sole wish of my kind spiritual friend,
and that they reach the great city of the definitive guru.

May the new moon of the supreme incarnation
emulate entirely the life and deeds of his predecessor,
and by the great festival of light of his composition, teachings, and debate,
may the teachings of the Buddha illuminate the four continents.

I pray that I too in the garland of my lives
will place with devotion my head to your feet
and quickly perfect the youthful vigor of the ten powers
to become a great warrior who saves all beings.

I WAS FORMALLY REQUESTED by the Ling Labrang manager Losang
Lungrik to compile for the benefit of future disciples a biography of the
life and deeds of this incomparably kind tutor, the Vajradhara throneholder
and Ling incarnation whose name I cannot bring myself to say, but out of
necessity I mention it as the most venerable and glorious Thupten Lungtok
Namgyal Trinlé. These deeds in the eyes of his ordinary disciples consisted
of entering the gateway of the precious teaching of the Buddha, followed by
study, contemplation, and meditation on the vast ocean of scripture, composition, teaching, and debate, and working for the Buddha's teaching and
living beings through his wisdom, pure ethics, and compassion. From my
side I agreed to do this with the great joy that came from recalling his kindness. So that the work would not be delayed because of the constant call
of my religious and secular duties, I asked Ratö Khyongla Tulku Ngawang
Losang to collect all relevant documents and to interview Losang Lungrik
and others who were close to him. I have added at the appropriate places
and where necessary some of the teachings I received, special advice and
instruction I received in conversation, and other suitable material.

Jewel Pendant: A Brief Account of the Commonly Perceived Deeds of
Mañjunātha, the Regent of the Buddha, the Protector and Great Tutor, the
Vajradhara Ling Incarnation, Venerable Thupten Lungtok Namgyal Trinlé
Palsangpo was completed by his disciple, the Śākya monk Tenzin Gyatso,
of the line of the Holders of the White Lotus, at a time of auspicious planetary conjunction, on the day of the first bhādra division of the waning half
of the jyeṣṭha month of the Tibetan earth-dragon year, in the seventeenth
sixty-year cycle, 2,532 years after the Buddha's passing according to the Theravada tradition, in the year 1988 of the Common Era, in Thekchen Chöling,
Dharamsala, in the district of Kangra, in the state of Himachal Pradesh, in
the noble land of India. May all who see, hear, recall, or come into contact
with this work be joyfully cared for by a Mahayana spiritual mentor such as
this great master.

Afterword

His Eminence the Seventh Ling Rinpoché, Tenzin Lungtog Trinley Choephag, was born November 18, 1985, and two years later His Holiness the Dalai Lama recognized Rinpoché as the reincarnation of his senior tutor, the Sixth Kyabjé Ling Rinpoché. Rinpoché joined Drepung Monastic University in South India as a pre-novice in 1990, and his enrollment was celebrated with large and elaborate religious ceremonies. Rinpoché received his novice monk's vow from His Holiness at Drepung in 1993, and at age ten he began his studies at Drepung and has been engaged in rigorous spiritual training under the special care and guidance of His Holiness the Fourteenth Dalai Lama ever since. On March 3, 2004, on the fiftieth anniversary of His Holiness's own monastic ordination, which he received from the Sixth Ling Rinpoché, His Holiness conferred full-ordination bhikṣu vows upon the Seventh Ling Rinpoché at His Holiness's residence in Dharamsala, India.

Rinpoché has traveled extensively both in India and around the world. Rinpoché receives frequent invitations to teach overseas and is always warmly received by Tibetan communities and international students. In 2015, His Eminence commenced a series of international teaching tours, with visits to Singapore, Australia, and North America. Rinpoché plans to visit Israel and the United States in 2017 and Europe in 2018. Rinpoché attended the World Peace Puja in Bodhgaya in January 2005; the International Conference on Vinaya in Sarnath, India, in January 2011; the Global Buddhist Congregation in New Delhi in November 2011; and the First Founding Members Conclave of the International Buddhist Confederation in New Delhi in September 2013. He is a regular attendee of the Mind and Life conferences in India.

He also organized and hosted His Holiness the Dalai Lama's historic Jangchup Lamrim Teachings at the great seats of learning in South India—Sera, Drepung, Ganden, and Tashi Lhunpo monasteries—from 2012 to 2015. In these teachings, His Holiness gave commentaries on eighteen classic treatises on the stages of the path to enlightenment. More than 35,000 people attended each year, including as many as 4,000 foreign attendees from seventy countries, while hundreds of thousands watched worldwide via live webcast. More information about these events is online at jangchuplamrim.org.

In November 2012, while driving to Goa Airport to greet His Holiness the Dalai Lama for the Jangchup Lamrim Teachings, the Seventh Ling Rinpoché was in a catastrophic car accident. The driver of the vehicle was killed, and other passengers sustained serious injuries. Rinpoché himself required lengthy surgeries and was unable to walk for several months. His complete rehabilitation and recovery took several years.

The Seventh Ling Rinpoché has now completed all five subjects in the monastic curriculum (Logic and Epistemology, Perfection of Wisdom, Madhyamaka Philosophy, Abhidharma, and Vinaya) and has been awarded his geshé degree from Drepung Loseling Monastic University. The auspicious occasion of Rinpoché's geshé ceremony was celebrated in November 2016 at Drepung (see plate 46), following which Rinpoché commenced the traditional one year of studies at the tantric college of Gyütö in Dharamsala.

Thupten Tsering, a long-time member of the staff of Ling Labrang, says, "The previous Kyabjé Ling Rinpoché was one of the greatest Geluk lamas of the twentieth century. His compassion had no bounds, and his genuine concern extended to all living beings and things. He was a genuine and pure lama and did not care for fame or reputation, always maintaining a simple life. I have been most blessed and fortunate to have been with him through many times and events, both happy and sad.

"The new incarnation from a young age showed much intelligence and displayed many traits of his previous incarnation. It is my greatest wish and prayer that the Seventh Kyabjé Ling Rinpoché will continue to follow in the footsteps of his previous incarnation."

The Editors

Appendix. Lineage Prayer

TRANSLATOR'S NOTE

As noted in the text above on pages 171–72, a prayer supplicating the past lives of the Sixth Ling Rinpoché was composed by Trijang Rinpoché in Tibet in 1954. As inspiration for the prayer, Trijang Rinpoché followed depictions of the past incarnations painted on the wall of Garpa Hermitage. These paintings were a result of visions had by the Fifth Ling Rinpoché Losang Lungtok Tenzin Trinlé.

Later, when the Sixth Ling Rinpoché lived in India, new sets of these paintings were produced. Following prolonged research by Venerable Tenzin Chönyi, or Kungo Tara, who was the senior secretary to His Holiness the Fourteenth Dalai Lama, and aided by Ven. Losang Yönten, a book was eventually produced with detailed biographies of all but five of the incarnations. The translation below is of Trijang Rinpoché's prayer, and the homage and colophon by these compilers is included because it contains a prayer to the present twenty-second Ling incarnation.

The First Ling Rinpoché, Hor Döndrup Gyatso (1655–1727), is incarnation 16 in this lineage prayer. The order of the incarnations below, based on recent research, differs in two places from Trijang Rinpoché's original text. The original text also included a twenty-second future incarnation, which the compilers omitted. As is customary with these kind of supplications, the names of the incarnations are woven into the Tibetan text. I have tried to highlight these in bold, but it was not always possible to replicate them exactly.

Gavin Kilty

Precious Necklace of the Most Powerful Wish-Fulfilling Jewels

A brief account of the deeds of the past lives of the Ganden Throneholder, the Vajradhara Ling incarnation, entity of Vajrasattva, the all-pervading master of the vast ocean of tantric families and mandalas

COMPILERS' HOMAGE

Fully enlightened Buddha, whose qualities of abandonment and
    insight are supreme,
sacred Dharma, which destroys all suffering and its causes,
noble Sangha, who hold the treasury of the ārya jewels of freedom and
    insight,
you Three Precious Jewels, bestow upon me every auspiciousness.

Arising as the complete ripening of the two kinds of merit,
which was accumulated over many eons,
the unknown friend to the world, unrivaled teacher, most powerful
    of the sages,
I bow in complete faith with body, speech, and mind.

Every accumulation of the wisdom, compassion, and power
of every conquering buddha brought together as one,
Mañjuśrī, in the dance of a spiritual teacher,
glorious Losang Drakpa, great pioneer of our snowy land,
I bow my head to you.

You achieved the power to make full use of the treasury
of the **scriptures** and **insights** within the **teachings** of the **Buddha**.
Your profound and **victorious activity**, long ago perfected, never
    diminishes.
As the great successor to the second Buddha,
the great protector of the doctrine and living beings in our snowy land
devoted himself to you as his peerless master,
may I be nourished by this actual Vajradhara.

The studded beautiful precious stones of your past lives,
which include famed and lesser-known practitioners of India and Tibet
as well as scholar practitioners and powerful rulers,
all performed the dance of the miraculous manifestation
of the three mysteries of the enlightened body, speech, and mind
in perfect accord with myriad types and dispositions of living beings.

Although this limitless ocean of extraordinary life stories
could not be told even by a chorus of ten million voices,
just this little drop of consecrating water
taken on the tip of a stalk of *kuśa* grass
and sprinkled with great faith will have great meaning.

In order to bring extraordinary benefit and happiness
to the **lands** and mountains of the teachings and living beings,
while never stirring from the realm of nonconceptuality,
like the many reflections of the moon in myriad clear lakes,
your magical dance of **incarnations appeared** as births and deaths,
well beyond the parameters of ordinary histories bound by the restraints
    of time,
simultaneously and **successively** without contradiction,
a feature only enjoyed by the great ārya beings.

TRIJANG RINPOCHÉ'S PRAYER

Oṃ svasti
All-pervading, **all**-doing, great bliss Vajrasattva,
the youthful dance of the **space** vajra as vast as **space**,
nondual master and guide, **dualistically** emanating and withdrawing,
I make this prayer to the lord of the **family** of all **families**.

I make this prayer to the one
whose beautiful and illusion-like autumn moon forms of exalted knowing,
all of which are one taste with the pacification of all signs of elaboration,
play simultaneously thousands upon thousands of times
in the lakes of the minds of living beings.

1. **Revealing** the light of miraculous display
to **destroy** the **enemy** of mental afflictions,
you were the friend that opened the white lotus
of purification and freedom for countless fortunate beings.
I make this prayer at the feet of Arhat Udayin.

2. You distributed the untied **golden** sheaves of scripture,
born from the **knowledge** of Mahābrahma,
as a nourishment of happiness for oneself and others.
I make this prayer at the feet of the brahman Veda Survarṇa.

3. With ascetic practice you **nourished** the yoga of the little child
of the spontaneously **accomplished** and uncontrived primordial mind,
becoming attached to the **glorious** and excellent qualities
of the beautiful mother of **great** bliss and emptiness.
I make this prayer at the feet of Mahāsiddha Śrīpāla.

4. As adornments for the ears of those fortunate beings in **Oḍḍiyāna**,
you created a bunch of a thousand **lotuses** of the profound reality
that lies at the heart of the **conqueror's** thinking.
I make this prayer at the feet of Oḍḍiyāna King Padminī.

5. The great light of your sun and moon of the two types of ethics
was **victorious** in the battle against the non-Dharma dark forces
and illuminated the **excellent** path of supreme happiness.
I make this prayer at the feet of King Suśubha.

6. With your virtuous **rule** you were the swift and excellent **horse**
that quickly brought order and tranquility to the world
with the miraculous gait of the blessings of the supreme vehicle.
I make this prayer to King Rathika.

7. With the sharp hook of wisdom you brought under control
the powerful and crazed **elephant** of the unruly mind
and **cared for** it within the forest of tranquility and liberation.
I make this prayer to the incomparable Hastipāla.

8. In the dense forest of karmic appearance,
within the **graveyard** that is samsara,
a **place** where the zombies of dualism wander,
you developed the ascetic practice of one-taste fearlessness.
I make this prayer to Siddha Śmāśānika.

9. Merely by brandishing your powerful sharp **horns**,
your buffalo face destroys the world of the hinderers.
With your blazing **renown** as a **Vajra** Bhairava practitioner,
I make this prayer to Ra Lotsāwa Dorjé Drak.

10. Intoxicated by the nectar **juice** of the syllable *a*,
whose significance is that of the unborn,
you performed some skillful magic,
sometimes expressed with **anger**, sometime with desire,
leaving all opponents with their pride shattered.
I make this prayer to the unrivaled Akhu Trothung.

11. Through practices that were difficult to **perform**,
you devoted yourself to the supreme and sacred **object**,
thereby nourishing the **youthful** moon of experience and insight,
and radiating its light of love and compassion
to living beings nurtured by their mother's **milk**.
I make this prayer to Jayülwa Shönu Ö.

12. The guru **master** arose, not just **partially**, but all-pervading
as the **ornament** of the moon within your heart.
In this **world** you were a great knowledge holder
who opened the way for the profound treasure tradition.
I make this prayer to Yarjé Orgyen Lingpa.

13. You were masterly at radiating the five-ray light,
the illusory-like Samantabhadra and the jewel essence
of this mind of clarity and **awareness** stripped away
of the bark of **holding** consciousness and held object,
to the all-pervading **vajra** space.
I make this prayer to Drupchen Rikzin Dorjé.

14. With the blazing light of the hundred-pronged **vajra** of clear light
in the realm of space of the complete absence of all elaboration,
you were supreme in **taming** the difficult-to-tame outer and inner
 hindrances.
I make this prayer to courageous Nanam Dorjé Düdül.

15. By developing the strength that comes from
a **vast** accumulation of the two merits,
you were able to brandish the sword of wisdom
to hack down the thousand ignorance vines of the two impure
 obscurations.
I make this prayer to the great scholar Gyamawa.

16. You who placed within the **lake**-born lotus at your heart
the **mahāmudrā** knowledge elixir of the ten million kinds of **siddhas,**
the essence of the eighty-four thousand Dharmas,
I make this prayer to the unparalleled Döndrup Gyatso.

17. You possess the glory of holding a treasury of the precious **teachings,**
a store of limitless **virtue,** a great treasure fulfilling all deepest desires.
You are wise in bringing the auspicious rains that announce
victory over the troubles of the three realms.
I make this prayer to the **authentic** lama Gendün Tenpai Gyaltsen.

18. You bring to bloom the lotuses of the **intelligent** and **fortunate,**
a beacon within samsara lighting up the skies of the **teachings** of the
 Buddha,
the wisdom of every **conquering** buddha appearing as the very essence
of the thirty-two **excellent** marks of an enlightened being.
I make this prayer to Losang Tenpai Gyaltsen,
an unparalleled sun of the sacred Dharma.

19. With your camphor-like moonlight of guiding **instructions**
that have been passed on from the great masters,
you are the moon of orators increasing the milk **lake** of vast qualities,
accompanied by the fresh **insights** of genuine **realizations**
that are born from **scripture** and reasoning.
I make this prayer to Yongzin Ngawang Lungtok Yönten Gyatso.

20. The garlands of utpala lotuses of your **scripture** and **insight**
bring beauty to the grove of complete **goodness**;
they give pleasure to those possessing the **mind** treasure of great wisdom
and pervade the delightful earth of the Buddha's **teachings**.
You whose enlightened **activities** are unceasing,
I make this prayer to Yongzin Losang Lungtok Tenzin Trinlé.

21. For the **teachings** of the **Buddha**, you are like the second Buddha,
acting out the dance of the pure enlightened **activities**
of every enlightened guide and **conqueror**
to correctly spread the Dharma of **scripture** and **insight**.
You who are the protector of those without a protector,
I make this prayer to Yongzin Thupten Lungtok Namgyal Trinlé.

22. I make this prayer to the one who in the future
will appear from the land of the Kalkī leading an **army** of gods,
having risen to a peak above a hundred thousand **generals**,
and with the splendor of the jewel of courage beyond **price**,
destroy the **great** darkness of the barbarians.

In short, I make this prayer to the one
whose ten million ocean waves of mysteries of body, speech, and mind,
all in accord with the dispositions of his variety of disciples,
reveal themselves effortlessly and for every purpose
as all-pervading clouds of inconceivable mandala assemblies.

This jewel garland of your past incarnations
is strung on the thread of words well composed,
designed to be worn around the heads of the fortunate and faithful
and offered as a prayer with a devoted and single-pointed mind.

By its merit, may the feet of the kind guru,
who is the glory of the wisdom, compassion, and power of the myriad
    buddhas
appearing in the form of a master for us disciples,
remain unmoving upon the vajra throne for a hundred eons.

May all bad karma arising from wrong practice toward the guru,
such as a lack of faith, disrespect, not doing as he has instructed,
brought about by being for a long time under the sway
of ignorance and a lack of conscientiousness, be quickly purified,
 and may these beings become suitable receptacles for your teachings.

With the rain of the elixir of your words and teachings
falling constantly on the fields of the minds of the faithful,
may there grow a hundred thousand jeweled wheat stalks
of the excellent paths of the sutras and tantras,
weighed down with the glory of the kernels of liberation.

In all my lives, whether worshiping at your feet,
listening to your words, or following your instructions,
may I, like Sadāprarudita and the youth Sudhana,
tirelessly emulate the deeds of your life.

By the power of doing so, may I quickly achieve
the stage of union, the supreme state of the lama,
and for as long as space exists, may I be able to fulfill,
like the wish-granting tree and the wish-fulfilling jewel,
the hopes of limitless living beings.

By the truth of the power of the compassion
of the myriad buddhas and bodhisattvas,
the *dharmadhātu* noncontradiction of emptiness and appearance,
and by the auspicious conjunction of pure samaya and faith
between the guru and his disciple,
may this prayer be effortlessly realized.

This *Precious Necklace of the Most Powerful Wish-Fulfilling Jewels*, a request
in verse, comprising thirty-two verses corresponding to the thirty-two
physical features of an enlightened being, and made to the previous incarnations of the Vajradhara Ling incarnation Thupten Lungtok Namgyal Trinlé,
the Shartsé Chöjé, supreme object of refuge for the omniscient holder of
the lotus, the senior tutor, entity of Vajrasattva, our great guide and all-

pervading master of all the tantric families and mandalas, was composed with single-pointed faith—not only in response to the request made by Amdo Ngakrampa Losang Nyima of the glorious Gyütö Monastery, but because I too am connected by great faith to such a master—by this devoted disciple who has made use of the elixir words of this supreme and venerable guru, the junior tutor, Ganden Losang Yeshé Tenzin Gyatso, holder of the name of the Trijang incarnation, in the male wood-horse year (1954), in the waxing half of the month of miracles, in the Losang Dunsa room at the great Potala. May I be joyfully cared for by the unparalleled guru.

Maṇgalaṃ.

Compilers' Colophon

The dance of the many deeds of the glorious buddhas
is performed in millions of realms in a state of effortlessness
brought about by the two accumulations created over countless eons.

Such is far beyond the horizons of the inferior mind
and is perceived solely by the mighty beings of the ten levels.
However, in order to give a mere indication to ordinary beings,
twenty-two images have been created as ambrosia for the eyes.

The topic to be expressed is in the form of a hundred thousand jewel
beads,
the words and grammar are the ornamented thread on which they are
strung,
the Dharma is the light of the confidence of precision that they radiate,
the reality is a precious necklace of the most powerful wish-fulfilling
jewels.

Under the instruction of the supreme incarnation,
this brief and sequenced garland of births taken from that necklace
was compiled with whatever could pass through the needle eye of my
intellect,
with a faith and devotion that shone like the morning star.

These days it is rare for the leaves and branches of the speech
to move in praise of the qualities of the great beings,
and those who listen and follow are akin to stars in the daytime.
Therefore, so that these events may remain for a long time to come,
this has been a worthy undertaking,
and may the virtue gained from the effort in this work
shine as bright as the stainless autumn moon.

And by the power of that virtue,
may the glory of our Land of Snow live a long time.
May his wishes speedily be fulfilled,
and may the splendor of temporal and spiritual rule shine on.

May the present supreme incarnation, the **noble** one of the **Dharma,
shouldering** the responsibility of the **teachings,**
have the power to sustain the lives of the previous incarnations.

Notes

1. Phabongkha Rinpoche (1878–1941), whose personal name was Jampa Tenzin Trinlé, was a highly influential Geluk lama in the early twentieth century. A prolific author and a charismatic teacher, most of the luminaries of the Geluk tradition of the last century, including the two tutors of the present Dalai Lama, were disciples of Phabongkha. His most well-known work is *Liberation in the Palm of Your Hand*, which exists in at least two different English translations.

2. All secondhand recollections recounted in this introduction are from personal communications unless otherwise indicated.

3. For an explanation of the different categories of Vajrayana practices in general, and the distinction between father and mother tantras, see Tsongkhapa, *A Lamp to Illuminate the Five Stages* (Boston: Wisdom Publications, 2013), 25–41.

4. Source: Personal email communication with the present Ling Rinpoche.

5. A *labrang* is the monastic household of an incarnation.

6. See page 383.

7. Dalai Lama, *The Universe in the Single Atom* (New York: Morgan Road Books, 2005), 44.

8. For a historical perspective on the controversy of Shugden practice, see George Dreyfus, "The Shugden Affair: The Origins of a Controversy," which can be accessed at www.dalailama.com/messages/dolgyal-shugden/ganden-tripa/the-shugden-affair-i.

9. For a rare collection of essays exploring the various aspects of the Dalai Lama's person and what he means for the world, see Rajiv Mehrotra, ed., *Understanding the Dalai Lama* (New York: Viking, 2004), which contains my own contribution, "The Dalai Lama and the Tibetan Monastic Academia."

10. For a detailed account, based on extensive archival study from the period of British India, of the ignorance of international affairs on the part of the Tibetan establishment, see Melvin Goldstein, *A History of Modern Tibet 1913–51: The Demise of a Lamaist State* (Berkeley: University of California Press, 1989). See also a firsthand account in the autobiography of the Tibetan minister Rinchen Sadutshang, *A Life Unforeseen: A Memoir of Service to Tibet* (Boston: Wisdom Publications, 2016).

11. As is described below on page 284, Rinpoché was requested to compose his autobiography, and he responded with short account. This was later translated by Losang Norbu Tsonawa in the *Tibet Journal*, a publication of the Library of Tibetan Works and Archives: "The Autobiography of Kyabje Ling Rinpoche," *Tibet Journal* 8.3 (1983): 45–61. The excerpt here has been slightly modified for accuracy and style..

12. "Master of the enemy of time" (*dus dgra'i dbang po*) is an epithet of Yamāntaka, the "slayer of Yama," a well-known meditation deity referred to in the previous verse who is recognized as a wrathful form of Mañjuśrī.

13. Some words in this verse play up Ling Rinpoché's name: Mighty Sage's doctrine =

Thupten; scripture and insight = Lungtok; victorious = Namgyal; enlightened deeds = Trinlé.

14. "Precious tutor" (*yongs 'dzin rin po che*) is the main way the Dalai Lama refers to the Sixth Ling Rinpoche, although sometimes he refers to him as Guru Vajradhara. This whole chapter and the next one appear in the back of the Tibetan editon.

15. All references to Serkong Rinpoché or "assistant tutor Serkong Rinpoché" in this book refer to Serkong Tsenshap Ngawang Losang Thupten Topjor (Ngag dbang blo bzang thub bstan tobs byor, 1914–83).

16. *Mi chos bla ma'i rdzun.*

17. See note 11.

18. Songtsen Gampo (seventh century), Trisong Detsen (eighth century), and Tri Ralpachen (ninth century).

19. Ü was divided into Uru and Yoru, and Tsang into Yeru and Rulak.

20. *Chos 'byung.* In Buddhist tantra this triangular feature represents the source of all deities and inanimate phenomena of the mandala. The aspects of its shape and color also represent qualities or goals of high tantric achievement.

21. *Yab.* Literally "father," but also used to refer to the main male deity of the mandala, here being Cakrasaṃvara.

22. "Stage of union endowed with its seven features" is an epithet of the fully enlightened state of buddhahood according to Vajrayana tradition.

23. The Tibetan text has 1902, in which the bulk of that water-rabbit year falls. However, the eleventh month of that year would be in 1903.

24. Holder of the White Lotus is an epithet of Avalokiteśvara, the bodhisattva of compassion, with whom the Dalai Lamas are identified in Tibet.

25. *Chu srin rgyal mtshan,* literally, "the sea-monster banner," a type of hindering demon.

26. Kalsang Palace here is the first palace built in the Norbulingka complex, named after the Seventh Dalai Lama Kalsang Gyatso.

27. Meaningful to Behold is an epithet often used to refer to a great spiritual being. Here it refers to the Thirteenth Dalai Lama.

28. These are the pacifying, controlling, increasing, and wrathful activities that protectors are ordered to carry out.

29. Lit. "great king"; referring to the Nechung protector.

30. A famed eleventh-century Tibetan mystic and a yogi of Vajrabhairava tantra.

31. These are ten outer and ten inner abilities of a qualified vajra master. They are listed in the last chapter of the *Ornament of Vajra Essence Tantra* (*Vajrahṛdayālaṃkāratantra*).

32. The fifteenth-century master and the founder of Gyütö Monastery.

33. Tenzin Gang is a Tibetan settlement in Arunachal Pradesh, in northeastern India, and Gyütö was reestablished there initially. Today, the main monastery has moved to Sidhpur, near Dharamsala, and only a small branch remains in Tenzin Gang.

34. Collected Topics, or *dura* (*bsdus grwa*), an initial topic of study in the monastic curriculum that presents basic philosophical phenomena in a dialectical format, in order to train students in the art of debate based on basic principles of logic. Although drawn from the eighth-century classical Buddhist work on logic and epistemology *Treatise of Valid Cognition* by Dharmakīrti—hence the title "collected topics"—the twelfth-century Tibetan thinker Chapa Chökyi Sengé is credited with the invention of the *dura* method of debate and dialectical inquiry. For a contemporary description of the *dura* method of debate and its practice as part of early education in Tibetan

monasteries, see Dreyfus, *Tibetan Monastic Education*, http://www.thlib.org/places
/monasteries/drepung/moned.php#!essay=/dreyfus/drepung/monasticed/.

35. The "six ornaments" are the Indian masters Nāgārjuna and his principal student Ārya-
deva, the two Yogācāra masters Asaṅga and Vasubandhu, and the founders of Buddhist
epistemology Dignāga and Dharmakīrti. The "two supreme beings" refers to Guṇaprabha and Śākyaprabha, whom the Tibetan tradition recognizes as authorities on Vinaya
monastic disciplinary codes.

36. Panchen Sönam Drakpa (1478–1554) was a highly influential author within the
Geluk school of Tibetan Buddhism. A historian, literary expert, philosopher, and
tutor to the Third Dalai Lama, Sönam Drakpa's commentarial works became the textbook for Drepung's Loseling College and Ganden Monastery's Shartsé College. Ling
Rinpoche, being a student at Drepung Loseling, was required to use Sönam Drakpa's
writings as the main textbook to read the great Indian Buddhist classics as well as their
exposition by the founders of the Geluk school, namely Tsongkhapa and his two principal disciples, Gyaltsap Jé and Khedrup Jé.

37. *Rgyal po rgyal phran.* A board game popular in many parts of Tibet.

38. The four are being content with (1) basic clothing, (2) alms, and (3) bedding, and (4)
taking delight in meditation and ascetic practices.

39. *Rdo.* Other sources have Kong (*kong*). These are houses of the Loseling College of
Drepung Monastery.

40. This refers to the Loseling uprising in 1921 initiated by the arrest of these three monks,
who were the managers of the three houses as briefly related here, although the time of
these events is not in keeping with the chronology of the text.

41. Takdrak Rinpoché (1874–1952) became junior, and later senior, tutor to the Fourteenth Dalai Lama, and in 1941 he took over as regent of Tibet.

42. *Dbang sdud 'khor lo,* a ceremonial object used in the ritual for gaining control over others.

43. "Conqueror Losang" here refers to Tsongkhapa, who is revered in the Tibetan tradition as an emanation of Mañjuśrī, the bodhisattva of wisdom.

44. The practice of White Mañjuśrī composed by Lalitavajra and passed down from Sasang
Mati Panchen (Sa bzang Ma ti paṇ chen, 1294–1376).

45. See note 11.

46. Maitreya, *Ornament of Realization* 4:6.

47. Ibid., 4:12.

48. This refers to Candrakīrti's rebuttal of Bhāvaviveka's critique of Buddhapālita for
only employing consequences as a means of negating opponents' views. Bhāvaviveka
insisted that to give rise to any valid inference, one must employ syllogisms, not just
reveal internal contradictions in the opponent's standpoint.

49. *Kāśyapa Chapter.*

50. These refer to the five categories that make up the core of the metaphysics of early Buddhist Abhidharma schools: material form, primary consciousnesses, mental factors,
nonassociated phenomena, and the unconditioned.

51. During the time of the Great Fifth Dalai Lama the title Lhaden Rapjampa ("master of
numerous treatises from Lhasa") was conferred during the great Lhaden (Lhasa) prayer festival on a student who had mastered all five great topics of classical Buddhist scholarship.
This term was shortened to become lharampa, which is now the highest rank of geshé.

52. *Bka' rams pa.* A geshé of the individual colleges who has studied the entire curriculum
syllabus and sat in debate within that college but not in all three monastic seats. Synonymous with a *kachupa* (*bka' bcu pa*) geshé.

53. This was outside the main Jokhang temple.

54. Site of Gyütö Monastery.

55. *Snyan seng dge rgan.* This is a particular post in the tantric college, one whose role is to help guide new entrants during their first few days.

56. One of the Buddha's first five disciples.

57. A special attraction of the fifteenth-day offerings is the public display of elaborate colored butter sculptures prepared by monk artists from the two tantric colleges.

58. This was in the northeastern part of the Barkhor.

59. The Thirteenth Dalai Lama's point is that if the entire long *Monastic Disciplinary Sutra* is not recited in its entirety, at least during the rainy-season retreat, it will never be done. This means that the announcement made regularly at the short recitation of the sutra during the bi-monthly sessions will be false.

60. The crowned Buddha that was the main sacred object of Ramoché temple.

61. Known popularly as Choné Lama Rinpoché, this scholar monk was a highly revered figure in the Geluk tradition. He was known especially for his *Interwoven Praise* (*Spel mar bstod pa*), which is a verse work elaborating on Tsongkhapa's praise to the Buddha entitled *Praise of Dependent Origination*. English translation of a selection of Choné Lama Rinpoché's verses can be found in *Songs of Spiritual Experience* (Shambhala: Boston, 2001), translated by Thupten Jinpa.

62. Known widely as Changkya Rölpai Dorjé (1717–86), he was a highly learned and influential Geluk teacher and author in the eighteenth century. His work on classical Indian philosophies, *Ornament of the Great Mountain of Buddha's Teachings* (*Grub mtha' thub bstan lhun grub mdzes rgyan*), is admired to this day as one of the best presentations on the views of classical Indian Buddhist schools. As the chief editor, Changkya oversaw the ambitious project of translating the entire Tibetan canonical collection the Tengyur into Mongolian. To a large measure, Changkya's influence stemmed from his close association with the Qianlong emperor of the Ching dynasty, for whom he was the high priest.

63. *Rdob rdob.* Recognized group of monks at a monastery, known for their undisciplined and rough manner. They did not pursue advanced study—stopping after the recitation exam—and instead did a lot of the work of running the monastery, such as working the kitchen, business with nomads, and security at big events.

64. Panchen Losang Yeshé's year of birth is usually given as 1663. These are the teachings that became *Liberation in the Palm of Your Hand.*

65. Akhu Sherap Gyatso was a great Amdo teacher and custodian of numerous lineages of instructions and oral transmissions.

66. *Ma dros mtsho.* Lake Manasarovar near Mount Kailash in western Tibet.

67. This verse uses a type of alliteration in which part of a proper noun or name is repeated as the third syllable in the line to form the allegory. Perfection of wisdom is here rendered as "mother of the buddhas" (*rgyal yum*) from which "buddha" is taken and repeated as the third syllable. "Nāga" is taken from "Nāgārjuna," "moon" is the "candra" of Candrakīrti, and "mind" (*blo*) is the first syllable of Losang.

68. This is a poetic rendering of the Jataka tales, the Buddha's birth stories, composed in Sanskrit by the Kashmiri king and scholar Kṣemendra in the twelfth century.

69. Tibetan grammar speaks of the *la don* prepositional particles, such as *na*, as having five distinct functions. One of these indicates position (*rten gnas*). Of the variant *la don* forms, it is rare that the *na* particle is used to indicate location. The latest book edition

of the biography has "adjectival" (*de nyid*) *la don* form, but the earlier *pecha* edition has the locative (*rten gnas*), which makes more sense.

70. *Srin pho glang.* Severe stomach pains akin to being gored by a bull (*glang*) due to disturbance of the tiny internal organisms (*srin pho*).

71. *Bya ba bsdus pa, Kriyāsaṃgraha.* If this is the work of the same name in the Tengyur, it is attributed to Kuladatta.

72. Known also as Losang Tamdrin, this Mongolian scholar was a prolific author composing numerous works on classical Buddhist themes, especially philosophy, as well as producing an abbreviated translation of Faxian's travel journals.

73. *Miktsema* refers to a verse of praise to Tsongkhapa that is widely recited like a mantra. There evolved an entire collection of texts, primarily ritual, connected with this praise verse, all of which later came to be compiled by Khyenrap Tenpa Chöphel as a collection called the *Miktsema Compendium.*

74. The Tibetan erroneously has "eighth century."

75. Thuken was an influential Tibetan author in the eighteenth century. A student of Changkya Rolpai Dorjé, Thuken is known most for his widely popular *Crystal Mirror of Philosophical Systems*, an English translation of which is in *The Library of Tibetan Classics* series.

76. Oath-bound protectors are bound by the oath they made. Rinpoché was now committed to this project and could not back out.

77. Thupten Kunphel was arrested for neglecting the illness of the Dalai Lama and later sent into exile.

78. The fourth Tibetan month, whose full moon is commemorated as the time of the Buddha's enlightenment.

79. This refers to the Geluk tradition, which is named after Tsongkhapa's main seat, Ganden, located on a mountain.

80. This is a citation from the *Lotus Sutra.*

81. *Skar ma.* Lowest denomination of Tibetan currency. Ten *karma* make one *sho*, a hundred karma make one *sang* (Goldstein's *New Tibetan to English Dictionary*).

82. For an accessible contemporary account of the Kadam school and its key early masters, see *Wisdom of the Kadam Masters* (Boston: Wisdom Publications, 2013), translated and introduced by Thupten Jinpa.

83. A *stupa* is an outdoor shrine or reliquary of a recognizable standard format. Its middle is terraced like farm fields on the side of a hill. The point being made by the protector is that he may be a mere nonhuman spirit, but his commitment to protect the Dharma remains unchanged. The terraced part of the stupa, being in the middle, will remain in the middle even when turned upside down.

84. Deity and protector of the Yarlung area of Tibet, tamed by Padmasambhava.

85. Namkha Gyaltsen was a revered master in both Kadam and Nyingma traditions from whom the great Tsongkhapa received teachings, especially those of more esoteric lineages.

86. Ra Lotsāwa is regarded as being a former birth of Ling Rinpoché.

87. *Rab gnas dge legs char 'bebs*, a consecration ritual that formed part of the Gyütö liturgy.

88. The *samaya beings* are the objects to be consecrated, such as statues, paintings, and even oneself. The *wisdom beings* are the actual beings represented by these objects that merge into and consecrate them.

89. *Tshul shing*, short yellow sticks used as a way of keeping count of the monks when they were out of the monastery.

90. *Ho thog thu.* Title bestowed upon high-ranking lamas by the Manchu emperor.

91. Entrants to the tantric monasteries who had not gone through the geshé degrees were known as generation-stage students.

92. *Abhidharmakośa* 6:54. Gendun Drup in his commentary states that this verse is describing the path of no interruption on the path of seeing. This path is the way to Brahma (nirvana). It is also the wheel of Brahma (the Buddha), turned by the Buddha for his disciples.

93. This concerns only one verse. Rinpoché recited the first line, and the monk went straight to the fourth line.

94. *'Brum nad.* Refers generally to poxes and rashes of different kinds, but also specifically to smallpox.

95. *Srid pa ho.* A common representation of the various trigrams and number-based divination diagrams, often used as protection.

96. From the *Guhyasamāja Root Tantra* (114b4).

97. Both editions of the Tibetan text have "the sixth month," or June. This cannot tally with the eighth Tibetan month later in the sentence. Shakabpa refers to the day of entering Lhasa as being October 8, 1939, or the twenty-fifth of the eighth Tibetan month; see *Tibet: A Political History* (New Haven: Yale University Press, 1967), 285.

98. The oracle lake close to the monastery where visions would be seen revealing the whereabouts of rebirths of high lamas.

99. This is a description of the past deeds of the lama recited during the mandala-offering ceremony of a long-life ritual.

100. Like the verse in the opening homage of this work, the words in bold play upon Ling Rinpoché's name: doctrine of the mighty sage = Thupten; scripture and realization = Lungtok; victorious = Namgyal; enlightened deeds = Trinlé.

101. These lines and the previous line come from the beginning of the first chapter of the root tantra. They have been translated according to Candrakīrti's *Bright Lamp* commentary.

102. A well-known estate close to Lhasa, whose family was that of the Twelfth Dalai Lama. Lady Yangtsé was a widow who was devoted to Phabongkha Rinpoché.

103. *Tshogs mchod.* Held after the full moon of the second Tibetan month, originally to commemorate the passing of the previous Dalai Lamas.

104. A grassy plain to the west of Lhasa, near the Norbulingka.

105. *Bstan 'bar ma,* an oft-recited prayer taken from the sutras, with the last verse added by Tibetans.

106. *Mkha' mnyam ma.* This is a hymn to the Buddha in verse composed by Rendawa Shönu Lodrö, one of the principal teachers of Je Tsongkhapa. As is common with Tibetan prayers, this prayer is given a title corresponding to the first few words of the first line.

107. Śiva or Mahādeva (*bde 'byung dbang*) lives in the Himalayas. "Lion" here is *gdongs lnga pa,* which is also a synonym for certain Indian gods.

108. *Mtshams 'byor,* rules on changes to pronunciation due to conjunctions of syllables in Sanskrit gammar.

109. First the extensive explanation is given, followed by a less extensive explanation, a brief explanation, and finally a summary.

110. In the previous reference to these two, they had been described as being from Drakpa House and Amdo House respectively.

111. This is probably a slightly abridged version of *Instructions on the Guru Puja: Treasury of Core Instructions from the Oral Transmission.*

112. "The regent of Mañjunātha" is an epithet for the Ganden Throneholder. "Mañjunātha" refers to the great Tsongkhapa, the founder of Ganden Monastery. The Jangtsé Chöjé and Sharpa Chöjé alternate in the succession to become Ganden Throneholder.

113. The new edition has 1949; the older edition does not mention the year. We have changed it to 1950 because the text goes on to say that the Dalai Lama assumed temporal power "in that year," and that occurred in 1950.

114. Town on Tibet's southern border between Sikkim and Bhutan.

115. This is Dorjé Shukden, or Dölgyal, about whom there would be much controversy later. It was also at this time that the Fourteenth Dalai Lama established his first connection with Shukden by summoning him through an oracle and putting forward questions concerning their precarious situation. However, in a sentence above, His Holiness only speaks about a dough-ball divination, which does not involve an oracle.

116. The text has "seventh" but July corresponds with the fifth more than the seventh, and Shakabpa (*Political History*, 304) confirms this month for the Dalai Lama's departure.

117. By way of direct perception, valid inference, and scriptural testimony.

118. *Dza sag*, a third-rank government officer.

119. The only text I can find with the name *Testament Carried on the Wind* is the Geluk mahāmudrā work by Tsultrim Nyima of Drepung Monastery, *Phyag chen gyi 'khrid yig man ngag zhal shes dang bcas pa'i kha chems rlung la bskur ba'i 'phrin yig*.

120. Takdrak Rinpoché, the previous senior tutor, passed away in 1952.

121. The council of ministers, or *kalons*, is the *kashak*. The secretarial and revenue committee, the *drungtsi*, was comprised of four monastic secretaries (*drung*) and four lay officials (*tsi*) with the revenue ministry.

122. A translation of this prayer appears as an appendix in the current volume.

123. Geshé Sherap was an influential scholar monk from Amdo. A sharp debater and an eloquent author, he was also a key figure in the renaissance of Tibetan Buddhism that took place among a small elite of ethnic Chinese during the Nationalist Kuomintang era. For a contemporary historian's perspective on this movement and Geshé Sherap Gyatso's role in it, see Gray Tuttle's *Tibetan Buddhists in the Making of Modern China* (New York: Columbia University Press, 2005).

124. Kumbum was the birthplace of Jé Tsongkhapa.

125. Probably monastic official Chöphel Thupten from Bumthang Monastery.

126. The three great stupas of Nepal are Boudhanath, Swayambhunath, and Namo Buddha.

127. A depiction of the past lives of the Buddha drawn from Kṣemendra's *Wish-Fulfilling Tree of the Bodhisattva's Lives*.

128. Lochen Rinpoché is the incarnation of the great translator Lochen Rinchen Sangpo (958–1055) and is traditionally associated with Tashi Lhunpo Monastery.

129. As noted previously, the only work found by this title appears to be a work on mahāmudrā practice.

130. These two collections consist of various practices related to Vajrabhairava and were compiled or composed by Ra Lotsāwa Dorjé Drak and Palzin Sangpo (fifteenth century).

131. A form of the protector Pehar, or Nechung.

132. *Rta thog ma*. A consecration ceremony so brief, it is apparently possible to perform it without getting off your horse. Nevertheless, the ceremony can last a few hours. I am grateful to Yael Bentor, who provided me this information.

133. White Tārā, Uṣṇīṣavijayā, and Amitāyus.

134. The first two weeks of the Tibetan new year celebrate the Buddha defeating the heretic teachers with a display of miracles.

135. One of those scholars, Geshé Lhundub Sopa, writes about this experience in his autobiography, *Like a Waking Dream* (Boston: Wisdom Publications, 2012), 205–8.

136. "A large uncultivated area west of Lhasa that had been used as a source of fodder for the Norbulingka stables" (Goldstein, *History of Modern Tibet*, 256).

137. *Phyu pa*, the traditional Tibetan long-sleeved outer coat for men, wrapped with a sash around the waist.

138. According to Trijang Rinpoché's autobiography the full names of these ministers were Surkhang Wangchen Gelek, Neshar Thupten Tharpa, and Shenkhawa Gyurmé Sönam Topgyal.

139. A sect of Tibetan Buddhism that had degenerated to the extent of monks wearing lay clothes.

140. This is a set of five aspiration prayers popularly recited as part of funeral rites. The prayers are (1) *Prayer of Samantabhadra*, (2) *Aspirations of Maitreya*, (3) the dedication chapter of Śāntideva's *Guide to the Bodhisattva's Way of Life*, (4) Tsongkhapa's *Prayers of Auspiciousness at the Beginning, Middle, and the End*, and (5) Tsongkhapa's *Prayer for Rebirth in Sukhāvatī*.

141. Idiomatic expression stressing the effectiveness of the ritual.

142. Bakula Rinpoche, though a prince belonging to the Ladakhi royal family, was a monk in the Geluk tradition. He later served in various senior positions in the Indian government, including being the Indian ambassador to the Republic of Mongolia. The main airport of Ladakh in its capital Leh is named after him.

143. The shrine here is the Bodhi Tree and the adjacent Mahabodhi Stupa, which houses a small temple within.

144. Protector ritual regularly held on the eighth day of the third month.

145. Dekhar Tsewang Rapten, commonly known as Lukhangwa.

146. The Tibetan text has "Doctor Hunter" inserted in brackets.

147. Chebulic myrobalan, one of the most potent and well-known herbal medicines in the Tibetan medical system.

148. This has been translated by Gavin Kilty and published in 2012 by Norbu Chöphel, a former attendant of Trijang Rinpoché, together with the Tibetan text in loose-leaf *pecha* format.

149. *Bla ma dri ma med pa*, Indian master and fourth in the line of the previous births of Trijang Rinpoché.

150. *Srog 'khor*, mystic diagrams or circles containing mantras and other powerful protection symbols.

151. Tsongkhapa's nirvana anniversary falls on the twenty-fifth of the tenth Tibetan month. It is celebrated widely as a light festival, with butter lamps being displayed outside on the roofs and windowsills of the monasteries as well as private homes. In the evening after the day's ceremonies are over, the monks circumambulate the main temples, or the entire campus of the monastery, carrying incense sticks and chanting the verse praise to Tsongkhapa known as the *miktsema*.

152. The fivefold self-arisen statue is a statue of eleven-faced Avalokiteśvara in a chapel of the Jokhang temple in Lhasa. It contains within a self-arisen sandalwood statue of the same deity. King Songtsen Gampo and his two brides also dissolved into the main statue, hence the five aspects.

153. This is a prayer in verse composed by the Dalai Lama himself, soon after coming to

India, invoking the power of the words of truth and praying for the welfare of all beings and the world at large, especially for the people and the country of Tibet.

154. *Rgyal ba rgya mtsho*, a red form of Avalokiteśvara.

155. Bamboo gum, saffron, clove, nutmeg, small cardamom, and greater cardamom.

156. A district southwest of Lhasa, where the previous Ling Rinpoché died when he was thrown from his horse, as mentioned below.

157. *Mnyes thang lha chen mo*, a large stone Buddha carved in a rock in Nyethang in Chushur district.

158. The Tibetan text describes the lion as "not having the two" (*gnyis med*). It was explained to me by two monks from Drepung that the analogy refers to the lions of India that lack the beautiful mane and ferocious claws of the Himalayan snow lion. Thus it refers to someone who lacks reasoning and learning.

159. The noble (*ārya*) Buddha, noble bodhisattva, noble self-enlightened ones (*pratyeka-buddha*), and the noble disciple (*śrāvaka*). These are the four āryas who, together with the wisdoms they embody, are the objects of homage at the beginning of Maitreya's *Ornament of Realization*.

160. Sudhana is a youth from the *Avataṃsaka Sutra* renowned for his reliance upon his gurus.

161. *Bkra shis gso sbyong*. The vow purification ceremony is a regular twice-monthly ceremony for monks and nuns held at full-moon and no-moon days, but occasionally it is held at times other than these to mark a special event.

162. This institute, now the Central University of Higher Tibetan Studies, is in Sarnath, Varanasi, UP, India.

163. Both versions of the text have January, but this is almost definitely an error.

164. Whether this should be the twenty-eighth or the eighteenth of a later month is difficult to say.

165. A spun-pipe factory at a remote location in Bihar, set up as an investment by D. N. Tsarong with funds from the sale of gold and silver from His Holiness's private treasury. A brief history of this ill-fated enterprise, which ultimately went under and lost its entire investment, is recounted in Sadutshang, *A Life Unforeseen*, 241–47.

166. G. S. Mandidip Paper Mills in Sehore, Madhya Pradesh, another industry set up with funds from the Dalai Lama's trust. See Sadutshang, *A Life Unforeseen*, 247–48.

167. A ritual dagger or stake around which there is a cycle of initiations and practices.

168. A revered ancient wooden statue of Avalokiteśvara that resided in the region of Mangyul Kyirong in western Tibet. In the wake of the Tibetan uprising in 1959 and the subsequent exodus of Tibetans into exile in India, the statue was brought to India by its custodian, the monks of Dzongkar Chödé Monastery, and offered to the Dalai Lama. This statue is recognized as one of the "four noble brothers," namely, Ārya Wati Sangpo, Lokeśvara in the main Lhasa temple, and two brother icons in Nepal, Ukhang and Jamali. All four are revered as self-arisen during the reign of Songtsen Gampo in the seventh century.

169. A fire offering completes a retreat. "One tenth" refers to the one tenth of the total mantras accumulated in retreat to be recited at the fire offering.

170. As the Dalai Lama was born in 1935, he would have become thirty-three on July 6, 1968, and so had entered his thirty-fourth year.

171. Also known as the Tibet Institute Rikon.

172. Although the Tibetan version has August as the month here, this is clearly an error,

because Rinpoché was still in India during all of August, as can be seen from previous entries.

173. *Bkra shis snye ma*, by Choné Lama Drakpa Shedrup (1675–1748) from northeastern Amdo.

174. The mother of the Buddha died seven days after his birth and was reborn in the celestial realms. After he had attained enlightenment the Buddha spent three months in these celestial relams teaching her and the other gods. The day he returned to the human world, which corresponds to the twenty-second of the ninth Tibetan month, is celebrated by this religious holiday.

175. *Snang srid zil gnon.*

176. *Cha phreng chos mdzad*, probably a patron monk from Chatreng Monastery.

177. Assembly where no tea or food is served.

178. Temple in Dharamsala where the Avalokiteśvara fasting practices took place.

179. A form of praise in which the constituent parts of the name of the person being praised are used and highlighted within the verse.

180. The fulfillment (1) of the gathered deities as a result of the offerings, (2) of the practitioners as a result of the vajra food and drink, (3) of the wisdom beings as a result of the nectar, (4) of the deities as a result of the pure awareness of bliss and emptiness, (5) of the outer and inner ḍākinīs as a result of melodic song, and (6) of the worldly spirits as a result of the torma offerings.

181. From 1966 onward, after conditions had deteriorated at the Buxa Duar monastic settlement, Drepung and Ganden monasteries were reestablished in a Tibetan settlement near Mundgod in the southern state of Karnataka, while Sera Monastery was set up in Byalkuppe in the same state.

182. These are the root treatises of the five main subjects of the monastic curriculum: Pramāṇa, Abhidharma, Perfection of Wisdom, Madhyamaka, and Vinaya. They are Dharmakīrti's *Treatise of Valid Cognition*, Vasubandhu's *Treasury of Abhidharma*, Maitreya's *Ornament of Realization*, Nāgārjuna's *Verses on the Fundamental Wisdom of the Middle Way*, and Guṇaprabha's *Vinaya Sutra*.

183. Lingsé is a particular rank of geshé. Literally it means "mixing of the communities" and dates to a time when candidates were examined by more than one monastic community, such as was the tradition of Sangphu Monastery.

184. The bodhisattva aspiration is the wish to attain enlightenment for the sake of all living beings, and the pledge of engagement is the vow to actually engage in bodhisattva activities.

185. *Dgra lha dpang bstod*; there are several works of this name.

186. Tashi Rapten was the name of Trijang Rinpoché's residence in the governmental area of Gangchen Kyishong.

187. *Rgyal po byed chas*. Appears to be a particular form of Pehar.

188. This collection of more than a hundred empowerments was compiled by the Sakya master Loter Wangpo (1847–1914).

189. That is, Dzokchen Rinpoché Jikmé Losal Wangpo (b. 1964).

190. This day is also called the day of the offerings of the twenty-fifth. The Tuṣita buddha realm (Ganden Yiga Chözin) is a realm separate from the Tuṣita heaven of the desire realm.

191. A way of referring to someone without mentioning their name. Gowo is a monastic house within Ganden Jangtsé, and Chözé is a title given to sponsors, especially those from within the monastery.

192. This may well be the Canadian monk Jhampa Zangpo, who interpreted for Ling Rinpoché as mentioned in the introduction. However, Jhampa Shaneman, as he is now called, cannot recall with any certainty.

193. Sadu Rinchen, or Rinchen Sadutshang, was a longtime official in the Tibetan government, having served as His Holiness's private secretary and interpreter in the early years of exile. At this point, he was in charge of the Dalai Lama's New Delhi office. See Sadutshang, *A Life Unforeseen.*

194. This center is affiliated with the Dharamsala center of the same name, both founded by Lama Thubten Yeshe and part of the Foundation for the Preservation of the Mahayana Tradition. The Delhi center opened in 1979.

195. Religious group dedicated to performing rituals on the tenth and twenty-fifth of each Tibetan month, regarded as special days in tantric practice.

196. The modern book format version of the Tibetan text has July 29, which cannot be correct because of dated events below. So we have corrected the date to June 29, which accords well with the subsequent dates. The older xylograph edition does not mention the month.

197. A name for Padmasambhava or Guru Rinpoché.

198. A center in Le Mont-Pèlerin founded by Geshé Rapten in 1977, it has since been renamed Rabten Choeling.

199. Both Tibetan editions have November, but this seems to be an error.

200. These two lines were spontaneously uttered by the Tibetan official Pholhané Sönam Topgyé (1689–1747) as the Seventh Dalai Lama, saddled on his horse, was about to leave central Tibet. Overcome by emotions, Pholhané could not complete a traditional four-lined stanza. So the Seventh Dalai Lama completed it by way of a response, adding, "May the influence and wealth of benefactors of the teachings prosper, / and may all be auspicious for the teachings of the Buddha to last a long time."

201. The rotund and jovial figure often referred to as "laughing Buddha."

202. Alexandra David-Néel died in 1969, and when Rinpoché visited, her house had become a museum.

203. The black protector is Palden Lhamo, and the red is Nechung.

204. This Kālacakra initiation, His Holiness's first in North America, took place near Madison, Wisconsin, at Deer Park Buddhist Center. See Lhundub Sopa and Paul Donnelly, *Like a Waking Dream: The Autobiography of Geshé Lhundub Sopa* (Boston: Wisdom Publications, 2012), 281–86.

205. This was the well-known doctor Ama Losang who lived in her Khangkar residence in Dharamsala.

206. *Dge ldan gtsug lag slob gnyer khang.*

207. See note 182.

208. A mountain to the west of the Potala.

209. Sallie confirms that she attended this teaching but said that the interpreter was not Sharpa Tulku, as he had left Dharamsala by then.

210. Remote Himalayan region of northern India.

211. Kalsang Yeshé at that time worked in the Department of Religious and Cultural Affairs, having served in the Assembly of Tibetan People's Deputies representing the Gelukpa for three years.

212. The Tibetan edition translated says "fourteen," whereas the first edition says "eight." This could well be an error due to the copier's eye slipping down a couple of lines to

where "fourteen ritual monks" is mentioned. Also, fourteen monks seems too large a number to be reciting in the small room in front of the body.

213. While there are many works that elucidate the stages of the path to enlightenment, eight works, headed by *Great Stages of the Path to Enlightenment*, have been singled out to make up this collection.

214. *Kha sbyor yan lag bdun.* This is a synonym for Vajradhara, the Buddha as the teacher of tantras, and refers to seven constantly present characteristics.

215. The Sixth Ling Rinpoché was born on the estate of the Tenth Dalai Lama, as described in chapter 4.

216. "Five" refers to the present era of the five degenerations, and the "hundred" refers to the hundred-year lifespan of humans.

217. The words of the Buddha are intoned and the plea made that by the power of their truth may the prayer be answered.

218. Each of these letters in Tibetan is the first in a phonetically related grouping of four letters, and so each of these three groups has four subgroups, as indicated below.

219. Small Tibetan settlement in Himachal Pradesh two hours away from Dharamsala.

220. The present Ling Rinpoché's attendant, Tenzin Khentse, told me that although it is officially stated that the Seventh Ling Rinpoché was born in Bir, his mother was sick during pregnancy and had traveled for treatment to Dharamsala, where she gave birth.

221. Tibetan colloquial word for a nun.

222. In this verse the words underlined spell out the Tibetan name Thupten Lungtok Namgyal Trinlé, the full name of Ling Rinpoché.

Glossary

Abhidharma (*mngon pa'i chos / chos mngon pa*). One of the five main subjects of the monastic curriculum, systematically presenting phenomena (*dharma*) of the base, path, and result, whose analysis and contemplation will make manifest (*abhi*) a wisdom that brings one closer to nirvana. Also a genre of texts epitomized by Vasubandhu's *Treasury of Knowledge*.

Akṣobhyavajra (*mi bskyod rdo rje*). The Buddha in the form of the main deity of the Guhyasamāja mandala. He is usually black with three faces and six arms.

Amitāyus (*tshe dpag med*). One of the three main deities for the practice of longevity. He is usually red with one face and two arms.

approach retreat (*bsnyan*). A retreat on the generation stage of a particular highest yoga tantra, by which the practitioner becomes closer to or "approaches" the meditation deity. The length of the retreat is usually determined by a fixed number of mantras to be recited.

ārya (*'phags pa*). Strictly speaking, a Buddhist practitioner who has reached the path of seeing by gaining a direct and nonconceptual perception of no-self.

aspiration and engaged bodhicitta vows (*smon sems 'jugs sems sdom pa*). Respectively, the pledge of aspiration to attain enlightenment for the sake of all living beings, and the pledge to engage in the practices of the six perfections that will accomplish that aspiration.

assistant tutor (*mtshan zhabs*). Literally, an attendant to a lama who helps him in his philosophy studies.

Avalokiteśvara Who Liberates All Beings from the Unfortunate Realms (*spyan ras gzigs ngan song kun grol*). A form of Avalokiteśvara, the buddha of compassion.

Bhagavan (*bcom ldan 'das*). Title applied to the Buddha as well as certain tantric meditation deities.

bodhicitta ceremony (*sems bskyed cho ga / mchod pa*). Ceremony for taking the aspiration and engaged bodhicitta vows.

body mandala (*lus kyi dkyil 'khor*). Tantric practice where one's body is taken to be the mandala of the particular tantra.

Buxa Duar. Fort in West Bengal where the main Tibetan monasteries were given sanctuary after first going into exile in 1959.

Cakrasaṃvara (*'khor lo bde mchog*). Highest yoga tantra whose meditation deity

Phabongkha Rinpoché was a renowned practitioner of. He has many forms but is usually dark blue in color.

Causing the Rain of Goodness to Fall (*dge legs char 'bebs*). Consecration ritual that formed part of the Gyütö liturgy.

chant leader (*dbu mdzad*). Monk trained in chanting techniques and styles who leads the assembly in ritual chanting.

Chö (*gcod*). "Cutting off" practice introduced into Tibet by the twelfth-century Indian adept Phadampa Sangyé. The term refers to the practice of cutting off self-cherishing (the root of samsara) and the four *māras*, or hindrances.

clear light (*'od gsal, prabhāsvara*). Also translated as "luminosity," it refers to the dawn-like luminous appearance occurring at the last stage of the death process before the consciousness enters the intermediate state. A facsimile of this state for the purposes of practice is designated to the period of dreamless sleep.

Collected Topics (*bsdus grwa*). A preliminary topic of study in the monastic curriculum that presents basic philosophical phenomena in a dialectical format in order to train students in the art of debate based on basic principles of logic.

counting sticks (*tshul shing*). Short yellow sticks used as a way of keeping count of the monks when they were out of the monastery.

ḍākinī (*mkha' gro ma*). A female practitioner or yogini who has gained high spiritual realizations, or is able to perform supernatural feats. She may be human, in human form, or from a celestial realm. The name means "sky-goer," thereby indicating her supernatural powers. There are twenty-four places sacred to the ḍākinīs, which are either geographically located in this world or designated to parts of the body mandala.

daylong Mahayana vows (*theg chen gso sbyong gi sdom pa*). Eight vows taken, typically before sunrise, for the duration of a single day.

deputy abbot (*bla ma dbu mdzad*). Literally, "lama chant-leader" (*lama umzé*), but in Gyütö Monastery it refers to the deputy abbot.

dhāraṇī (*gzungs*). The power of retention developed through meditative practices. The term is also used for certain mantras, such as those placed within a sacred object during consecration. It can also be applied to a genre of short texts found in the Kangyur that are recited as spells or charms to dispel unwanted phenomena such as eclipses.

Dharma protectors (*chos skyong / srung ma*). A group of deity-like beings dedicated to protecting the Dharma as a whole, specific traditions, or individuals.

dharmakāya (*chos kyi sku*). At the level of the complete enlightenment of a buddha it refers to the body of enlightened qualities that make up the enlightened mind, and to the ultimate-truth emptiness of that mind.

disciplinarian (*dge skos*). Proctor or monk in charge of enforcing monastic discipline.

dorampa (*rdo rams pa*). Lower rank of geshé, first awarded by the Fifth or Seventh

Dalai Lama. So called because the debates were held in front of a large stone (*do*) on which was placed the throne of the Dalai Lamas. Not a rank universally accepted by all three monastic seats.

eight auspicious substances (*bkra shis rdzas*). A mirror, yogurt, *durva* grass, *bilva* fruit, a right-spiraling conch, *giwang* medicine, vermillion powder, and white mustard seed.

eighth-day torma (*brgyad gtor*). Protector ritual held on the eighth day of the third month.

fire-offering ritual of the four feats (*las bzhi'i sbyin sreg*). Ritual accomplishment, by way of a tantric fire rite, of the feats of pacifying, controlling, increasing, and wrathful activities.

five exalted wisdoms (*ye shes lnga*). Mirror-like, equality, individual discernment, accomplishment, and dharmadhātu wisdom attained at the accomplishment of enlightenment and representing the enlightened transformation of the five aggregates.

four enlightened bodies (*sku bzhi*). "Bodies" in the sense of four distinct aspects of enlightenment, they are those of the qualities of the enlightened mind (*dharmakāya*), the ultimate truth emptiness of that mind, or naturally existing body (*svabhāvakāya*), the emanated body (*nirmāṇakāya*), and the body of enjoyments (*saṃbhogakāya*).

five king emanations (*rgyal po sku lnga*). Often regarded as five emanations of Pehar, a king-spirit, who in turn is identified with Nechung. The five emanations correspond to those of body, speech, mind, activity, and qualities and were originally tamed as protectors of Samyé Monastery by Padmasambhava.

four marks of contentment of an ārya (*'phags pa'i rigs bzhi*). A general contentment with food, clothing, dwelling place, and possessions, all of which are conducive to developing the insights of an ārya being.

four types of activities / four feats (*las bzhi*). Supernatural feats of pacifying, controlling, increasing, and wrath aimed at other beings or external phenomena and carried out by nonhuman protectors or powerful tantric practitioners.

Gangchen Kyishong (*gangs can skyid gshongs*). The area in between McLeod Ganj and Dharamsala where the offices of the Tibetan government-in-exile, the Library of Tibetan Works and Archives, and so on are situated.

Gangloma (*gang blo ma*). A praise of Mañjuśrī, so called because of the Tibetan habit of taking two or three syllables from the first line to create a title. Some say it was composed by the Indian pandit Vajraśāstra. Others say that an ancient Indian king asked a number of pandits to compose a praise of Mañjuśrī, and they simultaneously came up with this same praise.

general accomplishment of the three Buddha families (*rigs gsum spyi sgrub*). A practice focusing on the meditation deities Mañjuśrī, Avalokiteśvara, and Vajrapāṇi for the accomplishment of their qualities.

geshé (*dge bshes, kalyāṇamitra*). Literally "spiritual friend." Originally used as a general title for Buddhist teachers and mentors, but these days in the Geluk tradition it is a degree or title awarded to monks who have passed a rigorous examination of their studies. It is of varying grades, the highest of which is lharampa, awarded to those who have successfully sat in debate in all three monastic seats (see note 51). Lower grades are karampa, tsokrampa, lingsé, and dorampa.

Great Prayer Festival (*smon lam chen mo*). Great festival held to commemorate the time when the Buddha in Śrāvastī, India, defeated six teachers from other traditions in a contest of supernatural powers. It is traditionally held over the first half of the first month of the Tibetan year.

Guhyasamāja (*gsang ba 'dus pa*). Highest yoga tantra whose central deity is Akṣobhyavajra and is regarded as the king of tantras.

Guru Puja (*bla ma mchod pa*). Rite of offering and praise focused on the guru as the personification of all the buddhas, meditation deities, ḍākinīs, and so on.

guruyoga (*bla ma'i rnal 'byor*). Practice in which one's root guru is seen as the Buddha, during which praise, offering, and requests are made with single-pointed faith.

Halting the Ḍākinīs' Escort (*mkha 'gro bsu zlog*). A long-life ritual designed to prevent the ḍākinīs from coming to take the lama away to a pure land.

Hayagrīva secret-accomplishment ritual (*rta mgrin gsang grub*). Ritual focused on red Hayagrīva with three faces and six arms in the form of a fierce protector, performed to thwart unwanted events.

Hayagrīva, Vajrapāṇi, and Garuḍa (*rta phyag khyung*). Three deities whose permission initiations are often given together, and whose sādhana practice is known as the Three Wrathful Forms Combined (*drag po gsum dril*).

highest yoga tantra (*rnal 'byor bla na med pa'i rgyud*). Highest of the four classes of tantra.

horseback consecration (*rta thog ma*). A brief consecration, so called because it can be performed without dismounting from your horse.

house (*khams tshan / khang tshan*). Monastic houses within a monastery, often named after districts of Tibet.

hungry ghost (*yi dwags, preta*). A wretched class of beings, akin to ghosts, who wander in desperate and vain search for food, drink, and shelter.

illusory body (*sgyu lus, māyākāya*). Third of the five stages of the completion stage of tantra. A form created during completion-stage practices that is composed of the subtle winds and able to separate itself out from the ordinary body. In the aspect of the deity, it is the substantial cause for the resultant form body at the enlightened stage.

intermediate state (*bar do*). The state of existence between death and the start of the next rebirth. The being of the intermediate state has a body composed of subtle wind. In advanced completion-stage practice, this state is replaced by the illusory body in the form of a deity.

iron fortress (*lcags mkhar*). A torma used in a wrathful ritual constructed in the shape of Yama's iron fortress and with nine or sixteen sides.

isolate (*ldog pa*). The conceptualization and terminological designation of a phenomenon or aspect of a phenomenon.

Jangtsé Chöjé (*byang rtse chos rje*). Literally "Jangtsé Dharma master." Along with the Sharpa Chöjé, these two positions are the second highest in the Geluk order. They alternate in the succession to become Ganden Throneholder.

Kālarūpa/Dharmarāja (*chos rgyal*). Wrathful oath-bound protector associated with the deity Vajrabhairava. He is black in color with a single buffalo head, two arms, and an equally wrathful female companion.

karampa (*bka' rams pa*). A geshé of the individual colleges who has studied the entire curriculum syllabus and sits in debate within that college, but not in all three monastic seats. Synonymous with a *kachupa* (*bka' bcu pa*) geshé.

kyabjé (*skyabs rje*). Master for refuge and protection. A term of great respect given to high lamas.

labrang (*bla brang*). The monastic household of an incarnated lama.

lama (*bla ma, guru*). In the Geluk tradition a term of respect afforded to a revered spiritual teacher.

lharampa (*lha rams pa*). Highest rank of geshé. During the time of the Fifth Dalai Lama the title Lhaden Rapjampa ("master of numerous treatises from Lhasa") was conferred during the Great Lhasa Prayer Festival on a student who had mastered all five great topics of classical Buddhist scholarship. This term was shortened to become lharampa.

life entrustment (*srog gtad*). Often taken to mean a ritual whereby the practitioner entrusts their life to a protector, but according to His Holiness the Dalai Lama should be the practice of the protector entrusting itself to the practitioner.

lingsé geshé (*gling bsres dge bshes*). Lower rank of geshé. See note 183.

lion position (*seng ge nyal stabs*). Sleeping position of lying on one's right, thereby emulating the position of the Buddha when he passed into nirvana.

lion-face ḍākinī (*seng gdong ma*). Wisdom ḍākinī used as a protector.

Lokeśvara (*'jig rten dbang phyug*). Outside of Buddhism this term is used for different gods, but in Buddhism it usually refers to Avalokiteśvara.

Lord Chamberlain (*rtse mkhan mgron che ba*). The highest monk official in the Potala in charge of day-to-day matters, such as arranging audiences, forwarding applications and other submissions to the Dalai Lama, and so on. He had a staff of sixteen.

Madhyamaka (*dbu ma*). As a topic of study, it refers to the Middle Way philosophy propounded by Nāgārjuna and elucidated by Candrakīrti and others.

magical wheel (*'phrul 'khor / 'khor lo*). Mystical diagrams drawn as part of a repelling rite.

Mahākāla (*mgon po*). Deity having numerous forms and aspects, some of which are seen as manifestations of Avalokiteśvara and others as worldly protectors.

Mahayana precepts. *See* daylong Mahayana vows.

mandala (*dkyil 'khor, maṇḍala*). A particular celestial circle of deities, sacred objects, and an inestimable mansion as described within that tantra and into which one is initiated. Alternatively, it is a representation of the world according to traditional Buddhist scripture, often constructed ad hoc using heaps of grain topped with gemstones and so forth.

maṇi **mantra** (*ma ṇi*). The six-syllable mantra of Avalokiteśvara.

Mañjuśrī (*'jam dpal dbyangs*). Peaceful personification of the exalted wisdom of all the buddhas in the form of a deity. In his wrathful form he is Vajrabhairava, and as a disciple of the Buddha he was a bodhisattva. He is usually a reddish gold color with one face and two arms.

māra (*bdud*). An obstruction to spiritual progress, sometimes personified. There are four types: the aggregates, mental afflictions, death, and *devaputra*. The last, literally "god-realm son," is the personification of intoxication with pleasures.

master as longevity-deity initiation (*rje tshe 'dzin ma*). Longevity initiation by way of Tsongkhapa in the form of a long-life deity.

middle way. *See* Madhyamaka.

miktsema (*dmigs brtse ma*). A verse of praise written by Tsongkhapa for his lama, who then replaced his name for that of Tsongkhapa and offered it back to him. It is commonly recited as a mantra. There is an entire collection of ritual texts associated with this verse, which later came to be compiled as the Miktsema Compendium (*be'u bum*) by Khyenrap Tenpa Chöphel.

mind training (*blo sbyong*). A system of practice designed to take everyday life and its occurrences as opportunities and causes for training one's mind in the Mahayana path.

nāga (*klu*). Semi-divine creatures associated with snakes, who often need to be appeased by way of torma offerings, incense cleansing rituals, and so on.

nāga torma (*klu gtor*). Torma offered to placate the nāgas. *See* torma.

Nechung (*gnas chung*). The main protector, and counsel by way of oracle, for the Ganden Phodrang Tibetan government and the Dalai Lama.

Niguma (*ni gu ma*). Mahāsiddha sister of the Indian pandit Nāropa.

offerings of the twenty-fifth (*dga' ldan lnga mchod*). Anniversary of Tsongkhapa's nirvana on the twenty-fifth of the tenth Tibetan month. It is celebrated as a light festival, with butter lamps displayed outside on the roofs and windowsills of the monasteries and homes.

Palden Lhamo (*dpal ldan lha mo*). Female protector deity of Tibet with a close connection to the first and subsequent Dalai Lamas. She is wrathful in appearance, dark blue, and riding a mule.

Perfection of Wisdom (*shes rab gyi pha rol tu phyin pa / phar phyin, prajñāpāramitā*). As a topic of monastic curriculum it is the systematic study of the Perfection of Wisdom sutras from the perspective of their concealed teachings on the paths, levels, and practices leading to the goals of nirvana and enlightenment. It takes as its root text Maitreya's *Ornament of Realization*, a brilliant elucidation of these concealed teachings.

Pramāṇa (*tshad ma*). As a topic of the monastic curriculum it is the study of epistemology using Dharmakīrti's *Treatise of Valid Cognition* as a root text.

pratyekabuddhas (*rang rgyal / rang sangs rgyas*). Non-Mahayana disciples who prefer to practice without reliance upon a teacher, especially in their last life before attaining nirvana. They are solitary practitioners and in that sense are compared to the rhinoceros. Some tenets classify them as more intelligent than the śrāvakas.

rapjampa (*rab 'byams pa*). "Master of numerous treatises from Lhasa," later shortened to *rampa*. It is affixed to the varying grades of geshé. *See* lharampa.

regent (*rgyal tshab*). The administrator of Tibet in the interregnum between successive Dalai Lamas. It also used to refer to the holders of the throne of Tsongkhapa.

rinpoché (*rin po che*). A term of high respect meaning "precious one" bestowed by disciples. Unlike *tulku* it is not an official title, but it is most typically applied to reincarnated lamas.

ritual assistant (*mchod gyog*). Monk skilled in the creation and arrangement of the various offerings and tormas on the assembly hall altar.

sādhana (*sgrub thabs*). Text for a generation-stage practice focused on a particular deity.

samaya being (*dam tshig sems dpa', samayasattva*). The visualization of the practitioner as the meditation deity for the subsequently invited wisdom beings to enter into. So called because it is the definitive (*samaya*) place for the wisdom beings to enter.

samaya (*dam tshig*). A bond or pledge made by a practitioner in the presence of their lama or meditation deity. It also refers to the bond that exists between followers of the same lama.

sandhi (*mtshams 'byor*). Rules on changes to pronunciation due to conjunctions of syllables in Sanskrit grammar.

sang (*srang*). Tibetan silver coins.

self-generation (*bdag bskyed*). Generating oneself into a deity through the discipline of visualization together with associated practices.

seven-limb prayer (*yan lag bdun pa*). Seven individual preparatory practices assisted by chanted verses and physical activities: prostration, offering, confession, rejoicing, entreating the lamas to teach, requesting the lamas to not enter nirvana, and dedication.

seven-point meditative posture of Buddha Vairocana (*rnam snang gi chos bdun*). Seven physical features of a meditation posture resembling that of Buddha Vairocana: legs in full or half lotus position, right hand on left with thumbs touching, back straight as an arrow, lips and teeth as normal with tongue touching palate, head slightly bent forward, eyes naturally directed toward the nose, and shoulders straight and not raised or lowered. Sometimes counting twenty-one breaths is added to make eight.

shapdrung (*zhabs drung*). Monk who has studied under and spent time with a great lama.

Sharpa Chöjé (*shar pa chos rje*). *See* Jangtsé Chöjé.

Shijé (*zhi byed*). A Perfection of Wisdom practice belonging to the Chö tradition, brought to Tibet by Phadampa Sangyé, and involving the pacification (*zhi*) of the sufferings of samsara.

Shingja Chen (*shing bya can*). One of the five king emanationss (see above), who acts as counsel via the oracle of Gadong Monastery.

Sitātapatrā (*gdugs dkar*). A female protector who emanated from the crown of the Buddha and is particularly effective for warding off obstacles. She is usually white, with a thousand arms and faces, and is named after the white parasol that accompanies her.

six-session guruyoga (*thun drug bla ma'i rnal 'byor*). Tantric practice accompanied by visualization and recitation performed six times a day in order to maintain the pledges (*samaya*) of the five Buddha families.

sixteen elders (*gnas brtan bcu drug*). The sixteen disciples of the Buddha to whom the doctrine was entrusted until the coming of the next Buddha, Maitreya.

sixty-four-part ritual (*drug bcu ma*). The sixty-four-part torma-offering ritual made to protector Dharmarāja and the fifteen direction protectors.

śrāvaka (*nyan thos*). "Hearers" or "listeners." Non-Mahayana Buddhist disciples who hear the Buddha's teachings and pass them on to others. The goal of the śrāvaka path is arthatship, the cessation of personal suffering.

stages of the path (*lam rim*). The graduated practices, insights, and spiritual developments on the path or paths leading to enlightenment.

sugata (*bde gshegs*). "One who traveled to happiness"; epithet for a buddha.

Tārā Thread-Cross Ritual Repelling Attacks (*sgrol ma g.yul mdos*). A thread-cross is a ritual designed to repel harm, in which a substitute or effigy of the victim, or ransom substances, are offered within a structure made, in its simplest form, of two crossed sticks woven with colored thread. They are often associated with protecting deities such as Tārā.

ten powers (*stobs bcu*). Ten exclusive powers related to the wisdom of enlightened beings. These illustrate the unobstructed knowledge of the buddhas with regard to living beings, past and future, paths, and so on.

tenma (*bstan ma*). Twelve female protectors indigenous to Tibet.

three representations (*rten gsum*). A buddha statue, scripture, and a stupa as representations of the body, speech, and mind of the buddhas; traditional offering to a lama.

three wrathful forms combined (*drag po gsum dril*). Obstacle-repelling practice. *See* Hayagrīva, Vajrapāṇi, and Garuḍa.

thukdam (*thugs dam*). The period of meditation entered into by a tantric practitioner who has passed through the death process and abides within the state of clear light. It can also mean a vow or pledge made by a lama and is sometimes used honorifically to refer to the casting of a divination.

thukpa (*thug pa*). Noodles in soup, and a staple of the Tibetan diet.

torma (*gtor ma*). "That which is thrown"; an edible-substance offering for deities, protectors, nāgas, sprits, and so forth. It is cast away at the end of the ritual in order to reduce attachment. In Tibet tormas were usually made of tsampa, then shaped and decorated according to the description laid down for that particular object of offering.

tsampa (*tsam pa*). Roasted barley flour.

tsenshap (*mtshan zhabs*). *See* assistant tutor.

tsok (*tshogs*). Literally "gathering." The gathered food and other offerings amassed at an offering rite, which is ritually transformed, offered to the sacred objects, then enjoyed by the gathering. It can also refer to the actual gathering of yogis and yoginis at the feast.

tsokrampa (*tshogs rams pa*). Middling rank of geshé awarded to those who sit in debate during the assembly (*tsok*) of the Ganden Prayer Festival.

tulku (*sprul sku*). "Emanated being." Strictly, a term applied to emanations of buddhas and deities in forms visible to ordinary disciples appropriate to their mindset. More commonly used to refer to officially recognized incarnations of high lamas. Not all tulkus are lamas, and not all lamas are tulkus.

two obscurations (*sgrib gnyis*). Mental obstacles that prevent the attainment of higher spiritual stages. *Mental afflictions* prevent the attainment of nirvana and the *imprints* of those afflictions prevent the attainment of complete enlightenment.

two truths (*bden pa gnyis*). The conventional and ultimate levels of reality on which the Buddha's teachings are founded and which pervade all phenomena.

***vaiśākha* month** (*sa ga zla ba*). The fourth Tibetan month, whose full moon is commemorated as the time of the Buddha's enlightenment.

Vaiśravaṇa (*rnam thos sras*). Protector of the north direction and deity of wealth. Usually portrayed to resemble an ancient Indian king.

vajra master (*rdo rje slob dpon, vajrācārya*). Tantric master, especially when conferring initiations.

Vajrabhairava (*rdo rje 'jigs byed*). Deity of highest yoga tantra, a wrathful emanation of Mañjuśrī. Commonly referred to elsewhere as Yamāntaka. He is wrathful, dark blue, with nine heads, the main one of which resembles that of a buffalo, and has thirty-four arms and sixteen legs.

vajrācārya. *See* vajra master.

Vajradhara (*rdo rje chang*). The Buddha as the teacher of tantra. Also used as an affix to a lama's name to indicate his prowess in tantra.

Vajrapāṇi (*phyag na rdo rje*). Deity personification of the Buddha's power, designated to guard the tantras after the Buddha passed into nirvana. He is usually portrayed as a type of Indian demon known as a *yakṣa*, dark blue in color, with one face and two arms.

Vajrasattva (*rdo rje sems pa*). Meditation deity very effective in the purification of past misdeeds. Also often used as a synonym for Vajradhara. He is usually white with one face and two arms, holding a vajra and bell.

Vajravidāraṇa (*rdo rje rnam 'joms*). Female deity sourced from Indian texts and used for cleansing and purifying rites. Can be white, green, or blue, with one face and two arms, and is usually seated in peaceful or semi-wrathful form.

Vajrayoginī (*rdo rje rnal 'byor ma*). Mother tantra deity belonging to the highest yoga tantra class. She evolved from the Cakrasaṃvara tantra, where she acts as consort. One of the commonest Vajrayoginī lineages is that stemming from Nāropa. She is usually red in color, with one face, two arms, and standing in a particularly striking pose.

Vasudhārā (*nor rgyun ma*). Female wealth deity, popular in Nepal. She is of a golden color, with between two and six arms, seated with one leg touching the earth.

vetala (*ro langs*). A "risen corpse" usually taken over and inhabited by a spirit.

Vighnāntaka (*bgegs mthar byed*). Wrathful spirit invoked at the beginning of initiations and so on to clear away hindrances. He is wrathful, dark blue, and with one face and two arms.

Vinaya (*'dul ba*). The monastic discipline or code set down by the Buddha for the ordained, as well as a genre of texts in the Buddhist canon that elucidates these rules, often with elaborate stories about the Buddha and his disciples. Vinaya is one of the main curriculum subjects for monks, with Guṇaprabha's treatise the *Vinaya Sutra* serving as root text.

wisdom being (*yes shes sems dpa', jñānasattva*). The meditation deity invited to sit at the heart of the samaya being. So called because it is the exalted wisdom of bliss and emptiness in the form of a deity. *See* samaya being.

Yongzin (*yongs 'dzin*). As an official title it refers to the junior and senior tutors of the Dalai Lamas in their early years. More generally it is a lama who has the ability to completely (*yong*) protect or hold (*zin*) his disciples from the perils of samsara.

Bibliography

Abhayākaragupta. *Vajra Garland Mandala Procedures. Vajrāvalimaṇḍalalopāyikā. Dkyil 'khor gyi cho ga rdo rje phreng ba.*

Abridged Perfection of Wisdom. Prajñāpāramitāsañcayagāthā. Shes rab kyi pha rol tu phyin pa sdud pa tshigs su bcad pa. shes phyin.

All Wishes to Be Spontaneously Fulfilled. Bsam pa lhun grub. Author unknown.

Amé Shap Ngawang Kunga Sönam. *Teachings on the Central Channel. Rdzogs rim rtsa dbu ma.*

Anubhūti. *Sarasvatī Grammar Treatise. Sarasvatīvyākaraṇasūtra. Dbyangs can sgra mdo.*

Āryaśūra. *Garland of the Buddha's Birth Stories. Jātakamālā. Skyes pa'i rabs kyi rgyud.*

Asaṅga. *Stages of the Bodhisattva from Stages of the Yogacaryā. Yogacaryābhūmau-bodhisattvabhūmi. Byang chub sems dpa'i sa'i gzhi'i rnal 'byor gyi gnas.*

Aśvaghoṣa. *Fifty Verses on the Guru. Gurupancāśikā. Bla ma lnga bcu pa.*

Atiśa. *Lamp on the Path to Enlightenment. Bodhipathapradīpa. Byang chub lam gyi sgron ma.*

Butön Rinchen Drup. *Annotations on the Kālacakra Stainless Light Great Commentary. Dri med 'od kyi mchan.*

Cakrasaṃvara Condensed Tantra / Cakrasaṃvara Root Tantra. Laghusaṃvaratantra. Bde mchog nyung ngu rgyud.

Candragomin. *Twenty Verses on the Bodhisattva Vow. Bodhisattvasaṃvaraviṃśaka. Byang chub sems dpa'i sdom pa nyi shu pa.*

Candrakīrti. *Bright Lamp. Pradīpoddyotana. Sgron ma gsal bar byed pa zhes bya ba'i rgya cher bshad pa.*

———. *Entering the Middle Way. Madhyamakāvatāra. Dbu ma la 'jug pa.*

Causing the Rain of Goodness to Fall. Rab gnas dge legs char 'bebs. Author unknown.

Changkya Yeshé Tenpai Drönmé / Changkya Rölpai Dorjé. *Lamp Illuminating Great Bliss. Bde chen gsal ba'i sgron me.*

———. *Recognizing My Old Mother: A Song on the View. Lta ba'i mgur a ma dngos 'dzin.* An English translation by Thupten Jinpa can be found in *Songs of Spiritual Experience* (Boston: Shambhala, 2000).

Chekawa, Geshé. *Seven-Point Mind Training. Blo sbyong don bdun ma.*

Chim Jampaiyang. *Ornament of Abhidharma: A Commentary to the Abhidharma-kośa. Mngon mdzod kyi 'grel pa mngon pa'i rgyan.*

Choné Geshé Losang Gyatso. *Interwoven Praise Based upon Tsongkhapa's Praise of Dependent Origination: Opening Wide the Door to the Limitless Skies of Treasure That Is Its Explanation, a Great Cloud of Melody from a Golden Age.*

Choné Lama Drakpa Shedrup. *Sheaves of Auspiciousness. Bkra shis snye ma.*

Collected Rituals on Vaiśravaṇa. Rnam sras be'u bum. Various authors.

Core Instructions on Mind Training. Blo sbyong man ngag. Author unknown.

Dakpo Losang Jinpa. *Review Meditations on the Stages of the Path, Encompassing All Essential Points. Lam rim shar sgom gnad don kun tshang.*

Dalai Lama. *See under* Gendun Drup (First), Gendun Gyatso (Second), Ngawang Losang Gyatso (Fifth), Kalsang Gyatso (Seventh), Thubten Gyatso (Thirteenth), and Tenzin Gyatso (Fourteenth).

Darpaṇa Ācārya. *Compendium of Activities. Kriyāsamgraha. Bya ba bsdus pa.* (Attributed in all editions of Tengyur to Kuladatta.)

Desi Sangyé Gyatso. *Mirror of Beryl: A Historical Introduction to Tibetan Medicine. Gso ba'i rig pa'i khog 'bugs legs bhad bai dūrya'i me long.*

Dharmakīrti. *Treatise of Valid Cognition. Pramāṇavārttika. Tshad ma rnam 'grel gyi tshig le'ur byas pa.*

Dharmarakṣita. *Wheel of Sharp Weapons. Blo sbyong mtshon cha'i 'khor lo.*

Dignāga. *Compendium of Valid Cognition. Pramāṇasamuccaya. Tshad ma kun las btus pa zhes bya ba'i rab tu byed pa.*

Drati Rinchen Döndrup. *Explanation of the Thirty Verses / Clarifying the Thinking of Samantabhadra, Together with the Grammatical Ornaments: An Explanation of the Grammar Work "Thirty Verses." Bod kyi brda'i bstan bcos sum cu pa zhes bya ba'i rnam bshad kun tu bzang po'i dgongs pa rab gsal rgyan bcas.*

Dromtönpa (compiler). *Kadam Father and Son Teachings / Book of Kadam. Bka' gdams pha chos bu chos / Bka' gdams glegs bam.*

Drupchok Losang Namgyal. *Instructions on the "Navigator for Those Who Seek Liberation." Thar 'dod ded dpon gyi ṭī kā.*

Gendun Drup, First Dalai Lama. *Precious Garland: A Commentary on Vinaya. 'Dul ṭik rin chen phreng ba.*

———. *Illumination of the Path to Freedom: A Commentary on the Abhidharma-kośa. Mdzod ṭik thar lam gsal byed.*

Gendun Gyatso, Second Dalai Lama. *Offerings and Homage to the Sixteen Elders. Gnas brtan phyag mchod.*

Guhyasamāja Root Tantra. Guhyasamājatantra. Gsang 'dus rtsa rgyud.

Guṇaprabha. *Vinaya Sutra. Vinayasūtra. 'Dul ba'i mdo.*

Gungthang Tenpai Drönmé. *Powerful Weapon Wheel: Protecting Circle and Repelling Torma Ritual of the Ten Wrathful Protectors. Khro bcu'i bsrung zlog ngar ma'i rno mtshon.*

————. *Praise of Jé Tsongkhapa: Meaningful to Behold. Tsong kha pa'i bstod pa don dang ldan pa.*

————. *Prayer for the Flourishing of Tsongkhapa's Teachings. Rje'i bstan pa'i rgyas pa'i smon lam.*

————. *Profound Instructions on Drawing and Executing Ensnaring Yantras. Dra sdom 'khor lo bris sgrub bya tshul gyi zab khrid.*

————. *Ramblings of an Old Man. Nyams myong rgan po'i 'bel gtam.*

————. *Summary of Advice on the Three Vows. Sdom gsum bslab bya'i sdom tshig.*

————. *The Way to Study the Texts of Sutra and Tantra. Mdo sngags kyi gzhung la slob gnyer byed tshul.*

Gyalrong Chözé Losang Thokmé. *Kutsap Stages of the Path. Sku tshab lam rim / Lam rim myur lam dang lam rim bde lam gyi khrid yig.*

Gyaltsap Darma Rinchen. *Essence Ornament to Haribhadra's Clarification of the Meaning of the Ornament of Realization. Shes rab kyi pha rol tu phyin pa'i man ngag gi bstan bcos mngon par rtogs pa'i rgyan gyi 'grel pa don gsal ba'i rnam bshad snying po'i rgyan.*

————. *Illuminating the Path to Freedom: Explanation of Treatise of Valid Cognition. Rnam 'grel thar lam gsal byed.*

Gyurmé Tsewang Chokdrup. *Hundred Rays of Light: Commentary to Sarasvatī Grammar Treatise. Dbyangs can ma'i sgra mdo'i rnam bshad slob ma la phan pa rtogs dka'i mun pa sel ba'i 'od zer brgya pa.*

Haribhadra. *Clarification of the Meaning of the Ornament of Realization. Abhisamayālaṃkāravṛtti. Shes rab kyi pha rol tu phyin pa'i man ngag gi bstan bcos mngon par togs pa'i rgyan zhes bya ba'i 'grel pa. 'Grel pa don gsal.*

Heart Sutra. *Bhagavatīprajñāpāramitāhṛdaya. Bcom ldan 'das ma shes rab kyi pha rol tu phyin pa'i snying po.*

Hortön Namkha Pal. *Rays of the Sun: Training the Mind in Bodhicitta. Byang chub sems sbyong gi gdams pa blo sbyong nyi ma'i 'od zer.*

Hundred Deities of Tuṣita. *Dga' ldan lha brgya ma.* Attributed to Dulnakpa Palden Sangpo (1402–73).

Individual Liberation Sutra. *Pratimokṣa Sutra. Pratimokṣasūtra. So sor thar ba'i mdo.*

Jampal Lhundrup. *Preparatory Practices: Necklace for the Fortunate. Sbyor chos skal bzang mgrin rgyan.*

Jamyang Lama Choklha Özer. *Ratö Collected Topics. Rwa stod bsdus grwa.*

Jamyang Shepa Dorjé Ngawang Tsöndrü. *Great Vajra Words on the Exclusive Practice of Combining of the Peaceful and Wrathful Forms of Mañjuśrī. 'Jam dbyangs zhi khro sbrags sgrub thun mong ma yin pa'i rdo rje'i tshig sbram.*

————. *Peaceful and Wrathful Forms of Mañjuśrī Combined: Fulfilling the Hopes of the Fortunate. Skal ldan re ba kun skong gnyis sbrag.*

————. *Precious Garland of the Oral Transmission: Annotations on the Vajrabhairava Seven-Chapter Root Tantra*. Rgyud rtog bdun gyi mchan 'grel snyan brgyud rin chen 'phreng ba.

Kālacakra Tantra / Condensed Kālacakra Tantra. Laghutantra / Paramādibuddhoddhṛtaśrīkālacakra-nāma-tantrarājā. 'Phag pa'i dang po'i sang rgyas las phyung ba rgyud kyi rgyal po dpal dus kyi 'khor lo.

Kalsang Gyatso, Seventh Dalai Lama. *Guide to the View: A Song of the Four Recollections*. Lta khrid dran pa bzhi ldan.

————. *Instructions on the Hundred Deities of Tuṣita: Source of All Siddhis*. Dga' ldan lha brgya ma'i khrid yig dngos grub kun 'byung.

————. *Praise of Avalokiteśvara*. 'Phags bstod.

Kalsang Khedrup / Chökyi Dorjé. *Secret Path of the Vehicle of Means*. Thabs kyi theg pa'i gsang lam.

————. *Chö Text: Beautiful Adornment to the Teaching of the Ganden Practice Lineage*. Gcod gzhung dga ldan sgrub brgyud bstan pa'i mdzes rgyan.

Kāśyapa Chapter. Kāśyapaparivarta. 'Od srung gi le'u.

Khedrup Jé. *Bridge of Faith: Account of the Extraordinary Life of the Venerable Lama Tsongkhapa*. Rje btsun bla ma tsong kha pa chen po'i ngo mtshar rmad du byung ba'i rnam par thar pa dad pa'i 'jug ngogs.

————. *Dose of Emptiness: Opening the Eyes of the Fortunate*. Stong mthun skal bzang mig 'byed.

————. *Great Exposition of the Vajrabhairava Generation Stage*. 'Jigs byed kyi bskyed rim chen mo tshigs bcad du byas pa.

————. *Ocean of Attainments*. Dngos grub rgya mtsho.

Khyenrap Tenpa Chöphel. *Miktsema Compendium*. Dmigs brtse ma'i be'u bum.

Könchok Tenpai Drömé. *See* Gungthang Tenpai Drönmé.

Kṣemendra. *Wish-Fulfilling Tree of the Bodhisattva's Lives*. Bodhisattvāvadānakalpalatā. Byang chub sems dpa'i rtogs pa brjod rin po che dpag bsam gyi 'khri shing.

Langri Thangpa Dorjé Sengé. *Eight Verses on Mind Training*. Blo sbyong tshig brgyad ma.

Losang Döndrup. *Navigator for Those Who Seek Liberation*. Thar 'dod ded dpon.

Losang Gyaltsen Sengé. *Vajra Diamond: Sādhana of Wisdom Ḍākinī Siṃhamukha*. Ye shes kyi mkha' gro ma seng ge'i gdongs pa can gyi sgrub thabs rdo rje pha lam.

Losang Khyenrap. *Quick Path to the Ḍākinī Realm*. Mkha' spyod bgrod pa myur lam.

Losang Lungtok Tenzin Trinlé, Fifth Ling Rinpoché. *Eighteen-Step Guide to Vajrabhairava*. Them skas bco brgyad.

————. *Three Chapters*. Le tshan gsum.

Losang Namgyal. *Commentary on Navigator for Those Who Seek Liberation*. Thar 'dod ded dpon gyi ṭī kā.

Lotus Sutra. Saddharmapuṇḍarīkasūtra. Dam pa'i chos padma dkar po'i mdo.

Mahākāla Who Enters the Heart: Requests Made to the Guru and Mahākāla as One—A Hook that Draws in the Attainments. Mgon po snying zhugs bla ma mgon po dbyer med la gsol ba 'debs pa mngos grub 'gugs pa lcags kyu.

Maitreya. *Differentiating the Middle Way and the Extremes. Madhyantavibhaṅga. Dbus dang mtha' rnam par 'byed pa'i tshig le'ur byas pa.*

———. *Ornament of Realization. Abhisamayālaṃkāra. Shes rab kyi pha rol tu phyin pa'i man ngag gi bstan bcos mngon par rtogs pa'i rgyan zhes bya ba'i tshig le'ur byas pa.*

———. *Uttaratantra / Mahāyānottaratantraśāstra / Ratnagotravibhāga. Theg pa chen po rgyud bla ma'i bstan bcos.*

Minling Terchen Dharma Śrī. *Wonderful Wish-Granting Vase Sādhana. 'Dod 'jo'i bum bzang.*

Nāgārjuna. *Letter to a Friend. Suhṛllekha. Bshes pa'i spring yig.*

———. *Verses on the Fundamental Wisdom of the Middle Way. Mūlamadhyamaka-kārikā. Dbu ma rtsa ba'i tshig le'ur byas pa shes rab.*

Ngawang Losang Gyatso, Fifth Dalai Lama. *Boat to Enter the Great Ocean of the Mahayana: Explanation of the Great Treatise Entering the Middle Way. Bstan bcos chen po dbu ma la 'jug pa gsal bar byed pa theg chen rgya mtshor 'jug pa'i gru rdzings.*

———. *Exegesis of Ornament of Realization and Its Commentaries: Ornament to the Thought of Losang Drakpa. Mngon rtogs rgyan rtsa 'grel rnams gsal bar byed pa blo bzang dgongs rgyan.*

———. *Melody to Delight Sarasvatī: Commentary to Daṇḍin's Mirror of Poetics. Snyan ngag me long gi rtsa ba dang dka' 'grel dbyangs can dgyes glu.*

———. *Oral Transmission of Mañjuśrī: Instructions on the Stages of the Path to Enlightenment. Byang chub lam gyi rim pa'i khrid yig 'jam dpal dbyangs kyi zhal lung.*

———. *Pure Visions: The Sealed Secrets. Dag snang gsang ba rgya can.*

Ngawang Phuntsok Lhundrup. *Illuminating Treatise Explaining the Sarasvatī Grammar Treatise. Dbyangs can sgra mdo'i 'grel pa rab tu bya ba gsal ldan.*

Orgyenpa, Lama. *Compendium of Poetic Examples. Dpe brjod khams pa.*

Padmasambhava. *Removing Obstacles to the Path. Bar chad lam sel.*

Palkhang Lotsāwa Ngawang Chökyi Gyatso. *Lexicon Lamp of Speech. Dag yig ngag sgron.*

Palzin Sangpo. *Palzin Sangpo Collection on Vajrabhairava. Bcom ldan 'das dpal rdo rje 'jigs byed kyi chos skor dpal pod du grags pa.*

Paṇchen Losang Chökyi Gyaltsen, compiler. *Torma Offering Rites. Gtor ma brgya rtsa.*

Paṇchen Losang Chökyi Gyaltsen. *Guru Puja. Bla ma mchod pa.*

Paṇchen Losang Yeshé. *Swift Path Direct Instructions. Myur lam.*

Panchen Sönam Drakpa. *Analysis of the Perfection of Wisdom. Phar phyin mtha'
dpyod.*

———. *Analysis of Vinaya. 'Dul ba'i mtha' dpyod.*

———. *Elucidation of the Difficult Points: Commentary to Treatise on Valid Cognition. Rgyas pa'i bstan bcos tshad ma rnam 'grel gyi dka' 'grel dgongs pa rab gsal.*

———. *Lamp Illuminating the Meaning of the Mother Wisdom: An Overview of the
Perfection of Wisdom. Phar phyin spyi don yum don gsal ba'i sgron me.*

———. *Middle Way Analysis. Dbu ma mtha' dpyod.*

———. *Middle Way Overview. Dbu ma spyi don.*

———. *Utpala Garland. Utpal 'phreng ba.*

*Perfection of Wisdom in Eight Thousand Lines. Aṣṭasāhasrikāprajñāpāramitā. Shes
rab kyi pha rol tu phyin pa brgyad stong pa.*

*Perfection of Wisdom in Twenty-Five Thousand Lines. Pañcaviṃśatisāhasrikāpra-
jñāpāramitā. Shes rab kyi pha rol tu phyin pa stong phrag nyi shu lnga pa.*

Phabongkha Dechen Nyingpo. *Guru Yoga: Blessings That Are a Treasury of All
Desires. Bla ma rnal 'byor byin rlabs 'dod rgu'i gter mdzod.*

———. *Heart Scalpel: Evoking the Awareness of Impermanence. Mi rtag dran bskul
snying gi thur ma.*

———. *Increasing Great Bliss: Actualization of the Bhagavan Cakrasaṃvara Body
Mandala in the Tradition of the Mighty Siddha Ghaṇṭapāda. Grub pa'i dbang
phyug dril bu zhabs lugs kyi bcom 'das 'khor lo sdom pa'i lus dkyil gyi mngon par
rtogs pa bde chen rab 'phel.*

———. *Jewel Pendant of Cittamaṇi. Citta maṇi'i do shal.*

———. *Liberation in the Palm of Your Hand. Rnam grol lag bcangs.*

———. *Longevity Ritual for Self and Others by Way of Cittamaṇi White Tārā. Sgrol
dkar yid bzhin 'khor lo'i sgo nas rang bzhan tshe sgrub bya tshul.*

Praises to the Twenty-One Tārās. Sgrol ma phyag 'tshal nyer gcig ma.

Prayer for the Teachings to Flourish. Bstan 'bar ma. (Compiled from the sutras.)

*Prayer of Samantabhadra. Bhadracaryāpraṇidhānarāja. Bzang po spyod pa'i smon
lam gyi rgyal po.*

Puṇḍarīka. *Stainless Light Commentary / Great Commentary. Vimalaprabhāṭīkā.
Bsdus pa'i rgyud kyi rgyal po dus kyi 'khor lo'i 'grel bshad rtsa ba'i rgyud kyi rjes su
'jug pa stong phrag bcu gnyis pa dri ma med pa'i 'od.*

Ra Lotsāwa. *Ra Lotsāwa Collection on Vajrabhairava: Oral Transmission of the
ḍākinīs. Rwa khrid mkha' 'gro snyan brgyud.*

*Remembering the Three Jewels Sutra. Buddhadharmasaṃghānusmṛti. Dkon mchog
rjes dran gyi mdo.*

*Removing All Opposing Hindrances: An Unelaborated Curse-Weakening Ritual.
Spros med gtad rul mi mthun bar chad kun sel.* Author unknown.

Śāntideva. *Guide to the Bodhisattva's Way of Life. Bodhicaryāvatāra. Byang chub
sems pa'i spyod pa la 'jug pa.*

Sarvavarmā. *Kalāpa Sutra. Kalāpasūtra. Ka lā pa'i mdo.*

Secret Teachings on Four-Faced Great Vajra Mahākāla, Protector and Robber of Strength. Dpal rdo rje nag po chen po zhing skyong stobs 'phrog dbang po'i gsang khrid. Author unknown.

Seven-Chapter Vajrabhairava Root Tantra. Vajrabhairavakalpatantrarāja. Rdo rje 'jigs byed kyi rtog pa'i rgyud kyi rgyal po.

Shakabpa, Tsepon W. D. *Tibet: A Political History.* New Haven, CT: Yale University Press, 1967.

Shamar Pandita, the Fourth Amdo Shamar, Gendun Tenzin Gyatso. *Stages of the Path. Zhwa dmar lam rim.*

Sharchen Ngawang Tsultrim. *Vinaya Summary. 'Dul sdom.*

Shönu Lodrö. *Extensive as Space. Mkha' mnyam ma.*

Speaking the Names of Mañjuśrī. Mañjuśrīnāmasaṃgīti. 'Phags pa 'jam dpal ye shes sem dpa'i don dam pa'i mtshan yang dag par brjod pa (part of the *Māyājāla Tantra*).

Sutra of Immeasurable Wisdom and Life. Aparimitāyurjñāna. 'Phags pa tshe dang ye shes dpag du med pa'i mdo / Tshe mdo.

Takphu Losang Tenpai Gyaltsen. *Stairway of Refined Vaidūrya. Baidūrya zhun ma'i them skas.*

Tamboura of Devotion and Respect: Requests Invoking the Essence of Ārya Cittamaṇi Tārā. 'Phags ma yid bzhin 'khor lo'i thugs dam gnad nas bskul ba'i gsol 'debs mos gus kyi tam bu ra.

Taranatha, compiler. *Cycle of the Hundred Rinjung Initiations and Sādhanas. Rin 'byung brgya rtsa.*

Tenpa Rapgyé. *White Mahākāla Treasure Vase Accomplishment. Mgon dkar bum sgrub.*

Tenzin Gyatso, Fourteenth Dalai Lama. *Prayer of the Words of Truth. Bden tshig smon lam.*

Thönmi Saṃbhota. *Thirty Verses. Lung du ston pa'i rtsa ba sum cu pa.*

Thuken Chökyi Nyima. *The Way to Follow the Instructions for Repairing Weakened Pledges by Relying upon the Five Yamāntaka Families Performed in Conjunction with the Guruyoga of Glorious Vajrabhairava. Rdo rje 'jigs byed kyi bla ma'i rnal 'byor dang 'brel bar gshin rje gshed rigs lnga la brten nas dam tshig nyams chag gso ba'i gdams pa nyams su blang tshul.*

Thupten Gyatso, Thirteenth Dalai Lama. *Nectar for the Supreme Granting of All Wishes: A Long-Life Prayer. Smon tshig 'chi med 'dod rgu'i mchog stsol.*

Trijang Rinpoché Losang Yeshé. *Gateway to the Ocean of Great Bliss. Bde chen rgya mtsho'i 'jug ngogs.*

———. *Precious Necklace of the Most Powerful Wish-Fulfilling Jewels. Bsam 'phel dbang gi rgyal po'i do shal.*

Tsonawa Sherap Sangpo. *Sunlight Explanation. 'Dul ba mdo rtsa'i rnam bshad nyi ma'i 'od zer legs bshad lung gi rgya mtsho.*

Tsongkhapa. *Abridged Stages of the Path. Lam rim bsdus don.*

———. *An Elucidation of the Meaning of the Mandala Rite for the Complete Emptying of the Lower Realms by way of Vairocana. Rnam par snang mdzad kyi sgo nas ngan song thams cad yong su sbyong ba'i dkyil 'khor gi cho ga rgyud don gsal ba.*

———. *Annotations on the Emptying the Lower Realms Tantra. Ngan song sbyong rgyud mchan dang bcas pa.*

———. *Clarifying the Intention: Explanation of Entering the Middle Way. Dbu ma la 'jug pa'i rnam bshad dgongs pa rab gsal.*

———. *Elucidation of All Hidden Points (of the Cakrasaṃvara Condensed Tantra). 'Khor lo bde mchog bsdus rgyud rgya cher bshad pa sbas don kun gsal.*

———. *Essence of Excellent Explanation: Differentiating the Definitive and the Provisional. Drang nges legs bshad snying po.*

———. *Fire Offering Rituals: An Ocean of Attainments. Sbyin sreg dngos grub rgya mtsho.*

———. *Five Stages Complete on One Seat. Rim lnga gdan rdzogs.*

———. *Foundation of All Good Qualities. Yon tan bzhir gyur ma.*

———. *Golden Garland of Excellent Explanation. Legs bshad gser 'phreng.*

———. *Great Exposition of Secret Mantra. Sngags rim chen mo.*

———. *Great Stages of the Path to Enlightenment. Byang chub lam rim chen mo.*

———. *Great Yoga of the Completion Stage. Rdzogs rim rnal 'byor chen po'i khrid kyi rim pa mdor bsdus pa.*

———. *Guide Endowed with the Three Convictions. Khrid yig yid ches gsum ldan.*

———. *Highway to Enlightenment: An Exposition of Bodhisattva Ethics. Byang chub sems dpa' tshul khrims kyi rnam bshad byang chub gzhung lam.*

———. *Jewel Box Sādhana of the Thirteen-Deity Vajrabhairava. Rdo rje 'jigs byed lha bcu gsum ma sgrub thabs za ma tog.*

———. *Lamp to Illuminate the Five Stages. Rim lnga gsal sgron.*

———. *Middle-Length Stages of the Path. Lam rim chung ba.*

———. *Ocean of Reasoning: The Great Commentary. Tik chen rigs pa'i rgya mtsho.*

———. *Praise of Dependent Origination. Rten 'brel stod pa.*

———. *Praise of Mañjuśrī. 'Jam dbyangs bstod sprin rgya mtsho.*

———. *Prayer for Rebirth in Sukhāvatī. Bde ba can du skye ba'i smon lam.*

———. *Prayer of Auspiciousness at the Beginning, Middle, and End. Thog mtha' ma.*

———. *Precious Sprout. Mtha' dpyod rin chen myu gu.*

———. *Spiritual Autobiography. Rtogs brjod mdun legs ma.*

———. *Stages of the Path: A Song of Experience. Lam rim nyams mgur.*

———. *Testimony of Aspirations Well Realized. Rtogs brjod mdun legs ma.*

———. *Three Entrustments. Zab lam nā ro'i chos drug gi khrid yid ches gsum ldan.*

———. *Three Principal Aspects of the Path. Lam gyi gtso rnam gsum.*

Vairocana Enlightenment Tantra. Mahāvairocanābhisaṃbodhi. Rnam par snang mdzad chen po mngon par rdzogs par byang chub pa rnam par sprul pa byin gyis rlob pa shin tu rgyas pa mdo sde'i dbang po'i rgyal po.

Vasubandhu. *Treasury of Abhidharma. Abhidharmakośa. Chos mngon pa'i mdzod.*

Yangchen Drupa Dorjé. *Pillar of the Indestructible Life Force: The Way to Perform a Longevity Ritual by Way of Yellow Bhairava. 'Jigs mdzad ser po'i sgo nas tshes sgrub byed tshul 'chi med srog gi ka ba.*

Yeshé Gyaltsen, Yongzin. *Biographies of the Lineage Masters of the Stages of the Path. Lam rim bla ma brgyud pa'i rnam thar.*

———. *Instructions on the Guru Puja: Treasury of Core Instructions from the Oral Transmission. Bla ma mchod pa'i khrid yig snyan rgyud man ngag gi gter mdzod.*

———. *Jewel Garland Summary. Sems dang sems byung gi sdom tshig rin po che'i phreng ba.*

———. *Ornament for Those with Intelligent Minds: Clear Teachings on Mind and Mental Factors. Sems dang sems byung gi tshul gsal bar ston pa blo gsal mgul rgyan.*

Photograph Credits

BLACK AND WHITE PHOTOS

Yongzin Lingtsang Labrang
frontispiece and pages 3, 5, 9, 15 (© Brian Beresford), 30, 59, 96, 107, 145, 172, 178, 179, 204, 209, 216, 239, 244, 262, 276, 314, 337, 346, 368

Lama Yeshe Wisdom Archive
pages 4, 331

Tibet Documentation Project
pages 6, 164, 201, 205, 251 top, 251 bottom

© Pitt Rivers Museum, University of Oxford
page 14 © Charles Bell 1998.285.89-O
page 55 © Hugh Richardson 2001_59_19_139-O
page 76 © Hugh Richardson 2001.59.1.58.1-O
page 84 © Frederick Spencer-Chapman 1998_131_354-O
page 85 © Hugh Richardson 2001_59_2_45_1-O
page 86 © Hugh Richardson 2001_59_1_43_1-O
page 100 © Charles Bell 1998_285_196-P
page 105 © Hugh Richardson 2001_59_19_123-O
page 112 © Frederick Spencer-Chapman 1998_131_308-P
page 116 © Harry Staunton 1999_23_1_31_2-O
page 135 © Hugh Richardson 2001_59_14_48_1-O
page 144 © James Guthrie 2009_112_208_1-O
page 147 © Frederick Spencer-Chapman 1998_131_340_1-O
page 152 © Amaury de Riencourt 1998_131_634-O
page 161 © Charles Bell 1998_286_248-O

Tibet Images Collection
pages 44 (© Leslie Weir, courtesy Maybe Jehu), 82 (© Hugh Richardson), 134 (Archibald Steele), 177, 186 top (© Homai Vyarawalla), 191, 192, 200, 224

© Dundul N. Tsarong
pages 133, 165, 180

© Trustees of the British Museum
pages 136 & 187 © Arthur J. Hopkinson
page 146 © Hugh E. Richardson

Courtesy Marist College Archives
page 163 © Lowell Thomas

Tibet Museum
page 176

Office of His Holiness the Dalai Lama
pages 184, 186 bottom, 209

Library of Tibetan Works and Archives
page 267

Color Plates

Yongzin Lingtsang Labrang
plates 4, 8, 17, 18, 21, 23, 24, 26, 27, 28, 29, 30, 31, 32, 34, 35, 38, 40, 41, 42, 43, 45

Lama Yeshe Wisdom Archive
plates 1, 2 (© Brian Beresford), 33 (© Danilo Ghirardi), 36 (© Jeff Nye), 37, 39

© Matt Linden & Joona Repo
plate 5

José Cabezón and Tibetan & Himalayan Library
plate 6 © Michael Cox

© Pitt Rivers Museum, University of Oxford
plate 7 © Frederick Spencer-Chapman 1998_157_31-0
plate 9 © Frederick Spencer-Chapman 1998_157_67-P
plate 15 © James Guthrie 2009_112_17_1-R

Tibet Images Collection
plates 10 (© Jirina Simajchlova), 19

© Thomas L. Kelly
plate 11

© The Trustees of the British Museum
plates 13 & 14 © Hugh E. Richardson

Magnum Photos
plate 20 © Estate of Marilyn Silverstone

© Sonam Tsering
plate 22

Courtesy Namgyal L Taklha
plate 25

Office of His Holiness the Dalai Lama
plates 3, 16, 44

© Paolo Regis
plate 46

© Nicholas Vreeland
plates 47, 48

Index

Note: Titles of works are listed under author name, when known.

About the Author

 TENZIN GYATSO, the Fourteenth Dalai Lama, is the spiritual leader of the Tibetan people. He frequently describes himself as a simple Buddhist monk. Born in northeastern Tibet in 1935, he was as a toddler recognized as the incarnation of the Thirteenth Dalai Lama and brought to Tibet's capital, Lhasa. In 1950, Mao Zedong's Communist forces made their first incursions into eastern Tibet, shortly after which the young Dalai Lama assumed the political leadership of his country. He passed his scholastic examinations with honors at the Great Prayer Festival in Lhasa in 1959, the same year Chinese forces occupied the city, forcing His Holiness to escape to India. There he set up the Tibetan exile administration in Dharamsala, working to secure the welfare of the more than a hundred thousand Tibetan exiles and prevent the destruction of Tibetan culture. In his capacity as a spiritual and political leader, he has traveled to more than sixty-two countries on six continents and met with presidents, popes, and leading scientists to foster dialogue and create a better world. In recognition of his tireless work for the nonviolent liberation of Tibet, the Dalai Lama was awarded the Nobel Peace Prize in 1989. In 2012, he relinquished political authority in his exile administration and turned it over to democratically elected representatives.

His Holiness frequently states that his life is guided by three major commitments: the promotion of basic human values or secular ethics in the interest of human happiness, the fostering of interreligious harmony, and securing the welfare of the Tibetan people, focusing on the survival of their identity, culture, and religion. As a superior scholar trained in the classical texts of the Nalanda tradition of Indian Buddhism, he is able to distill the central tenets of Buddhist philosophy in clear and inspiring language, his gift for pedagogy imbued with his infectious joy. Connecting scientists with Buddhist scholars, he helps unite contemplative and modern modes of investigation, bringing ancient tools and insights to bear on the acute problems facing the contemporary world. His efforts to foster dialogue among leaders of the world's faiths envision a future where people of different beliefs can share the planet in harmony.

GAVIN KILTY has been a full-time translator for the Institute of Tibetan Classics since 2001. Before that he lived in Dharamsala, India, for fourteen years, where he spent eight years training in the traditional Geluk monastic curriculum through the medium of class and debate at the Institute of Buddhist Dialectics. He also teaches Tibetan language courses in India, Nepal, and elsewhere, and is a translation reviewer for the organization 84000, Translating the Words of the Buddha.

THUPTEN JINPA LANGRI was educated in the classical Tibetan monastic academia and received the highest academic degree of geshé lharam (equivalent to a doctorate in divinity). Jinpa also holds a BA in philosophy and a PhD in religious studies, both from the University of Cambridge, England. Since 1985, he has been the principal English translator for the Dalai Lama, accompanying him to the United States, Canada, and Europe. He has translated and edited many books by the Dalai Lama, including *The World of Tibetan Buddhism*, *Essence of the Heart Sutra*, and the *New York Times* bestseller *Ethics for the New Millennium*.

Jinpa has published scholarly articles on various aspects of Tibetan culture, Buddhism, and philosophy, and books such as *Songs of Spiritual Experience: Tibetan Poems of Awakening and Insight* (co-authored) and *Self, Reality and Reason in Tibetan Thought*. He serves on the advisory board of numerous educational and cultural organizations in North America, Europe, and India. He is currently the president and the editor-in-chief of the Institute of Tibetan Classics, a nonprofit educational organization dedicated to translating key Tibetan classics into contemporary languages. And he also currently chairs the Mind and Life Institute.

ALSO AVAILABLE
BY HIS HOLINESS THE DALAI LAMA

from Wisdom Publications

Buddhism
One Teacher, Many Traditions
With Thubten Chodron
Foreword by Bhante Gunaratana

The Compassionate Life

Essence of the Heart Sutra
The Dalai Lama's Heart of Wisdom Teachings
Translated and edited by Thupten Jinpa

The Good Heart
A Buddhist Perspective on the Teachings of Jesus
Translated and annotated by Thupten Jinpa
Edited and with preface by Robert Kiely

Imagine All the People
A Conversation with The Dalai Lama on Money, Politics,
and Life As It Could Be
With Fabien Ouaki

Kalachakra Tantra
Rite of Initiation
Translated, edited, and introduced by Jeffrey Hopkins

Meditation on the Nature of Mind
With Khöntön Peljor Lhündrub and José I. Cabezón

The Middle Way
Faith Grounded in Reason
Translated by Thupten Jinpa

Mind in Comfort and Ease
The Vision of Enlightenment in the Great Perfection
Foreword by Sogyal Rinpoche

MindScience
An East–West Dialogue
With Herbert Benson, Robert Thurman, Howard Gardner,
and Daniel Goleman

Opening the Eye of New Awareness
Translated and introduced by Donald S. Lopez, Jr.

Practicing Wisdom
The Perfection of Shantideva's Bodhisattva Way
With Thupten Jinpa

Sleeping, Dreaming, and Dying
An Exploration of Consciousness
Edited and narrated by Francisco Varela

The Wheel of Life
Buddhist Perspectives on Cause and Effect
Translated by Jeffrey Hopkins
Foreword by Richard Gere

The World of Tibetan Buddhism
An Overview of Its Philosophy and Practice
Translated, edited, and annotated by Thupten Jinpa
Foreword by Richard Gere

About Wisdom Publications

Wisdom Publications is the leading publisher of classic and contemporary Buddhist books and practical works on mindfulness. To learn more about us or to explore our other books, please visit our website at wisdompubs.org or contact us at the address below.

Wisdom Publications
199 Elm Street
Somerville, MA 02144 USA

We are a 501(c)(3) organization, and donations in support of our mission are tax deductible.

Wisdom Publications is affiliated with the Foundation for the Preservation of the Mahayana Tradition (FPMT).

CALGARY PUBLIC LIBRARY

NOV   2017